TEACHING LINGUISTICALLY HANDICAPPED CHILDREN

TEACHING LINGUISTICALLY HANDICAPPED CHILDREN

MILDRED FREBURG BERRY, Ph. D.

PRENTICE-HALL, INC., Englewood Cliffs, New Jersey 07632

Library of Congress Cataloging in Publication Data

BERRY, MILDRED FREBURG.
   Teaching linguistically handicapped children.

   Includes bibliographies.
     1. Language disorders in children.
2. Language acquisition—Psychological aspects.
3. Language arts. I. Title.
LC4019. B425   371.91'4   80–325
ISBN 0–13–893545–9

Editorial/Production supervision: Richard C. Laveglia
Interior design by Barbara Alexander
Cover design by Maureen Olsen
Manufacturing buyer: Harry P. Baisley

Printed in the United States of America

10 9 8 7 6 5 4 3 2 1

Prentice-Hall International, Inc., *London*
Prentice-Hall of Australia Pty. Limited, *Sydney*
Prentice-Hall of Canada, Ltd., *Toronto*
Prentice-Hall of India Private Limited, *New Delhi*
Prentice-Hall of Japan, Inc., *Tokyo*
Prentice-Hall of Southeast Asia Pte. Ltd., *Singapore*
Whitehall Books Limited, *Wellington, New Zealand*

To James

To my colleagues in the public schools who "gladly wolde
. . lerne and gladly teche."

CONTENTS

FOREWORD   *xi*

chapter 1   **DIMENSIONS AND DIRECTIONS IN TEACHING LINGUISTICALLY HANDICAPPED CHILDREN**   *1*

Introduction   *1*
The Place of the Special Language Teacher in the Programs   *4*
Inadequacy of Formal Tests and Measurements   *7*
Evaluation of Selective Knowledge of the Special Language Teacher   *9*
Alteration of Traditional Materials and Methods   *14*
Hallmarks of Oral Language Acquisition   *15*
Pragmatics of Language Learning   *18*
References   *20*

chapter 2   **THE MEDIATION OF ORAL LANGUAGE IN THE CENTRAL NERVOUS SYSTEM**   *25*

The Neurobiological Basis of Linguistic Handicaps: An Introduction   *25*
Aspects of Neural Function   *28*
Integrative Systems in Oral Language   *41*
Cortical Mechanisms in Oral Language   *49*
The Final Common Path to Speech: Comprehension-Oral Expression   *64*
References   *67*

chapter 3 NEURAL-PSYCHOLOGICAL SUBSTRATES
OF ORAL LANGUAGE *75*

Motivation, Attention, Memory *75*
The Psychological Aspects of Motivation *79*
The Psychological Aspects of Attention *87*
Problems of Attention in Language-Retarded Children *91*
Neuro-Psychological Aspects of Memory *97*
Short-Term and Long-Term Memory *98*
Training Memory: The Skills *105*
References *107*

chapter 4 HALLMARKS OF ORAL LANGUAGE *112*

Introduction *112*
Variables Affecting Teaching and Learning Hallmarks of Language *115*
Hallmark 1: Perceptual-Semantic Development *121*
References *147*

chapter 5 HALLMARKS OF ORAL LANGUAGE *152*

Hallmark 2: Phonatory (Prosodic) Development *152*
Hallmark 3: Phonological Development *162*
References *176*

chapter 6 HALLMARKS OF ORAL LANGUAGE *183*

Hallmark 4: Syntactic Development *183*
References *201*

chapter 7 POSITIVE MARKERS OF
PROGRESS IN LANGUAGE ACQUISITION *206*

Introduction *206*
Stage 1 Beginning Oral Language *207*
Stage 2 Early Intermediate Stage of Language Development *211*
Stage 3 Later Intermediate Stage of Language Acquisition *218*
Stage 4 Continuing Education Stage:
Priority of the Major Hallmark, Perceptual-Semantic Development,
in Language Learning *223*
References *225*

chapter 8   A GLOBAL-ONTOGENIC
TEACHING PROGRAM   *228*

Introduction   *228*
Basic Concepts and Terms   *229*
The Language Learning Environment   *232*
Unit 1 Teaching Oral Language with Emphasis on
Prosody and Phonology   *244*
Teaching Oral Language with Emphasis on
Perceptual-Semantic Skills   *255*
References   *274*

GLOSSARY   *295*

INDEX   *311*

FOREWORD

In *Language Disorders of Children* (Prentice-Hall, Inc., 1969), I presented the bases and diagnoses of oral language development and its deficits. This book on teaching linguistically handicapped children is its sequel. It is directed to teachers and students who are or will be engaged in teaching children handicapped by delay in the development of oral language or by language disorders.

The importance of this subject was underscored by the American Speech and Hearing Association in 1971 when it made an unfavorable report on the preparation of the average teacher in this branch of our field. The survey revealed a woeful lack of preparation in oral language. The extent to which students were prepared in normal language acquisition, retarded language development, and communication patterns of dialect communities was minimal.[1] When confronted with the demand to institute language programs for the handicapped, the "speech clinician" used the tools at hand. They dealt principally with strategies of *speech remediation*.

The tocsin was sounded for specific preparation in the new field. Speech therapists from the public schools and habilitation centers crowded summer classrooms, inservice workshops, conferences and convention short courses in order to retool. Unfortunately some teachers in the public schools returned to their positions only to find that they were

[1] J. Stark, "Current Clinical Practices in Language," *Asha*, 13(4) (April 1971), 217–220.

unable to break the lockstep of the established organization, curriculum, and methods employed in speech therapy. It was business as usual, the business of teaching children how to improve their articulation in individual fifteen-minute sessions twice a week. Change was in the wind, however, and educators finally realized that a radical revision in the philosophy and methodology of "speech therapy" must be instituted. The need for revision was brought on first by the general recognition that the "clinical" approach in the public schools was uneconomic and unproductive, and secondly by PL 94-142 (1975) which mandated the schools and habilitation centers to provide appropriate services for *all communicatively handicapped persons* (three years to twenty-one years of age). As a consequence, the preparation of teachers who must provide these "appropriate services" moved to "prime time" in college and university curricula.

Throughout the writing of this text I have referred to the professional in this field of communication handicaps as the *special language teacher* or simply as the language teacher. It is the most accurate and laudatory title I know. It is not a popular title at present. The major professional groups in our field, lacking authentic ID cards, have not yet decided what to call themselves. Particularly are they in a quandary over an appropriate cognomen for the worker in the vineyard, the public schools, where two-thirds of the professionals in our field are to be found. Clinician, therapist, consultant, communicologist: all by turns have been tried and found wanting. The focus of this book is on teaching a specialty, oral language; hence it seems appropriate to designate these professionals as special teachers. Incidentally, I shall use the feminine gender in referring to them, inasmuch as 83.2% of the membership in the American Speech-Language-Hearing Association is female. But when I write about a child I use the generic word, *him* or *his*. I do so because to alternate the male with the female gender would cause unnecessary confusion. Unfortunately, the English language does not offer a pronoun that can refer to either sex.

What kinds of preparation are needed for this important program in the field of speech, hearing, and language sciences? A line from an old musical provides the answer: "You've got to know the territory." Indeed the special language teacher must know the territory—its contents and its boundaries. Boundary and content, however, involve more than the acquisition of prosody, sounds, morphemes, words, and syntax. The special language teacher must be able to interpret the child's language retardation in more fundamental ways. She must draw upon and apply her knowledge of the psychological, neurobiological, and socioeconomic determinants of oral language to the specifics of its development: perceptual-semantic, phonatory, phonological, and syntactic. The special language teacher must go even farther; she must have the knowledge, perspective, and the courage to implement a program that will be effective with children who are handicapped in oral language.

The use of the term, perception, instead of cognition or discrimination or apperception may be unacceptable to some readers. All are listed as synonyms in general and special dictionaries. In my view, perception is more meaningful because it implies more than recognizing stimuli, more than differentiating or discriminating between sensations, associations, or ideas. Apperception, once used to distinguish between recognition of the stimulus and its interpretation, is contained within the term, perception. Brain charts no longer show defined boundaries between areas of reception and interpretation of sensorimotor impulses. Perception is primarily concerned with understanding the *relationship* between sensations, associations, and ideas. It is not enough for the child to recognize that there is a relationship; he must know what the relationship *means,* its ramifications, and its connections, near and far. The relationship involves activity, not passive recognition. Other synonyms of perception are understanding, comprehension, insight, and acumen. In my view, perception is the most accurate term to describe the listener's response in terms of "(1) literal meaning, (2) presupposition and inference, and (3) illocutionary acts," (the semantic intention of speech acts).[2] In this text I have linked perception with semantics in order to articulate emphatically their common purpose, that is, to understand meanings and to comprehend the semantic intention of the speaker and the listener. To be sure, perception of syntax and morphology is necessary if one is to comprehend the literal meaning of a sentence, but such perceptions really tell us little about the child's ability to comprehend the interactions underlying the semantic intentions of the speaker and his use of language *in context.*

Where are the objective tests of oral language development? They are not included in this book because they do not evaluate oral language as children comprehend it and use it. What they assess is information about the child's abilty to perceive syntactic, phonologic, and morphologic forms in unrelated tidbits of language. Tests of auditory perception or discrimination do not evaluate the child's ability to comprehend the *continuum* of oral language. Other perceptual items borrowed from general intelligence tests measure such nonverbal skills as similarities and differences in form, color, use, and so on. But they are a far cry from the percepts needed in the language situations that these children encounter every day. They take no account of the pragmatic nature of language, or of the context of language set in a particular environment. And almost all tests are set against the conventional metric of chrono-

2 N. S. Reese and M. Shulman, "I Don't Understand What You Mean by Comprehension," *J. Speech Hear Dis,* 43(2) (May 1978), 208–219.

logical age. A more valid and comprehensive evaluation, I have maintained, may be obtained through the study of tapes made over a period of time of children's comprehension-expression of oral language when they are participating with their peers in real situations in and out of the classroom.[3]

Another question which undoubtedly will trouble the reader is, can children whose language retardation stems from different causes be taught in one self-contained classroom? It *has* been done successfully in many schools and centers. An itinerant special language teacher has frequently assisted by conducting a special one-hour session twice a week with a severely retarded group in order to reinforce their learning in the self-contained class. The chief fear of these children was that they would miss a part of the activity in which their more advanced peers were engaged!

I am indebted to my colleagues in the public schools in many states for their reception of the program as I have presented it in summer sessions, seminars, workshops, and conferences. Subsequent observation of the innovative skills of many of these teachers in adapting the program to their needs is encouraging. Their feedback has been of inestimable value. At my home base I have been the consultant of T.A.L.K. (Teaching Activities for Language Knowledge) (Appendix A-1). To these farsighted and innovative special language teachers, Joyce Vee and Ann Guedet and psychologist, Harold Bauer, who together planned and executed the program, my salute! I have learned much from them and also from Lucille Nicolosi, diagnostician in speech, hearing, and language for the Rockford Public Schools. Frank Parrino, Regional Superintendent of Schools, has provided valuable materials on current educational philosophies. My friends in the Rockford Public Library have been invaluable assistants. My aides in typing the manuscript, Joan Casarotto and Mary Lou Yankaitis, have also been my helpful editors. And to those closest to my daily life—my understanding family and friends—words are a useless tribute. In the great realities of life, we are dumb; we cannot speak.

---

[3] M. F. Berry, *Language Disorders: The Bases and Diagnoses.* Englewood Cliffs, N.J.: Prentice-Hall, Inc., 1969, chap. 6.

TEACHING
LINGUISTICALLY
HANDICAPPED
CHILDREN

chapter 1

DIMENSIONS AND DIRECTIONS IN TEACHING LINGUISTICALLY HANDICAPPED CHILDREN

INTRODUCTION

This book is intended primarily for the people who are teaching or who are preparing to teach children in public schools or speech and hearing centers. The children are handicapped by delay or disruption in the acquisition, comprehension, or utilization of linguistic symbols in oral communication. The extent of the delay or disruption must be judged in its relation to age, class, and cultural and community standards of normality.[1] The teaching program may be adapted to serve three principal groups of children:

1. *Those handicapped by severe language disorders and taught in small groups outside the academic classroom.* In the main they are children in whom neurophysiological or psychological conditions affect the input, integrative functions, or output of oral language. Some children in this group may exhibit maturational delay or disturbances in auditory or tactile-kinesthetic perception; others exhibit a faulty integration of sensorimotor impulses (neural assemblies) which may occur at subcortical levels, and still others may exhibit maturational delay or confusion in cortical organization or dominance.

---

[1] This description of language impairment is abstracted from the definition found in *Terminology of Communication Disorders* by L. Nicolosi, E. Harryman, and J. Kresheck. (Baltimore: Williams & Wilkins, 1978).

2. *Those retarded in oral language development and taught in a self-contained classroom, preschool through the third grade.* Here we are teaching children

    a. whose language age is significantly below their mental age,

    b. who manifest subtle sensorimotor deficits in bodily rhythms and general motor coordination which are also reflected in sensorimotor coding of oral language, or

    c. who are psychologically maladjusted in oral communication.

3. *Those who are in need of language enrichment, whose oral language is behind age expectation usually because of cultural or economic disadvantages in their environment.* They also will be taught in a self-contained classroom.

The distinction among these groups can be clarified by example although the lines of differentiation are not clear-cut.

A Child in Group 1

Steve, four years of age, is being taught in Group 1. He has a medical history of encephalitis at 18 months, confirmed by a pediatrician but later questioned by other medical specialists. Although the impairment of the central nervous system is evident in many facets of sensorimotor behavior: stance, balance, running, and eye-hand coordination, it is most apparent in retarded comprehension-expression of oral language. Auditory perception fluctuates, not only from hour to hour, but apparently also within the sentence he is comprehending. He does not readily or completely understand what he has heard. The result is confusion in telling what he has comprehended. He makes his wants known in monosyllabic phrases uttered in a monotone (kinesthetic-motor deficits; dysprosody). Only when he is truly excited by a story or "play" in which he has a part does his utterance become more melodic and accompanied by bodily gesture. The specific involvements of the central nervous system (CNS) will be discussed in Chapter 2.

A Child in Group 2

Mary, five years old, is a lively girl who is aware of and comprehends events in her immediate environment. She is determined to participate in the non-verbal activities in the classroom although she has problems in motor coordination. She has a peculiar gait and often falls over the very obstacle she is determined to avoid, thereby giving the impression of the "clumsy child syndrome." She refuses to read the captions in her cartoon books, preferring to guess "what it says." She uses either hand in printing her name, but without respect to the hand, she generally inverts the

M and transposes the loop in Y. Her language age is far below her mental age. In her kindergarten class she excels in non-language activities. Her oral language deficits are most noticeable in comprehending and using new melodic patterns of expression, new words, and structures. She feels safe with the rigid, simple structures and lexicon she has learned. Are the following items from the mother's report clues to the problems that must be overcome? The oldest sibling, a male, (Mary is the youngest) was similarly delayed in oral language, development, attended a reading clinic for two years, "made it through high school by having his mother type his papers or record them on tape," went on to college, majored in mathematics and biology (a different symbolic system), and now teaches science in high school. The mother also reported that several members of the father's family did not talk "on time" or "much" until they were adults. Does Mary's language retardation stem from a genetically atypical nervous system? We believe that Mary is a brain-different, not a brain-injured child. She suffers from no lesions in CNS but has an atypical neural organization affecting sensorimotor coding. Mary is progressing rapidly in a self-contained class in learning disabilities taught jointly by the language and learning disability specialists with the assistance of two aides!

A Child in Group 3

One cannot select one type of language problem or one child as illustrative of the language enrichment program because the children who are in this self-contained classroom come from several very different environments. Some come from culturally deprived environments, but their families are neither poor nor living in a ghetto area; some children are from bilingual families; others, from economically depressed families, both black and white. *T.A.L.K.* (Teaching Activities for Language Knowledge is an innovative program of language enrichment. The Joint Dissemination Review Panel in the Education Division of the Department of Health, Education and Welfare approved it as an "Exemplary Educational Program," (July 1979). This program, now designated Title IV C, is more fully described in Appendix A-I, p. 23.

Names and Places

In this book I shall refer to those of you who teach linguistically handicapped children as special language teachers. In my view, you are not clinicians or therapists; you are educators. If you want to know more precisely my reasons for not designating even university educators as clinicians, therapists, or pathologists (the most flagrant misrepresentation), you will find them in a letter, "For want of a name—," in *Asha,* Forum section, July 1977. I shall use the feminine gender simply because women represent the great (but not silent) majority of public school professionals.

THE PLACE OF THE SPECIAL
LANGUAGE TEACHER

She has many places, many roles today. Traditionally she has directed the program for those children handicapped by severe language disorders and taught outside the academic classroom (Group 1). Instead of tutorial instruction on a one-to-one basis, she now will teach them in small groups. Although she is the director, she does not teach alone. She will take advantage, one hopes, of assistance from consultants and aides both in and outside the school: the classroom teacher, psychologist, counsellor, pediatrician, nurse, playground supervisor, music, art, and drama teachers, and the family and community agencies which may provide resources of great value. In some school systems she will have the help of an itinerant language teacher who can assist her and also give special attention to the language-retarded in self-contained classrooms who present difficult problems.

Early Childhood Education

The special language teacher is needed in other programs of special education in which language skills are essential to learning. Until recently her knowledge and skill in the area of early childhood education have not been recognized. One rarely sees the special language teacher as a consultant or even as a lecturer in this program. Yet I cannot think of any behavior more critical to the young child's development than oral language. By definition, courses in early childhood education embrace the study of the physical, cognitive, and behavioral characteristics and processes underlying human development. Perhaps the most critical perceptual-semantic dimension underlying human development is oral communication. Until the child achieves a measure of proficiency in oral communication, he does not belong to that special class, *homo loquens* (man as a talking animal), "separated by an unbridgeable gulf from the rest of the animals." [2]

[2] Dennis Fry, *Homo Loquens* (Cambridge, England: Cambridge University Press, 1977), 1.

Learning Disabilities

The special language teacher is urgently needed in teaching children with learning disabilities. In fact the distinction between a learning disability and a language disability seems obscure. A learning disability is defined in a professional journal as "due to a significant deficit in one or more of the central learning processes (e.g., perception, attention, memory, integrative skills, thinking processes, etc.)" [3] These are the same skills that must be taught in language learning (although the writer is confounded by the term, "thinking processes"). The author reserves receptive and expressive language skills, however, for the specialist in language disabilities. But is not receptive language completely dependent upon one's perceptive ability? Are they not one and the same skill? [4]

From reviewing textbooks and reading lists used in courses in learning disabilities and from lecturing to these classes, I am convinced that when these students engage in teaching the learning-disabled, they will need the help of the specialist in oral language. In the textbook survey I found only collections of tidbits about oral language. It was a kind of cafeteria ware, all of it without framework or integral relation to the field. I am puzzled by the fact that language specialists rarely participate in writing texts or in training teachers majoring in learning disabilities. I ask these questions:

1. Are not learning and language interlocked, perception being the basis both of language and learning?

2. Is not learning blocked
   a. if you do not perceive (understand) the meaning of what you hear or read;
   b. if you do not have a framework on which to hang your ideas (syntax);
   c. if you do not have a vocabulary that goes beyond naming (semantics)?

3. Is not the potential for learning impaired when physiological or neurological deficits affect not only comprehension, but also such expressive attributes as phonology, prosody, voice, articulation?

[3] D. Hantman, "Speech and Language-Learning Disabilities: Semi-Autonomous Department," *Isha* 9(2) (February 1976), 9–13.

[4] An equally ambiguous and all-inclusive definition of a "specific learning disability" is provided in Public Law 94–142 (Federal Register 94–142–121a.5): "a disorder in one or more of the basic psychological processes involved in understanding or in using language, spoken or written, which may manifest itself in an imperfect ability to listen, think, speak, read, write, spell, or to do mathematical calculations. The term includes such conditions as perceptual handicaps, brain injury, minimal brain dysfunction, dyslexia, and developmental aphasia. The term does not include children who have learning problems which are primarily the result of visual, hearing, or motor handicaps, of mental retardation, of emotional disturbance, or of environmental, cultural, or economic disadvantage."

At this point let me say that in all these highly specialized fields: early childhood education, learning disabilities, the educable mentally handicapped (EMH), it is unrealistic to expect students to engage in specialization in their own major subject and also to complete comprehensive courses in another area of special education: oral language development.[5] But until recently I found no expert in oral language assisting the teacher in the classroom in learning disabilities, the teacher who so urgently needed her services. Instead I found the language specialist in the recesses of the teachers' lounge or behind the stoves in the closed home economics department, teaching a child whose articulation was marred by a central-s lisp! This year I observed a turn of events. Two directors of programs in learning disabilities as an experiment included special language teachers as a part of the teaching team. Indeed the two teachers shared equal responsibilities; they were codirectors! They developed a master plan in which oral language had a major role. The results were excellent. Mary, Group 2 [6] was a super-achiever in this class. The good news spread to other classes for learning-disabled children. Now other school systems have adopted the plan.

Mental Impairment

Language specialists are providing services as consultants or as cooperating teachers in programs for the mentally impaired (MI), a third area in special education. By definition these children probably do not have a language deficit or disorder if there is little disparity between their language age and their mental age, judged either by verbal or by performance scores. The help of the special language teacher, however, is of inestimable value to the MI teacher who may not be adequately prepared in the area of oral language development.[7]

The Learning Opportunities Program which I have observed in one community [8] has had signal success through the formation of a teaching team composed of MI teachers, special language teachers, a psychologist, a physical therapist, and a social worker. The MI teacher and the special language teacher, codirectors of the program, have devised a master plan and have enlisted the support of their colleagues. All children in these

[5] F.P. Connor, "The Past is Prologue: Teacher Preparation in Special Education," *Exceptional Children* 42(7) (April 1976), 366–378.

[6] R.L. Schiefelbusch, ed., *Language of the Mentally Retarded* (Baltimore: University Park Press, 1972).

[7] R.L. Schiefelbusch and L.L. Lloyd, eds., *Language Perspectives—Acquisition, Retardation, and Intervention* (Baltimore: University Park Press, 1974).

[8] LOP was the innovation of the Department of Special Education, Rockford (Ill.) Schools.

self-contained classrooms are mentally impaired, but many have additional handicaps of cerebral palsy, deafness, and visual or other neuromotor disorders. They are taught academic skills, including rhythmics and drama, in a setting of oral language development.

In these three areas: early childhood education, learning disabilities, and the mentally impaired, the language specialist may act as a consultant in defining goals and strategies to be employed in advancing the perceptual-semantic, phonatory (prosodic), phonological, and syntactic development of oral language. Or the special language teacher may be a generalist and assume partial or complete responsibility for the planning and teaching of a self-contained classroom in which language competencies necessary for academic and social growth are the primary considerations. Ideally she should join up with a team in which every member has a part in planning, directing, and teaching language-retarded children.

Language Enrichment

In the third area, language enrichment, the oral language teacher is the supervisor, the leader. With the help of many colleagues in direct participation: classroom teachers, physical educationists, teachers of drama, rhythmics, and so on, she directs a program called the "language enrichment program." In this classroom the staff teaches ethnic groups whose parents may not speak English, the economically disadvantaged, the culturally deprived, black and white students whose oral language may be impoverished or deviate because of the environment in which they live. I have watched this program grow. The pervading atmosphere is enjoyment of communication. All children in Group 3 are in this class. This program of language enrichment will be described more fully in Appendix A-1.

INADEQUACY OF FORMAL TESTS AND MEASUREMENTS

Students and teachers may be disconcerted by the absence of diagnostic tests. They have been omitted from all discussions of evaluation in this book because formal assessment measures rarely tell us what we need to know about the true status of a child's language development. Oral language must be evaluated in pragmatic terms, that is, in terms of the child's use of language in the context in which it was generated. Tests do not ferret out the problems the child has in comprehending or expressing his intentions and his dynamic interactions in oral communication with children in his environment.[9] Instead commercial tests evaluate isolated segments of language: the literal meaning of words and sentences, the comprehension of lexical items, the understanding of grammatical "rules." [10]

Some measures, for example, are supposed to determine a child's knowledge of a receptive vocabulary determined in a game of picture identification (Peabody Picture Vocabulary Test). Others appraise cognitive skill by posing questions of judgment of behavior (what-to-do questions) (Revised Stanford-Binet Scale). And still others place their reliance on tests which assess the comprehension-use of grammatical segments (Northwestern Syntax Screening Test). The essential aspects of oral language, however, are not appraised: the child's intentions in oral communication, his sensorimotor actions surrounding the utterance, and his use of language in interacting with children (not adults) in a natural communicative environment.

I repeat *natural communicative environment* because the examiner's usual practice is to collect information about some features of the child's language through tests administered in an artificial "clinic" environment. At no time is the child's ability to understand and use the language of everyday conversation assessed. This cannot be done because there is no chance to appraise a total communicative environment and the child's interaction with children (not adults) in the environment.

Because I found years ago that these tests were of little value in determining what and how to teach these children, I advocated videotapes or auditory tapes recording samplings of the children's language in a free and familiar environment while the children were engaged in a language task or activity. Such a procedure allows the teaching team to study the use of oral language of children and their linguistic progress in the context of the communicative experience. In an earlier text, *Language Disorders of Children* (Prentice-Hall, Inc., 1969), I devoted a chapter to diagnostic teaching which included discussion of appropriate kinds of language activity through which the teachers in the course of six weeks could trace a true language profile. Others are now suggesting child-to-child conversations eliciting oral language samples or developing "language tasks." [11]

[9] Lynn S. Snyder, "Communicative and Cognitive Abilities and Disabilities in the Sensorimotor Period," *Merrill-Palmer Quarterly* 24(3) (July 1978), 161–180.

[10] N.S. Rees and M. Shulman, "I Don't Understand What You Mean by Comprehension," *J Speech Hearing Disorders* 43(2) (May 1978), 217.

[11] L.B. Leonard and others, "Nonstandardized Approaches to the Assessment of Language Behaviors," *Asha* 20(5) (March 1978), 371–379; T.M. Longhurst and J.J. File, "A Comparison of Developmental Sentence Scores from Head Start Children Collected in Four Conditions," *Language, Speech and Hearing Services in Schools* 8(1) (January 1977), 54–63.

SELECTIVE KNOWLEDGE OF THE SPECIAL LANGUAGE TEACHER

At the outset the competent teacher has mastered knowledge in the subject areas of departmental study: oral language development, its deficits and disorders; articulation; voice; hearing; stuttering; cleft palate speech; and cerebral palsied speech. It is presumed that she also has knowledge of the basic sciences such as biology, physiology, psychology, phonetics, and allied scientific courses: anatomy, neurology, behavioral and physiological psychology, psycholinguistics as well as educational theory and principles. To these we would add another requirement: a rich background in literature and the arts.

The corpus of materials to be included in departmental topic areas and basic sciences has been well established. Literature and the arts certainly are creeping under the big top again probably because they are the stuff out of which lively oral language is made.[12] The debate comes over the professional sciences: psycholinguistics, learning theories, neurophysiology, experimental phonetics, and behavioral psychology. What and how much do we select from these fields that undergird oral language? What knowledge shall we take from psycholinguistics, from psychology, from neurophysiology, from educational theories? Our difficulties, I think, spring from our failure to be analytical, to be selective. We are not in agreement in sorting out the knowledge that we can use most effectively. As you read the succeeding pages, you may well disagree with the inclusion and exclusion of knowledges; particularly does this seem to be so in excluding traditional practices. One person's feat is another's defeat.

Linguistic Information: Evaluation

We have been caught up with feature components of phonemes, sound systems of phoneticians, with Chomsky's theories of transformational grammar, and with semantic theories. None of the writers in these areas is a special language teacher (or, if you prefer, language "clinician"). By definition linguistics is the science of language; it is not the science of human communication. Consequently linguists can only describe language behavior; they cannot explain it. As Staats says in his discussion of linguistics:

> If you wish to produce a behavior or to prevent a behavior from developing, you must have contact with the biological or learning events—for these

[12] P.C. Boomsliter, "Language Capacity and Language Learning." (Unpublished paper, Copyright 1970.)

are the determinants of behavior. In the realm of linguistics there is no study of explanatory events of either the biological or learning kind. . . . Linguistic theory cannot make explanatory statements. The linguist has no contact with the determining conditions, only with the behavior (language) itself . . . [Linguists only] assume that there are cognitive structures or processes that correspond to their rules . . . their description of language behavior is just that; it is not an *explanation of language behavior.* For explanation one must make contact with the events that "cause" the language behavior.[13]

The special language teacher cannot separate the language behavior of the child from the events in the environment, of which it is a part. She must understand the interaction in order to deal with it.

We should remember, too, that most linguistic research has been done on what one might call immaculate prose. Such prose consists of grammatically correct sentences with nouns, verbs, and other parts of speech in their proper places. Words are spelled correctly, and rules of punctuation are observed. All computer programs based on what is called natural language require immaculate prose because the sentences that are fed into the computer are parsed in one way or another so that the meaning of the ensemble can be inferred from conventional rules of syntax. This is not the oral language which you want to teach children because children, no more than adults, speak in complete sentences. Indeed, the majority of adults have not learned grammar by rule or by rote; they could not pass a grammar test. Has anyone learned to speak a foreign language by memorizing and practicing grammatical rules? Among the Fulbright associates of the author in three countries it was easy to identify the ones who had tried—and failed. As Ortony has concluded, educators find the work of modern psycholinguists of little value because they have ignored the fact that "language is for the people." They are people whose statements may not be grammatically correct but are acceptable by a person competent in the language.[14]

Young children do not use "immaculate prose." They rarely speak in sentences at any time during language acquisition. They are not born with a sense of grammar. "They have (1) no intuitions of grammaticality and (2) make no judgments of acceptability, both of which are crucial to transformational methodology (grammar). In short, there is no unequivocal evidence that children of this age know anything about sentences, or that their utterances are guided by an unconscious knowledge of sentences. Indeed, Langendoen (1972) suggests that children may not have

---

[13] A. Staats, *Learning, Language, and Cognition* (New York: Holt, Rinehart and Winston, 1968), 155–157.

[14] A. Ortony, "Language Isn't For People: On Applying Theoretical Linguistics to Practical Problems," *Review of Educational Research* 45 (1975), 485–504.

a grammar in the transformational sense for many years. They may have some skills for talking and listening, but Langendoen claims that these skills arise and develop long before grammar arises and develops." [15]

We have wallowed too long, I think, in the psycholinguistic thickets of competence and performance, transformational-generative grammar of Chomsky, theories of syntax, immediate constituents, deep and surface structure. It may give one confidence to know the difference between "John is eager to please" and "John is easy to please" but in teaching a language-retarded child, knowledge of this fact has limited use. The linguist does not deal with the competence and performance of children learning to speak. That is our business. The first order of our business in dealing with grammar is to determine the structure that young children actually use, and our second is to assist them in perceiving and developing further the form of their language. How best to accomplish these aims are detailed in succeeding chapters.

General Educational Information:
Evaluation of Theories and Practices

Students in courses in childhood education are frequently taught that the social learning theory satisfactorily explains a child's language development. These educational theorists tell us that a child's learning of language is the result of observation and imitation of a model's behavior with or without reinforcement. Modeling, they claim, is highly influential in the development of children's social response. Experimental studies of the effects of verbal modeling in young children, however, have not been highly successful. We will grant that imitation undoubtedly plays a role in vocabulary growth and in learning something about grammatical structure, yet the theory falls short in explaining the essential aspects of lexical and syntactic development. It would be virtually impossible for a child to memorize all language structures that he hears and associate a particular conceptualization with each structure.[16] If you have observed the remarkable rate at which children in all societies learn language without respect to their social environment, you will question such a theory. Furthermore the theory does not take into account the highly creative nature of children's language. Any language teacher knows that from early on, chil-

[15] J. Dore, "Holophrases, Speech Acts and Language Universals," *J Child Language* 2(1) (April 1975), 21–40; D.T. Langendoen, "Is the Theory of Generative Grammar Relevant to Neurobiology?" (Paper presented at Neurosciences Research Program Work Session on *Language and the Brain: Developmental Aspects,* November 20, 1972.)

[16] L.G. Butler, "Language Acquisition of Young Children: Major Theories and Acquisitions," *Elementary English* 51(8) (November-December 1974), 1120–1137.

dren understand novel sentences and, more importantly, construct completely new sentences—sentences they have not heard before and which therefore could not be imitations of adult speech. Such directives from a five-year-old as "Grandpa, *higher* the swing; my feet are dragging" or "*Fall* the cup in the basket" are logical and ingenious inductions from the syntax he knows. They convey clear meaning to others.

Moreover many parents and teachers have found that little children are highly resistant to alteration of the forms and vocabulary they employ in oral expression. That the process of imitation, modeling, and reinforcement (modified social learning theory) goes a short way toward an explanation of learning theory is attested to by a classic study of communication without a language model. A group of six deaf children (17 to 49 months) who had no experience either with oral language or manual sign language developed a structured sign system expressing *semantic relations* in a systematic way, that is, by following the syntactic rule based on the semantic role of each of the sign units.[17]

Behavioral Psychology: An Evaluation

Behavior modification, achieved through methods of operant conditioning, has received widespread attention from workers in our field. A highly controversial subject, it has been pursued enthusiastically and successfully by some special language teachers and researchers; for others it has seemed to be old domestic beer with a foreign label recently tacked on. I know that it has been effective in teaching useful sentences to the mentally trainable. I remember, however, that here we are not dealing with language delay or disorder if there is little or no disparity between the language age and the mental age. If stuttering, on the other hand, might be classified one day as a language disorder, then we would have an example of the effectiveness of behavior modification. The issue is not settled.

In my view behavior modification has merit in educating children handicapped by serious disorders of language. Its premise is simple. Operant conditioning basically involves the establishment of new relations between a stimulus and an overt response. Well and good. But I do not believe that a collection of new and old S-R connections necessarily will result in perception. We cannot teach ideation by operant conditioning; we cannot teach the child how to reach a generalization on the basis of analysis and synthesis by operant conditioning. In sum, it is a poor tool in teaching the

[17] S. Goldin-Meadow and H. Feldman, "The Development of Language-Like Communication Without a Language Model," *Science* 197(4301) (22 July 1977), 401–404.

child how to comprehend oral language and how to make inferences from the language—how to think. The Skinnerian psychologist regards the child as a hollow organism who responds only to external stimulation and reinforcement. True, the psychologist can shape rather elaborate response patterns by reward and punishment but what is the effect on the child? He could well become an automaton, not a thinking individual. Learning—or relearning—language is more than a complex series of computerlike conditioned responses made possible by maturing pathways and an innate ability to imitate. The Skinner box will go a short way in our field of oral language development. We must take account of something more important—*the contribution of the child to language comprehension and performance.*

Neurophysiological Information

Special language teachers must understand the neurophysiological principles that have a role in the acquisition and breakdown of oral language. But, as in other allied fields, they must be selective in information. The chemistry of the muscle spindle response during speech, for example, does not share equal importance with the intricacies of neural coding in order to locate the level of breakdown or the obstacles to the normal development of language. Other illustrations of essential information come to mind. Students of oral language development must know that the effect of a cerebral lesion on adult communication is far different from its effect on the language of a child whose lesion is the result of trauma. The capacity of the child brain to surmount anatomical deficits or physical pathologies also is clearly different from that of the mature brain. If the teacher understands the nature of developmental failures and how they may affect cortical fields and/or neural routes mediating oral language, such knowledge will stand her in good stead in teaching these children. (See Figures 2-9, 2-10 on pp. 54–55.)

Phonology: Evaluation

The feature system involving the sound or phoneme patterns and the rules governing their combination has received great attention in the study of the phonology of language. Teachers in the public schools, having had extensive education in articulatory deficits, are prone to make articulation and the production of phonemes the center of oral language learning. No child learns his language, however, by adding sound to sound in a string-of-beads fashion any more than an adult learns a second language by those means. And certainly the child cannot be nearly so concerned with the phoneme /s/ in its addition to the word *cat* as he must be in developing the *percept of possession* in *cat's* or *of number in cats*. The special language teacher must select those phonological principles that she considers applicable to the development of the child's use of oral language.

It is time that we language teachers set our house in order, evaluating, modifying, and adopting those concepts which are relevant to our field. We must sort out the knowledge of high applicability from all these fields: linguistics, behavioristic psychology, neurophysiology, and theoretical phonetics. True, we are the Academy's best borrower but we must be circumspect in what we borrow; otherwise uncertainty and frustration will continue to pervade our teaching.

ALTERATION OF TRADITIONAL MATERIALS AND METHODS FROM SPEECH AND HEARING SCIENCES

If we must exercise choice in what we borrow from allied fields, we also must be ready to abandon or modify the use of materials and methods in our own field which are not applicable to the teaching of oral language.

Here are some concepts traditionally associated with and perpetuated in teaching that must be omitted or given new direction in our teaching of linguistically handicapped children.

1. We shall not be concerned exclusively, or even primarily, with articulation and articulatory deficits because oral language is predicated on a totally different goal: communication. We cannot target in on the sound in isolation, for oral language is neither comprehended nor expressed that way; sound sequences, a group of syllables (syntagma), yes,—single sounds, no. "The child's earliest multiple-word utterances are organized as syntagmas which represent conceptual schemas in terms of phonetic strings." [18]

Had we examined more critically the long-term results of public school programs in speech and hearing we might have turned our attention much earlier from "target sounds" to the target of intelligible communication. Some readers may say that I am beating a stillborn horse to death. They will insist that "it can't happen here any more"—but it does. I have surveyed countless programs in action in all sections of the country. I have observed the teaching and examined the teaching materials at first sight and hand. It does happen here! Eighty percent of the speech, hearing, and language programs in one year in one state was devoted to the "correction" of the sounds: /s/, /th/, /1/ and /r/. Year after year, the teacher imprinted on a child's mind his "defective sound," a badge that he must wear like Hester Prynne's adulterous A. Generally the first step in the operation was the period devoted to "listening for speech sounds,"—for *his* sound. Enchanted as some teachers were with exercises in passive "listening for speech sounds"—particularly on Friday—the

---

[18] J. Dore and others, "Transitional Phenomena in Early Language Development," *J Child Language* 3(1) (February 1976), 25.

period proved to be counter-productive. The writer remembers the small child who was enjoined to "listen, listen, and you'll get better." He shook his head; "Naw," he said, "I could get worse!" The results? The writer is all too familiar with the bottom line on the final report: "In *structured speech* situations he is able to produce a good /s/!" In free speech? On that point: no report. And today we have observed the extension of this approach to oral language programs in some public schools. Obsolescence long since has set in; the vehicle should find a place in an antiquarian corner. Yet it is amazing how long an idea persists after the brains have been knocked out of it.

2. Since oral language is not perceived or produced as single sounds or phones, phonemic feature analysis is not central to our purpose in teaching linguistically handicapped children.[19] Phonological considerations, however, are a part of the analysis of a linguistic feature system in that it includes such phonological aspects as the perception and production of morphophonemic sequences in syllable, word, phrase strings, and in sentences of many syllables.

3. There is no general agreement among colleagues on the importance of the physiology of speech production in the oral language curriculum. Teachers must understand the physiology of respiration, phonation, resonation, and articulation, if for no other reasons than because of its special application to phonatory (prosodic) and phonological development. In oral language activities, the special language teacher uses her knowledge, for example, in teaching children rhythmic coordination of body with the melodic or prosodic patterning of oral language (pitch, stress, and duration). She also may have to motivate some children to project their voices or to articulate consonants clearly. In a language program for which I was consultant, I opposed the plan to teach children in the second and third grades, the anatomy and physiology of speech production as a project in perceptual-semantic development. I was wrong. The children were enchanted with the plaster of Paris models and with the acquisition of knowledge and a vocabulary which impressed children in upper grades for whom they gave demonstrations. It was successful.

4. Some critics have dismissed oral language programs, calling them exercises in speech improvement. The major concern of oral language is not voice and diction, the main topics of courses in speech improvement. They are but one aspect of oral production, namely, phonology. But this differentiation is not meant to denigrate courses in speech improvement. Plainly the philosophy undergirding the two programs is entirely different. They do not share methods or goals.

HALLMARKS OF ORAL LANGUAGE ACQUISITION

Language programs, whether for children with a developmental lag or disorder, should follow the course of normal language development, that is,

[19] H. Walsh, "On Certain Practical Inadequacies of Distinctive Feature Systems," *J Speech Hearing Disorders* 39(1) (February 1974), 32–43; I. Lehiste, "The Units of Speech Perception," *Speech and Cortical Functioning*, ed. J.H. Gilbert (New York: Academic Press, 1972); J.H. Abbs and H.M. Sussman, "Neurophysiological Feature Detectors and Speech Perception," *J Speech and Hearing Research* 14(1) (February 1971), 23–36; A.M. Liberman, I.G. Mattingly, M.T. Turvey, "Language Codes and Memory Codes," *Coding Processes in Human Memory,* eds. A.A. Melton and E. Martin (New York: John Wiley, 1972), 313–314; 317.

the ontogenic schedule. The primary target is the growth of comprehension and expression of ideas through the motivation and development of specific skills essential to these processes. Considered ontogenically the order of the hallmarks of language development is perceptual-semantic, phonatory, phonological, and syntactic.

Perceptual-Semantic Development is the first ontogenic principle, the major hallmark which will determine progress in all successive steps. Some writers refer to this principle as discrimination or cognition. Historically and currently leaders in the brain sciences use perception.[20] In my view, neither term—discrimination nor cognition—is a true synonym. Cognition has a more restricted meaning than perception which Guilford explains in a symposium on creativity and learning: "I prefer to restrict it (cognition) to *simple awareness* (italics mine) of knowing or being in possession of information." [21] Earlier in the discussion he refers to cognition as *recognition* of information. It is the recognition or identification of information derived from sensations from one or several modalities. We are aware of the warmth of the fireplace, for example, because of visual sensations alone or in conjunction with several sensory modalities. The term, discrimination, by derivation is a separating process, a process differentiating or detecting differences. It may be a process by which one builds perceptions. Perception, in the context in which it is used by leaders in neurophysiology, means much more than cognition or discrimination; it means the interpretation and affective appreciation of information in all its relational aspects. It follows then that in perceptual-semantic development, the child is advancing in the comprehension and/or expression of interpretation of information in meaningful language.

That all hallmarks are subordinate to perceptual-semantic development is manifested in infant behavior. Very early in life infants demonstrate by their behavior an awareness, a rudimentary comprehension of their immediate environment. They are aware of objects, people, events, and the rhythms of oral language; they form hypotheses or schemata of their meanings.[22]

Very soon these babies respond in bodily movements and elementary prosodic patterns, crude but meaningful forms of communication: This is the second ontogenic step. At first the perception is indeed rudimentary;

[20] See: D.O. Hebb, *The Organization of Behavior* (New York: John Wiley, 1949); W. Penfield and L. Roberts, *Speech and Brain Mechanisms* (Princeton, N.J.: Princeton University Press, 1959); A.R. Luria, *Higher Cortical Functions in Man* (New York: Basic Books, 1966); J.C. Eccles, *The Understanding of the Brain* (New York: McGraw-Hill, 1973); Karl Pribram, *Languages of the Brain* (Englewood Cliffs, N.J.: Prentice-Hall, Inc., 1977); G.M. Shepherd, "Microcircuits in the Nervous System," *Scientific American* 238(2) (February 1978), 92–104.

[21] J.B. Guilford, "Creativity and Learning," J.B. Lindsley and A.A. Lumsdaine, *Brain Function Vol. IV: Brain Function and Learning,* eds. J.B. Lindsley and A.A. Lumsdaine (Berkeley: University of California Press, 1967).

[22] J. Kagan, "Do Infants Think?" *Scientific American* 226(3) (March 1972), 74–82.

the patterns of movement, a generalized bodily response; and the prosodic vocalization, emotional in intent. Progression from these achievements to prosodic or melodic expression (*phonatory development*) accompanied by discrete gestural expressions is an important second step in the comprehension-expression of oral language. As perceptual-semantic growth continues, the child takes the third ontogenic step: *phonological acquisition*. He utters syllable, word, and phrase strings reflecting comprehension of elementary morphemic changes and word order. Now the child progresses rapidly partly through the interaction of thought and language and partly through the synthesis of his knowledge of phonatory, phonological and presyntactical (word order) elements in oral expression. Language grows as thought develops, and thought is aided by expression. Armstrong explains the interaction: "Once thought has been linguistically expressed, the expressions can be perceived and react back upon the mind, eventually creating more complex and sophisticated thought which in turn can be given linguistic expression. And so speech gives birth to thought." [23] —and thought to speech, we add. What thoughts? What speech? Our program is set in a framework of sensorimotor experiences because this is what children in the early elementary grades talk about; this is the stuff out of which they create their thoughts and develop their language.[24]

The fourth ontogenic step is *syntactical development*. By incorporating form or syntax in the skills associated with perceptual-semantic growth, we avoid formal instruction in structure which tends to dissociate ideas from their expression in a natural situation. This principle of the inseparability of perceptual-semantic development and syntax has received increasing theoretical support from philosophers and linguists. "Syntactic structure," Bennett maintains, "is an abstraction, a selection of certain aspects from this larger whole (semantics)." Bennett vigorously opposes Chomsky's view that "syntax stands on its own feet and if all goes well, carries semantics on its shoulders." [25] It is quite the opposite; the form is empty unless meaning dictated it. Syntactic classes and operations, in fact, are governed by perceptual-semantic relations. To express new relations, for example, among objects, persons, or events, the child perceives a likeness to structures already in his repertoire or he creates a structure based on word order.[26] The perceptual-semantic level will determine the syntactic

[23] D.M. Armstrong, "Meaning and Communication," *Philosophical Review* 80 (1971), 427–428.

[24] P. Minuchin and B. Biber, "A Child Development Approach to Language in the Preschool Disadvantaged Child," *Monographs Society for Research in Child Development* 33(8) (30 December 1968), 10–18.

[25] Jonathan Bennett, *Linguistic Behavior* (Cambridge, England: Cambridge University Press, 1976), 244–248.

[26] Melissa Bowerman, "Semantic Factors in the Acquisition of Rules for Word Use and Sentence Construction," *Normal and Deficient Child Language,* eds. D.M. Morehead and A.E. Morehead (Baltimore: University Park Press, 1976), 99–181; D.I.

forms the child needs. If he does not need and will not use complex noun phrases or verbs in the passive voice in order to communicate his sensori-motor experiences, why are we testing and drilling children on these structures? It is clear that we shall prescribe no drills or exercises or rigidly structured stories stressing syntactical forms.[27]

THE PRAGMATICS OF LANGUAGE LEARNING

Such an experiential program as the one we advocate has been facetiously called "romantic." [28] It may be romantic in the classical definition of the term in that it subordinates form to content and emphasizes imagination and emotion in oral communication. It also may be characterized as adventurous. The majority of children we have taught and observed have found it an enjoyable and profitable adventure in learning the language in the context of their own experiences and needs. That is what we mean by the pragmatic approach to teaching: teaching language in the context and environment in which it is generated. It involves the interpretation of the child's utterance; the meaning intended by the child; his sensorimotor actions that precede, accompany, and follow the utterance; the knowledge shared by the communicative dyad. The pragmatic approach makes use of speaker-listener intentions and relations and all the elements in the environment surrounding the message.[29] From this explanation, it is clear that pragmatics cannot be limited to the intent of word meanings in structured units although research has centered largely on this aspect.[30]

Why does a baby learn language? For pragmatic reasons, to intervene in his environment in order a. to satisfy his wants, and b. to interact socially with the people in his immediate environment for pleasure and interchange of information.

Slobin, "Cognitive Prerequisites for the Development of Grammar," *Studies of Child Language Development,* eds. C.A. Ferguson and D.I. Slobin (New York: Holt, Rinehart and Winston, 1973), 175–208.

[27] J. Limber, "Unravelling Competence, Performance and Pragmatics in the Speech of Young Children," *J Child Language* 3(3) (October 1976), 309–318.

[28] G.G. Abkarian, "The Changing Face of a Discipline: Isn't it Romantic?" *J Speech Hearing Disorders* 42(3) (August 1977), 422–435.

[29] Lynn S. Snyder, "Communicative and Cognitive Abilities and Disabilities in the Sensorimotor Period," *Merrill-Palmer Quarterly* 24(3) (July 1978), 161–180; E. Bates, *Language and Context: The Acquisition of Pragmatics.* (New York: Academic Press, 1976).

[30] Laurence B. Leonard and others, "Understanding Indirect Requests: An Investigation of Children's Comprehension of Pragmatic Meaning," *J Speech Hearing Research* 21(3) (September 1978), 528–537.

Infantile language must be useful language, producing returns, and hence must be taught as it is used by people—in its contextual sense. But as we have indicated, context includes much more than "sentence learning." The difference between sentence learning and pragmatic learning is analogous to the difference between cognition and perception. The autistic child may be cognizant of the meaning, the bare bones of the sentence, addressed to him but he does not perceive the social and semantic relationships embodied in the sentence. Moreover, he does not interpret the physical-emotional responses: movement patterns, facial expression, and gestures which are also a part of the "illocutionary act." [31]

Because we believe so firmly that children must comprehend and use language in its true contextual sense *as* they learn or relearn it, Chapter 8 is devoted to materials and methods to be employed in a global program. If we are to be successful in the pragmatic approach to oral language, we must include in our definition of contextual use, the child's intentions; his social interactions of anger, pleasure, approval, or indifference; his bodily movements, and gestures and facial expressions. Following pragmatic tenets we must teach the language the child needs in the form and lexicon for which he has use at *his* level of development and which is adapted to *his* environment.

Order of Teaching Hallmarks of Oral Language

In the first stage of language learning, the sensorimotor period, bodily and vocal rhythmic patterns communicate more information in a contextual sense than verbal utterance, referred to in linguistic research as "linguistic performatives." [32] We regard these gestural signals (bodily and vocal) first as precursors and then as reinforcers of verbal communication. We shall begin, therefore, teaching the *phonatory elements:* the employment of body language, out of which are developed the basic melody patterns, the *prosody* of oral language. [33] From the phonatory or prosodic elements *phonological patterns*—morphemes and syllable strings—will emerge to communicate more specific intentions and meanings. With the development of word order, phrases and sentences gradually appear. The struggle to master the *syntax,* the grammatical construction of language

[31] J. Dore, "Children's Illocutionary Acts," *Discourse Production and Comprehension,* ed. R. Freedle (Norwood, N.J.: Ablex, 1977), 227–244.

[32] Snyder, "Communicative and Cognitive Abilities and Disabilities in the Sensorimotor Period," 161–180.

[33] Phonatory or prosodic development is frequently called a *paralinguistic* feature of oral language. In our view, it is not an adjunct to language. Rhythmic bodily patterns are the first signs of communication in the newborn. Their sequellae in prosodic or melody patterns are an essential part of oral language development.

begins. In all these attributes (phonatory, phonological, and syntactical), perceptual-semantic development has played a major role. It is the base of oral communication.

Program Adaptations

Modifications in the time schedule and in the methods and materials of this program may be necessary to meet the special needs of the linguistically handicapped. For example, children who are mentally handicapped or have learning disabilities will progress at a slower rate. Gestural communication and prosodic training undoubtedly will be modified for the orthopedically handicapped. Children with special perceptual deficits may spend an extensive period of time developing a scheme for perceptual organization. Bilingual or economically disadvantaged youngsters may require more extensive teaching than others in the phonological and syntactic constituents.

REFERENCES

ABBS, J.H., and H.M. SUSSMAN, "Neurophysiological Feature Detectors and Speech Perception," *J Speech and Hearing Research,* 14(1) (February 1971), 23–36.

ABKARIAN, G.G., "The Changing Face of a Discipline: Isn't it Romantic?", *J Speech Hearing Disorders,* 42(3) (August 1977), 422–435.

BENNETT, JONATHAN, *Linguistic Behavior.* Cambridge, England: Cambridge University Press, 1976.

BUTLER, L.G., "Language Acquisition of Young Children: Major Theories and Acquisitions," *Elementary English,* 51(8) (November-December 1974), 1120–1137.

CONNOR, F.P., "The Past is Prologue: Teacher Preparation in Special Education," *Exceptional Children,* 42(7) (April 1976), 366–378.

CRYSTAL, D., "The Case of Linguistics: A Prognosis," *British J Disorders of Communication,* 7(1) (April 1972), 3–16.

DORE, J., "Holophrases, Speech Acts and Language Universals," *J Child Language,* 2(1) (April 1975), 21–40.

DORE, J. and others, "Transitional Phenomena in Early Language Development," *J Child Language,* 3(1) (February 1976), 13–28.

ECCLES, J.C., *The Understanding of the Brain.* New York: McGraw-Hill, 1973.

FERGUSON, C.A. and D.I. SLOBIN, eds., *Studies of Child Language Development*. New York: Holt, Rinehart and Winston, 1973.

FREEDLE, R., ed., *Discourse Production and Comprehension*. Norwood, N.J.: Ablex, 1977.

FREEDMAN, P.P. and R.L. CARPENTER, "Semantic Relations Used by Normal and Language-Impaired Children at Stage I," *J Speech Hearing Research,* 19(4) (December 1976), 784–795.

FRY, D., *Homo Loquens*. Cambridge, England: Cambridge University Press, 1977.

GILBERT, J.H., ed., *Speech and Cortical Functioning*. New York: Academic Press, 1972.

GOLDIN-MEADOW, S. and H. FELDMAN, "The Development of Language-Like Communication Without a Language Model," *Science,* 197 (4301) (22 July 1977), 401–404.

HOCKETT, C.F., *A Course in Modern Linguistics*. New York: Macmillan, 1958.

KAGAN, J., "Do Infants Think?" *Scientific American,* 226(3) (March 1972), 74–82.

LANGENDOEN, D.T., "Is the Theory of Generative Grammar Relevant to Neurobiology?" Paper presented at Neurosciences Research Program on *Language and the Brain: Developmental Aspects* (20 November 1972).

LEONARD, L.B. and others, "Understanding Indirect Requests: An Investigation of Children's Comprehension of Pragmatic Meaning," *J Speech Hearing Research,* 21(3) (September 1978), 528–537.

LEONARD, L.B. and others, "Nonstandardized Approaches to the Assessment of Language Behaviors," *Asha,* 20(5) (May 1978), 371–379.

LIBERMAN, A.M. and others, "A Motor Theory of Speech Perception," *Proceedings of the Speech Communications Seminar*. Stockholm: Royal Institute of Technology, 1963.

LIMBER, J., "Unravelling Competence, Performance and Pragmatics in the Speech of Young Children," *J Child Language,* 3(3) (October 1976), 309–318.

LONGHURST, T.M. and J.J. FILE, "A Comparison of Developmental Sentence Scores from Head Start Children Collected in Four Conditions," *Language, Speech and Hearing Services in Schools,* 8(1) (January 1977), 54–63.

LURIA, A.R., *Higher Cortical Functions in Man*. New York: Basic Books, 1966.

MC LEAN, J.E. and LEE K. SNYDER-MCLEAN, *A Transactional Approach to Early Language Training*. Columbus, Ohio: Chas. E. Merrill, 1978.

MELTON, A.A. and E. MARTIN, eds., *Coding Processes in Human Memory.* New York: John Wiley, 1972.

MILLER, L., "Pragmatics and Early Childhood Language Disorders: Communicative Interactions in a Half-Hour Sample," *J Speech Hearing Disorders,* 43(4) (November 1978), 419–436.

MINUCHIN, P. and B. BIBER, "A Child Development Approach to Language in the Preschool Disadvantaged Child," *Monographs Society for Research in Child Development,* 33(8) (30 December 1968), 10–18.

MOREHEAD, D.M. and A.E. MOREHEAD, eds., *Normal and Deficient Child Language.* Baltimore: University Park Press, 1976.

NICOLOSI, L., E. HARRYMAN and J. KRESHECK, *Terminology of Communication Disorders.* Baltimore: Williams & Wilkins, 1978.

ORTONY, A., "Language Isn't For People: On Applying Theoretical Linguistics to Practical Problems," *Review of Educational Research,* 45 (1975), 485–504.

PENFIELD, W. and L. ROBERTS, *Speech and Brain Mechanisms.* Princeton, N.J.: Princeton University Press, 1959.

PRIBRAM, KARL, *Languages of the Brain.* Englewood Cliffs, N.J.: Prentice-Hall, Inc., 1977.

REITMAN, W.R., *Cognition and Thought.* New York: John Wiley, 1965.

SCHIEFELBUSCH, R.L. and L.L. LLOYD, eds., *Language Perspectives— Acquisition, Retardation, and Intervention.* Baltimore: University Park Press, 1974.

SCOTT, C.M., "A Comparison of Home and Clinic Gathered Language Samples," *J Speech Hearing Disorders,* 43(4) (November 1978), 482–495.

SHEPHERD, G.M., "Microcircuits in the Nervous System," *Scientific American,* 238(2) (February 1978), 92–104.

SNYDER, LYNN S., "Communicative and Cognitive Abilities and Disabilities in the Sensorimotor Period," *Merrill-Palmer Quarterly,* 24(3) (July 1978), 161–180.

STAATS, A., *Learning, Language and Cognition.* New York: Holt, Rinehart and Winston, 1968.

STUDDERT-KENNEDY, M. and others, "Motor Theory of Speech Perception," *Psychological Review,* 77(3) (1970), 234–249.

WALSH, H., "On Certain Practical Inadequacies of Distinctive Feature Systems," *J Speech Hearing Disorders,* 39(1) (February 1974), 32–43.

Appendix A-1

T.A.L.K. (TEACHING ACTIVITIES FOR LANGUAGE KNOWLEDGE)[34]

The philosophy underlying the program and its purposes are extracted from the published statements of the consultant and the staff. T.A.L.K. is an exciting adventure in language enrichment. It is a unique adventure for it signals the abolition of traditional boundaries of speech and language programs. It marks a turning from narrow concepts of speech therapy, from teaching the minutiae pertaining to expressive language, from clinical setting and individual training to group education in communication. Originally its program was designed for low socioeconomic and low achieving schools. The present purpose of T.A.L.K. is to improve the oral language skills of all children in kindergarten through the fifth grade by providing education in the comprehension and expression of meaning in the everyday setting of the school. The major divisions of the manual indicate more precisely the organization of the program:

1. *Making friends through T.A.L.K.; other uses of oral communication;*
2. *personal and social awareness; listening skills; prosody of language; grammatic skills; cognitive skills; T.A.L.K. applied to other subjects.*

This barebones outline of the program gives little indication, however, of the social dynamics which must enter into the teaching from the very beginning. As consultant, I have observed it firsthand. Children are motivated to see, to feel, and to know the difference between enjoyable communication and the language of crisis; they learn communication, not estrangement; information, not empty exercise; friendship and mutual respect in communication, not avoidance and indifference. Articulation and voice training undoubtedly have a part in the program, but they are not primary hallmarks. Syntactic relations are stressed but only in the context of their use in everyday dialogue. They learn language melody through role playing and dramatization of familiar stories. In handling ideas, the language specialist and the classroom teachers make use of familiar events or situations at first and then teach the children to generalize and extend their competence to other subjects. I have watched these children take delight in the exploration of ideas, in suppositions about situations or events

[34] The program was developed in the Rockford Public Schools (Rockford, Illinois) in 1974 under the direction of Joyce Vee, M.S., Language Specialist, with the cooperation of the Superintendent of Schools. The staff included Ann Guedet, the language specialist in charge of teaching the program; Harold Bauer, psychologist; and a language consultant outside the school system. In July, 1979 it was approved by the Joint Dissemination Review Panel in the Education Division of the Department of Health, Education and Welfare as an Exemplary Educational Program.

and about causal relations. Essentially the goal of language enrichment could be put into a single sentence: To teach children *what* to think about, *how* to think about that which is important to them, *how* to express these thoughts in a language that will pass muster, and *how* to use language so that they live in a world in which friendship, not fight, predominates.

chapter 2

THE MEDIATION OF ORAL LANGUAGE IN THE CENTRAL NERVOUS SYSTEM

THE NEUROBIOLOGICAL BASIS OF LINGUISTIC HANDICAPS: AN INTRODUCTION

Oral language is the distinctive mark of man. Apparently it develops normally about the same time in all cultures, in all lands. The motivation to communicate seems to be the same all over the universe, so when children have something to talk about they generally begin to talk. The taproots of oral language are embedded in neurobiology, but we cannot define exactly all the mechanisms by which it emerges from these taproots. How does the nervous system order and integrate the oral information to which we attend? How do we make those connections between comprehension and verbalization, between the understanding and the telling? How do we adults remember what we have said, or more importantly, what we had planned to say? But loss of direction is not unique to adults. You teachers have observed children who also lose their way. Less able than an adult to cover for his loss of direction, a child says, "I forget," and registers a startle reaction as he realizes that the focus of the story is lost. The child may have begun well enough but was unable to remain on track to complete the specific semantic intentions. How like the adult aphasic with whom we have worked! At some point in the telling, *linguistic confusion* sets in; the focus is lost. Is this condition caused by a deficit or breakdown in the neural connections so that the child (or adult) cannot continue to draw from his memory storage? Or are false cues pulled from memory? Perhaps extraneous impulses crowd out the proper ones. If you have experienced the mixing of two channels in the receiver of your television set (a regular occurrence in cable transmission), you can appreciate the effect of conflicting messages on the individual. And finally how do you sort out the psychogenic from the neurogenic factors?

Is *cluttering* then a similar language disorder since the clutterer presents the same response pattern but expresses it motorically? Perhaps the production mechanism breaks down because the programming in the integrative processes of the cortex or subcortex is either in deficit or it short circuits. If the block in coding appears between comprehension and expression, how can you help the child to jump the hurdle? In certain children with deviant language, you know that an increase in basal metabolism incites greater activity of the limbic and reticular-activating systems and, as a consequence, the comprehension-expression cycle is facilitated. How can you stimulate the metabolic gradient?

You teachers also must have observed that many *dyslexic children* enrolled in a special reading program are also in your program for the speech handicapped. Perhaps developmental dyslexia is a perceptual deficit since not only reading but also speech, spelling, and fine motor coordination are often deficient. In one scientific report [1] it is suggested that

> . . . dyslexia may be associated with (1) bi-hemisphere representation of *spatial functions* (italics mine), in contrast to the right-hemisphere specialization observed in normal children, and (2) typical left-hemisphere representations of linguistic functions, as is observed in normal children.

As a consequence, the bilateral neural involvement in spatial processing could interfere with the left hemisphere's processing of its own specialized functions and result in deficient linguistic, sequential processing.

Do you still ask: Why do I need this knowledge? If the need is not sufficiently clear from the questions raised in the preceding paragraphs, let me cite other reasons. If we are ever to find explanations of deviant language and hence be certain of the soundness of our teaching, we can do it best by observing the language behavior of *children,* not adults, who suffer from this handicap. The great population of these children is in the public schools, but if teachers are not trained to make these observations or trained to interpret what they observe, then neither teaching nor research profits. A second reason is that although we have understanding of certain "pieces" of neurological information which we now use with profit in teaching, we need more. We have followed Ariadne's thread but not to its end. We need more extensive knowledge of the neurologic as-

[1] S.F. Witelson, "Developmental Dyslexia: Two Right Hemispheres and None Left," *Science* 195(4275) (21 January 1977), 309–311.

pects of certain central auditory mechanisms, for example, if we are to teach children who suffer, not from a loss in peripheral hearing, but from central auditory dysfunction.[2] You teachers have the best opportunity to study the language behavior of these children, but if you do not understand the neurobiology of auditory perception you will not be able to sort out the significant from the insignificant in your observations. You will not be able to use the clues in modifying the language behavior. Here are two children in a second grade classroom. Both have normal peripheral hearing. They attend closely as you read the story, but when they are to tell the story to the class, they miss several essentials of the plot. Now you allow them to read the story silently and then dictate the story to you. The result is entirely different. When the visual coding system assists by "feeding into" or making connections with the auditory perceptual areas and memory storage, the production or motor areas of expression perform well. Then their language competence and performance seem quite normal.

In order to find answers, even partial answers, we must understand the operation of certain systems of neural organization and integration although we may not understand the intricacies of structure. Indeed in this discussion we shall be concerned chiefly with function, assuming that the student will return to basic texts in our field if he wishes a review of the anatomy underlying function.

The nervous system must not be thought of as a static structure. Like all other bodily systems it is a growing, dynamic, changing structure, a complex of fibers, ninety billion glia cells that act as buffers and ten billion neurons. The brain itself triples in weight within the first twelve months of life. Nerve fibers acquire myelination in order of their importance to developing integration. Neurons grow in size, the ratio of nucleus to cytoplasm changes, and their dendritic processes increase in number. The perceptual, sensorimotor and adaptive integrative development will depend largely on the extension and modification of the neuronal assemblies. In contrast to the commonly accepted belief of a static structure, we have to think of the brain as being structurally plastic—some bodies being mature; others, developing; others, regressing. In this dynamic process, however, we cannot assume that growth is undirected or nonselective. Quite the opposite is true. "Neural circuits for behavior are definitely grown in, pre-functionally, *under genetic control*—and with great precision in an enormously complex, pre-programmed, biochemically controlled system." [3] In this dynamic process, the synapse assumes prime importance.

---

[2] D.D. Duane, "A Neurologic Perspective of Central Auditory Dysfunction," *Central Auditory Dysfunction,* ed. R.W. Keith (New York: Grune and Stratton, 1977), chap. 1.

[3] R.W. Sperry, "Left-Brain, Right-Brain," *Saturday Review* 2(23) (9 August 1975), 31.

ASPECTS OF NEURAL FUNCTION

Synapse: Basis of Function

Basic to all neural organization and integration is the synapse. (See Figure 2-1.) It is the true functional unit of the nervous system. We must understand, however, the kind of connection the synapse makes. Each neurone has hundreds of branches twisting away from it; in turn, each branch has hundreds of terminals along its membrane. As coded information in the form of an electrical impulse arrives at one of these terminals, it must cross the gap, the synapse, in order to pass itself along to the next neurone. It does so by "squirting a minute amount of a chemical neurotransmitter into the synapse." [4] This makes the membrane of the "receptor site" on the other side of the gap more permeable. The electrical impulse is carried across the gap. No physical union of the tracts has occurred. The synaptic junction is the site only of a functional contact between the neurons; there is no cytoplasmic continuity of neurons at the synapse.

The chemical, the neurotransmitter, "squirted" into the synapse apparently is some form of ribonucleic acid (RNA). However doubtful we may be about the specific form of RNA, we do know that it provides the electronic power to bridge the synaptic cleft. The current then flows into the postsynaptic cell; a functional connection has been made between the presynaptic and postsynaptic neurons. The remarkable feat in synaptic selection is that the neurons of the brain make orderly connections with each other by means of approximately 10^{14} synapses. It can be accounted for only if we assume genetic guidance of neuronal processes to the correct targets. [5]

Many brain-different children appear to suffer from deficits in potential, in genetic guidance, or in fiber connections. What has happened when the functional connections seem to be lacking or are misguided or when the potential is so reduced that the cleft cannot be jumped? We do not know; we can only surmise. According to one theory, the *quantum hypothesis,* [6] a large number of quanta or chemical packets are stored in the nerve terminals or at the synapse and are "released" or fired by the action potentials of nerves in response to stimuli. [7] If the firing fails, a defective genetic code may account for the fact that the number of chemical packets (RNA)

[4] H. Rosenfeld and K. Klivington, "Inside the Brain," *Saturday Review* 2(23) (9 August 1975), 13.

[5] S.H. Barondes, ed., *Neuronal Recognition* (New York: Plenum, 1976).

[6] L.P. Swisher, "Auditory Intensity Discrimination in Patients with Temporal-Lobe Damage," *Cortex* 3(2) (1967), 179–193.

[7] J.A. Nathanson and Paul Greengard, "Second 'Messengers' in the Brain," *Scientific American* 237(20) (August 1977), 108–119.

FIGURE 2-1   Diagram of Sensory (Proprioceptive) and Motor Impulses from the Muscle Spindle of the Tongue. Note Feedback Circuit.

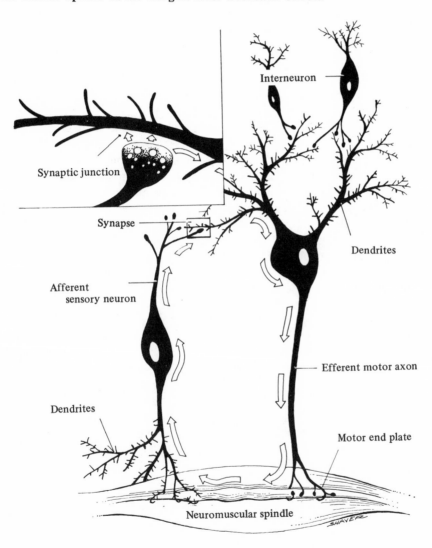

is insufficient or the electrical potential is low. Or unfavorable uterine conditions in the mother may have resulted in malnutrition, infection, or toxemia. Postnatal disease such as encephalitis or pertussis or idiosyncratic blood patterns such as the Rh factor may have damaged or destroyed whole bundles of nerve fibers. In some children it could well be an inability to shut out neural connections that have a negative or disruptive effect on the integration of a response. The nervous system presumably has lost its ability to sort out the extraneous from the purposive, or germane, stimuli so that a gallimaufry of sensations and associations enters the integrative complex. Chaos results, and the child either makes nonpurposive, hyperactive behavioral responses or "unable to put the blocks together," makes no response. We shall discuss the subject again in connection with the role of excitation and inhibition in neural integration.

We must abandon any concept of the central nervous system as a fixed action structure. As a child develops, new connections among neurons are made until a network, or a system, develops under the guidance of the genetic code. At every stage in life some synaptic connections will be mature, others will develop, and yet others will regress. Geriatricians are fond of saying that an individual is as old as "the grease in his joints." From a physical standpoint that may be right. Mentally the individual is as old as the "juice at the synapse."

Homeostasis

As a prologue to the discussion of specific aspects of neural function, it is well to review a major neurophysiological principle dominating human behavior, that is, the *closed-loop control system* in establishing *homeostasis*.

Homeostasis may be defined as the regulated balancing of nervous and endocrine factors in the organism in order to preserve an internal steady state. A homeostat is stable, however, only so long as it maintains an adaptively modifiable equilibrium. The thermostat regulating the heating system in one's home does not maintain an absolute temperature. In practice, the actual temperature fluctuates about the preset temperature control. To achieve and maintain this state of *labile stability* in temperature, the thermostat becomes a part of the closed-loop system employing feedback. An increase in the temperature of the home is followed by lowered activity in the furnace with a consequent decrease in heat production. When the temperature goes down below the thermometer setting, heat production increases.

Biologically analogous control systems have the same goal: to compensate for the difference between the actual and the predetermined operation through the utilization of feedback. The maintenance of a relatively constant body temperature; fluid balance; hormonal levels of adrenalin, thyroxin, and other hormones in the blood stream; and the smooth integration among voluntary muscles in all activities: these are examples of the closed-loop control system employing feedback. The central nervous system, in conjunction with the endocrine system, acts as a master homeostat exercising control over minor homeostats—respiratory, thermal, vascular, and lymphatic. Its physiological purpose is to achieve a labile stability of the internal environment of the individual. Note again that static ability is not the goal of the control. Just as the simple thermostat designed to maintain temperature keeps oscillating slightly above and below the desired value, so the neuroendocrine controls of feedback-feedforward in the individual do not achieve an exact goal. "Here you miss or there exceed the mark." The result in muscle response, for example, is a slow, imperceptible tremor.

Feedback

The phenomenon of *feedback* (see Figures 2-1, 2-2, 2-3) in which output controls or regulates input pervades every daily activity, determining at every step whether the operation is overshooting or falling short of the mark. Few sensorimotor skills can be learned except as one performs the action. One cannot be taught to dance, for example, by verbal analysis of the steps involved. He is aided, to be sure, by visual, auditory, and tactile perception, but he must rely fundamentally upon proprioceptive feedback from the muscles involved in dancing. How does one check the spelling of a word about which he is in doubt? He writes it quickly without looking at the word, "lest his eyes make the fool of his other senses." He is relying solely on tactile-proprioceptive feedback, a muscle memory pattern shutting out for the moment other sensory modalities. In language learning, feedback acts mainly as a negative mechanism restricting and correcting input, integration, and output so that the goal of accurate communication is achieved. Inhibitory impulses (negative feedback) may shut out all information presented to it by other sensory receptors. Irrelevant auditory materials, for example, can be excluded in the medulla (ventral and dorsal cochlear nuclei); or they can be turned back by means of feedback loops higher in the brain stem, in the thalamus or in the cerebral cortex. In the primary auditory areas of the cerebral cortex, subtle inaccuracies in the auditory percept also must be ironed out by the feedback mechanism. Even in the process of utterance, at the "tip-of-the-

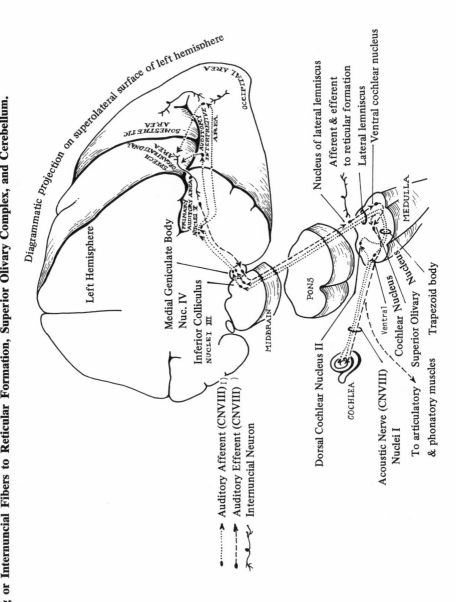

FIGURE 2-2 Schematic Diagram of Auditory Afferent (Primary Sensory) and Efferent (Feedback) Systems Instrumental in Perception-Expression of Oral Language. Nuclear Orders I–V Indicate Synaptic Levels of Auditory Afferent Pathway. Note Correlating or Internuncial Fibers to Reticular Formation, Superior Olivary Complex, and Cerebellum.

FIGURE 2-3 Schema of Integrative Mechanisms (Feedforward-Feedback) for Oral Language Mediating Tactile-Kinesthetic (Proprioceptive) Impulses from Tongue and Mandible-lip Area. Impulses Originate in Hypoglossal Nerve (CNXII) and Mandibular Section of the Trigeminal Nerve (CNV).

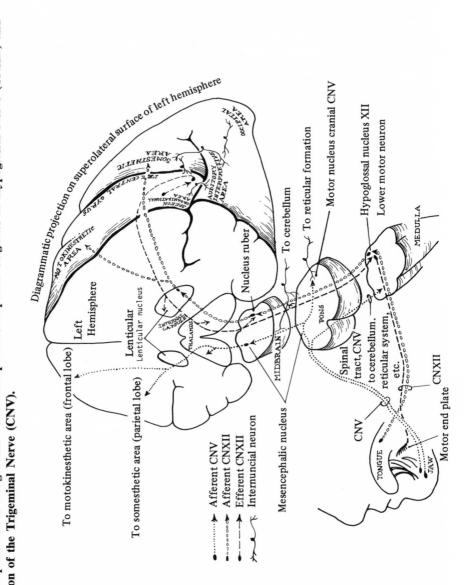

33

tongue," feedback is operative making subtle corrections in the percept. If inhibitory control is interrupted, the resulting increase in the afferent activity produces sharp increases in sensitivity to any changes in auditory intensity.[8]

Feedback Delay and Oral Language

If there is a delay in feedback, perception may be markedly attenuated. This delay may account for the finding that some linguistically handicapped children may need 75–100 msec in contrast to a linguistically proficient child's reaction time of 5–10 msec in order to perceive a syllable sequence at the acoustic level.[9] Other oral language deficits assigned to feedback delay or interference and exhibited in oral expression are repetitive verbalization, distorted speech rhythms (dysprosody), and persistent phonemic deviations.[10]

Consider feedback in relation to another determinant of oral communication, the endocrines. One speaks generally of a "stress syndrome" controlled by pituitary and adrenal hormones.[11] When the secretion of the stimulating hormones reaches a certain level in the bloodstream (in normal states), the feedback mechanism connected with the hypothalamus shuts down or reduces the amount, thus avoiding a crisis in oral behavior.

Feedforward

The neurobiological control system also must utilize the *feedforward* (FF) mechanism. (See Figure 2-3.) In contrast to feedback, it increases neural activity, accelerates its conductance (by lowering resistance at the synapse), and heightens the response by preparing specific cortical fields for the reception of sensorimotor patterns. In verbal coding, for example, certain areas in the temporal and parietal areas of the brain will display a sudden spurt in electrical potential. Feedback and feedforward loops acting through subcortical systems presumably are responsible for the heightened activity in these cortical areas and, at the same time, for the

---

[8] L.P. Swisher, "Auditory Intensity Discrimination in Patients with Temporal-Lobe Damage," *Cortex* 3(2) (1967), 179–193.

[9] W.G. Hardy, "Hearing in Children—Panel Discussion," (Sixth International Congress on Audiology). *Laryngoscope* 68 (1958), 224–228.

[10] G.J. Borden and E.D. Mysak, "Feedback Systems: Research and Therapy." Short course presented at American Speech and Hearing Association Convention, Houston, Texas, November 1976.

[11] S. Levine, "Stress and Behavior," *Scientific American* 224(1) (January 1971), 26–32.

reduced electrical potential of surrounding nonstrategic areas. In short, they prepare these areas to "attend" to certain kinds of incoming neural patterns and inhibit surrounding fields from getting into the act. In augmenting and directing signal patterns, FF eliminates a common characteristic of servomechanisms known as velocity lag. Like feedback, FF also acts as a goal-seeking control, but it does so by a positive force of selecting, augmenting, and directing sensorimotor patterns. The process is analogous to a *timer,* or *modulator,* on your house thermostat. The timer changes the setting, raising it early in the morning and lowering it at night. It acts as a *modulator* of the thermostat. In the regulation of body temperature, the hypothalamus acts by means of *feedback* as the thermostat in the regulation of body temperature, but other neuroendocrine glands act as the *timer,* or *modulator,* over the process. So in the production of oral language the FF mechanism in the neuroendocrine system *modulates* sensorimotor patterns by aiding and abetting those patterns and integrative areas most significant to the realization of the goal.

The neural operation underlying the feedback-feedforward mechanism in oral language will be better understood after you have read the sections on the subsystems of neural integration. Suffice it to say here that multiple feedback-feedforward circuits are in operation in language learning. Countless feedforward-feedback loops and loops within loops, many of which are part of the subcortical reticular system (to be discussed later), intercede between input and output. They must determine the priority, segregation, and integration of sensorimotor processes. At the cortical level tactile, kinesthetic, and auditory impulses must be conjoined in the appropriate sequences with respect to time and space. Neuronal assemblies that mediate the retrieval of memory patterns of linguistic sequences, for example, may be suppressed or brought actively into the percept. Finally, if the muscle synergies are to be organized so that we "speak the speech" expertly, the feedback circuits governing the muscle spindles (gamma fibers) of the larynx, jaw, palate, tongue, and lips must operate in near-perfect synchrony. The mechanism of feedback-feedforward begins at the periphery and operates throughout every phase of linguistic coding. Where the master homeostats, or integration centers, are for these biological activities have not been determined. The hypothalamus probably acts as the integration center for the regulation of temperature, but undoubtedly there are higher controls influencing this regulation center. Other researchers believe that the reticular system is the "bias wheel," the major homeostatic control. Still others associate the limbic system with the master homeostats.[12]

---

[12] K. Pribram, "Control Systems and Behavior," *Brain and Behavior,* ed. M.A.B. Brazier (Washington, D.C.: American Institute of Biological Sciences, 1963) II, 376.

Homeostatic Control and Feedback
in Language Learning

Developing oral language demands much of a plastic, slightly unstable nervous system so its homeostatic overseers must be on constant alert. They must be sensitive to such factors as traffic load, potential strength of neural circuits, efficacy of feedback, and the diverse components to be patterned. In every case homeostatic controls will be governed by the relation of the neural events to the total behavior of the individual.[13] Normally the milieu during 'attention intérieur' will not be disturbed by unexpected events of a certain magnitude. In motor speech, for example, a considerable margin of safety may be exercised before homeostatic controls are taxed. Note the adaptations that one must make in respiration, phonation, resonation, and articulation for speech, yet equilibrium normally is maintained. Study of a single aspect, respiration, reveals that it is markedly different from the patterns of quiet breathing. The number of breaths per minute is sharply reduced. Inhalation is shorter and more shallow than exhalation. The normal CO_2-O_2 balance regulating quiet respiration is upset. Electrical activities of the inhaling muscles may continue through part of the exhaling phase. Despite all these modifications of breathing for speech, the individual normally is able to tolerate them without adverse effect. Homeostasis operates. A cerebral-palsied child whose homeostasis is impaired, on the other hand, complains frequently of dizziness during speech production probably brought on by dysrhythmia of the respiratory musculature.

As neural integration for oral language proceeds, feedback from areas directing phonatory, phonological, syntactic, and semantic patterns becomes more complex. The child's initial trials are often inexact with numerous random oscillations from the target. Gradually the random efforts displayed in "overproduction" of bodily and articulatory gestures, word finding, syntactical circumlocutions, and so on are reduced and refined, and the oscillations from the preset target become less frequent and less noticeable.

Defective Homeostasis and Language Learning

In the normal process of learning a language, we presume that the systems of neural-endocrine control are in a state of stable lability. The central

[13] P. Hernandez-Peon, H. Scheer, and M. Jouvet, "Modification of Electrical Activity in Cochlear Nucleus During 'Attention' in Unanesthetized Cats," *Science* 123 (24 February 1956), 331–332; R. Galambos, "Suppression of Auditory Activity by Stimulation of Efferent Fibers to Cochlea," *J Neurophysiology* 19 (September 1956), 424–437; R. Galambos, G. Sheatz, and V.G. Vernier, "Electrophysiological Correlates of a Conditioned Response in Cats," *Science* 123 (2 March 1956), 376–377.

regulators, the reticular and limbic systems, are set at an optimum at the level of equilibrium. The child is set to attend, to learn. Homeostatic controls, however, vary greatly both because of genetic and adventitious factors. Some children from birth are not able to achieve an operative biological equilibrium. The physical organism succumbs to every ill wind; the constitution is a frail reed, indeed. The higher functions of the nervous system show a similar failure in adaptation. In the actuation of synergies of excitation and inhibition, of attention and motivation, the neural and hormonal machinery seems weak, ineffective, or out of gear. It cannot produce a state of stable lability.

In another group of children, physiochemical events have conspired to upset homeostasis. Disease or trauma has left its effect, sometimes only a subtle effect, upon learning. Feedback triggering in the neurocouple of the reticular activating system may have broken down either partially or completely. It is no longer sensitive to the changing milieu and hence does not contribute effectively to stability. Another subcortical system of control, called the limbic system, may attempt to stabilize the emotional matrix and if the events are of short duration, it may be successful. In such an unstable and uncontrolled state of "free energy," auditory, visual, and tactile-kinesthetic streams of impulses course through the nervous system, but the integrative mechanisms are unable to organize them into spatio-temporal patterns of perception. Sometimes such an individual attempts to block certain impulses from entering the CNS. A ten-year-old child who had suffered serious cortical injury in an accident found that he was more successful in the first stages of relearning language when all stimuli except auditory impulses were eliminated. As he proceeded, however, he discovered that language was imprinted more effectively in terms of recall when tactile-kinesthetic and visual modalities were linked with auditory impulses.

The S-R Concept

We can no longer describe neural activity mediating oral language simply in terms of stimulus and response. (See Figure 2-4.) Indeed we are unable to describe the simplest behavior of man this way. Oral language involves operations much more sophisticated and creative than is implied in any S-R concept. Human speech is not the automatic response of a neuromechanical robot whose button has been punched by the programmer. Neither can verbal behavior be described as a simple transmission of tactile-kinesthetic and auditory impulses to some prescribed area in the cortex from which the motor mechanism of speech will be set in operation. A baby of three months does not rely entirely upon immediate S-R patterns. Very early on, the infant forms a hypothesis about the object, the event, the person and makes a behavioral response. Communication

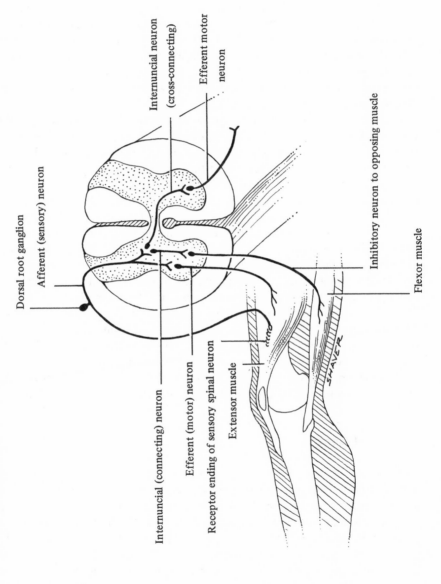

FIGURE 2-4 Direct and Crossed Reflex Arc.

38

for him is thus a creative process, not a matter of an automatic S-R arc. If the toy is an old one, he may take no notice of it. If it is a toy animal making the familiar sounds of a barking puppy, he fits it into his percept of *puppy* and reaches for it. If it is a different toy animal, the like of which he has not seen before, and which emits unearthly sounds, the toy is not fitted into any scheme. The baby screams, gesticulates, or moves away from it, if possible. What he cannot fit in his scheme of things he rejects.

The child developing oral language learns early to link past objects, events, persons, and associated behavioral patterns with stimuli in the current environment. And here is the most creative aspect of his language growth. He begins to predict future happenings in terms of past and present knowledge of his world. He asks questions and comments about stimuli no longer in his immediate environment. Joe (18 months) cannot find Pogo in his toy box. He points to the bedroom and repeats the first syllable, *po-po-po,* over and over. He not only remembers that Pogo went to bed with him last night, but he also "talks" about Pogo. Jerry (three years) looks at storm clouds and urges Mommy to run to their car. In other words, he predicts future events in terms of past and present knowledge. His notions about happenings in the world of objects, events and relations may not always be correct but they are *his* notions, *his* percepts. Sometimes he gets a faulty notion because of double meanings in adult language. To my granddaughter, under three years of age, I said: "I don't think we can go now. Look, it's spitting snow." Kim responded by showing how one spits. She was entranced by the word "spitting" so she demonstrated several times how a person spits. She had one percept for the word and could not fit the new percept immediately into the action of spitting. It is this predictive, creative capacity effectuated through high neural synergies which precludes language learning—or any learning—from being defined as stimulus and response. Some behaviors, chiefly those of habituation, indeed may be the product of S-R conditioning, instrumental learning, or operant conditioning. For rats, rabbits, and chimps, operant conditioning may be the manual of operation. For the lively, normal baby of two years, this writer finds it a half-price cookbook. The complex, creative behavior of oral communication involving the knowledge and manipulation of symbolic elements of a high order deserves a more dynamic and sophisticated approach to learning than S-R conditioning.

"The Reflex Arc"

Because conditioned and unconditioned reflexes are associated with the motor patterns of oral communication, we include the reflex arc in aspects of neural function, albeit with some reluctance. (See Figure 2-3.)

Unconditioned reflexes are supposed to have essentially innate mechanisms, are a part of the genetic code of the species, regular in appearance, and independent of previous experience. We concede that they are basic to all visceral activity, but are they truly automatic, invariable responses in man? Probably not. Certainly few "reflexes" employed in speech—and possibly in all human behavior—are innate, completely automatic, and independent of influence, either of facilitation or inhibition from other neural circuits. Behavior in man is generally subjected to control by the brain stem and cortex even in such vital processes as breathing, circulation, muscle tone, posture, and laryngeal valving. In speech production we know that these activities are highly modifiable.

Perhaps the simple knee-jerk, a *two-neurone extensor response,* is the least modifiable. Tapping the tendon of the muscle that extends the knee joint suddenly stretches the muscle and the neuromuscular spindle within the muscle. The stretched spindle excites the afferent neuron endings that discharge to the fast conducting motor neurons terminating in motor end plates; the result, a sudden contraction of extensor muscle fibers. A continuous stretch, on the other hand, is dependent on a three-neurone arc. Again this "reflex" may be altered by cortical inhibition.

We think of walking as an "automatic," reciprocal action of muscle groups involving four or five neuron arcs, yet these arcs are not free of sensorimotor controls in brain stem and cortex. As another example of the "automatic" response, on one occasion your response to smoke in the receptors of your nostrils may be automatic although it could involve several neuron chains. On another occasion—when you are reading a good mystery story—inhibition may operate to shut out all response to the smoke information, including a cortical interpretation of the origin and kind of the stimulus. In sum, neural circuits mediating excitation, inhibition, summation, and interpretation may modify responses at the brain stem and cortical levels whether they be "reflex" or voluntary. In this sense the reflex arc is a misnomer; it is rarely a reflex or an arc, although it may be a useful diagnostic sign of the integrity of the CNS.

Facilitation-Inhibition

Oral communication—or any other behavioral response—would not be possible without the exercise of the principle of facilitation-inhibition manifested in neural function. Although all sectors of the nervous system operate on this principle, its effect on oral communication can best be demonstrated by the performance of two systems: the reticular and the limbic.

INTEGRATIVE SYSTEMS IN ORAL LANGUAGE

The Reticular Activating-Adapting System

Historically this network in the brainstem was simply described as a kind of reticule of fibers to which was assigned nebulous properties of association or transfer. (See Figures 2-3, 2-4, 2-5.) Today, its functions as an activator and adapter mechanism extend to all aspects of oral language.

> It awakens the brain to consciousness and keeps it alert; it directs the traffic of messages in the nervous system; it monitors the myriads of stimuli that beat upon our senses, accepting what we need to perceive and rejecting what is irrelevant; it tempers and refines our muscular activity and bodily movements. We can go even further and say that it contributes in an important way to the highest mental processes—the focusing of attention, introspection and doubtless all forms of reasoning.[14]

In sum, the reticular system plays a primary role in augmenting and inhibiting impulses coursing via conventional tracts through the nervous system. It acts as an energizer and organizer. Through its direct influence over cerebellar, brainstem, and cortical function, it insures efficient operation of all sensorimotor pathways. Particularly cogent to our concern in language learning are its activities associated with arousal and drive-setting mechanisms.

How does the reticular system exercise its alerting function? First, it probably sensitizes certain cortical fields to respond to stimuli significant to them, surrounding these "fields of influence" at the same time by high threshold areas. Second, it may act to inhibit or facilitate the transmission of neural information, even through the specific primary cortical-spinal pathways. Third, it apparently establishes priority of attention among stimuli by methods not completely clear. In establishing motivation leading to attention, it probably acts in conjunction with the limbic system, to be discussed later. Together they may accomplish this end by excluding or interrupting certain impulses when others of greater importance to the individual must be attended to. According to Galambos [15] attention may be so powerful that the reticular-limbic system will exclude the incoming signal either at the peripheral or pickup point of sensory input or

---

[14] J.D. French, "The Reticular Formation," chap. 3, *Altered States of Awareness* (San Francisco: W.H. Freeman and Company, 1972), 29; Walle J.H. Nauta and Michael Feirtag, "The Organization of the Brain," *Scientific American* 241(3) (September 1979), 88–111.

[15] Galambos, "Suppression of Auditory Nerve Activity by Stimulation of Efferent Fibers to Cochlea," 424–437.

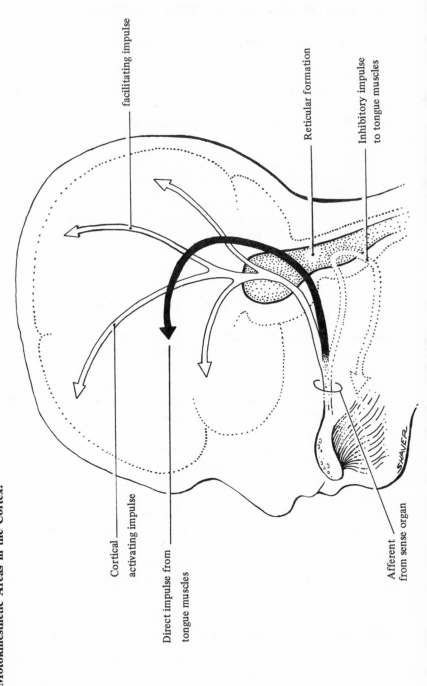

FIGURE 2-5 The Reticular System. Schema of its Role in Activation and Inhibition of Sensory Impulses (Tactile-proprioceptive) from the Tongue to Cortical and Subcortical Areas. In Addition Specific Information is Conveyed to the Somesthetic and Motokinesthetic Areas in the Cortex.

at several points after it has entered the CNS. Unless the pattern is deeply set and motivation keen, sensations from the viscera will take precedence over such sensory modalities as vision, audition, proprioception, and taction.

Exactly how the reticular system effects a synchrony, a harmonious pattern, we do not know beyond the fact that it possesses all the "materials" for selection, modification, and organization. Presumably it must reset the excitability cycles of many neuron assemblies so that they can be fitted into the matrix of sustained excitatory or inhibitory patterns held in the reticular formation and the dendritic meshwork of the cortex.

Is *facilitation or inhibition* the stronger agent in the reticular organizing process? Probably inhibition. The reticular system is a main thoroughfare to and from the cortex and consequently is loaded with sensorimotor traffic. In producing coordination and interaction among impulses, the reticular monitor necessarily must be busy weeding out or trimming impulses that do not contribute effectively to the total patterns of perception and expression.

In recapitulation, the reticular system assists perception and motor response in these ways: It has altered the cortex, sensitizing certain "fields of influence" and decreasing the potential of adjacent areas. By determining the rate (frequency code) and patterning of nerve impulses, it brings those of a kind into a space relation and shunts to particular areas certain packets of information. In order to effect this organization and direction, it must shut out extraneous impulses, increase the potential of faint but significant impulses, modulate slightly the form of some temporal patterns, and thus bring the whole complex of sensorimotor charges into a meaningful whole. It governs, in short, the coding of all varieties of integration, including perception, and learning and motor response. It is solely or largely responsible for the development and maintenance of a dynamically ordered economy of behavioral response and adjustment.[16]

Linguistic Handicaps and Adaptive Failures of the Reticular System

Our observation of the breakdown of facilitation and inhibition in linguistically handicapped children leads us to conclude that in some of these children the deficit is in the reticular system. The child is not able to discriminate or organize afferent impulses. It is as if the major networks are battered by an army of disorganized impulses and excitability cycles which

[16] Levine, "Stress and Behavior," 26–32.

bear no spatial and—what is more important—no temporal relation to each other. It is conceivable that in these children the alerting mechanism operates—perhaps too well—but the reticular system is not selective. It does not inhibit those sensorimotor patterns which are not useful to the present behavioral response. These children may try to shunt into the background sensations deleterious to perception and learning, but they rarely are successful. The sluice gates are open. They overreact to class bells; the light is too bright; the room too warm. On a higher level they experience even greater difficulty. "I try," one says, "but I cannot see what you see in that picture." Another complains, "I always seem to fall over the very thing I am trying to avoid." "I get that tune mixed up with other songs I know," yet another says. We presume that reticular networks, or the cortex in conjunction with the reticulum, cannot suppress aberrant impulses, step up necessary potentials, and modulate still others. The effect on speech perception may be likened to visual perception in a fog. Words and phrases have no faces; they do not emerge as clear figures upon a ground.[17]

In its integrative function, the reticular system also contributes to the regulation of such sensorimotor aspects of behavior as phasic movement, muscle tone, and righting reactions. Impairment of these functions, *sensorimotor* in origin, can be observed in cerebral palsy. In severe cases, excitations flow in uninhibited fashion until tonic contraction has virtually paralyzed, for instance, the movement of the articulators in speech. The fine gradations of tension and relaxation which one sees normally in posture and movement are gone. The system responds nonselectively; all stimuli apparently share equal time and force. A frequent accompaniment to these manifestations is a lack of control of the righting reflexes. As the cerebral-palsied child develops, the head and neck assume bizarre positions. Voluntary effort to control them only results in more extreme responses. Little wonder that the athetoid exclaims, "But the harder I try to relax, the more tense I become."

Injury to the motor cortex has been the classical explanation of cerebral palsy. This explanation is being supplanted by etiologies that include the reticular-activating-adaptive system. In some types of cerebral palsy, undoubtedly this system, not the motor cortex, has suffered insult. "In higher forms, it (the reticular complex) is thus directly responsible for postural reflexes and righting reactions, and plays a critical role in phasic movement and in maintenance of muscle tone."[18]

---

[17] D.B. Lindsley and W.F. Adey, "Availability of Peripheral Input to the Midbrain Reticular Formation," *Experimental Neurology* 4 (October 1961), 358–376.

[18] A.A. Ward, "Efferent Functions of the Reticular Formation," *Reticular Formation of the Brain,* eds. H.H. Jasper and others (Boston: Little, Brown, 1958), 263–264.

Voluntary Motor Activity

The reticular system also must be concerned with the efficient projection of voluntary motor impulses in such a complex process as the articulation of speech. It demands a satisfactory range, level, and duration of tonic attack which must extend beyond the requisites of single sounds or syllables. In the rapid fire of the speech continuum, is the reticular control able to effect smooth coordination? Or is the whole synergy out of tune? Speech characterized by an "awkward tongue," a "slightly spastic tongue," or "cluttering" may be the result of a breakdown in reticular controls or in their integration with an impaired motor cortex.

The explicit nature of control of corticoreticular bidirectional loops has been demonstrated in experimentally produced lesions of the reticular system. Impulses initiated by the primary motor neurons in the cortex may travel as usual in the pyramidal tract, *but* they do not result in contraction. Some neurologists believe that what has been lost is the ability to *initiate* motor movement. Since muscles do not respond singly but in patterned synergies, motor impulses probably cannot be started because they cannot be organized into synergies without the help of the reticular system. In this connection one remembers the muscular rigidity characteristic of the Parkinson syndrome. Rigidity, per se, however, is not the central problem in speech. The greater handicap is the inability to initiate organized movement patterns of the jaw and tongue. This disability could result from the deterioration of circuits connecting cortex, basal nuclei, and the reticular formation.[19] The rigidity of Parkinsonism may be likened to that of the cerebral-palsied child or the stutterer who is also unable to initiate movement patterns of the speech organs.

The Limbic System

A second neural complex contributing to facilitation and inhibition is the limbic system. (See Figures 2-6 and 2-7.) Its composition is not easy to define. Probably it is a functionally integrated system, but certainly it is not a structural unit. Presumably such substructures of the cortex as the hippocampal gyrus lying in the posterior horn of the lateral ventricle, the cingulate gyrus, and the adjacent nuclear masses in the thalamus, mamillary bodies, and hypothalamus belong to the limbic system. Considerable support also has been found for the inclusion in the limbic complex of the

[19] A. Brodal and B. Kaada, "Cutaneous and Proprioceptive Impulses in the Pyramidal Tract of the Cat," *Acta Physiologica Scandinavica* 29 (August 1953), 131–132; Nauta and Feirtag, "The Organization of the Brain," 108.

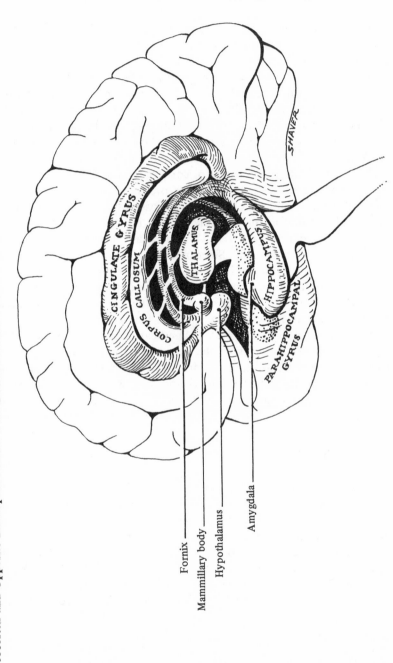

FIGURE 2-6 Major Processing Stations of the Limbic System. Both Input and Output Pathways from the Temporal Lobe, Neocortex and Opposite Hemisphere Make Connections in these Nuclear Masses.

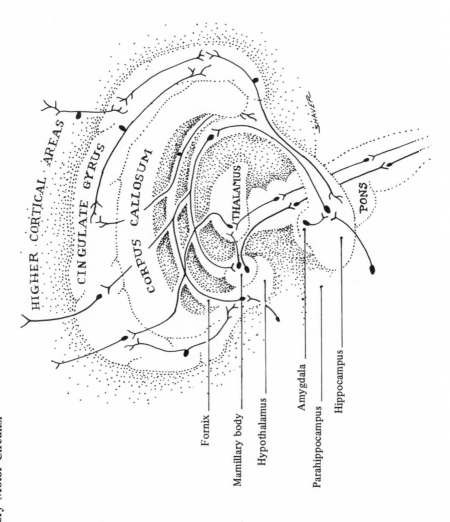

FIGURE 2-7 Schema of Some Functional Connections of the Limbic System which Mediate Motivating and Emotional Processes in CNS. Cortical Limbic Feedback Circuits Interact Within the Limbic System and with Cortex Reticular System and Other Brain Stem Sensory Motor Circuits.

amygdala, habenula, and the basal section of the fronto-temporal cortex. As you will note in the diagrammatic sketch, these nuclear masses are located in the basal portion of the cerebrum. Their influence on other sectors of the nervous system, however, is thought to be far reaching and significant. The wealth of fiber connections within the limbic system and with the cortex, with nuclear assemblies in the reticular formation, and with the autonomic system suggest that it plays an important role in language behavior.

Function

Certainly the limbic system is more primitive, and therefore its mediation and control of affective states of the individual may be unstable.

> One scientist proposed a striking model of how the cerebral cortex works with the more primitive limbic system. He likened the thinking brain to the rider of a horse; the older brain to the horse. They are interrelated and have vaguely similar perceptions, evaluations, goals, reactions, but are not exactly alike. Both systems are efficient and competent. But, their interaction is far from completely efficient and smooth. Just so, the interaction between the "higher" intellectual centers and the more primitive centers controlling attention, mood, affect, arousal . . . may be unstable, incompetent, and variable.[20]

The control of metabolism by the limbic system will not be considered, although the link between extreme emotional states and hunger or thirst, for example, is well known. Limiting our discussion to its role in language learning we may say that the limbic system operates in three areas:

1. emotional reinforcement and motivation,
2. recent memory, and
3. mastery of purposive motor response.

Memory and purposive motor patterning, however, might well be assisted by emotional dynamics and therefore be subject to indirect mediation by the limbic system.

The dominant effect of limbic activity on language learning is a general emotional coloration, a pervasive reinforcement and motivation. Excitation of the hippocampus (a part of the limbic system), by haptic, auditory, and visual impulses, for example, will elicit trains of rhythmically recurring potentials which persist well beyond the duration of stimulation

[20] G.W. Brown, "Temperament and Child Development," *J Learning Disabilities* 6:9 (November 1973), 560.

and will outlast the rapid activity of the neocortex.[21] Presumably this is the emotional resurgence that continues beyond the stimulus. At what point does emotional facilitation by the limbic system become great enough to stimulate learning; at what point does it paralyze thought? The control over emotion and motivation may lie in the gating power of the reticular system discussed in the preceding section.

Recent memory may be disturbed by interference specifically with limbic areas in the deep masses of the fronto-temporal lobes.[22] Milner in her study of impaired recall of verbal material assigns the loss to these areas.[23] Others would assign "primary" or short-term memory specifically to the hippocampal formation.[24] The question is whether these tracts contribute specifically to the retention of what has been learned or whether they are instrumental in sharpening the focus of the pattern by emotional reinforcement and hence aiding recall.[25]

Another nuclear mass, the thalamus, and especially the hypothalamus, is intimately related to the limbic and the reticular systems. In fact, certain sections are included in the two systems. Most of the fiber pathways to the hypothalamus, both from rostral and caudal sources, have come to be identified with the limbic and reticular systems. The thalamus and hypothalamus, whether considered separately or as integral parts of the limbic and reticular systems, are important emotional and motivational matrices of language behavior.

CORTICAL MECHANISMS IN ORAL LANGUAGE

Hemispherical Dominance

Hemispherical dominance refers to horizontal superiority, to the preeminence of one cerebral hemisphere over the other in such specialized activities as hand control, language, analytical processes, and memory. (See Figure 2-8.) Although left hemisphere specialization is thought to be largely genetic in origin and tends to be dominant even in left-handed

---

[21] J.W. Papez, "A Proposed Mechanism of Emotion," *Archives of Neurology* 38 (Chicago) (October 1937), 725–744.

[22] W.R. Adey, "Brain Mechanisms and the Learning Process," *Federal Proceedings* 20 (1961), 617–627.

[23] B. Milner, "Laterality Effects in Audition," *Interhemispheric Relations and Cerebral Dominance,* ed. F. Mountcastle (Baltimore: Johns Hopkins Press, 1962), 179.

[24] R.L. Isaacson, "Memory Processes and the Hippocampus," chapter 12, *Short-Term Memory,* eds., D. Deutsch and J.A. Deutsch (New York: Academic Press, 1975).

[25] W.R. Adey, "Studies of Hippocampal Electrical Activity During Approach Learning," *Brain Mechanisms and Learning,* ed. J.F. Delafresnaye (Oxford: Blackwell Scientific Publications, 1961), 585.

FIGURE 2-8 **Diagrammatic Sketch of Hemispherical Dominance Designating Functions of Major (Left) and Minor (Right) Hemispheres.**

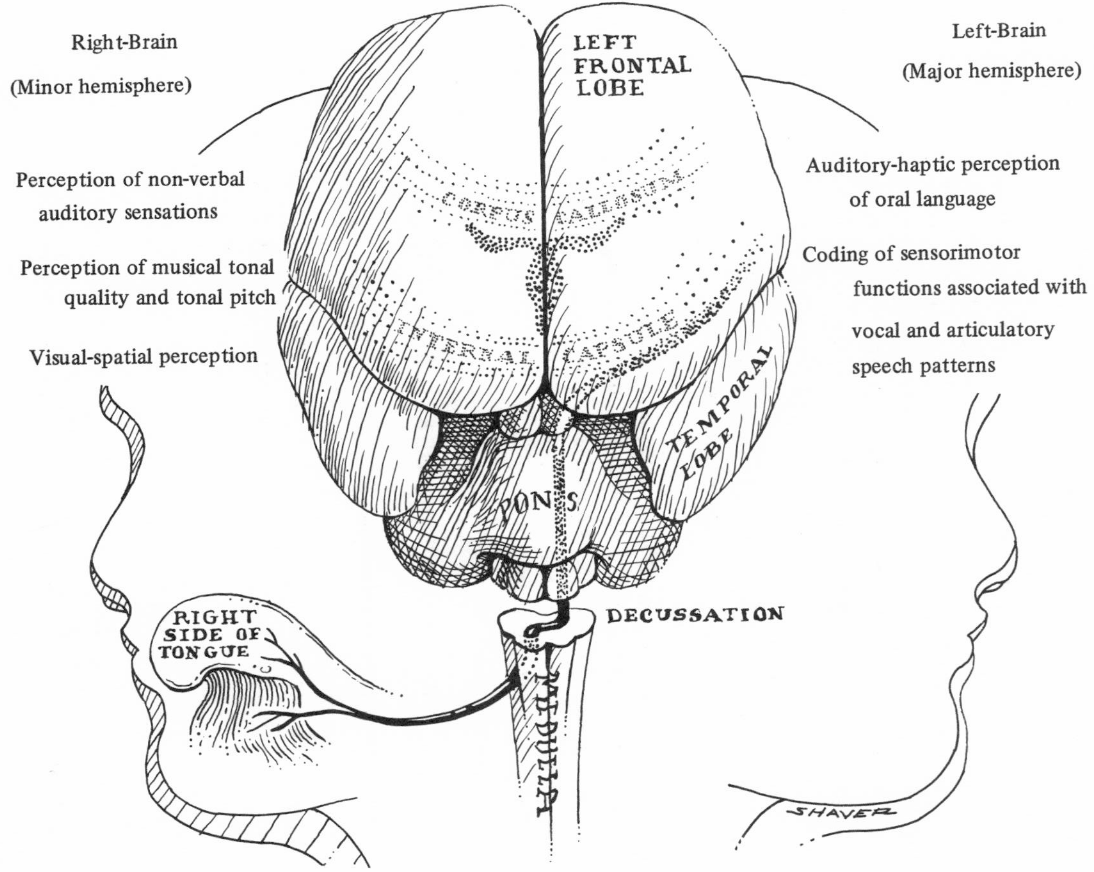
Right-Brain
(Minor hemisphere)
Perception of non-verbal auditory sensations
Perception of musical tonal quality and tonal pitch
Visual-spatial perception
Left-Brain
(Major hemisphere)
Auditory-haptic perception of oral language
Coding of sensorimotor functions associated with vocal and articulatory speech patterns
LEFT FRONTAL LOBE
CORPUS CALLOSUM
INTERNAL CAPSULE
TEMPORAL LOBE
PONS
DECUSSATION
MEDULLA
RIGHT SIDE OF TONGUE
SHAVER

persons, few positive statements on this subject can be made because research results are contradictory and inconclusive.[26] One day the tangled skeins of research and observation may be combed straight and braided neatly. Until that time we can only make assumptions that may rest on the merest substructure of fact.

Development of Dominance

The hemispheres may be equipotential at birth, and hence very young children probably employ diffuse areas in both hemispheres in learning to comprehend and use speech. As the child learns, cortical and subcortical fields of influence are more clearly defined. Neural circuits mediating perception and expression of oral language tend to develop high potentials in the major (left) hemisphere. (See Figures 2-8; 2-9; 2-10.) From the age of three years, most children develop progressive lateralization in the left hemisphere. Dominance for oral expression seems to be completed in a rudimentary way by the age of five or six years although some functional plasticity persists up to the twelfth or thirteenth year.[27] Hand preference develops in the same period but may not be established before the seventh or eighth year.

We have even less clear evidence of the respective roles of the hemispheres in the discriminative processes of oral language. Auditory and tactile-kinesthetic discrimination seem to be more diffusely represented in the right than in the major left hemisphere.[28] Although each cochlea, for example, has fiber connections with both hemispheres, apparently the quality of projection to the two sides is different. In the major (left) hemisphere, auditory perception of linguistic units has been localized. The minor hemisphere is able to make high-level auditory discriminatory responses on the *nonverbal* plane especially in temporal processes pertaining to

[26] M. Critchley, "Speech and Speech-Loss in Relation to Duality of the Brain, *Interhemispheric Relation and Cerebral Dominance,* ed. V. Mountcastle (Baltimore: Johns Hopkins University Press, 1962); R. Hicks and M. Kinsbourne, "Human Handedness: A Partial Cross-Fostering Study," *Science* 192(4242) (28 May 1976), 908–910; S. Krashen, "The Development of Cerebral Dominance and Language Learning: More New Evidence," *Developmental Psycholinguistics: Theory and Applications,* ed. D. Dato (Washington, D.C.: Georgetown University School of Languages and Linguistics, 1975); A. Smith and C.W. Burklund, "Dominant Hemispherectomy: Preliminary Report on Neuropsychological Sequelae," *Science* 153 (9 September 1966), 1281–1282.

[27] D. Kimura, "Functional Asymmetry of the Brain in Dichotic Listening," *Cortex* 3 (June 1967), 167–169; J.B. DeQuiros and O.L. Schrager, *Neurophychological Fundamentals in Learning Disabilities.* (San Rafael, Ca.: Academic Therapy Publications, 1978).

[28] Milner, "Laterality Effects in Audition," 187–188.

musical pitch and quality; [29] it also may account for fairly complex emotional responses, but its power of oral response is feeble. A parietal lesion in the minor hemisphere also produces deficits in spatial discrimination, an important requisite of proprioception. The resulting pattern may not be "lost," but it is not sufficiently intense to produce discrimination. As maturation proceeds even in left-handed persons, the dominant circuits employed in perception and expression seem to be clustered in the left hemisphere.

We have discussed the development of dominance as it occurs in the average child, but we know that cerebral lateralization varies in children just as maturation of the nervous system varies both in rate and extent. In some individuals dominance is never completely realized. Even as adults, they possess a type of cerebral organization particularly vulnerable to all types of stress. Their neural organization is not truly ambilateral (equal potential in major and minor hemispheres); on the contrary, it reflects a lack of dominance in either hemisphere.

Shift in Dominance

A very practical question on cerebral dominance is frequently raised: Can the minor hemisphere assume the language functions in the event of deficit in or injury to the major hemisphere? The answer depends upon not one, but several factors. The sensorimotor circuits and integrative and association areas for oral language in the left hemisphere generally have a higher potentiation than their counterparts in the right hemisphere. Hence we would expect congenital deficits in the major hemisphere and lesions in that hemisphere, particularly in children over six years of age, to affect more frequently and more seriously the perception and use of oral language. The common mistake, I believe, is the assumption that a deficit or lesion produces only a *motor* speech disorder.[30] This is the obvious *external* manifestation, but the *act* of expression cannot be divorced from the neural circuits and areas involved in *comprehension*. The sensory arm of the sensorimotor components and the integrative and association areas all are a part of the final pattern of expression.

---

[29] Ibid.; L. Roberts, "Central Brain Mechanisms in Speech," *Brain Function Vol. III: Speech, Language and Communication,* ed. E.C. Carterette (Berkeley: University of California Press, 1966), 18–19; J.W. Brown, "On the Neural Organization of Language: Thalamic and Cortical Relationships," *Brain and Language* 2 (1975), 18–30; H.M. Sussman, "Evidence for Left Hemisphere Superiority in Processing Movement-Related Tonal Signals," *J Speech Hearing Research* 22(2) (June 1979), 224–235; N. Geschwind, "Specializations of the Human Brain," *Scientific American,* 241(3) (September 1979), 190–199.

[30] F. Darley and A. Aronson, *Motor Speech Disorders* (Philadelphia: W.B. Saunders Co., 1975).

We conclude that the ability of the minor hemisphere to take over the sensorimotor and integrative and association functions of oral language when the major hemisphere is impaired depends, as does the development of hemispheric dominance, on these factors: *intelligence, genetic capacity of the minor hemisphere for neural potential and organization, the age of the individual at the time of insult,* and *the level of premorbid mental maturity.*

Integrating Neural Signals:
Perception of Oral Language

Perception is the interpretation and affective appreciation of meaning resulting initially from sensorimotor impulses and their integration with earlier neural patterns embracing past experience. Perception involves the highest integrative neural mechanisms in which the cortex plays a prominent role. Perhaps the stages in the intellectual development in the child are somewhat analogous. *Identification* is the most elementary process, *description* comes next, and *interpretation* is the highest and most complex. One interprets, and by association enlarges, the meaning of a complex of stimuli in relation to past experience or knowledge.

The perceptual process is complex probably because our knowledge is incomplete. In this area we are data rich and theory poor—poor because the data bits do not make a consistent theory. Pieces of the puzzle are left over after we have completed it. The process of integration itself is difficult to analyze. In terms of comprehension of oral language it must involve the organization of a "brain state," for nerve impulses, in themselves, do not produce "immediate awareness" much less perception.[31] Integration also demands the superposition in the same system and at the same moment of time of two phenomena which are separated in time or space. In comprehending an auditory message, for example, one must compare the acoustical structure with another which one has known previously. In addition to this comparison with past experience, all sensory modalities connected with the stimulus—auditory, tactile-kinesthetic, and visual—must merge in a neuronal assembly in a perceptual area. Figures 2-2, 2-3, 2-9 and 2-10 present a diagrammatic sketch of the integration of sensorimotor modalities in oral language.

Auditory Perception

Auditory perception may no longer be considered the only route to language learning. Although it still holds prime time with scholars in this

[31] Karl Pribram, "The Brain," *Psychology Today* 5(4) (September 1971), 45–90.

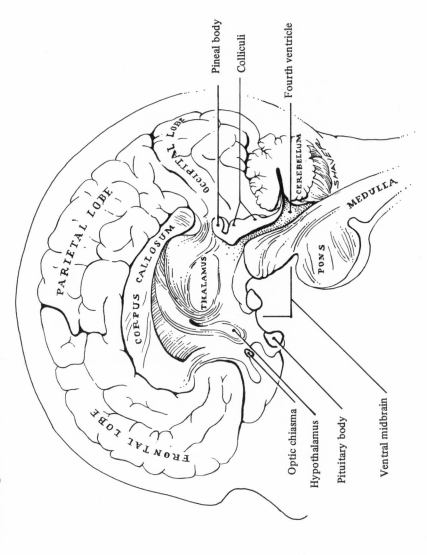

FIGURE 2-9 Median Sagittal Chart of the Brain.

54

FIGURE 2-10 The Superolateral Surface of the Left Cerebral Hemisphere Showing Cortical Areas Associated with the Perception-Expression of Oral Language.

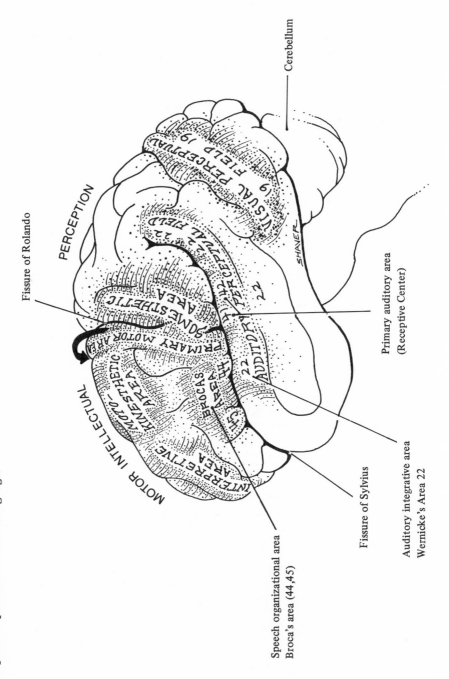

field, tactile-kinesthetic and, to a lesser degree, visual perception are important contributors to language comprehension. (See Figures 2-2, 2-3 and 2-10.) Many auditory tests assess the baby's response to nonsocial, nonverbal pure-tone sounds and environmental noises. These sounds may have some bearing on the child's peripheral hearing; they can scarcely be used to measure his ability to interpret auditorially the continuum of oral language. Auditory acuity and auditory perception are not equivalent terms, although the latter is not possible without the former. Put another way, a deficit in auditory perception resulting from CNS damage can occur even when auditory sensitivity (peripheral hearing) is normal. A disability in speech perception may be the result of conditions interfering with the transmission of a battery of neural impulses in the auditory pathways. Such conditions may follow upon its accommodation, or conversely, its inhibition of other impulses—auditory, haptic, or visual—in the neuronal pool at the same CNS level at the same moment.

Teaching sounds or syllables.   Although few scholars hold to the theory of phonetic perception of speech, many teachers continue to teach oral language sound by sound, the string-of-beads strategy. We know that speech sounds follow one another far too rapidly in connected speech for the nervous system to analyze each one separately. In discussing the complexity of the speech code, Liberman and others state,

> If speech were a cipher on the phonetic message, that is, if each segment of the message were represented by a unit sound, then the limit would be determined directly by the rate at which the phonetic segments were transmitted. But given that the message segments are, in fact, encoded into acoustic segments of roughly syllabic size, the limit is set, *not by the number of phonetic segments per unit time, but by the number of syllables* (italics mine).[32]

Although the unit of perception of oral language is the syllable, perception also is dependent on what happens between syllables, between phrases and clauses. It follows that tests of auditory discrimination of single phonemes have little value in determining auditory perception of speech.

Nature and the process of auding.   We know, first of all, that it is a temporal phenomenon, that is, it is based on a time pattern. Such auditory phenomena as frequency variations, the duration of input signals, the periodicity of neural excitation and segmentation of the stream of speech into syllabic elements, and finally, the identification and match of elements

[32] Alvin M. Liberman, Ignatius G. Mattingly, and Michael T. Turvey, "Language Codes and Memory Codes," *Coding Processes in Human Memory,* eds. A.W. Melton and E. Martin (New York: John Wiley, 1972), 317; A.L. Robinson, "More People Are Talking to Computers as Speech Recognition Enters the Real World," *Science* 203(4381) (16 February 1979), 634–636.

are temporal in nature and must be so interpreted. In the last phase, the match of elements, note how much depends on the time order of the morphemic or syllabic unit in such words as *lips* and *lisp* or in *kingdom* and *dumb king*. Even when units arrive simultaneously, they must be converted by the hearer into sequential patterns. [33]

In the process of auding verbal units certain major steps can be identified, namely,

1. the analysis at the initial stage of rapidly successive bits of information;

2. primary patterning through feedback-feedforward processes until new patterns are joined with wave patterns from other modalities (see Figures 2-2 and 2-3), and

3. further modification of wave patterns affected, in part, by earlier patterns that are reactivated in cortical and subcortical areas. Modalities mediating bits of information do not operate, however, in isolation. Words and word strings assume sharp profiles, "faces," in auditory comprehension because motor speech, through tactile-kinesthetic feedback, helps to provide them. In fact, the tactile-kinesthetic gnostic field must act as a "programming agent" because it has direct connections with such cortical integrative mechanisms as Wernicke's area (auditory perception), Broca's area (organizing area for motor speech), association areas, and primary motor projections areas (frontal lobe) mediating speech in much the same way that visual perception can act to reinforce or modify auditory-perceptual patterning. (See Figure 2-10.)[34]

The division of auding speech into temporal phases is arbitrary and a kind of convenient abstraction. It is useful in the sense that specific neural activity can be matched with each temporal phase.

Phase 1. Activation of neurons requires (1) a chemical mediator responsible for the specific sensitivity of the end organs, and (2) generator potentials to transform the change in end organs into a form of energy capable of discharging the nerve terminals. In the organ of Corti, mechanical pressure on its hair cells fires the chemical catalyst. It, in turn, incites a potential of sufficient magnitude to initiate impulses in a rhythmic flow in the acoustic nerve. The modification of these impulses by feedback probably begins immediately in the cochlea and continues throughout the brain stem and cortex. A few tracts conceivably could bypass the lower stages and carry as much temporal detail as the nervous system can re-

---

[33] E.E. Maccoby, "Selective Auditory Attention in Children," *Advances in Child Development and Behavior, III,* eds. L.P. Lipsitt and C.C. Spiker (New York: Academic Press, 1967), 100.

[34] Mildred F. Berry, *Language Disorders of Children* (Englewood Cliffs, N.J.: Prentice-Hall, Inc., 1969), 59–60; W.H. Fay, *Temporal Sequence in the Perception of Speech* (The Hague: Mouton, 1966), 19; Jerry Konorski, *Integrative Activity of the Brain* (Chicago: University of Chicago Press, 1967); N.P. Erber, "Auditory-Visual Perception of Speech with Reduced Optical Clarity," *J Speech Hearing Research,* 22(2) (June 1979), 212–223.

tain all the way to the cerebral cortex. The usual pattern, however, is a cyclical process in which constant erosion or modification occurs from the millisecond the stimulation is received in the cochlea until the response of perception is made.[35]

What is coded in the first phase is hypothetical. Possibly the stream of impulses is partially differentiated in terms of fundamental frequency, amplitude, and duration. Some impulses may diminish in strength or fade out in this phase, either because the generator potential is insufficient to maintain a flow of impulses required for the formation of a rhythmic pattern or because feedback has inhibited them from entering central channels.

Phase 2.   Modification and discrimination of the auditory pattern continues as the wave pattern makes connections with the ventral and dorsal cochlear nuclei, inferior colliculi, medial geniculate body, and other nuclear assemblies along the lemniscal or direct auditory route.

The indirect route via the reticular system may be even more important in organizing and focusing the perceptive field of audition since interconnections are rich and multisensory convergences abound in this system.[36] Many circuits embracing nuclear masses in the brain stem and cortex send information to the reticular system. Within the reticular networks several events have been postulated. Waves similar in frequency, amplitude, and duration may be joined through facilitation at synaptic junctions. Inhibitory processes in the same millisecond may hold up or prevent other impulses from entering the channel. Waves mediating visual and tactile-kinesthetic patterns may converge upon the auditory pattern. One effect of intermodal organization in this phase may be the completion of synthesis of pitch, amplitude, and duration so that intonational patterns now emerge and are recognizable. This critical stage in interpreting auditory information depends heavily upon the temporal resolving power of the nervous system, that is, its ability to resolve time patterns, and, in this phase, to resolve them in terms of basic intonation patterns.[37] Since the perception of intonation contours is aided by the breath group employed in speech, motor patterns of speech also must enter the coding process.[38]

[35] W.K. Livingston, F.P. Haugen, and J.M. Brookhart, "Functional Organization of the Central Nervous System," *Neurology* 4 (Minneapolis, July 1954), 485–496.

[36] Neurons making up the reticular network are multisensory or plurivalent, that is, they are not specific for one modality. The same cell may fire in response to visual, auditory, or somatic stimuli—A. Fessard, "The Role of Neuronal Networks in Sensory Communication Within the Brain," *Sensory Communication,* ed. W.A. Rosenblith (Cambridge, Mass.: M.I.T. Press, 1961), 585–606.

[37] P. Lieberman, *Intonation, Perception, and Language* (Cambridge, Mass.: M.I.T. Press, 1967), 48–107; H.L. Teuber, "Summation," *Brain and Behavior I,* ed. M.A.B. Brazier (Washington, D.C.: American Institute of Biological Sciences, 1961), 393–417.

[38] P. Lieberman, *Intonation, Perception, and Language,* 41–47.

Success in this phase will depend, in large part, on power at *synaptic junctions* and on interconnection patterns within the reticular system.

Phase 3.   Bearing in mind the continuous nature of coding, we suggest, nonetheless, certain neural events that may occur in the third phase in order to further perceptual processes of audition. Research now in progress suggests that the decoder categorizes the acoustic cues only when they are heard as speech and not when they are presented and perceived as nonspeech. If that is so, then we should suppose that the decoder is not merely an extension of the auditory system, but is, more properly, an integral part of the mechanisms that underlie our use of language.[39] In this phase, the rostral reticular system, the thalamus, and the cortex probably combine forces of integration through numerous bidirectional pathways. Gastaut believes that the thalamocortical pathways, which he calls the "rostral reticular stem," are of particular importance in differentiating between two sets of neural events that differ only in temporal patterning.[40] In order to make such a differentiation between time patterns, Neff postulates a short-term memory (between a fraction of a second and a few seconds) to be essential.[41] In this phase, the reticular activating system alerts and sensitizes such specific cortical fields in the dominant (left) hemisphere as the auditory fields in the temporoparietal area; the kinesthetic receptive and gnostic areas and Broca's area in the premotor cortex; and the primary motor field in the frontal cortex. The limbic system, separately or in conjunction with the reticular system, is simultaneously activated to provide motivational and emotional reinforcement.[42] As a result, wave fronts coursing through dendritic-glial layers in the sensitized areas of cortex and subcortex are able to impose their temporal patterns upon patterns similar in form and derived from earlier inputs. In this phase of analysis by synthesis, the determinant again is the temporal resolving power to order and sequence syllables, words and sentences. Perception is approaching completion. (See Figures 2-2; 2-10.)

Right ear–left ear.   Dichotic listening techniques have established the right ear and left hemisphere to be superior in the transmission and per-

---

[39] A.M. Liberman, "Some Characteristics of Perception in the Speech Mode," *Perception and its Disorders,* eds. David Hamburg and others (Baltimore: The Williams & Wilkins Company, 1970), 252.

[40] H. Gastaut, "The Neurophysiological Basis of Conditioned Reflexes and Behavior," *Neurological Basis of Behavior,* eds. G. Wolstenholme and C. O'Connor (Boston: Little, Brown, 1958), 265.

[41] W.D. Neff, "Neural Mechanisms of Auditory Discrimination," *Sensory Communication,* ed. W.A. Rosenblith (Cambridge, Mass.: M.I.T. Press, 1961), 274.

[42] J.C. Eccles, *The Neurophysiological Basis of Mind* (London: Oxford, 1953), 273–286.

ception of verbal symbols, the left ear (right hemisphere) of nonverbal symbols.[43] Considerable intercortical activity, however, must enter into coding oral language. The discrimination of such tonal characteristics as pitch, intensity, duration, and timbre, for example, is thought to take place in the minor (right) hemisphere, but because they are constituents of speech melody (prosody), they also must enter into language coding in the dominant hemisphere.[44] This may be the reason why the aphasic suffering from a left-brain lesion responds well to intonation therapy.[45]

We have presented one view of the way in which auditory information is handled in the nervous system. It is the most complex process of all sensory modalities. The primary auditory pathway (Figure 2-10), familiar to most students in our field, has its nuclei of origin in the spiral ganglion of the cochlea, an aggregation of bipolar cells from which the short processes extend to the hair cells in the Organ of Corti (inner ear). The longer central processes enter the brain stem at the medulla-pons border as the *cochlear nerve* and synapse immediately in the ventral and dorsal cochlear nuclei. The majority of fibers decussate (cross the midline to the opposite side) in the trapezoid body and ascend in the lateral lemniscus to synapse in the inferior colliculi of the midbrain and the adjacent nuclei in the medial geniculate body. Auditory radiations from these nuclei sweep through the internal capsule to terminate finally in the primary auditory areas of the superior temporal and lower parietal lobes. In its course the primary auditory pathway has contributed fibers to the reticular and limbic systems, both of which play a significant role in the coding process. But this is not the end of the track. Auditory perception involves feedforward-feedback loops extending from cochlea to the cortex and from cortex to cochlea, thus forming cyclical rings of facilitation and inhibition. They produce a multiplicity of modal and intermodal connections embracing motokinesthetic, visuomotor, and audiomotor circuits. Finally, coding rarely takes place except as similar neural patterns derived from earlier input are activated from memory storage.

Determination of deficits in auditory perception. At this juncture we are interested in the differentiation between peripheral and central

[43] C.I. Berlin and others, "Dichotic Speech Perception: An Interpretation of Right-Ear Advantage and Temporal Offset Effects," *J Acoustic Society America* 53 (1973), 699–709; A. Knox and D. Boone, "Auditory Laterality and Tested Handedness," *Cortex* 6(2) (June 1970), 164–173.

[44] T. Bever and P. Chiarello, "Cerebral Dominance In Musicians and Nonmusicians," *Science* 185(4150) (9 August 1974), 537–539; D. Deutsch, "Pitch Memory: An Advantage for the Left-Handed," *Science* 199(4328) (3 February 1978), 559–560.

[45] M.L. Albert, R.W. Sparks, and N.A. Helm, "Melodic Intonation Therapy for Aphasia," *Archives of Neurology* 29(2) (1973), 130–131; R.W. Sparks and A.L. Holland, "On: Melodic Intonation Therapy for Aphasia," *J Speech Hearing Disorders* 41(3) (August 1976), 298–300.

hearing losses in the perception of oral language. We must emphasize that we are concerned with a very highly integrated and specific function. Many evaluations of auditory perception, however, are based on a baby's response to environmental sounds, to single phones, to phonemes, or to words. None of these measures will assess the baby's comprehension of syllable "strings," of the speech continuum. Granted that a four-week-old infant may distinguish phonemic contrasts (determined by heart-rate changes), but that is a far cry from his need to distinguish phrase and sentence cues at 15 months. We grant, too, that experimental studies in which babies of 14 months perceive the difference between a stranger's voice and the mother's voice are an affirmative sign of the integrity of perception, but only for vocal attributes of pitch, intensity, quality, and duration contributing to the melodic (prosodic) pattern of utterance. We are, nevertheless, some way from the assignment of this ability to auditory perception alone and a long way from the comprehension of oral language in a situation demanding sustained attention.

A second troublesome question is the delineation of the neurological level beyond which the problem no longer can be considered a deficit in acoustic acuity and becomes a loss in central hearing and hence perceptual in nature. Probably integration of auditory information mediating verbal symbols begins above the ventral and dorsal cochlear nuclei in the medulla-pons area. Integration of binaural signals and lateralization of auditory impulses may occur at the pontine-midbrain level. The temporal and parietal fields of the cortex are primary agents of integration leading to auditory comprehension of oral language, but they are not the only areas. Through facilitation and inhibition the reticular system organizes subcortical tracts contributing to auditory discrimination and heightens the potential of cortical auditory fields in relation to surrounding fields. In combination with the reticular system or separately, nuclear masses of the limbic system (hippocampus, thalamus, hypothalamus, and basal nuclei), which have direct fiber connections with the primary auditory fields, provide motivating, attentional and emotional control in the final stages of auditory perception.

It is apparent that a loss in auditory perception, per se, is not easy to determine and is often difficult to differentiate from a loss in hearing acuity. The disorder certainly could be partially peripheral, partially central. As Katz explains the relation, "Conductive hearing losses are like earplugs in that they restrict the sounds of the environment from stimulating the cochlea, thereby depriving the auditory system of normal activity." [46] As a result, the retrocochlear system and the brain both suffer from this deprivation and consequently perception is impaired. Further,

[46] J. Katz, "The Effects of Conductive Hearing Loss on Auditory Function," *Asha* 29(10) (October 1978), 879–886.

one cannot easily determine whether another perceptual modality, tactile-kinesthesis, for example, which contributes to the perception of rhythmic patterns of language, may be seriously deficient and hence affect the comprehension of certain aspects of oral language.

Tactile-Kinesthetic (Haptic) Perception of Oral Language

The haptic modality embraces both tactile and kinesthetic sensations which are so intimately related in function that they must be considered together. Taction includes all perceptions of the environment such as geometric information (size, shape, line, and angles), texture, pain, and pressure derived from the sensory end-organs in the skin and subcutaneous tissue. Kinesthetic perception or proprioception is an awareness and appreciation of those sensations derived from bodily movement including the position of the body in space, its static limb positions, dynamic movement patterns, and sensitivity to direction.[47] Since kinesthetic perception is determined by motor feedforward and feedback, the total perceptual process should really be called haptic-motor perception.

As infants develop highly skilled action patterns, four phases of the complex patterns are central to success:

1. Intention or feedforward, a form of internal excitation anticipating and signaling an intended action.
2. Feedback proper from the respiratory, phonatory, and articulatory synergies employed in speech.
3. The discrimination and integration in the brain of tactile-kinesthetic-motor, visual-motor, and auditory-motor phenomena.
4. Smooth, temporally ordered sequences of action demanded in oral expression.[48]

Roots of Prosody

The dynamic movement patterns in speech control another important aspect of perception and expression: prosody, the melody patterns of oral language. ". . . the prosodic aspects of language are the most primeval aspects of language which man . . . uses to convey his emotional state as

---

[47] J. Chalfant and M.S. Scheffelin, *Central Processing Dysfunction in Children* (Bethesda, Md.: National Institutes of Health, 1969).
[48] J.S. Bruner, "Organization of Early Skilled Action," *Child Development* 44(1) (March 1973), 1–11.

well as the formal emotion-free aspects of language." [49] It is the earliest dimension to be employed in language-specific patterns. [50] From the primitive, nonsegmental sentences of infancy to their return in old age, prosody will continue to be the critical marking that makes one's speech peculiarly his own. Yet it is flexible varying with one's bodily state, mood, thoughts, and with his psychosocial environment. To what extent each characteristic of tone—pitch, quality, intensity, and duration—enters into the making of prosodic features we do not know. Writers enumerate such prosodic features as intonation (the contour of melody), stress, rhythm, duration, nuance, and phonetic configurations, but they are not separate, distinctive features. Speech rhythm, for example, is sometimes regarded as synonymous with intonation. It is not, although intonational contours influence rhythm just as syntactic and semantic patterns indirectly contribute both to rhythm and to prosody. Recognizing their interdependence, Crystal groups prosodic features with a common basis in four *prosodic systems:* pitch, loudness, tempo, and rhythmicality. [51]

Recognition of the importance of prosody in language learning has been prompted by observation of its significance in the communicative responses of babies. Weir found that early intonation patterns are the means of "segmenting utterance into sentence-like chunks, regardless of the intelligibility of the utterance to an adult listener." [52] In a more recent study Condon and Sander report that infants less than fifteen days old changed the ongoing pattern of their body movements to conform with the speech patterns of the adults they heard. The authors point out that if an infant, from the beginning, moves in precise, shared rhythm with the organization of the speech structure of his culture, then he participates developmentally through complex, sociobiological entrainment processes in millions of repetitions of linguistic forms long before he uses them in speaking and communicating. By the time he begins to speak, he may have already laid down within himself the form and structure of the language system of his culture. [53] Other observers have noted that a four-month-old

[49] P. Lieberman, K.S. Harris, M. Sawashima, "On the Physical Correlates of Some Prosodic Features," *Prosodic Feature Analysis*, eds. P.R. Leon, G. Faure, and A. Rigault (Ottawa: Marcel Didier (Canada), LTEE 1970), 35.

[50] D. Crystal, "Prosodic Systems and Language Acquisition," *Prosodic Feature Analysis*, eds. P.R. Leon, G. Faure, and A. Rigault (Ottawa: Marcel Didier (Canada), LTEE 1970), 79.

[51] David Crystal, *The English Tone of Voice* (London: Edward Arnold, 1975), 94–95.

[52] R. Weir, "Some Questions on the Child's Learning of Phonology," *The Genesis of Language*, eds. F. Smith and G.A. Miller (Cambridge, Mass.: M.I.T. Press, 1966), 153.

[53] G.D. Allen, "Speech Rhythm: Its Relation to Performance Universals and Articulatory Timing," *J Phonetics* 3 (1975), 75–86; W.S. Condon and L.W. Sander,

baby will make a rhythmic bodily and vocal response to the pattern connoting pleasure or displeasure. Say *bye-bye* or *no-hot!* The baby will attempt an imitation, not of the sounds, but of the prosodic pattern in the
rough. He communicates, in the first instance, his response of pleasure and
anticipation. In the second instance, the entire body may join in communicating negation. As oral language develops, prosodic interpretations
antedate and may determine grammatic structure. Certainly a dominant
perceptual component of the speech signal is prosodic in nature.

Prosodic development is dependent on haptic-motor development. Many
scholars have documented the thesis that prosodic patterning is heavily
dependent on the integration of and feedback from haptic-motor assemblies.[54] Moreover they suggest that little children comprehending and expressing oral language rely on prosody entirely for their perception of
phrasing, syntax, and meaning. Older persons also depend on it to a significant degree in comprehending oral language. Prosody is essential to
language learning.

THE FINAL COMMON PATH TO SPEECH
COMPREHENSION-ORAL EXPRESSION:
A CONTINUOUS PROCESS

We cannot separate brain stem feedforward-feedback circuits or the
reticular and limbic systems from cortical areas mediating the final integrative stages of perception and expression. (See Figures 2-2, 2-3, 2-7 and
2-10.) Since coding is a continuous process, these systems belong to a single
ring of operation, and no circuit or process is autonomous, going its own
independent way. Even the cortical and subcortical circuits engaged in the
final stages of coding are composed of bidirectional neurons, and the
areas of the cortex associated with the comprehension-expression of oral
language are not "centers" to which information comes and from which

"Neonate Movement is Synchronized with Adult Speech," *Science* 183 (1974), 99–
101; A.N. Meltzoff and M.K. Moore, "Imitation of Facial and Manual Gestures by
Human Neonates," *Science* 198(4312) (7 October 1977), 75–78.
[54] G. Kaluger and C.L. Heil, "Basic Symmetry and Balance—Their Relationship to
Perceptual-Motor Development," *Progress in Physical Therapy* I (2) (1970), 132–
137; K.S. Lashley, "The Problem of Serial Order in Behavior" L.A. Jeffress, *Cerebral Mechanisms in Behavior* (New York: John Wiley, 1951); A.M. Liberman and
others, "A Motor Theory of Speech Perception," *Proceedings of the Speech Communications Seminar* (Stockholm: Royal Institute of Technology, 1963); A.M. Liberman and others. "The Discrimination of Relative Onset-Time of the Components of
Certain Speech and Non-Speech Patterns," *J Experimental Psychology* 61 (1961);
P.F. MacNeilage, "Motor Control of Serial Ordering of Speech," *Psychological
Review* 77(3) (1970), 182–196; J. Martin, "Rhythmic (Hierarchical) Versus Serial
Structure in Speech and Other Behavior," *Psychological Review* 79(6) (November
1972), 487–509.

information is projected. They are, instead, integral parts of a ring. Patterned impulses are contained in circular or closed networks, providing interchanges for ingress and egress but at no point on the circle can we say, "Here sensory impulses end and the motor impulses begin." In this circle of neuronal assemblies, the sensorimotor cortical fields, from which primary effectors join the circle, may be thought of as "funnels of convergence" of the stream of impulses that have gone into the making of the final common path to oral expression.[55]

So auditory, tactile, visual, proprioceptive, and somatic stimuli begin the transmission of their brand of information to the nuclear processing centers of the brain stem. Wave patterns (sensory impulses) produced by these stimuli have several components: intensity (a quantitative function); duration (a temporal function); frequency (number of stimuli per unit time); and the dimensions of shape and motion. As these spatial-temporal wave patterns, evoked by generator potentials, surge forward, feedback-feedforward cycles come into play. They will modify the message perhaps at the receptor level. It is thought that all efferent neurons in the CNS project axons to the receptors, either to facilitate or inhibit the sensor. They will suppress those input channels that do not contribute to the central code. If extraneous noise is inhibited, for example, by cochlear efferent fibers to the hair cells in the cochlea, the wave patterns central to auditory perception will be sharpened or brought into focus. So at every nuclear station, inhibitory and facilitatory neuronal assemblies play both presynaptically and postsynaptically upon the nuclear assemblies containing the coded signals. The reticular system (Figure 2-5) alerts critical areas of the cortex by interrupting the alpha rhythm, raising the potential, and surrounding these areas by a zone of inhibition. Thalamic reticular nuclei are known to assist in this preparation of phasic activation of the cerebral cortex. Cortical areas thus are "set to attend." Fibers from the cerebellar-thalamo-cortical and cortico-striate-cerebellar pathways send collateral neurons to the reticular networks; their purpose is to synchronize and further refine the motosensory patterns essential for phonation and articulation. The limbic system (Figures 2-6; 2-7) will impress emotional reinforcement on the developing sensorimotor patterns. At some point in the coding process (not necessarily the last step), these patterns will converge in critical regions of the temporal, parietal, occipital and frontal lobes. These integration and association areas for oral language are defined in Figures 2-2, 2-3, and 2-10. One region, know as Broca's area, is traditionally referred to as the motor speech area. This is a misconception,

[55] C. Terzuolo and W.R. Adey, "Sensorimotor Cortical Activities," *Handbook of Physiology: Sec. I: Neurophysiology II,* ed. J. Field (Washington, D.C.: American Physiological Society, 1958), 825.

for its fibers are not motor projection fibers coursing through the internal capsule and brain stem to synapse in the lower motor neurons. Broca's area is a *speech organizing area*. It receives information from the frontal, temporal, parietal and occipital cortices, organizes speech patterns and relays them to the primary motor cortex and adjacent motor projection areas. These tracts innervate the muscles of respiration, phonation, resonation and articulation.

The high point of cortical integration, however, does not seem to center in the traditional "association areas" of the frontal lobe but in temporoparietal fields where countless sensorimotor patterns converge. At least we know that lesions in these fields produce greater deficits in oral language than lesions in the traditional frontal areas.[56] Indeed it is in the temporoparietal regions of the cortex where previously laid down patterns (memory patterns) appear to be strongest.

We have presented a transactional view of neural operation. The message has undergone constant modification and elaboration from receptor to response through the elaborate feedback-feedforward mechanism. In this process a vast company of neuronal assemblies "with collaterals unlimited" have mediated, enlarged, and modified the code. The transaction began in the peripheral receptive systems where the code first may have been altered; it continued in classical sensorimotor routes, in multisensory convergences upon polyvalent neurones of reticular, limbic, subcortical, and cortical bidirectional systems, through specific and nonspecific sensorimotor fields in cortex and subcortex. The transaction is completed in the response, that is, in the *act* of perception, inner language, or explicit expression. All are responses. Contributing to the success of the transaction are homeostatic, motivating, facilitating, feedback-feedforward, and fixation mechanisms.

In this presentation we have taken little account of individual differences yet we know that individuals vary greatly in their neural ability to code oral language. The basic difference, of course, is the dynamic plasticity of the nervous system. More specifically we would name the following variables:

1. the competence of neural receptors;
2. the strength of spontaneous rhythms in neuronal assemblies;
3. the strength and speed of transmission of neural patterns;
4. the form and competence of synaptic potentials;
5. the power of presynaptic and postsynaptic feedback-feedforward mechanisms;

---

[56] M. Piercy, "The Effects of Cerebral Lesions on Intellectual Function: A Review of Current Research Trends," *British J Psychiatry* 110 (May 1964), 310–352.

6. the alerting power of the reticular system (arousal mechanisms set-to-attend);

7. the strength and efficiency of segregating, synchronizing, facilitatory, and inhibitory mechanisms (especially in reticular, limbic, and cortical networks);

8. the power and extent of fields of influence (sensitized areas of cortex and subcortex); and

9. the integrity, power, and speed of motor outlets.

This account of the neurobiological foundations of communication is obviously incomplete, perhaps inaccurate. Venerable canons of neurobiology have been challenged, but new ones are yet to be established. In Delbruck's discussion of neurobiology in his Nobel prize lecture (1969), he asks the question, "What is language?" and acknowledges his inability to answer because the neurobiologist knows very little about the neural mediators of language. He says,

> It simply is not enough to know that nerve fibers conduct, that synapses are inhibitory or excitatory, chemical or electrical, that sensory inputs can be transduced, that they result in trains of spikes which measure intensities, that all kinds of accommodations occur, and so forth. I believe that we need a much more basic and detailed understanding of these stimulus response systems, be the stimulus an outside one or a pre-synaptic signal. Sensory physiology in a broad sense contains hidden in its kernel an as yet totally undeveloped but absolutely central science: transducer physiology, the study of the conversion of the outside signal to its first "interesting" output.[57]

When Delbruck's prediction is realized, we may write a more complete, possibly a vastly different, account of the neurobiological operations involved in the perception-expression of oral language.

REFERENCES

ABBS, J.H. and H.M. SUSSMAN, "Neurological Feature Detectors and Speech Perception: A Discussion of Theoretical Implications," *J Speech and Hearing Research,* 14(1) (March 1971), 23–36.

ADEY, W.R., "Brain Mechanisms and the Learning Process," *Federal Proceedings,* 20 (1961), 617–627.

ALBERT, M.L., R.W. SPARKS, and N.A. HELM, "Melodic Intonation Therapy for Aphasia," *Archives of Neurology,* 29(2) (1973), 130–131.

BARONDES, S.H., ed., *Neuronal Recognition.* New York: Plenum, 1976.

---

[57] M. Delbruck, "A Physicist's Renewed Look at Biology: Twenty Years Later," *Science* 168(3937) (12 June 1970), 1313.

BERLIN, C.I. and others, "Dichotic Speech Perception: An Interpretation of Right-Ear Advantage and Temporal Offset Effects," *J Acoustic Society America,* 53 (1973), 699–709.

BERRY, M.F., *Language Disorders of Children.* Englewood Cliffs, N.J.: Prentice-Hall, Inc., 1969. Chapters 1–3.

BEVER, T. and P. CHIARELLO, "Cerebral Dominance in Musicians and Nonmusicians," *Science* 185(4150) (9 August 1974), 537–539.

BOLINGER, DWIGHT L., "Intonation Across Languages," J.H. Greenberg, ed., *Universals of Human Language, Vol. 2: Phonology,* Stanford, California: Stanford University Press, 1978, 471–524.

BOLINGER, DWIGHT L., "Intonation as a Universal," *Proceedings of the Ninth International Congress of Linguistics,* ed. H.G. Lunt. The Hague: Mouton, 1964.

BRENNER, D. and others, "Somatically Evoked Magnetic Fields of the Human Brain," *Science,* 199(4324) (6 January 1978), 81–83.

BROOKSHIRE, R.H., "Auditory Comprehension and Aphasia," chap. 2 *Clinical Management of Neurogenic Communicative Disorders,* ed. D.F. Johns. Boston: Little, Brown and Company, 1978.

BROWN, G.W., "Temperament and Child Development," *J Learning Disabilities,* 6:9 (November 1973), 557–561.

BROWN, J.W., "Language, Cognition and the Thalamus," *Confinia Neurologia,* 36 (1974), 33–60.

BROWN, J.W., "On the Neural Organization of Language: Thalamic and Cortical Relationships," *Brain and Language,* 2 (1975), 18–30.

BRUNER, J.S., "Organization of Early Skilled Action," *Child Development,* 44(1) (March 1973), 1–11.

CARPENTER, M.B., *Human Neuroanatomy,* 7th ed. Baltimore: The Williams & Wilkins Co., 1976.

CARTERETTE, E.C., ed., *Brain Function Vol. III: Speech, Language, and Communication.* Berkeley: University of California Press, 1966.

CHALFANT, J.C. and M.S. SCHEFFELING, *Central Processing Dysfunction in Children.* Bethesda, Md.: National Institutes of Health, 1969.

CHESNI, Y., "Sur le role des propriocepteurs dans le controle de la parole," *Review Laryngology* (Bordeaux), 84 (July-August 1963), 451–457.

CONDON, W.S. and L.W. SANDER, "Neonate Movement is Synchronized with Adult Speech," *Science,* 183 (1974), 99–101.

CRYSTAL, D., *Linguistics.* New York: Penguin, 1971. 133.

CRYSTAL, D., "Prosodic Systems and Language Acquisition," *Prosodic*

Feature Analysis, eds. P.R. Leon, G. Faure, and A. Rigault. Ottawa: Marcel Didier (Canada) LTEE, 1970.

CRYSTAL, D., *The English Tone of Voice.* London: Edward Arnold, 1975.

DELBRUCK, M., "A Physicist's Renewed Look at Biology: Twenty Years Later," *Science,* 168(3937) (12 June 1970), 1313.

DE QUIROS, J.B. and O.L. SCHRAGER, *Neuropsychological Fundamentals in Learning Disabilities.* San Rafael, Ca.: Academic Therapy Publications, 1978.

DEUTSCH, D., "Pitch Memory: An Advantage for the Left-Handed," *Science* 199(4328) (3 February 1978), 559–560.

DUANE, D.D., "A Neurologic Perspective of Central Auditory Dysfunction," chap. 1 *Central Auditory Dysfunction,* ed. Robert W. Keith. New York: Grune and Stratton, 1977.

ECCLES, J.C., *The Neurophysiological Basis of Mind.* London: Oxford, 1953. 273–286.

ECCLES, J.C., *The Understanding of the Brain.* New York: McGraw-Hill, 1973.

ERBER, N.P., "Auditory-Visual Perception of Speech with Reduced Optical Clarity," *J Speech Hearing Research,* 22(2) (June 1979), 212–223.

FAY, W.H., *Temporal Sequence in the Perception of Speech.* The Hague: Mouton, 1966.

FESSARD, A., "The Role of Neuronal Networks in Sensory Communication within the Brain," *Sensory Communication,* ed. W.A. Rosenblith. Cambridge, Mass.: M.I.T. Press, 1962, 585–606.

FLETCHER, S.G., "Time-by-Count Measurement of Diadochokinetic Syllable Rate," *J Speech and Hearing Research,* 15(4) (December 1972), 763–770.

FRENCH, J.D., "The Reticular Formation," *Altered States of Awareness.* Chap. 3. San Francisco: W.H. Freeman and Company, 1972.

GALAMBOS, R., "Electrical Events in the Brain and Learning," *Brain Function and Learning, Vol. IV: Brain Function,* eds. D.B. Lindsley and A.A. Lumsdaine. Berkeley: University of California Press, 1967. 49–77.

GESCHWINDT, N., "Specializations of the Human Brain," *Scientific American,* 241(3) (September 1979), 180–199.

GILBERT, JOHN H., *Speech and Cortical Functioning.* New York: Academic Press, 1972.

GOODGLASS, H. and others, "Some Linguistic Structures in the Speech of a Broca's Aphasia," *Cortex,* 8(2) (June 1972), 191–212.

HAMMILL, D.C. and N.R. BARTEL, *Teaching Children with Learning and Behavior Problems*. Chap. 8. Boston: Allyn and Bacon, 1975.

HARDY, W.G., "Hearing in Children," Panel Discussion, (Sixth International Congress on Audiology). *Laryngoscope,* 68 (1958), 224–228.

HOROWITZ, F.D., "Visual Attention, Auditory Stimulation, and Language in Young Infants," *Monographs,* 39(5–6), (1975).

ISAACSON, R.L., "Memory Processes and the Hippocampus," *Short-Term Memory,* eds. D. Deutsch and J.A. Deutsch. New York: Academic Press, 1975.

KALUGER, G. and C.L. HEIL, "Basic Symmetry and Balance—Their Relationship to Perceptual-Motor Development," *Progress in Physical Therapy,* I(2) (1970), 132–137.

KANDEL, E.R., "Nerve Cells and Behavior," *Scientific American,* 223(1) (July 1970), 57–71.

KATZ, J., "The Effects of Conductive Hearing Loss on Auditory Function," *Asha* 29(10) (October 1978), 879–886.

KAUFMAN, A.S., R. ZALMA, and N.L. KAUFMAN, "The Relationship of Hand Dominance to the Motor Coordination, Mental Ability, and Right-Left Awareness of Young Normal Children," *Child Development,* 49(3) (September 1978), 885–888.

KIMURA, D., "Functional Asymmetry of the Brain in Dichotic Listening," *Cortex,* 3 (June 1967), 167–169.

KIMURA, DOREEN, "The Asymmetry of the Human Brain," *Scientific American,"* 228(3) (March 1973), 70–80.

KLEINMAN, D. and E.R. JOHN, "Contradiction of Auditory and Visual Information by Brain Stimulation," *Science,* 187(4173) (24 January 1975), 271–273.

KNOX, A. and D. BOONE, "Auditory Laterality and Tested Handedness," *Cortex,* 6(2) (June 1970), 164–173.

KONORSKI, J., *Integrative Activity of the Brain*. Chicago: University of Chicago Press, 1967.

KOZHEVNIKOVA, V.A. and L.A. CHISTOVICH, *Speech Articulation and Perception*. Moscow-Leningrad, 1965, translated by National-Technical Information Services, U.S. Dept. of Commerce, Springfield, Va.

KRACKE, I., "Perception of Rhythmic Sequences by Receptive Aphasic and Deaf Children," *British J Communication Disorders,* 10(1) (April 1975), 43–51.

KRASHEN, S., "The Development of Cerebral Dominance and Language Learning: More New Evidence," *Developmental Psycholinguistics:*

Theory and Applications, ed. D. Dato. Washington, D.C.: Georgetown University School of Languages and Linguistics, 1975.

LAWSON, CHESTER A., *Brain Mechanisms and Human Learning,* ed. John E. Horrocks. The International Series in the Behavioral Sciences. Boston: Houghton Mifflin Co., 1967.

LEVINE, S., "Stress and Behavior," *Scientific American,* 224(1) (January 1971), 26–32.

LIBERMAN, A.M., "Some Characteristics of Perception in the Speech Mode," *Perception and Its Disorders,* eds. David Hamburg and others. Baltimore: The Williams & Wilkins Co., 1970.

LIBERMAN, A.M., "Some Results of Research on Speech Perception," *J Acoustic Society America,* 29 (January 1957), 117–123.

LIBERMAN, A.M., "The Specialization of the Language Hemisphere," *Haskins Laboratories Status Report on Speech Research,* SR–31-32, 1972.

LIBERMAN, A.M. and others, "A Motor Theory of Speech Perception," *Proceedings of the Speech Communications Seminar.* Stockholm: Royal Institute of Technology, 1963.

LIBERMAN, A.M., I.G. MATTINGLY, and M.T. TURVEY, "Language Codes and Memory Codes," *Coding Processes in Human Memory,* eds. A.W. Melton and E. Martin. New York: John Wiley, 1972.

LIEBERMAN, P., K.S. HARRIS, M. SAWASHIMA, "On the Physical Correlates of Some Prosodic Features," *Prosodic Feature Analysis,* eds. P.R. Leon, G. Faure, and A. Rigault. Ottawa: Marcel Didier (Canada) LTEE, 1970.

LIEBERMAN, P., *Intonation, Perception, and Language.* Chap. 4. Cambridge, Mass.: M.I.T. Press, 1967.

LINDSLEY, D.B. and W.R. ADEY, "Availability of Peripheral Input to the Midbrain Reticular Formation," *Experimental Neurology,* 4 (October 1961), 358–376.

LINDSLEY, D.B. and A.A. LUMSDAINE, eds., *Brain Function, Vol. IV: Brain Function and Learning.* Berkeley: University of California Press, 1967.

LING, D. and A.H. LING, "Communication Development in the First Three Years of Life," *J Speech and Hearing Research,* 17(1) (March 1974), 146–157.

LISKER, L., F. COOPER, and A.M. LIBERMAN, "The Uses of Experiment in Language Description," *Word,* 18 (August 1962), 103.

LLINAS, R.R., "The Cortex of the Cerebellum," *Scientific American,* 232(1) (January 1975), 56–71.

LURIA, A.R., *Higher Cortical Functions in Man.* New York: Basic Books, Inc., 1966.

MACNEILAGE, P.F., "Motor Control of Serial Ordering of Speech," *Psychological Review,* 77(3) (1970), 182–196.

MACCOBY, E.E., "Selective Auditory Attention in Children," Lipsitt, L.P. and C.C. Spiker, eds., *Advances in Child Development and Behavior, III.* New York: Academic Press, 1967.

MARTIN, J., "Rhythmic (Hierarchical) Versus Serial Structure in Speech and Other Behavior," *Psychological Review,* 79(6) (November 1972), 487–509.

MELTZOFF, A.N. and M.K. MOORE, "Imitation of Facial and Manual Gestures by Human Neonates," *Science* 198(4312) (7 October 1977), 75–78.

MENDELSON, M.J. and M.M. HAITH, "The Relation Between Audition and Vision in the Human Newborn," *Monographs Society for Research in Child Development,* 41(4) (1976).

MILNER, B., "Laterality Effects in Audition," *Interhemispheric Relations and Cerebral Dominance,* ed. F. Mountcastle. Baltimore: Johns Hopkins Press, 1962, 187–188.

MUSAK, E., *Speech Pathology and Feedback Theory.* Springfield, Ill.: Charles C. Thomas, 1966, 34–37.

NATHANSON, J.A. and P. GREENGARD, "Second Messengers in the Brain," *Scientific American,* 237(20) (August 1977), 108–119.

NAUTA, WALLE J.H. and MICHAEL FEIRTAG, "The Organization of the Brain," *Scientific American,* 241(3) (September 1979), 88–111.

NEFF, W.D., "Neural Mechanisms of Auditory Discrimination," *Sensory Communication,* ed. W.A. Rosenblith. Cambridge, Mass.: M.I.T. Press, 1961, 274.

NEWCOMBE F. and G. RATCLIFF, "Handedness, Speech Lateralization and Ability," *Neuropsychologia,* 11 (October 1973), 399–407.

NOBACK, CHARLES R., *The Human Nervous System: Basic Principles of Neurobiology.* 2nd ed. New York: McGraw-Hill, Inc. 1975.

NORTHERN, L. and M.P. DAWNS, *Hearing in Children.* Chap. 3. Baltimore: The Williams & Wilkins Co., 1974.

OJEMAN, G.A., "Language and the Thalamus: Object Naming and Recall During and After Thalamic Stimulation," *Brain and Language,* 2 (1975), 101–120.

PAPEZ, J.S., "A Proposed Mechanism of Emotion," *Archives of Neurology,* Chicago, 38 (October 1937), 725–744.

PRIBRAM, K., "Control Systems and Behavior," *Brain and Behavior,* ed.

M.A.B. Brazier. Washington, D.C.: American Institute Biological Sciences, II, 1963.

PRIBRAM, K.H., "Memory and the Organization of Attention," *Brain Function and Learning, Vol. IV: Brain Function,* eds. D.B. Lindsley and A.A. Lumsdaine. Berkeley: University of California Press, 1967, 79–113.

PRIBRAM, K., *Languages of the Brain.* Englewood Cliffs, N.J.: Prentice-Hall, Inc., 1971.

REES, N.S., "Auditory Processing Factors in Language Disorders: A View From Procrustes' Bed," *J Speech Hearing Disorders,* 38(3) (1973), 304–315.

ROBERTS, L., "Central Brain Mechanisms in Speech," *Brain Function, Vol. III: Speech, Language and Communication,* ed. C. Carterette. Berkeley: University of California Press, 1966.

ROBERTS, T.D.M., *Basic Ideas in Neurophysiology.* New York: Appleton-Century-Crofts, 1966, 88–90.

ROUTTENBERG, ARYEH, "The Reward System of the Brain," *Scientific American,* 239(5) (November 1978), 154–165.

SANDERS, D.A., *Auditory Perception of Speech.* Englewood Cliffs, N.J.: Prentice-Hall, Inc., 1977.

SCHUBERT, E.D., "The Role of Auditory Perception in Language Processing," *Reading, Perception and Language,* eds. D.D. Duane and M.B. Rawson. Baltimore: York Press, Inc., 1975, 97–130.

SMITH, A. and C.W. BURKLUND, "Dominant Hemispherectomy: Preliminary Report on Neuropsychological Sequelae," *Science,* 153 (9 September 1966), 1281–1282.

STUDDERT-KENNEDY, M. and SHANKWEILER, D., "Hemispheric Specialization for Speech Perception," *J Acoustical Society of America,* 48 (August 1970), 576–594.

SUSSMAN, H.M., "What the Tongue Tells the Brain," *Psychological Bulletin,* 77(4) (1972), 262–272.

SUSSMAN, H.M., "Evidence for Left Hemisphere Superiority in Processing Movement-Related Tonal Signals," *J Speech Hearing Research,* 22(2) (June 1979), 224–235.

TALLAL, P. and PIERCY, M., "Developmental Aphasia: Rate of Auditory Processing and Selective Impairment of Consonant Perception," *Neuropsychologia,* 11 (October 1973), 389–398.

TALLAL, P., "Rapid Auditory Processing in Normal and Disordered Language Development," *J Speech Hearing Research,* 19(3) (September 1976), 561–571.

TERZUOLO, C., and W.R. ADEY, "Sensorimotor Cortical Activities," *Handbook of Physiology: Sec. I: Neurophysiology II,* ed. J. Field, Washington, D.C.: American Physiological Society, 1958.

TEUBER, H.L., "Summation," *Brain and Behavior I,* ed. M.A. Brazier. Washington, D.C.: American Institute of Biological Sciences, 1961.

TEYLER, TIMOTHY, J., *A Primer of Psychobiology.* San Francisco: W.H. Freeman and Company, 1975.

VANBUREN, J.M., "The Question of Thalamic Participation in Speech Mechanisms," *Brain and Language,* 2 (1975), 31–44.

WARD, A.A., JR., "Efferent Functions of the Reticular Formation," chap. 12 *Reticular Formation of the Brain,* eds. H.H. Jasper and others. Boston: Little, Brown, 1958.

WEIR, R., "Some Questions on the Child's Learning of Phonology," *The Genesis of Language,* eds. F. Smith and G.H. Miller. Cambridge, Mass.: M.I.T. Press, 1966.

WEITHORN, C.J., "Hyperactivity and the CNS: An Etiological and Diagnostic Dilemma," *J Learning Disabilities,* 6(1) (January 1973), 46–50.

WHITAKER, H.A., *On the Representation of Language in the Human Brain.* Edmonton, Alberta, Canada: Linguistic Research, Inc., 1971.

WILLIAMS, P.L. and R. WARWICK, *Functional Neuroanatomy of Man.* Philadelphia: W.B. Saunders Company, 1975.

WITELSON, S.F., "Developmental Dyslexia: Two Right Hemispheres and None Left," *Science,* 195(4275) (21 January 1977), 309–311.

WITTROCK, M.S. and others, *The Human Brain.* Englewood Cliffs, N.J.: Prentice-Hall, Inc., 1977.

chapter 3

NEURO-PSYCHOSOCIAL SUBSTRATES OF ORAL LANGUAGE

MOTIVATION, ATTENTION, MEMORY

One might argue that perception should be considered a neuropsychological substrate and hence be included in this chapter. We have not done so because perception is the sum and substance of language, not a substrate. Without perception, meaningful communication in any form is not possible. The two, perception and language, are in an interlocking directorate. In Chapter 2 we discussed the major sensory modalities, neural pathways, and cortical areas engaged in the *primary perceptual processes*. We also have traced two *secondary neural systems,* reticular and limbic, which organize and facilitate the *act* of perception at subcortical levels. Certain functions of these secondary systems will be reviewed in this chapter. They are functions mediating motivation, attention, and memory. The major emphasis, however, will be on the psychosocial determinants of these substrates of oral language development.

Neurogenic Basis of Motivation, Attention, Memory

Motivation, attention, and memory all belong to an interactive ring participating in the learning event. Their neurological correlates seem to involve the same systems: reticular-activating and limbic systems. As we have noted earlier, the reticular system, like the starter in an automobile, starts the brain engine running and maintains its power by facilitating or inhibiting the flow of signals to the cortex.[1] The reticular system is not the sole motivating power, but because every sensory modality shunts impulses to it, it contributes mightily to motivation. The second neurological correlate is the limbic system, often called the motivational-affective system.[2] If learning is augmented by strong emotional reinforcement, then this complex must be active in directing a rapid fire of impulses into the learning event. The two systems act in concert to incite and maintain attention.

The neurological correlate of attention is also the alerting mechanism of the reticular system. This mechanism, Hebb says, provides "the immediate facilitation from one phase sequence or assembly action (of neurons) to the ensuing one. . . . This is the way the reticular system bids the individual 'to attend.' "[3] How the reticular system establishes priority of attention among stimuli is a moot question. We do know that some neurological mechanism operates to increase the potential in appropriate cortical and subcortical areas. In so doing, it awakens the brain and keeps it alert. It acts as a kind of traffic control system. We believe this mechanism is the reticular system producing the set-to-attend and the focusing of attention.[4]

Galambos and others have made interesting observations on attention to auditory stimuli in animals. They state that the neural processes responsible for attention play an important role in determining whether or not a given acoustic stimulus proves adequate.[5] Apparently auditory response to sound is secondary to visual-visceral stimuli in importance to some animals. The attention of a cat, for example, to a stimulus of prime importance (mice in a glass jar) resulted in complete inhibition of the auditory response to the sound. Competing stimuli were much stronger and hence commanded the cat's attention. According to Galambos the set-to-attend may be so powerful that the reticular system will exclude the incoming signal at the peripheral, or pickup point of sensory input, or at several points after it has entered the CNS. Unless conditioning is deeply set and motivation extraordinarily keen, sensations from the viscera will take precedence over such sensory modalities as vision, audition, proprioception, and tactation. But if visceral stimuli are held in abeyance,

[1] J.D. French, "The Reticular Formation," chap. 3, *Altered States of Awareness* (San Francisco: W.H. Freeman Company, 1972).

[2] R. Melzack, *Perception and Its Disorders,* 48:277, Research publication of the Association for Research in Nervous and Mental Disorders (Baltimore: Williams & Wilkins, 1970).

[3] D.O. Hebb, *The Organization of Behavior* (New York: John Wiley, 1949), 152.

[4] French, "The Reticular Formation," 23–29.

[5] R. Galambos, "Suppression of Auditory Nerve Activity by Stimulation of Efferent Fibers to Cochlea," *J Neurophysiology* 19 (September 1956), 424–437.

then vision probably will take precedence over audition, providing the intensity of the competing stimuli are equal, or nearly so. The auditory potential, in other words, will be reduced or erased in favor of the visual potential.

In the normal baby, attention matures as the nervous system matures. We have referred in an earlier text to the resting rhythmic activity of the cortex and other parts of the nervous system.[6] This resting activity, sometimes called the alpha wave, changes in form and frequency as the child matures. In a four-month-old baby, the wave has a frequency of 3–4 cycles per second (cps); at one year the rhythm has increased to 5–6 cps; by the age of 10–12 years, it has reached the average adult frequency of approximately 11 cps. Feedback loops contribute to the maturation process by inhibiting information that does not contribute to the main focus of attention, thus allowing important information to preempt the pathways.

Memory is the third substrate of language learning and it, too, probably is mediated by the same neural complex. Books have been written on the neural coding processes of memory; yet the subject is still moot.[7] Current debate centers on the difference in time, quantity, and quality of the coding mechanisms of short-term recognitive memory and long-term retention. Short-term memory, surviving for minutes to an hour, probably is dependent upon the initial strength of the synaptic impulses (synthesis of deoxyribonucleic acid, DNA), reinforcement by the reticular-activating and limbic systems, pretraining of the individual, and the absence of interfering input. Long-term memory probably depends on the same factors, but the mechanism of transfer from one to the other is purely theoretical. Whatever this mechanism is, the same synapses and neuronal assemblies are presumed to participate in both processes. In the brain the structures showing a persistence of stimulus-evoked activity are localized mainly in the hippocampus (inner surface of temporal lobe) and diencephalon (thalamus). The assumption is that they are involved in the postperceptual coding for memory of stimulus events, but they must not be thought of as memory storage bins.

The Genetic Drive

Behind the reticular and limbic systems, behind all nervous activity contributing to motivation, attention, and memory is a variable we can affect in a very limited way. It is the genetic drive, an inherited built-in force or

[6] Mildred F. Berry, *Language Disorders of Children* (Englewood Cliffs, N.J.: Prentice-Hall, Inc., 1969), 40–41; 89.

[7] D. Deutsch and J.A. Deutsch, eds., *Short-Term Memory* (New York: Academic Press, 1975); A.W. Melton and E. Martin, eds., *Coding Processes in Human Memory* (Washington, D.C.: V.H. Winston and Sons, 1972); N. Geschwind, "Specializations of the Human Brain," *Scientific American* 241(3) (September 1979), 189–190.

energizer that varies with the physical constitution and determines the neural potentials of the reticular and limbic systems. That its potential varies widely among individuals every teacher knows. Joe's mother says, "he is always in low gear." Can parents and teachers help this child, Joe, to maximize the genetic force to its limits? Increased physical activity which will enhance energy metabolism [8] seems to be the best way. It, in turn, will augment the blood flow and thus increase the oxygen available to the nervous system.[9] One purpose in initiating our teaching program (Chapter 8) with basic rhythmic activities involving walking, running, skipping, and so on is to increase the energy metabolism of children who apparently are lacking in drive.

In the majority of children, this dynamic drive exhibited in motor activities is evident from birth.[10] It is particularly noticeable in early infancy when the baby intervenes in his environment by reaching, position changes, locomotion, and so on to get what he wants. Such a drive, or "push," initially brings on a phase of discomfiture that is followed by action to reduce the discomfiture. Some authorities describe this action as a biased homeostat, building up tension and restoring homeostasis when the act of learning has been accomplished. So by the act of living and learning, a child resolves his needs and thereby reduces his tension states which are manifested in increased activity.[11] A college student experiences a similar state in preparing the term paper. He suffers days of tension until the evidence has been assembled and the final outline is in hand. All seems comparatively easy after that; he attacks the writing furiously, the action increases, and homeostasis is finally restored.

It is apparent that motivation may be genetic, organismic, and intrinsic in origin, although one cannot say at any time that even in infants, it is completely intrinsic or that it is extrinsic in the sense that behavior is controlled through psychosocial forces in the environment. Emotional behavior illustrates the mixture of the two, intrinsic and extrinsic. Emotion, properly controlled by the limbic system, is a powerful accessory to, if

---

[8] Energy metabolism: the physiologic activities concerned with the intake, interchange, and output of energy.

[9] The demonstration of the dependence on blood flow of activity in cortical fields mediating comprehension and expression has been graphically revealed with the aid of radioactive isotopes.—Niels A. Lassen, David H. Ingvar, and Erik Skinhoj, "Brain Function and Blood Flow," *Scientific American* 239(4) (October 1978), 62–71.

[10] Nancy Bayley, "The Development of Motor Abilities During the First Three Years," *Monographs Society for Research in Child Development* (1935), No. 1; Nancy Bayley, "Comparisons of Mental and Motor Test Scores for Ages 1–15 Months by Sex, Birth Order, Race, Geographical Location, and Education of Parents," *Child Development* 36 (1965), 379–411.

[11] R.L. Shelton, W.B. Arndt, and J.B. Miller, "Learning Principles and Teaching of Speech Language," *J Speech Hearing Disorders* 26 (November 1961), 368.

not an integral part of, genetic drive. Contrariwise, emotion, uncontrolled or prolonged in duration by extrinsic forces, upsets the biased homeostat of innate drive so that motivation deteriorates. Ordinarily frustration and fear produce a disruptive increase in drive. Hope may come in to reduce the excessive drive and when it does, it usually wins out over fear and frustration.[12] Then learning is facilitated. Hopefulness, in short, supplies the probability of success and becomes an adjuster of homeostasis. A master teacher in any field is constantly aware of the need to keep hope going by intermittent reinforcement. Hope is the "future tense" of life. We turn now to those constituents of extrinsic motivation that are dominantly psychosocial in nature.

THE PSYCHOSOCIAL ASPECTS OF MOTIVATION

The Troika

In language learning, motivation, attention, and memory form a troika of interdependent substrates. If a child is motivated, he attends, and if he attends with positive intent, recall is heightened. Motivation acts as a specific hypothesized determinant of the direction and/or strength of action or of a line of action.[13] Although the prime purpose of motivation is to arouse, to cause the individual to attend more closely to his environment, motivation also influences the direction, selectivity, and persistence of his attention.[14] The result is that it will increase the probability that the child will respond to one class of stimuli rather than other classes of stimuli.[15]

Extrinsic Motivation: An Archaic Concept Revisited

The extent to which intrinsic motivation can be stimulated is limited by physiological forces. Potentially the psychosocial constituents present a greater scope for motivation because they develop out of repeated affective experiences connected with certain types of situations and types of behavior. Extrinsic motivation could be and frequently is a powerful ingredient of achievement. That it is not always so is the counter influence of a

---

[12] John Jung, *Understanding Human Motivation, A Cognitive Approach* (New York: Macmillan, 1978), 33.

[13] Ibid., 4–5.

[14] Fred McKinney, Raymond P. Lorion, and Melvin Zax, *Effective Behavior and Human Development* (New York: Macmillan, 1976), 14–24.

[15] R.C. Johnson, "Linguistic Structure Related to Concept Formation and to Concept Context," *Psychological Bulletin* 59 (November 1962), 468–476.

changing society, one sector of which is opposed to the work ethic, another sector, too affluent to be motivated. The slogans, which both groups live by, denigrate motivation: "I couldn't care less" (and thousands of children in our public schools really don't care); "Who cares?"; "Doin' what comes naturally"; "What's in it for me?"; "Let George do it"; "I'll get by"; "So what?" All these expressions are symptomatic of a society questioning its direction. The stimuli of the child's world frequently are limited to television, a deadly soporific, setting apathetic behavior patterns which he shortly will employ in school. His parents, his playmates, perhaps some of his teachers may accept his lethargic state, occasionally attempting to awaken him by trapping him into learning with such rewards as sweets or money.

But there is another "wind a-blowing" in the educational world, stirred by the knowledge that Johnnie can't read, write, or communicate, stirred too by the realization that Johnnie is not able to meet a society that ironically still demands a measure of competence. An ecologically oriented segment of our society is now looking critically at the needs of its children in relation to the demands of their immediate world.[16] The concern of parents and teachers alike is, or should be, the motivation of the very young to meet their world by affirmative action. Because the investigation of motivational factors that underlie child learning has been neglected, the list we present is probably incomplete, perhaps inaccurate. From our experience, we have found the factors discussed in the preceding paragraphs to be important even today in motivating children to learn oral language.

Sensorimotor Exploration

We know that the infant is motivated to make *exploratory responses*— eye movements, head turning, and so on but only if stimuli are intensified and if they are sufficiently long to be "categorized." A baby explores the world through his senses. As he learns oral language, he will be prompted to respond to stimuli that are novel, or ambiguous (raising questions about meaning), or collative (matching previous stimuli). His *why* questions, however, do not call for answers from others at this stage. When he reaches three years, he will demand explanations about verbal or physical events in his world. His questions are directed to those important others in his world.[17] Curiosity leading to exploratory behavior certainly is a basic factor of motivation. By the time he reaches kinder-

[16] "Classification options, A Conversation with Nicholas Hobbs on Exceptional Child Education," *Exceptional Children* 44(7) (April 1978), 494–497.

[17] Jung, *Understanding Human Motivation*, 163.

garten he is or should be even more intent, more highly motivated in sensory explorations of his world, and as a consequence, more aware (self-identity) of himself in relation to it.

Motivation through Competition

A second motivating factor in early learning is a child's sense of competition with his peers. Rivalry expressed in physical aggression is scarcely a healthy kind of competition. But friendly competition with one's peers can be a true goal to learning. A master teacher, particularly of little children, uses this tool of facilitation by stimulating youngsters to take their cues from a peer and successfully imitate the peer's responses, indeed to surpass them. So children learn to do what they see and hear others are doing. The importance of lively models in a stimulating physical environment cannot be exaggerated. Some children do not have this experience until they arrive in preschool or kindergarten. Oh, they may be told, warned, or admonished by their models, the parents, to do well in school. But if their adult models do not behave as if *they* valued intellectual skills, the child scarcely can be expected to be motivated to acquire them.

Once in school the child competes in other ways. He is motivated to take a high interest in *involvement*. He wants to be a part of the action, whether it is stirring the soup in the "cooking class," striking camp while on a Brownie trip, or carrying a message from his teacher to the principal's office. We also have observed the eagerness of children to compete in *problem solving*. Some child's dog has sneaked in through the door, left ajar, and is disrupting the scheduled activity in the class. His master or mistress is not in this room. He is lost but will not be coaxed out of the room. What to do? Almost every child has a solution to the problem and with obvious enjoyment pleads with his teacher to try *his* plan. Participation in problem solving certainly indicates high motivation.[18]

Sanctions

The power of rewards and penalties is extremely important in early life and particularly so in the first stages of learning. The forms that sanctions take, however, are clearly debatable. A baby's frustrations are reduced by rewards of pleasurable sights and sounds and by comfort and security. The act of communication, gestural or verbal, produces pleasur-

[18] Bernard C. Rosen and Roy D'Andrade, "The Psychosocial Origins of Achievement Motivation," *Readings in Child Behavior and Development,* 3rd ed., eds. Celia Stendler Lavatelli and Faith Stendler (New York: Harcourt Brace Jovanovich, 1972), 408–416; 413–414.

able responses within him and these internal responses are further reinforced by pleasurable or satisfying responses from his environment: food, clean clothing, fondling, and pleasant sounds. At first he accepts these rewards from any one's hands, from all hands. Later he becomes selective in his rewards, responding particularly to nurturance, praise, and recognition by his model, the *significant other person.* He is further rewarded and motivated as he increases his similarity to the model, for here is the image of what he wants to be. In play he first imitates his parents, then his teacher.[19] If he achieves identity like that "significant other person," he, too, will enjoy the reward of self-worth, competence, and control of his environment.[20] With this type of motivation he scarcely needs such external rewards as "M and M's" or "Cheerios." (Does he need them under any circumstances?) He incorporates within himself the model's strength and adequacy and very shortly adopts some of the model's complex integrated patterns. He *identifies* with "that other person." And all this is done without any formal method of operant conditioning.[21] There are risks today in a child's attachment to a model. In this day of a transitional culture posing changing values and life styles, a child may very suddenly find that his model has either been removed from the home or demeaned in public esteem and self-worth. Children have been known to stop talking altogether when this happens.

I have said earlier in this discussion that the form of sanctions, particularly rewards, is much debated these days. Recent research on the effect of verbal or tangible rewards on learning in the elementary school does not support their effectiveness. In one study it was found that when compared with a control group, the children given tangible or verbal rewards pursued the task less long and retained less of what they had learned.[22] In an earlier study Stevenson observed that the majority of children in the early years of elementary school were already highly motivated to learn. The high motivation, however, did not appear to be strongly dependent upon a desire to obtain material rewards. In fact the addition of an extrinsic reward to an intrinsically interesting task seemed to reduce the motivation to perform the task. The most important conse-

---

[19] Mollie S. Smart and Russell C. Smart, *Children, Development and Relationships,* 3rd ed. (New York: Macmillan, 1977), 642–646.

[20] J. Kagan, "Motivational and Attitudinal Factors in Receptivity to Learning," *Learning About Learning,* ed. J. Bruner (Washington, D.C.: Bureau of Research, U.S. Office of Education, 1966), 34–36.

[21] Paul H. Mussen, John J. Conger, and Jerome Kagan, *Child Development and Personality,* 4th ed. (New York: Harper and Row, 1974), 393f.

[22] Richard L. Sorensen and Martin L. Maehr, "Toward the Experimental Analysis of Continuing Motivation," *J Educational Research* 69(9) (May-June 1976), 319–322.

quences appeared to be *knowledge of the correctness of response, pleasing the parent or teacher* and, later, *pleasing themselves.*[23] If the task has an *intrinsic interest* for him, the child becomes the "operator," his own teacher. Let us hope that language learning has intrinsic interest, that it becomes a pleasant adventure, not a dull drill!

"That's very close, Scott."

Cartoon reprinted by permission of Jared D. Lee Studios and *Saturday Review* (June 23, 1979), p. 9.

Intermittent and Self-Motivation in Language Learning

No one enjoys constant extrinsic motivation, not even babies. As a learning task becomes interesting for its own intrinsic value, intermittent reinforcement of silent approval (a smile) is quite sufficient. And even intermittent reinforcement must be handled with considerable insight. Olver likens intermittent reinforcement to the continuous feedback of "getting warmer" or "getting colder" which children employ in guessing games.[24] But unlike the guessing games one does not finally say, "you're right"; to do so would mean complete homeostasis, a deterrent to new learning. It

[23] H.W. Stevenson, "Learning in Children," *Carmichael's Manual of Child Psychology, 1,* ed. P.H. Mussen (New York: John Wiley, 1970), 919.
[24] R. Olver, "Tutor and Learner," *Learning About Learning,* ed. J. Bruner (Washington, D.C.: Bureau of Research, U.S. Office of Education, 1966), 97.

is the mild uncertainty that spurs one at any age to mastery. Untermeyer recognized this goad to achievement when he wrote,

> From compromise and things half-done
> Keep me, with stern and stubborn pride.
> And when, at last, the fight is won,
> God keep me still unsatisfied.[25]

By the age of four self-reinforcement becomes a dominant means of learning oral language. In its practice, either overtly or implicitly, the child internalizes both the substance and the linguistic form of a conversation with the parent, and then runs it off independently. The child is his own paymaster, which is to say that by his mastery he provides his own continuing motivation and reinforcement.[26] This kind of activity is not random behavior produced by an overflow of energy. It is directed, selective, and persistent, and it continues because it satisfies an intrinsic need to establish his identity as a person and to deal competently with his environment.[27] The writer surrounded by four- and five-year-olds on a trip is under perpetual bombardment: "What's that?"; "What do you call it?" and "*Why* does it act that way?" They will do it at home, too, but there the attack seems less concentrated. More frequently at home or in the nursery school, the child may not ask questions of others, but he still is asking himself: "What is that thing?"; "*Why* does it do that?" He contemplates a thing; he scans it independently; he is searching for cues.[28] As a result of this activity and oral expression, the child establishes learned expectancies. He is becoming a real person in the sense that he knows what to expect from himself and his environment.

Motivation and Language Disorders

A major problem in teaching children with severe language handicaps is that many of them do not have the sense of identity to which we have just alluded. Lacking minimal competence in language, they seem to live in an existential vacuum, unable to say who they are, or worse, unable to *know* who they are. Perhaps the autistic child knows who he really is but he will not reveal his identity, at least to significant others. The non-

[25] L. Untermeyer, "Prayer," *Long Feud: Selected Poems* (New York: Harcourt Brace Jovanovich, 1962), 76. By permission of the publishers.

[26] J.S. Bruner, "The Act of Discovery," *Human Learning in the School,* ed. J.P. De-Cecco (New York: Holt, Rinehart and Winston, 1963), 264f.

[27] R.W. White, "Motivation Reconsidered: The Concept of Competence," *Psychological Review* 66 (September 1949), 297–333.

[28] J.S. Bruner, "On Perceptual Readiness in Perception," *Psychological Review* 64 (February 1957), 123–152.

autistic language-handicapped group frequently seems to lack the built-in drive, inherent in neural potential and organization, which is necessary for perceptual readiness. Consequently they do not expect to hear what they hear, see what they see, or feel what they feel. And the less their readiness, the stronger must be the input and redundancy of auditory, visual, and tactile-kinesthetic cues if they are to learn at all. Some of these faceless children were found every year in our resident summer Speech Center. As hope developed and fears and frustration diminished with speech training, and as expectancies were established, they emerged as children with distinct identities and with some competence in predicting and dealing with their environment.

Specific reinforcers employed in teaching these speech- and language-handicapped children follow the general pattern for all learning, but with some modifications. Tangible rewards became less necessary as curiosity, mastery, and the satisfaction of achievement entered into language learning. Such verbal praise as "That's a good try"; "Good boy"; and the approval of persons outside the circle of significant others (sometimes contrived) became effective reinforcers but only if they were used sparingly. One might wish that the child would develop early the motivation that comes with a favorable feedback from the task accomplished, but in the severely handicapped, the achievement may not meet the requisites even of early subgoals. If the child does attain a modicum of competence in oral language, this achievement becomes a motivating force with the supplementary benefits we alluded to earlier. He gains a sense of self-worth, he is able to exercise some control over his environment, and most importantly, he assumes responsibility for his own learning. All too frequently speech teachers fail to recognize the need to transfer responsibility from teacher to child. Ringing in the teacher's ears is the parent's injunction to "fix up" the youngster's "talk," a responsibility the teacher cannot and should not assume. Rarely does the teacher ask the child about the difficulties he has in understanding what is said to him or for ideas on how he could fix up his own speech. This is one way, nevertheless, of getting the child to be accountable for his own learning.

Some older language-handicapped children, preadolescent and adolescent, are singularly resistant to any form of reinforcement. Motivation seems to have been eroded by a series of environmental setbacks or by the realization that they will not overcome their handicaps. It is as if expectation of failure had replaced hope and intention. If the youngster is sensitive, his developing personality cannot withstand such assaults as the denigration of his self-image, his aspirational level, his effectance, or negative adult attitudes toward him day after day. Motivation slips away "like spilt milk over stone." The task of teachers and parents of these children is to find ways to negate comparison with the child's peers, his family members, and to develop in him genuine compensations for his handicap. It is not easily accomplished. In some instances social rewards, such as special privileges, may constitute immediate positive reinforcement. In other instances, negative reinforcers—the withdrawal of social reward following self-defeating language behavior or the use of imaginary, threat-inducing situations, for the purpose of enabling the individual to reduce anxiety by increased learning efforts—may work. And if the adolescent has been in a special speech class for three or four years, a semester's holiday could be a remarkable positive reinforcer.

Reinforcement, gained by matching a model, sometimes is not possible at any stage of language learning. Severely handicapped children, for example, early in life appreciate the fact that they cannot hope to become like those significant others in their home environment. What motivation can a cerebral-palsied lad substitute for the drive to emulate his handsome father-model? What model will this nine-year-old girl find who is handicapped by cleft palate, and who cried out recently, "Who would want a kid with this ugly face and speech?" Our best hope as teachers may be to have them model the leader in their group.

Lest this sound like a catalog of failures, let me cite examples in which either the materials or the environment provided motivation for a measure of success in habilitating children with serious linguistic handicaps.

A group of adolescent, acoustically handicapped children had been students in our Speech and Hearing Center for intensive teaching for two summers. Their schedule extended over eight weeks in three-hour daily sessions. The results of the first two summers were meager. When these children were scheduled for the third summer, the staff as a whole met to devise a new program for them. After lengthy consideration of our past failures, it was determined that the group should be engaged in a single, comprehensive activity of immediate interest to them for the entire summer. Drill on articulation, speech reading, distinctive phonetic features, auditory and visuomotor discrimination was abandoned. The instructors were to get completely away from clinic-oriented and clinic-limited speech to the real talk of life. It was a completely pragmatic approach, the language of use. The raw material of an electronics laboratory was supplied —borrowed or donated from electric research labs, Bell Telephone Company, and so on. The only requirement was that the children must talk about everything they were doing. They must make every effort to be understood by their peers and instructors. The result? We found that very often at five o'clock in the afternoon, they were still together in the lab, completing experiments, getting advice, and criticizing each other's work. When their achievements in oral comprehension and expression were evaluated at the end of the session, the average gain in speech proficiency of the group was 55 percent.

The motivation of a stimulating and pleasurable environment is much more important to language-handicapped children than to the normal child. The writer was a visiting consultant at a state institution for cerebral-palsied children in the Middle East. These children had had few experiences enjoyed by nonhandicapped children. The home was located in a rural setting with a village ten miles away, a village which they had not visited even at holiday time because the majority were nonambulatory. They saw few people except their caretakers and occasional family visitors. It was a totally gray environment—walls, furniture, people. Certainly their deprivation in stimulation accounted, in part, for their paucity of oral language. To be sure, these children had many sensorimotor handicaps; yet we concluded that deprivation in stimulation accounted, in large part, for their failure even to attempt to communicate with their peers. When they were given opportunities to participate in such minor experiences as watching a parade in the village, or creating holiday decorations for their home, or helping to put up brightly colored pictures on the dormitory walls, they made perceptible advances in communication.

Contrast these environments with a school for mentally retarded children in this country where the writer also served briefly as consultant. As we walked into a sunny corridor, we noted "talk" placards everywhere. We heard the voices and laughter of children and staff. The goal clearly was "get them to talk and always respond to their talk." In a guide for the staff, reinforcement techniques were described, for example, physical arousal and awareness, exploration, praise, responsibility for learning, and oral demonstrations to others. Motivation seemed to be a primary determinant of behavior throughout the school.

In our plan of situational, pragmatic learning of oral language, we are exceptionally dependent on the dynamics of interrelations between the child and his environment. People and forces in his world combine to accelerate his exploration, direction, and goal seeking, but his drive to learn oral language also will depend on his constitutional predisposition, self-reinforcement, and his need to use oral communication in adapting to his world.

THE PSYCHOSOCIAL ASPECTS OF ATTENTION

My friend, Jennie, mother of five-year-old Jamie, complained to me that her son "never listens" to what she says, never heeds her directives. A visit to Jennie's home provided the answer: Jennie never really talks *to* Jamie. She goes about her household tasks exhorting Jamie to pick up his toys, wash his hands, finish the puzzle, but actually addressing no one in particular, every one in general. As you will read later in this chapter, Jennie has violated almost every rule on attention getting.

I was consulted on the low achievement and high distractibility of a class of language-handicapped youngsters in the third grade. I decided to drop in on the class on a Friday morning. I found them in the learning center viewing a film about wild animals. The room was large. The children were seated in "scattered clusters." The film was at its climax when I entered. "In the gloaming" I finally located the teacher. She seemed to be intent on something other than the film; she was knitting! At the conclusion of the film and to our surprise, she stood up and asked questions about the plot. No one proffered a remark. Why did she expect responses? She had paid no more attention to the film than the children had. As we shall see later in this section, she too had violated the rules.

Neuropsychological Link between Motivation and Attention

As you noted at the beginning of this chapter, it is difficult to distinguish between the neuropsychological substrates, particularly between motivation and attention. Why does the individual attend to certain stimuli and not to others? Probably because some neural thresholds are lowered by the reticular system for certain classes of stimuli and raised in surrounding fields to exclude other stimuli. In more exact terms, when the differential thresholds for orientation become preferentially lower toward one class of events, relative to others, the person attends.[29] This is called *selective attention* because those stimuli not relevant to the oriented stimulus are shut out by suppression of their neural potentials. Attention is thus maintained until the child perceives the meaning. When attention is *diffuse,* on the other hand, the threshold of many classes of immediate stimuli is the same. Consequently attention is short; the child has inadequate perception of the event and hence faint or no recall. Is this the kind of attention the distractible child exhibits in your class? If it is, how can his or her motivation be stimulated, the factors producing distractibility be dealt with, and attention be made selective? The answer may lie partially in the alteration of the child's physical behavior, in part, in psychosocial adaptations. Some linguistically handicapped children quite regularly exhibit a kind of compulsive interruption of attention that probably is caused by disturbances in the CNS. They are thought to be metabolic or electric in nature, affecting the cortex or the reticular system controlling attention. An adult aphasic, with whom we have worked, experiences diurnal shifts in attention span. On Monday, Gordon is very receptive to language learning. He is alert and attends strictly to the problem at hand. He corrects his own mistakes in grammar and his errors in identification

[29] J. Kagan, *Perception and Its Disorders,* eds. D.A. Hamburg, K.H. Pribram, and A.J. Stunkard (Baltimore: Williams & Wilkins, 1970), 214–237.

of phrases. He notes his failure to catch quickly the significance of a passage and discusses it. His attention does not flag. Gordon returns for his second session on Wednesday, but on this day he learns little. He seems to be unaware of his errors, frequently looks away, and then must return to the beginning of the operation. He is listless and withdrawn. We resort to dictation. He asks us to repeat, again and again. Finally he shakes his head and gives up. Why? We know that fatigue, stress, and depression have an interruptive effect on attention. In Gordon's case one of these factors probably has lowered the synaptic potentials in the reticular system. He says, "Nothing registers today."

A short attention span in some language-handicapped children is associated with highly distractible behavior. It probably results from a complex of neuropsychological and environmental constituents. In neuropsychological terms, the gating or inhibitory power of the CNS may be poor, allowing a flood of impulses to come in, many of which are irrelevant, interfering with the central percept commanding attention.

Events Commanding Attention

To what kinds of "events" embracing a complex of stimuli does a child first attend? What stimuli seem to demand priority? We cannot name all the factors for they are as varied as the socioeconomic backgrounds of children. Here is a list of the priorities of the average child that should be of paramount concern to parents and teachers.

1. A child attends to an "event" to which he is initially *oriented by motivation,* and the length or direction of his attention generally is a rough index of how easy or difficult it is for him to understand it.[30] His behavior in attending may be characterized as a kind of search-and-sampling of the features of the event in order to interpret it, in order to perceive its meaning.

2. A child naturally attends to *the novel,* to that stimulus complex which has elements of the new, although it cannot be completely new.

3. Out of his attentional orientation response to the stimuli emerges a *communicative intention.* In the beginning stages of language development, he signals his intention with sensorimotor activity—positional changes toward the stimuli, visual shifts, and vocalizations—and later with some kind of meaningful utterance.[31] Communicative intention serves a double purpose. The child not only tries to understand the intention of the speaker, he also wants to express *his* intention to respond. In our plan of situational or pragmatic language teaching, communicative intention is essential to its success.

[30] Jerome Kagan, "Do Infants Think?" *Scientific American* 226(3) (March 1972), 74–82.

[31] Lynn S. Snyder, "Communicative and Cognitive Abilities and Disabilities in the Sensorimotor Period," *Merrill-Palmer Quarterly* 24(3) (July 1978), 161–180.

4. Children, particularly in the early stages of language development, attend to events that possess a *high rate of change*. In visual stimulation, changes in such physical characteristics as light, contour, and movement facilitate attention. Indices of attention to auditory events are more ambiguous, but it appears that stimuli having a high rate of change, such as intermittent sounds, produce more quieting and presumably more focused attention than continuous sounds.[32]

5. Children generally exhibit sustained attention to those visual events with which they have direct and uninterrupted *eye contact* or *focus*.[33] Although we can cite no research to verify our observation, we have noted the intermittent attention of children in the classroom when the teacher, half hidden behind her desk, presents oral directions for an activity. She directs her gaze at no one, and hence they reciprocate by glancing around the room, at the ceiling or the floor.

6. A child attends to those events which *satisfy his expectancy*. In oral communication, for example, he may attend to foreign speech because it is novel— but only for a short time because he does not know what to expect. Dialectal speech will hold his attention longer because it is novel and yet he can fit it into his schema of language perception.[34] His expectance is satisfied.

7. Children will sustain attention to an external event that *activates several schemata,* or associational patterns, within the brain. The extent to which they can activate associations will be determined by the intensity, selectivity, and duration of their attention. In teaching perceptual development of oral language, these attentional attributes assume critical importance. Programs devoted to sentence building with little or no contextual reference and with remote connections with a child's daily use of language can scarcely be expected to develop selective attention.

8. Children will exercise sustained attention on those events to which they are expected to respond. The poor intellectual return on children's television programs has been documented and publicized. One factor accounting for the poor record is that such programs rarely demand even an expectation of response. Attention is intermittent and completely passive. Learning is negligible. A similar situation frequently exists in auditory training in speech discrimination. Attention will be maintained in "listening for speech sounds" only if the children know that they are to respond. Since a dramatic development in set-to-respond (product of sustained attention) has been found to occur in children between six and seven years of age, it behooves special language teachers to capitalize on it.

[32] Jerome Kagan, "Attention and Psychological Change in the Young Child," *Science* 170(3960) (20 November 1970), 826–832; William Kessen, Marshall Haith, and Philip Salapatek, "Human Infancy: A Bibliography and Guide," *Carmichael's Manual of Child Psychology, I,* 3rd ed., ed. Paul H. Mussen (New York: John Wiley, 1970), 340.

[33] Antoinette Krupski and Patricia R. Boyle, "An Observational Analysis of Children's Behavior During a Simple-Reaction-Time Task: The Role of Attention," *Child Development* 49(2) (June 1978), 340–347.

[34] "A schema (plural: schemata) is a representation of experience that preserves the temporal and spatial relations of the original event, without being necessarily isomorphic with that event."—Jerome Kagan, "Attention and Psychological Change in the Young Child," 826.

PROBLEMS OF ATTENTION IN
LANGUAGE-RETARDED CHILDREN

Deficits in Attentional Behavior:
Expectancy and Intention

The spur that motivation gives to attention in the normal child has been stressed. In the language handicapped, strong and consistent motivation is essential. Its lack seriously affects the aspects of intention and expectancy. A group of special language teachers in a workshop complained that the language retardate showed little interest in language experiences, despite their efforts to make them novel and varied. After discussion they agreed that behind lack of interest were more fundamental problems they must attack: *lack of expectancy* in the event and *lack of intention* to participate in it. These teachers were not asking the children to engage in drills on phonemes or on sentences out of context and without connection to their pragmatic language needs. Attention, they knew, could not be facilitated by such an approach. They decided to motivate the children to develop selective and sustained attention with a unit on dramatization of familiar stories with the aid of puppets. Did all these teachers turn in success stories? Not all. A good many were enthusiastic about their results. Lest you think it is always easy to "turn on" the language retardate if you have the proper method, here is a report of one of this group who claimed very minimal success.

Using paper bag, hand, and sock puppets, this teacher had dramatized several familiar stories. The children, ten in all, had "tried out" the fuzzy finger puppet. Then one morning they came into their classroom to find a puppet stage and a semiprofessional performance in progress. To be sure, it was a new kind of experience in some respects: The story was new; the puppets and the staging were new. The teacher, nevertheless, expected a general reaction of eagerness, expectancy, and intention. But as the performance progressed, it was apparent by their posture, wandering gaze, and distracting movements that the majority of the group had little intention of entering into the experience. At the climax the action was interrupted, giving her the opportunity to ask the children, "And now, what do you think will happen?" Only three of the ten children apparently had anticipated the outcome. Perhaps some children had not *expected to respond*. Others possibly did not know *how to respond*. Teaching children intention and expectancy at a very early age (four to five years) may not be an easy assignment, but when it achieves positive results, language growth may be dramatic. I say *early* because the effect of this failure on later development is disastrous. Our experience with Peter, nine years of age, illustrates the problem. He does not anticipate what comes next in the story, what he is to do next in playing a game, or what he is to "think next" in pursuing an idea. Peter confounds his teachers and me. There should be a way, we agree, to train him in expectancy through the development of voluntary attention. If he attends, develops an attention span voluntarily, he should improve his ability to anticipate future action on the basis of his immediate past action. Piaget says that "as transports (temporospatial relations) become systematized or extended in time and space, they give rise to anticipatory attitudes (*einstellung* effects) or to real anticipations." [35]

Deficits in Selective Attention:
Their Effect on Schematic Development

From our discussion in an earlier section of this chapter, we know that selective attention normally *prepares and facilitates perception of oral language*. By the age of four months, the baby no longer attends to all sounds that have a high rate of change, have great intensity, or continue over a long period of time. He attends only to those auditory stimuli which he can fit into his scheme or meaningful organization of stimuli. If the auditory event has slightly discrepant factors, he will attend to it because he may mentally transform it into a form with which he is familiar, the schema. But if the event is completely discrepant, a total mismatch with his neuronal model, the baby will react only defensively (turning away, crying, and so on). If the event is completely familiar, if it is the same event in every detail, he also may fail to attend to it. Some schema in selective attention, however, the baby must have. For example, he must be able to recognize that a sequence of high pitched sounds in an intonation pattern is human speech rather than a bird song; he must have schemata for the human voice and for bird songs.[36] More applicable to language learning and more ominous in import is our recent observation of a five-month-old child who does not distinguish between the voice of his mother and other voices of women in the neighborhood. Will this child's attention sharpen and perception develop so that shortly he will begin to copy the prosodic patterns of speech in his environment? This is an early prognostic sign of the integrity of the attentional process facilitating perception.

Selective Attention and Perceptual Style

At a later period in language development, the retardate may experience more complex problems having to do with selective attention in organizing stimuli, in excluding irrelevant stimuli, and in putting together complexes

[35] J. Piaget, *The Mechanisms of Perception* (New York: Basic Books, 1969), 186.
[36] Kagan, "Do Infants Think?" 74–83.

of stimuli that belong together. Piaget, as you noted in the preceding section, stated that the development of anticipation, or expectancy, depended on systematization, the organization of stimuli into complex schemata. Returning to our experience with Peter, how do we teach him to systematize his perceptual schemes so that he has a consistent way of handling stimuli, a way resulting in a perceptual style?

Admittedly there are individual differences in the way nonhandicapped children deploy attention in developing a perceptual style. In some children the perceptual style is to scan the whole stimulus field; in others, the habitual mode is to focus immediately on the centrum. Peter focuses on an object or a person in the stimulus field, but it is not the core of the percept; frequently it bears little relation to the percept. Is his inability to exercise selective attention appropriate to the significant features of the percept caused, at least in part, by his incapacity to *understand* the nature of the situation? [37] Our study of linguistically handicapped children suggests that many of them do not employ selective attention and hence do not comprehend the significant features of the percept. Peter is but one example. A cerebral-palsied child with severe language handicaps protested: "But I never see what you see in that picture." A nontalking child of five years studies a bug in a corner of the picture but fails to see the boy whizzing down a hill on a bike in the center of the picture. An eight-year-old boy, aphasic following cerebral damage in an accident, examines every miniscule in background and foreground and then laboriously tries to integrate all in one percept. How can all four children be taught to organize attention-sets, thereby facilitating the perceptual processes?

Deficits in Sustained Attention: Attentional Shift and Fixation

Attentional shifts resulting in a short attention span affect all learning; yet we have little information on ways to inhibit shifts and thus lengthen the span. Earlier in this chapter we recognized certain neurological factors that may account for the problem in some children. In other children psychosocial forces alone may be the cause of shifts in attention. Evidence from research on both scores is inconclusive.

From infancy on, many a child today lives in a perpetually disturbing and changing environment. Threatened by the continuous melee of brilliant lights, loud sounds, and tense feelings, he is forced into habitual attention shifts. He responds to every noise, every change in light, every stimulus that comes into his purview. His attention skips, hops, and returns momentarily to the prime stimulus. If this is a description of the

[37] M.D. Vernon, *The Psychology of Perception* (Harmondsworth, Middlesex, England: Penguin Books, 1962), 157–195.

environment of a child in your class, family cooperation to change it must be sought.

In the classroom we have tried various methods to habituate these children to irrelevant stimuli. We do not teach them in soundproof, barren cubicles, devoid of all distracting stimuli, because they do not live in such a world. The initial objective is to secure attention quickly so that relevant cues have "maximum salience." Once this is accomplished, the likelihood of shift is lessened.[38] We search for a challenging, enjoyable activity in which they will become completely absorbed. Once attention is secure, we slowly increase distractions in the background. In one instance, even the recess bell did not produce a shift. The children continued to attend to the foreground. That is our best approach. Martin and Powers describe experimental efforts to increase the amount of time attending to a task by immediate reinforcement contingent on the time spent.[39] With some children we have succeeded in increasing the time spent on a task, but perhaps the task actually could have been completed in less time. Was the child truly attending the whole time he was engaged in the task? We do know that attention shifts are fewer in these children when we require them to *respond* either in action or speech than when they merely observe or listen.[40]

A problem that we associate, frequently but not exclusively, with the mental retardate is *fixation of attention*. Instead of shifting attention rapidly and nonpurposively, these children seem to be unable to leave one stimulus for succeeding stimuli. In the comprehension of oral language, successive auditory and haptic stimuli must be processed in milliseconds. A split-second fixation results in confusion and loss of meaning.[41] The inability to "move ahead" because attention remains fixed on one battery of stimuli is a significant deterrent to learning. Laurie, a five-year-old language retardate, shouts gleefully as she points to a cat in Norman Rockwell's portrayal of a scene from *The Adventures of Tom Sawyer*,[42] disregarding the determined Aunt Polly pushing a spoonful of medicine into Tom's mouth. "Tell us a story about the picture," I ask. She talks about the cat on which she has riveted her attention. Despite our urging, she

---

[38] D. Zeaman and B.J. House, "The Role of Attention in Retardate Discrimination Learning," *Handbook of Mental Deficiency,* ed. N. Ellis (New York: McGraw-Hill, 1963), 159–223.

[39] G.L. Martin and R.B. Powers, "Attention Span: An Operant Conditioning Analysis," *Exceptional Child* 33 (April 1967), 565–570.

[40] D. Premack, "A Functional Analysis of Language," *J Experimental Analysis of Behavior,* 14(1) (July 1970), 107–125.

[41] W.G. Hardy and M. Hardy, *Essays on Communication and Communicative Disorders* (New York: Grune and Stratton, 1977), 66.

[42] Picture No. 325, *The Adventures of Tom Sawyer* in *Norman Rockwell* by Thomas S. Buechner (New York: Harry N. Abrams, Inc., 1970).

does not shift attention in order to take a swift survey of all significant stimuli. She has not learned a "way of looking at things, a 'perceptual style.' " Consequently she does not comprehend the meaning of the whole. Older children frequently rivet their attention on one word in a phrase and are unable to progress to the next word. In reading they repeat a phrase over and over; they cannot get beyond it. Someone has said that these children continue the task long after it has been completed.

Teaching Facilitation of Attention

In the course of this discussion we have suggested general ways of developing controlled attention, but there are still unanswered questions pertaining to specific practices. Is the auditory route the exclusive pathway to language learning? If it is, then it is also the pathway to attention control. From the vast amount of literature on auditory discrimination training, it would seem to have exclusive rights to the territory. Now special language teachers are less sure that this assumption is entirely true. First they have found that the prime sensory modality varies greatly among the children they teach. In neurological terms modality primacy must depend upon the relative power and integrity of the sensory analyzer. Mark pays attention to auditory stimuli for comprehension of language because he understands more quickly by that route. Jay says, "Let me read it; then I'll get it." Ellen says, "Let me say it to you; then I will understand and remember it." The preference of Mark for audition, Jay for vision, Ellen for proprioceptive-motor analysis may lie in genetic or neurobiologic sources.

A second question to be answered concerns the specific stimulus properties of the preferred sensory modality. In Mark's preference, changes in pitch or volume or rate could trigger his attention. Some children attend immediately to parents who suddenly reduce the volume, slow the rate, or lower the pitch of the voice. These are "attention getters" with "parent-deaf" children, at least until they become habituated to these changes.

A third question concerns the ability to train specific sensory modalities. We believe that attentiveness can be trained although we do not have sufficient information on the way to do it. Children normally must experience an increase in the sharpness and power of auditory orienting responses as a developmental process in the comprehension of language. Training in rhythmics that depends on haptic-motor skills has advanced early language learning in a program with which we have been associated. We presume that the maturation of the sensorium in the language retardate does not progress by the same increment as in the nonhandicapped. The presumption is based, however, on the smallest substructure of fact.

A sensory modality that might have been the prime route may be negatively conditioned by the sociocultural environment. Bits of evidence support the argument that some children, particularly from economically or culturally disadvantaged homes, have lost the capacity to respond to auditory input. The noise level of this environment is presumed to be exceedingly high, thus negating all discriminative response in attention.

Teachers are asking many more questions for which we have no answers. As yet psychology has made only minimal contributions.[43] Until attentional sources and means for measuring individual differences in attention are established, we shall have to rely on experimental teaching programs and subjective judgment for answers to such questions as these: How well does a child attend to what he hears? To what he sees? To what he feels tactually and proprioceptively? What are the specific stimulus properties that gain and control attention across preschool and elementary school age ranges? Are the sensory modalities—auditory, visual, tactile, and kinesthetic—equally educable in developing attentional behavior? Is the prime determinant of strength of sensory input genetic, neurobiological or psychosocial? Does a combination of sensory modalities increase or decrease attention? Does the child attend more intently and longer when visual and auditory stimuli are combined? Does a consistently noisy environment contribute to habituation and, hence, to exclusion of all auditory stimuli in attention control? Is the stimulus complex focused on semantic and syntactic variables rather than on phonetic variables of language in attention behavior?

A teaching team for a class of first grade children with language handicaps set down these suggestions as aids in teaching control of attention.

1. The "response set." Select a group activity that demands good posture, alert expression, visual focus, intention, and positive emotional attitudes.

2. Attention timing. Encourage the children to respond only on signal in the group activity. Give "symbolic" rewards to those who inhibit the tendency to "beat the gun." Establish a tempo, however, that inhibits attentional fixation.

3. Warming up. Proceed from a warming-up activity which will provide the conditional stimulus to the activity demanding the imperative stimulus. The conditional stimulus may be the song or poem which the children have come to expect as the "first order of the day." Engage children who exhibit a slow reaction time in physical exercises (skipping, marching, and so on).

4. Partial familiarity. The completely new does not beget attentiveness so choose an activity with which the children have some knowledge. Introduce novel, but pertinent, stimuli from time to time.

5. Expectations. Before the announced activity begins, heighten expectancy and anticipation by demonstrating the kinds of activities and/or responses

[43] W.D. Rohwer, Jr., "Cognitive Development and Education," *Carmichael's Manual of Child Psychology, I,* ed. P.H. Mussen (New York: John Wiley and Sons, Inc., 1970), 1421–23.

you will expect from them. Induce negative "attention seekers" to participate by assigning special, "privileged" responsibilities.

6. Stimulus sensitivity. Select an activity that calls for an increase in the number of stimulus dimensions to be integrated with the primary stimulus. Identify and protect children who cannot sustain attention under multiple sensory input.

7. Perceptual styles. Demonstrate "perceptual styles" in attending to an activity (intention, general sweep, sequencing stimuli, exclusion of irrelevant stimuli, and unitary organization of consistent foci).

8. Voice tone. In talking about an activity or in giving directions, vary vocal pitch, time, and intensity in order to increase attention. Lower the volume occasionally so that the children will have to strain to hear. Use simple, clear language.

9. Reinforcement. Go around the circle encouraging each child by a nod, smile, gesture, or hand touch. Encourage the children also to respond to stimuli, verbal or nonverbal, *with feeling*.

10. Attention in a noisy environment. Before the activity begins, tell the children that some background noise may intrude at times. Remind them of ways, physical and mental, by which they can keep their attention on the activity, despite increasingly distracting and complex background noise.

11. Attention control. Attention control grows by what it feeds on—practice!

NEURO-PSYCHOSOCIAL ASPECTS OF MEMORY

In contrast to the scanty interest in motivation and attention until very recently, the topic of memory has been the subject of intensive investigation, both experientially and theoretically. Neurologists and psychologists for a decade or more have debated the relation of human learning and memory and specifically the bearing of the coding processes on retrieval. Yet memory remains an elusive phenomenon. Rarely has one subject engaged the attention of so many scientists with so little advance in its understanding. How are meaningful language events coded and stored? Are learning and remembering the same thing, that is, do language percepts and their recall have a common interface so that when we perceive clearly and completely, we have little difficulty in recalling the percept? What is the memory code for oral language? What is the difference between long and short memory stores in the coding process? How do we train memory skills in the language retardate? These are some questions we shall consider. In some instances our answers are reliable; in others they are hedged by theory.

Halstead defines memory as "a process whereby organized time-space events are carried forward in time." [44] These events, represented in the

[44]W.C. Halstead, "Thinking, Imagery and Memory," chap. 46, *Handbook of Physiology, Sec. 1: Neurophysiology III,* ed. J. Field (Washington, D.C.: American Physiology Society, 1960), 1675.

nervous system as substantive memory traces, constitute the time-bind feature of the brain. Establishment of a memory trace presumably depends upon the ability of the organism to retain in its neural organization a skeletal relationship among neuron assemblies that have responded together in earlier time-space events and to reproduce this related complex when needed. These "related complexes," or neuronal assemblies mediating memory functions, interestingly enough have been established in those temporoparietal regions of the brain which also serve the reticular and limbic networks.[45] We know that electrochemical activity in some form of ribonucleic acid, either RNA (an intermediate) or DNA synthesizes protein and increases sharply in amount in these areas as the learning curve rises. The synthesis of protein continues for some time afterward.[46] The extent to which the ribonucleic acid content rises and the length or duration of the chemical in critical fields presumably determines one's ability to recall. Duration, and hence retention, some scientists believe, varies not only with the amount of RNA or DNA, but also with the persistence of a theta rhythm (a cortical rhythm best recorded from the infero-temporal region, having a frequency of four to seven cycles per second).[47]

SHORT-TERM AND LONG-TERM MEMORY

Neurological evidence on the difference between short-term memory and long-term storage is inconclusive. Some scholars believe that short-term memory is dependent for its duration on the "reverberation in self-reexciting neural circuits." [48] What happens chemically in the reverberating system must be a limited alteration of the neurotransmitter substance which fades at the synapses at different rates. It may be a matter of seconds or minutes. Long-term memory presumably owes its duration to an autocatalytic process which synthesizes and resynthesizes the protein of the ribonucleic acid at the synapses in the temporoparietal brain. The connections endure, and under motivation by the reticular and limbic

[45] David S. Olton, "Spatial Memory," *Scientific American* 236(6) (June 1977), 82–98; Wilder Penfield and G. Mathieson, "Memory," *Archives of Neurology* 31 (September 1974), 145–154; Patricia Wallace, "Neurochemistry: Unraveling the Mechanism of Memory," *Science* 190(4219) (12 December 1975), 1076–1078.

[46] Peter Watson, "In Search of Memory," *The Illustrated London News* 259(6880) (November 1971), 42–43.

[47] Philip W. Landfeld, James L. McGaugh, and Ronald J. Tusa, "Theta Rhythm: A Temporal Correlate of Memory Storage in the Rat," *Science* 175(4017) (7 January 1972), 87–89.

[48] R.N. Haber, "How We Remember What We See," *Scientific American* 222(5) (May 1970), 104–112; H.B. Robinson and N.M. Robinson, "Mental Retardation," *Carmichael's Manual of Child Psychology, II,* ed. P.H. Mussen (New York: John Wiley, 1970), 637.

systems, events experienced months and years before can be recalled.[49] According to Pribram, the neurological process of memory storage is ordinarily thought to run something like this: An event occurs and is registered in short-term memory where it circulates for a time as a trace in neural loops from which it is finally transferred into a longer term molecular store. The transfer process is called the consolidation of the memory trace.[50]

Just as the interface between learning and remembering is thin so is the boundary between short-term and long-term memory. Memory has a dual nature, but the differences in mechanism and the manner of transposition of information from short- to long-term memory are nebulous. Some scholars describe short-term memory as a stimulus trace or momentary image—visual, acoustic, or haptic—lasting less than a second after perception and dependent for its duration on the "reverberation" in self-reexciting neural circuits.[51] Another group of researchers conclude that short-term memory may cover a period of minutes and is related to the retention of information beyond the immediate span of attention.[52]

Since the short-term store is the temporary working memory, its importance in language learning is crucial.[53] The stimulating event presumably is first received in a short-term mechanism (reverberating neural circuits) which then searches long-term memory for the "best fit." In the projected seconds or minutes, depending on the form and complexity of the event, the long-term store is activated, and the search or probe begins, not only to find the best fit or accommodation, but to bring in to short-term circuits closely related information. It must be consolidated with the current perceptions of which the child is momentarily aware. If the substance of immediate recall is rehearsed and not interrupted by extraneous or interfering stimuli, consolidation presumably goes on, turning short-term into long-term memory.

Perception and Memory

Perceiving and memorizing are functionally undifferentiated, that is, whatever aids perception aids memory. They are the product of the same

[49] Samuel H. Barondes, "Protein-Synthesis Dependent and Protein-Synthesis Independent Memory Storage Processes," *Short-Term Memory,* eds. Diana Deutsch and J.A. Deutsch (New York: Academic Press, 1975), 385–388.

[50] Karl H. Pribram, *Languages of the Brain* (Englewood Cliffs, N.J.: Prentice-Hall, Inc., 1971), 349.

[51] Haber, "How We Remember What We See," 104–112; H.B. Robinson and N.M. Robinson, "Mental Retardation," 637.

[52] R.L. Isaacson, "Memory Processes and the Hippocampus," chap. 12, *Short-Term Memory,* eds. D. Deutsch and J.A. Deutsch (New York: Academic Press, 1972), 314; E.R. Kandel, "Small Systems of Neurons," *Scientific American* 241(3) (September 1979), 67–76.

[53] R.C. Atkinson and R.M. Shiffrin, "The Control of Short-Term Memory," 82–91.

neural processing, the same coding operations. The ability to comprehend the complex of stimuli, to organize it, and to find a meaning, depends on the quality of search and organization in the process of coding. The image conveyed by the sensory input (auditory, visual, or haptic) to the perceptual-memory system must be accurate if it is to be recalled at all. It cannot be the source of error.[54]

Organization and Memory

The organization or sequencing of incoming information may take several forms. The individual may organize according to intentionality or temporospatial sequencing. Intention to perceive and remember owes much to motivation and attention but also to social forces in the home and school. The story is old, but it concerns intention, and it happened to the writer. Effie had been placed in a special speech class because of a severe lisp. When her mother heard the news, she appeared at my classroom door and without introduction challenged me: "Why you put my girl, Effie, in a peeth clath? Now lookere, I lithp an I got a huthbun and Effie theeth gonna lithp tho thee can get a huthbun." More recently an experience with José, enrolled in a linguistically handicapped group of Hispanic children, made me realize that a child who *will not* relate to his peers through language *and is determined not to,* will profit little from our effort to teach him to learn and to remember what he learns. José, only seven years of age but very tall and husky, was negatively disposed to oral communication. His behavior was consistent: He was completely noncommunicative with the other children in the class and with teachers—negatively disposed to academia in general. He exhibited *intentional forgetting.* On invitation his father visited school. "José—jus like me—" he said. "I don go school" (I wouldn't go to school); "I like play." On inquiry "play" meant baseball both for father and son. With the cooperation of the recreational staff, José was invited to participate in the fifth grade athletic program with the provision that he also must participate in our language program. José became a star in several sports; and *almost* a star in language learning in the second grade.

Sequencing in time or space is used frequently in recall of a narrative by employing the chaining method of "what happened next." In sequencing lines of poetry, children frequently intensify the rhythmic pattern in order to heighten the sequence and thus remember the poem. Rehearsal, spatial sequencing, is the practice most frequently used by children in language learning. Rehearsal may be overt or covert; either way it does something more than repeat the bare bones of the percept. It

[54] Haber, "How We Remember What We See," 104–112.

strengthens sequencing and unquestionably sets the perceptual-semantic chain in memory.

Other Organizing Practices

The activation of the semantic network, the practice of bringing in closely related verbal information from the memory store is a valuable organizing procedure, particularly for slightly "older" children (six to nine years). It involves intensification of feedforward and feedback in coding so that other neuronal complexes will join the code. As a result the verbalization of sets and subsets of information are related so that new concepts and experiences are added and the knowledge already in the semantic network may be recombined, discriminated, and generalized.[55] Another practice aiding recall with little children is *imaging* and covertly enacting motor patterns while listening to or reading directions, stories, and so on. With older children this was not an effective memory aid. We do not know why.

Visual, Auditory, Haptic Transformations in Memory Code

I have said that the length of time required for recall depends in part on the sensory form of the stimulating event. Pictorial or iconic (image) events must be translated into semantic or symbolic form. A picture that we see is not stored in words *unless* immediate association is made in language, and that demands immediate rehearsal. Consequently visual translation to speech takes time. I am sure that every teacher has observed children who "take in" the meaning of a picture quickly, but unless they translate it immediately into symbolic language, they have difficulty recalling its description or meaning in verbal symbols. Although visual imagery assists linguistic association, the latter is usually the more important key to long-stored memory of *language acts.*[56] But recall is also determined by the complexity of the event. Little children may comprehend the general sense of long and somewhat complex directions. Simultaneous haptic feedback may help some in the group to execute the direc-

[55] R.C. Atkinson and R.M. Shiffrin, "The Control of Short-Term Memory," *Scientific American* 225(2) (August 1971), 82–90; David E. Meyer and R.V. Schvaneveldt, "Meaning, Memory Structure and Mental Processes," *Science* 192(4234) (2 April 1976), 27–33; D.A. Norman and R.P. Abelson, "Intelligent Verbal Behavior," *Science* 175(4025) (3 March 1972), 1024.

[56] D.D. Wickens, "Characteristics of Word Encoding," *Coding Processes in Human Memory,* eds. Arthur W. Melton and Edwin Martin (Washington, D.C.: V.H. Winston and Sons, 1972), 212–231.

tions correctly. But symbolically they have not had time in which to analyze, organize, or elaborate the code. Since the percept is not complete, recall also will be uncertain or inaccurate.

The effort of some children to *repeat exactly* in recall what has been said to them is a lesson in futility. Like nailing jello to the wall, it can't be done. Why? Because an event is recalled by the *semantic relationships* of the language memory code. They are recalled in paraphrased sentences, in phrases, in semantic chunks of information, not in the exact words in which they are received in memory. Certainly recall of symbolic language is neither phonetic nor syntactic in nature.[57] If semantic relationships molded into an *idea* is the focus of language learning and of recall, it follows that phonetic instruction has doubtful value in developing memory skills. The language code undergoes a continuous change, eroded at some points, sharpened at others, as it travels from the acoustic signal through neural circuits to be phonemically molded finally into syllable, word, or phrase in the temporoparietal cortex. Here the phonemic strings, possessed of a form, syntactic and prosodic, are translated into meaning or semantic codes, a network of meaningful relations. It is the *semantic code* that becomes the object of our search in recall.[58] It will not be released in the same phonemic, syntactic, or even prosodic form in which it entered the memory store. The semantic code may be a complete transformation, different words, different structure.

MEMORY PROBLEMS OF LINGUISTICALLY RETARDED CHILDREN

Some problems discussed in these paragraphs are not peculiar to the language retardate. They are shared by the slow learner, the child with perceptual problems, the emotionally disturbed youngster. And the problems are not truly language problems: They are learning problems.

Mastery of the Percept; Overlearning

"Think it once more! Do you know all you need to know about it? Say it once more! Act it out once more! One more time please! Let's say and act it out once more—shall we?—" This teacher's persuasion to children

[57] S.G. Paris and G.J. Mahoney, "Cognitive Integration in Children's Memory for Sentences and Pictures," *Child Development* 45(3) (September 1974), 633–642.

[58] R.A. Cole, "Perceiving Syllables and Remembering Phonemes," *J Speech Hearing Research* 16(1) (1973), 37–47; J. Konorski, *Integrative Activity of the Brain* (Chicago: University of Chicago Press, 1967), 129; W.A. Wickelgren, "The Long and Short of Memory," chap. 2, *Short-Term Memory,* eds. D. Deutsch and J.A. Deutsch (New York: Academic Press, 1975), 46–47.

pleased me. It did not turn off the children. Obviously it increased their excitement, motivation, and intent to learn for they called out, "Yes— let's!" The major stumbling block in all learning is the failure of the child to perceive the image accurately in the first place. Whether the image is visual, auditory, or haptic, it cannot, it must not be in error. Like the slow learner, the linguistically handicapped child "forgets" because the percept is fuzzy, not clearly framed in a context.[59] But behind that "because" are other "becauses." The major problem is that he has not rehearsed the information immediately upon receipt and then repeatedly in spaced rehearsals. This practice would sharpen and clarify the original trace in the short-term memory store. It would stimulate continued dynamic reverberation in the neural circuits.

Transposition: Translation of Sensory Modalities into Verbal Images

A second stumbling block is the child's inability to transpose visual and haptic events into verbal symbols—into words, phrases, sentences. He sees and apparently appreciates the meaning of the picture but he cannot put it into words. Sometimes a child says, "I know it; let me draw it,"—and he does it quite well but he cannot put it into words. Another child listens to a story and then when asked to tell it attempts to repeat it in the exact words which were read to him. Of course he cannot do it for these are not his words. He has tried to remember words, not meaning. He remembers the first and last words of the sentence, the first and last direction, and the end of a story or activity. The middle remains in limbo recesses, not to be retrieved. The semantic code or network is missing.

Unisensory or Multisensory Input

A third practice, related to the second, is the dependence in comprehension on one sensory modality and on one only. The visual route for the majority of children (and adults) is superior. As I have explained earlier, it is a slower route because visual symbols must be translated into auditory-verbal symbols.[60] With linguistically handicapped children it may indeed be the best way to teach—to teach language through oral reading. The advantage in the three-pronged probe—auditory, visual, and haptic—is that any one of the three may call forth the memory. We all have had the

[59] Karl H. Pribram, "The Neurophysiology of Remembering," *Scientific American* 220(1) (January 1969), 73–84.
[60] C.G. Penney, "Modality Effects in Short-Term Memory," *Psychological Bulletin* 82(1) (1975), 68–94.

experience of enhanced recall by association. When the plane lands in my favorite foreign country where I have taught, visited, and revisited, I am completely aphasic. Not one word of that language beyond a greeting comes to mind as I pass through Customs. But on the other side are my friends waiting to meet me! We drive down the familiar avenues; the sights, sounds, smells; the prosodic patterns of speech, of my friends, of the cab driver, of the venders; the open market place, *my* hotel: All comes back to me—including the foreign tongue! Children normally have a strong tendency to use all sensorimotor avenues to construct semantic relationships among phrases and sentences and to integrate the relationships into holistic schemata in memory.[61] What one hopes is that the language-retarded child will be able to use the multimodal input without disturbing his margin of safety, his homeostat. Can the limbic and reticular systems tolerate the bombardment of multimodal stimuli?

Retrieval Interference

All individuals must counter retrieval interference, but the language retardate seems to have unusual trouble in this respect. One is reminded of the professor of icthyology who complained that each time he learned the name of a new student, he forgot the name of a fish. This is not just another joke about an absent-minded professor. It illustrates the interference theory of forgetting; that is, that attending to one group of stimuli may have an adverse effect on remembering other groups. Forgetting increases with time because storage becomes crowded and memory patterns not closely related to a specific retrieval are "pushed into the background." Hence each new search must be conducted over a broader area of memory. The interference experienced by the language retardate often comes from his inability to inhibit external and/or internal stimuli. The cerebral-palsied child's aberrant, uncontrolled movements of the head produce distortions of proprioceptive feedback in the articulatory organs resulting in changing language patterns and hence in inaccurate recall. Internally physical and neural disturbances conspire to defeat recall. The difficulty varies from day to day, frequently receding and reappearing within the hour.

Retarded Speech

A problem allied with interference is the influence of the child's retarded speech production on memory. If he cannot remember the syllable strings long enough to use them in reproducing speech or cannot hold

[61] Paris and Mahoney, "Cognitive Integration in Children's Memory for Sentences and Pictures," 633–642.

minimal stretches of connected speech in short-term memory, then recall will be impaired. He has neither the correct auditory nor haptic feedback to aid him in establishing or retrieving the information.[62]

TRAINING MEMORY: THE SKILLS

There may be many more ways to aid language-handicapped children in remembering than we list here. Memory systems are for sale; we abjure them. Tricks of phonemic, letter, or number associations are offered; they are broken crutches.

1. We must find ways to help the child to understand clearly the percept, the idea. He can be helped to achieve clarity in ideation by selective observation (attention), structuring, organizing, and sequencing stimuli. Clear definitions along the way will help, but the greater task is to categorize, to put together those items which belong together and to put them in a logical order.

2. Rehearsal, immediate rehearsal accompanying input, is imperative, but it cannot be a "barebones memorization." It must be a lively re-creation of the original design. It may be either covert or overt. Children who rehearse subvocally or vocally have an echoic store that facilitates recall. Of course, if the phonology of speech is faulty, rehearsal also is impaired.

3. Recall is aided by increasing semantic intersentential relations in the network. Since it is much more difficult to recall specific unrelated sentences, every means should be employed to help the child to "chain," or join subitems, in building the percept. Children enjoy "narrative chaining" in which the sequence of events of a story or situation is told and retold. And just as it is difficult for children to remember unrelated sentences, so it is also difficult for them to recall linguistic associations which are completely foreign to their language environment.

4. Recall is aided by the development of mental imagery and physical participation. The child describing an activity, a situation, or a scene will employ bodily action (postural changes, movement, and gesture) in order to sharpen the image and set the connections among subitems. The links are forged, not only with words but also by the actions, the bodily expressions inherent in the activity. Many an adult, trying to recall a name, a situation, or an idea will evoke the memory by repeating actions associated with the person or event.[63] Eccles argues that mental imagery is overwhelmingly important to the function of memory.[64]

5. Finally, the secret to all memory systems is overlearning. The story must be told one more time; the directions for the project, rehearsed one more time; the idea, the whole idea—with all its connectives: Say it again, one more time! Overlearning is the key to retention.

---

[62] J.L. Locke and K.J. Kutz, "Memory for Speech and Speech for Memory," *J Speech Hearing Research* 18(1) (March 1975), 176–191.

[63] J. Konorski, *Integrative Activity of the Brain,* 493–495.

[64] J.C. Eccles, "The Physiology of Imagination," chap. 4, *Altered States of Awareness. (Readings from Scientific American.)* San Francisco: W.H. Freeman and Company, 1972), 31–40.

Parents and teachers may put into practice all these suggestions and yet fail to improve materially the memory of certain language-retarded children. A frustrated eight-year-old once protested to me: "I don't want to remember. My forgetter may even get worse!" I, too, have held the damp hand of frustration of teachers as will be evident by these excerpts from the daily logs of one of my staff, an excellent team teacher:

> Josephus seems to have no imagination. We have tried multimodal input; it disturbs him so much that we have abandoned phonological reinforcement and rely only on auditory feedback, although this modality too seems blunted. . . Is the percept blurred because he cannot put a clear verbal handle on it? Because he cannot find the words or the frame by which to express an idea? Sometimes he reports that he has forgotten how the sentence begins by the time it is concluded. Or is it interference from other informational bits which produces the rapid deterioration of the rehearsed percept? Josephus fails to "overlearn" the story although he spends hours supposedly in rehearsal. We show him how to paraphrase, but he tries to repeat the story exactly as we told it. We demonstrate how to chain "particulars," to connect them, and then to generalize.

We have gone full circle; once again we are trying to teach Josephus how to group or "cluster" percepts—numbers, colors, objects, situations, key phrases—so that the recall elements, although not identical, are bound together.

There are strategies yet to be discovered, strategies we now know are worthless, and strategies we think are sound and should be developed. Certainly passive intake strategies restricting recall only to the most recently acquired information should be discarded. In our observation operant conditioning often becomes a passive pushbutton exercise in which all responses, successful and unsuccessful, are automatically rewarded. We believe that active rehearsal involving total bodily participation, immediate linking through clustering with associative tasks, and appropriate interpersonal, emotional reinforcement are strategies that may yield dramatic gains in memory. Operative conditioning, as it is now practiced, probably will not be the Sesame Street to memory.

No neuropsychological substrate is an independent factor in language learning. Possibly all substrates subtend from perceptual ability or intelligence. Our ability to perceive and to know motivates us to attend, and conversely we attend to the significant features in an environment which we perceive and understand. And finally we remember those objects, events, and ideas to which we have given maximum motivated attention, (often colored by emotional reinforcement) and which therefore we have perceived clearly. We are back to the taproots of language learning: perception or intelligence.

REFERENCES

APPEL, LYNNE F., and others, "The Development of the Distinction Between Perceiving and Memory," *Child Development* 43(4) (December 1972), 1365–1381.

ATKINSON, R.C., and R.M. SHIFFRIN, "The Control of Short-Term Memory," *Scientific American* 225(2) (August 1971), 82–90.

BARONDES, SAMUEL H., "Protein-Synthesis Dependent and Protein-Synthesis Independent Memory Storage Processes," *Short-Term Memory*, eds. Diana Deutsch and J.A. Deutsch. (New York: Academic Press, 1975), 385–388.

BAYLEY, NANCY, "The Development of Motor Abilities During the First Three Years," *Monographs Society for Research in Child Development* 1 (1935).

BAYLEY, NANCY, "Comparisons of Mental and Motor Test Scores for Ages 1–15 Months by Sex, Birth Order, Race, Geographical Location, and Education of Parents," *Child Development* 36 (1965) 379–411.

BEATTY, JACKSON, "Activation and Attention in the Human Brain," Chap. 3, *The Human Brain,* eds. M.C. Wittrock and others. Englewood Cliffs, N.J.: Prentice-Hall, Inc., 1977.

BERRY, MILDRED F., *Language Disorders of Children,* Englewood Cliffs, N.J.: Prentice-Hall, Inc., 1969.

BRUCK, MARGARET and G. RICHARD TUCKER, "Social Class Differences in the Acquisition of School Language," *Merrill-Palmer Quarterly* 20(3) (July 1974), 205–220.

BRUNER, J.S., "On Perceptual Readiness in Perception," *Psychological Review* 64 (February 1957), 123–152.

BRUNER, J.S., "The Act of Discovery," in *Human Learning in the School,* ed. J.P. DeCocco. New York: Holt, Rinehart and Winston, 1963.

CARROW, A.E. and M. MAULDIN, "Children's Recall of Approximations in English," *J. Speech Hearing Disorders* 16(2) (June 1973), 201–210.

CHALFANT, J.C. and M.A. SCHEFFELIN, *Central Processing Dysfunctions in Children: A Review of Research,* NINDS Monograph No. 9. Bethesda, Md.: U.S. Dept. of Health, Education and Welfare, 1969.

COLE, R.A., "Perceiving Syllables and Remembering Phonemes," *J. Speech Hearing Research* 16(1) (1973), 37–47.

DEUTSCH, D. and J.A. DEUTSCH, eds. *Short-Term Memory.* New York: Academic Press, 1975.

DIXON, THEODORE R. and DAVID L. HORTON, eds., *Verbal Behavior and General Behavior Theory.* Englewood Cliffs, N.J.: Prentice-Hall, Inc., 1968.

Eccles, J.C., "The Physiology of Imagination," *Altered States of Awareness:* Introduction by T.J. Teyler. San Francisco: W.H. Freeman and Company, 1972. 31–40.

Ferguson, Charles A. and Dan Isaac Slobin, *Studies of Child Language Development.* New York: Holt, Rinehart and Winston, 1973.

French, J.D., "The Reticular Formation," *Altered States of Awareness:* (Readings from Scientific American); Introduction by T.J. Teyler. San Francisco: W.H. Freeman and Company, 1972. 23–29.

Galambos, R., "Suppression of Auditory Nerve Activity by Stimulation of Efferent Fibers to Cochlea," *J. Neurophysiology* 19 (September 1956), 424–437.

Geis, M.F. and D.M. Hall, "Encoding and Congruity in Children's Incidental Memory," *Child Development,* 49(3) (September 1978), 487–861.

Geschwind, N., "Specializations of the Human Brain," *Scientific American* 241(3) (September 1979), 180–199.

Haber, R.N., "How We Remember What We See," *Scientific American* 222(5) (May 1970), 104–112.

Halstead, W.C., "Thinking, Imagery and Memory," chap. 46, *Handbook of Physiology, Sec. 1: Neurophysiology III,* ed. J. Field. Washington, D.C.: American Physiology Society, 1960.

Hardy, W.G. and M. Hardy, *Essays on Communication and Communicative Disorders.* New York: Grune and Stratton, 1977.

Hebb, D.O., *The Organization of Behavior.* New York: John Wiley, 1949.

Isaacson, R.L., "Memory Processes and the Hippocampus," chap. 12 *Short-Term Memory,* eds. D. Deutsch and J.A. Deutsch. (New York: Academic Press, 1972), 314.

Johnson, R.C., "Linguistic Structure Related to Concept Formation and to Concept Context," *Psychological Bulletin* 59 (November 1962), 469.

Jung, John, *Understanding Human Motivation, A Cognitive Approach.* New York: Macmillan 1978.

Kagan, Jerome, "Motivational and Attitudinal Factors in Receptivity to Learning," *Learning About Learning,* ed. J. Bruner. Washington, D.C.: Bureau of Research, U.S. Office of Education, 1966.

Kagan, Jerome, "Attention and Psychological Change in the Young Child," *Science* 170(3960) (20 November 1970), 826–832.

Kagan, Jerome, "The Distribution of Attention in Infancy," *Perception and Its Disorders,* eds. D.A. Hamburg, K.H. Pribram, and A.J. Stunkard. Baltimore: Williams & Wilkins, 1970.

KAGAN, JEROME, "Do Infants Think?" *Scientific American* 226(3) (March 1972) 74–82.

KAGAN, JEROME, "The Determinants of Attention in the Infant," *Readings in Child Behavior and Development,* 3rd ed., eds. Delia S. Lavatelli and Faith Stendler. New York: Harcourt Brace Jovanovich, 1972, 152–161.

KANDEL, E.R., "Small Systems of Neurons," *Scientific American* 241(3) (September 1979), 67–76.

KESSEN, WILLIAM, MARSHALL HAITH, and PHILIP SALAPATEK, "Human Infancy: A Bibliography and Guide," *Carmichael's Manual of Child Psychology I,* 3rd ed., ed. Paul H. Mussen. New York: John Wiley, 1970, 287–445.

KONORSKI, J., *Integrative Activity of the Brain.* Chicago: University of Chicago Press, 1967.

KRUPSKI, ANTOINETTE and PATRICIA BOYLE, "An Observational Analysis of Children's Behavior During a Simple-Reaction-Time Task: The Role of Attention," *Child Development* 49(2) (June 1978), 340–347.

LANDFELD, PHILIP W., JAMES L. MCGAUGH, and RONALD J. TUSA, "Theta Rhythm: A Temporal Correlate of Memory Storage in the Rat," *Science* 175(4017) (7 January 1972), 87–89.

LASSEN, NIELS A., DAVID H. INGVAR, and ERIK SKINHOJ, "Brain Function and Blood Flow," *Scientific American* 239(4) (October 1978), 62–71.

LOCKE, J.L. and K.J. KUTZ, "Memory for Speech and Speech for Memory," *J Speech Hearing Research* 18(1) (March 1975), 176–191.

MCKINNEY, FRED, RAYMOND P. LORION, and MELVIN ZAX, *Effective Behavior and Human Development.* New York: Macmillan, 1976.

MARTIN, G.L. and R.B. POWERS, "Attention Span: An Operant Conditioning Analysis," *Exceptional Child* 33 (April 1967), 565–570.

MELTON, A.W. and E. MARTIN, eds., *Coding Processes in Human Memory.* Washington, D.C.: V.H. Winston and Sons, 1972.

MELZACK, R., *Perception and Its Disorders,* 48: 277. Research Publication of the Association for Research in Nervous and Mental Disorders. Baltimore: Williams & Wilkins, 1970.

MEYER, DAVID E. and R.V. SCHVANEVELDT, "Meaning, Memory Structure and Mental Processes," *Science* 192(4234) (2 April 1976), 27–33.

MUSSEN, PAUL H., JOHN J. CONGER, and JEROME KAGAN, *Readings in Child Development and Personality,* 2nd ed. New York: Harper and Row Pub., 1965.

Mussen, Paul H., John J. Conger, and Jerome Kagan, *Child Development and Personality,* 4th ed. New York: Harper and Row, Pub., 1974.

Olton, David S., "Spatial Memory," *Scientific American* 236(6) (June 1977), 82–98.

Olver, R., "Tutor and Learner," *Learning About Learning,* ed. J. Bruner. Washington, D.C.: Bureau of Research, U.S. Office of Education, 1966.

Paris, S.G. and G.J. Mahoney, "Cognitive Integration in Children's Memory for Sentences and Pictures," *Child Development* 45(3) (September 1974), 633–642.

Penfield, Wilder and Gordon Mathieson, "Memory," *Archives Neurology* 31 (September 1974), 145–154.

Penney, C.G., "Modality Effects in Short-Term Memory," *Psychological Bulletin* 82(1) (1975), 68–94.

Peterson, R.G. and C.W. McIntyre, "The Influence of Semantic 'Relatedness' on Linguistic Integration and Retention," *American J of Psychology* 86(4) (1973), 697–706.

Piaget, J., *The Mechanisms of Perception.* New York: Basic Books, 1969.

Pick, H. L. and A.D. Pick, "Sensory and Perceptual Development," chap. 11 *Carmichael's Manual of Child Psychology, I,* ed. P.H. Mussen. New York: John Wiley, 1970.

Premack, D., "A Functional Analysis of Language," *J Experimental Analysis of Behavior* 14(1) (July 1970), 107–125.

Pribram, K.H., "The Neuro-Physiology of Remembering," *Scientific American* 220(1) (January 1969), 73–84.

Pribram, Karl H., *Languages of the Brain.* Englewood Cliffs, N.J.: Prentice-Hall, Inc. 1971.

Robinson, H.B. and N.M. Robinson, "Mental Retardation," chap. 27 *Carmichael's Manual of Child Psychology, III,* 3rd ed., ed. P.H. Mussen. New York: John Wiley, 1970.

Rohwer, William D., "Cognitive Development and Education," chap. 19 *Carmichael's Manual of Psychology, I,* ed. P.H. Mussen. New York: John Wiley, 1970.

Rosen, Bernard C. and Roy D'Andrade, "The Psychosocial Origins of Achievement Motivation," *Readings in Child Behavior and Development,* 3rd ed., eds. Celia Stendler Lavatelli and Faith Stendler. New York: Harcourt Brace Jovanovich, 1972. 407–416.

Shelton, R.L., W.B. Arndt, and J.B. Miller, "Learning Principles and Teaching of Speech Language," *J Speech Hearing Disorders* 26 (November 1961), 368.

SMART, MOLLIE S. and RUSSELL C. SMART, *Children, Development, and Relationships,* 3rd ed. New York: Macmillan, 1977.

SNYDER, LYNN S., "Communicative and Cognitive Abilities and Disabilities in the Sensorimotor Period," *Merrill-Palmer Quarterly* 24(3) (July 1978), 161–180.

SORENSEN, RICHARD L. and MARTIN L. MAEHR, "Toward the Experimental Analysis of 'Continuing Motivation,' " *J. Educational Research* 69(9) (May-June 1976), 319–322.

STEVENSON, H.W., "Learning in Children," chap. 12 *Carmichael's Manual of Child Psychology, I,* ed. P.H. Mussen. New York: John Wiley, 1970.

TALLAND, G.A., *Disorders of Memory and Learning.* Harmondsworth, Middlesex, England: Penguin, 1968.

VERNON, M.D., *The Psychology of Perception.* Harmondsworth, Middlesex, England: Penguin, 1962.

WALLACE, PATRICIA, "Neurochemistry, Unraveling the Mechanism of Memory," *Science* 190(4219) (12 December 1975), 1076–1078.

WATSON, PETER, "In Search of Memory," *The Illustrated London News* 259(6880) (November 1971), 42–43.

WHITE, R.W., "Motivation Reconsidered: The Concept of Competence," *Psychological Review* 66 (September 1949), 297–333.

WICKELGREN, W.A., "The Long and Short of Memory," chap. 2 *Short-Term Memory,* eds. D. Deutsch and J.A. Deutsch, (New York: Academic Press, 1975), 46–47.

WICKENS, D., "Characteristics of Word Encoding," *Coding Processes in Human Memory,* eds. Arthur W. Melton and Edwin Martin. (Washington, D.C.: V.H. Winston and Sons, 1972), 212–231.

WILDER, PENFIELD and G. MATHIESON, "Memory," *Archives of Neurology* 31 (September 1974), 145–154.

WITTROCK, M.C., "The Generative Processes of Memory," chap. 8 *The Human Brain,* eds. M.C. Wittrock and others. Englewood Cliffs, N.J.: Prentice-Hall, Inc., 1977.

ZEAMAN, D. and B.J. HOUSE, "The Role of Attention in Retardate Discrimination Learning," chap. 5 *Handbook of Mental Deficiency,* ed. N. Ellis. New York: McGraw-Hill, 1963.

ZUCKERMAN, P., and others, "Children's Viewing of Television and Recognition Memory of Commercials," *Child Development,* 49(1) (March 1978), 96–104.

chapter 4

HALLMARKS OF ORAL LANGUAGE

Perceptual-Semantic Development

INTRODUCTION

Priority Among Hallmarks

In an earlier chapter we discussed hallmarks in relation to their developmental schedule. Now we shall consider them from the vantage point of their importance in the educational process. In my view, perceptual-semantic development is the primary hallmark in language learning. My belief is reinforced by my study of the speech and language sciences and the neurobiological and psychological support underlying them; and, above all, by an extensive stretch covering a half-century of teaching language-retarded children. Only recently has this priority won general acceptance. For three decades the canon of psycholinguists that "grammar is all" has prevailed in research and teaching. Innumerable publications have appeared with these phrases in their titles: "transformational grammar"; "the structure of communication"; "surface and deep structure"; "structure, the language universal"; and "interventional skills in teaching linguistic structure." Chomsky,[1] to whom all psycholinguists are indebted for theory, predicted the complexity of the grammar possessed by the child would also predict the complexity of psychological processing. This did

[1] Noam Chomsky, *Syntactic Structures* (The Hague: Mouton, 1957).

112

not prove to be the case. When sentences differed in "transformational complexity" but had the same meaning, no differences in psychological complexity could be identified. The child still comprehended the more involved form as long as the *meaning* remained invariant. The problem did not lie in the number of grammatical transformations the child would make, but in the complexity of the *semantic* interpretation.

The case studies of the psycholinguists, on whom we also seem to have been overdependent, did not come from the classroom. They were generally based on their experience with a single child, or perhaps two or three children who usually were the atypical offspring of highly educated parents in a university environment. These studies did not stem from experiences in teaching twenty children four- and five-years old in a public school.

Interdependence of Hallmarks

Although we hold that perceptual-semantic growth is the sine qua non of language acquisition, we recognize the interdependencies of phonatory, phonological, syntactic, and perceptual-semantic development. Prosody, a phonatory attribute, is the infant's first perceptual key to meaningful communication. Phonemic and morphemic strings (phonological attributes) must be fitted into prosodic (melodic patterns). And, as the baby develops communication, his percepts must have a framework, a structure, which at first may be only word strings in some order but which later develops into a syntactic frame. We must emphasize, however, that *semantic complexity* seems to do a better job of predicting the acquisition of *word order* than does *grammatical complexity*.

Realistic Language: Realistic Goals

Teachers are concerned with the actual language children must use in order to intervene successfully in their environment. This is the language of reality of children, not the language adults may use or the artificial constructs of language derived from theories of what the language of children should be. In terms of oral production, what realistic goals in the skills of comprehension-expression—semantic, lexical, and syntactic—can be set for linguistically retarded children?

Semantic and Lexical Skills

A child's development in these areas also must be judged in terms of his linguistic needs, his developmental cycle, and his environment. Language development is not a continuous incremental process with developed accomplishments becoming part of the permanent range of competencies of the growing child. It is cyclical and varies widely among children. Someone has said that particularly in lexical and semantic development, it goes by "jerks and holds" and sometimes by a backing-up. Teachers from preschool through the elementary grades must recognize that competencies in perception-semantics, phonation, phonology, and syntax develop for a time and then go into a holding pattern, only to accelerate at a later age. Said another way, development is not a continuous linear process, but rather a series of waves with whole segments of development recurring repetitively.[2] Let me illustrate by reporting the contrast in development of my close friends who are twins. Jason and Julie will be four years old next week. Their environment and linguistic needs seem to be about the same, but their developmental cycles are different. Julie is articulate, fluent, and unabashed by person or place. She talks nonstop about everything and everyone in the immediate environment, stringing out word sequences, using words and structures which come and go, some of which may never appear again. Her vocabulary is not extensive, but repetitive. Jason, quiet and introverted, works to solve a problem in the operation of a mechanical toy. He explains in short, simple, structured phrases how "it" works—or should work. Many scholars use *mean length of utterance* as the common measure of acquisition of speech. If we used this measure, Julie would be accelerated; Jason, retarded. If we used the developmental scoring method based on fifty sentences, Julie probably would be ahead but if we observed Jason outside the test situation, we would find that he is using structures to which he did not choose to respond in the test. On the test of perceptual maturity as reflected in the *substance* of oral expression, Jason outranks Julie. Recently both Jason and Julie have been attending preschool. The mother's report which I can corroborate indicates that Jason now uses more new words and new forms than Julie. His structures are sometimes innovative, but he communicates his meaning. Julie's speech is more advanced in articulation, prosody, and simple grammatical forms. Jason is ahead of Julie in perceptual-semantic development and complex structure.

Syntactic Skills

We are centering our attention on teaching children from three to eight years of age although we recognize that language learning is not achieved by eight, or ten, or twelve—or fifty years! At the "advanced age" of eight

---

[2] T.B.R. Bower, "Repetition in Human Development," *Merrill-Palmer Quarterly* 20(4) (October 1974), 303–318.

years, what should the child have achieved in syntactic skills? Does he need to know the rules of syntax? Clinical manuals of language therapy are filled with exercises made up of isolated sentences employing unusual grammatical forms and set in situations totally foreign to the child—and frequently to the average adult. To be sure the ungrammatical English of adults in oral communication is a sad commentary on the state of the art. It should be, it must be, improved. But will the adult ever meet the syntactic standards we set for children who lag in development? In my view, these goals are unrealistic. Adults, for example, rarely use complete sentences in the hurly-burly of today's forum, but in the texts of language intervention which focus on grammar and structure, complete sentences and carefully honed prose are modeled and demanded. In one test of syntactical development, for example, a child of six is supposed to distinguish the correct usage from a pictured representation involving two people: "This is his wagon" or "This is their wagon." Children in certain programs of language intervention are taught to speak in complete sentences, sentences of "correct" adult language, yet a recent one-hour tape of an airport conversation among six adults produced only *four complete declarative sentences* and *three incomplete interrogative sentences*. In a toy barnyard a child of five years is supposed to be able to act out "The cow hit the pig that chased the deer"—an unlikely story or happening in the life of a four-or forty-year-old—and a sentence structure that he will have little occasion to use outside of class.

VARIABLES AFFECTING TEACHING AND LEARNING HALLMARKS OF LANGUAGE

We know that children learn language about the same time the world over. They seem to learn it without instruction from their elders. All they seem to need is a talking environment. But we also know that individuals vary widely in the rate of acquisition and in the realization of competence in oral language. Although general intelligence might be considered the universal variable, it is synonymous with perceptual-semantic development in the context in which we use it in language learning. We shall discuss their relation in a later section of this chapter. Among the variables which affect, but are not a part of, the perceptual process are these: the *learning environment, health status,* and *neurophysical handicaps.* We are rich in theory and anecdotal data, poor in facts to substantiate the specific ways and the degree to which each of these variables figures significantly in the child's acquisition of oral language and in our teaching.

The Learning Environment

Oral language "grows by what it feeds on" in its environment. The interaction between the child and his environment is vital. Before oral language emerges, the average child has already had a history of rich preliminary experiences, many of which are nonverbal. The parents and other members of the family usually have set up pleasurable and satisfying interchanges with the child. He has felt body contact, heard laughter, played "games," reacted to gestures and talk, and received attention by that "special someone" to his needs. In a sense he comes early to a participation in communication, to experiences and expectations centered in himself which he remembers. His communication may not be verbal, but nonetheless it is true communication of feelings and of emerging global, albeit fuzzy, percepts. Some parents who have provided the ideal language environment for the baby in his first years, however, forget that language development is not "finished," once the child learns to talk. The same kind of environment should continue to surround the child for many years. Television is no substitute for pleasurable social interactions among the family, offers no approval by "significant others," provides no physical contacts, and allows no participation in table talk. It is a mighty poor substitute for the sensorimotor experiences which the child encounters if he explores the world about him. The child flourishes linguistically in a stable lively environment, responsive to him and to which he can respond.

Many linguistically handicapped children do not have this kind of warm, supportive, and stimulating environment. During my residence in the Middle East as a Fulbright lecturer, I visited two institutions of child care. The children in these foundling homes were left lying supinely in their cribs until they could pull themselves into a sitting position. Some children were three years of age and were not yet able to do this. When they could sit alone, they were placed occasionally on a linoleum strip covering a section of a cement floor. No toys, no picture books, no music, no children's furniture except cribs were evident. Silent attendants took minimal care of the physical needs of the children. Gestural language was largely absent. A faceless environment, faceless children.

We have a different, but nevertheless real, deprivation in the language environment which pervades many homes today. And it is not limited to one socioeconomic class although it may be more prevalent among the poor. At one time, it was reported that "where the context is interpersonal, the middle class relative to the working class, moves markedly toward the use of language." [3] Presumably the child in the middle-class family

[3] Basil Bernstein and Dorothy Henderson, "Social Class Differences in the Relevance of Language to Socialization," *Readings in Child Development and Personality,* 2nd ed., eds. Paul H. Mussen, John Conger, and Jerome Kagan (New York: Harper and Row, 1970), 240–241.

was exposed to various and attractive stimuli which he explored on his own terms and thus was accelerated in the acquisition of motor, perceptual, and manipulative skills. He regulated his own learning of language in a carefully controlled environment. But is this a true picture of the average middle-class language environment today? And is it true, especially for children in the elementary schools? A fluid, ambient society with its attendant social changes suggests the possibility of a very different environment, a negative environment for *continuous language development*. The influx into the work force of middle- and upper-class career women, family patterns of increasing instability, the number and quality of family caretakers, regular patronage of fast food establishments, the fierce competition of society with its attendant stresses, continuous television entertainment, and the loss of the neighborhood school: all these factors may contribute to a negative environment for language development at all levels of our society. For many teenagers, home shortly may be the place where "when you have to go there, they have to take you in." [4]

The pragmatic global program of teaching the language retardate, a program to which we are committed, is predicated on the belief that we can unite home, school, and neighborhood in a common enterprise: teaching children to comprehend and express their meanings and feelings with a measure of competence in all the hallmarks of language development.

Health Status

Many psychologists have recognized the dependence of intellectual development on the general health of the child, but studies of the specific effects of a low physical index on perception and language development are rare. The exception is Jean Piaget, the eminent developmental psychologist, who made sensorimotor development the basis of perception and the emergence of oral language. In the sensorimotor stage the child must be physically active in the exploration of his environment if he is to progress in intellectual development. Knowledge is constantly linked with physical experience, with actions or operations. If the child is *not able* to manipulate his environment, Piaget contends at one point, that such perceptual factors as causality and space perception are definitely impaired.[5]

We know that viral diseases, such as rubella (measles) and pertussis (whooping cough) may invade the CNS resulting in encephalitis. Retarded

---

[4] "The Death of the Hired Man," *Collected Poetry of Robert Frost* (New York: Henry Holt and Company, 1930).

[5] Piaget, "Piaget's Theory," *Carmichael's Manual of Child Psychology, I,* 3rd ed., ed. Paul H. Mussen (New York: John Wiley, 1970), 703–733.

language development is a common aftermath. But the greater incidence of language arrest or retrogression in our observation occurs in children who suffer simply from recurring but low grade upper respiratory infections. Children, three to four years of age, will stop talking for a period of a month or two. They retrogress, not only in oral expression but in comprehension of and response to stimuli. In older children the arrest may be short-lived; they talk again, but fluency and articulation seem to have suffered a setback. In both groups something untoward has happened to the physical organism that seems to have permanently slowed the rate of acquisition and development of language. Possibly the learning process is retarded by the effect of any illness, acute or chronic, on the nutritional index and hence on the energy coefficient of the child.

In cooperation with the University of Wisconsin Research Foundation, I conducted a study of delayed speech and stuttering involving four hundred children who had been entered for routine pediatric care in outpatient clinics in Chicago.[6] One in three of these children who were entered because he "did not talk" or "did not talk plain" had a history of frequent upper respiratory infections accompanied by extreme elevations in temperature. And among the children who originally were entered for speech retardation, a high incidence of stuttering was reported later in their medical histories. The pediatricians concluded that these children suffered from a "rheumatic diathesis," that is, a *constitutional predisposition* producing a susceptibility to severe respiratory infections accompanied by a high fever. The final result was a lowered physical index of the entire body from which the child had not recovered by adolescence. Although the question of encephalitic sequellae was raised by the pediatric staff, it was not answered.

The Apgar score [7] which evaluates a newborn infant's physical status was not used by Bayley [8] in her early longitudinal study of the physical and mental development of infants from birth. She used other tests, however, to prove that early sensorimotor development and simple adaptations of infants exhibit the components of intelligence. In other words, those infants who were responsive and endowed with high energy co-

[6] Mildred F. Berry, "The Developmental History of Stuttering Children," *J Pediatrics* 12(2) (1938), 215.

[7] *Apgar Score:* Evaluation of a newborn infant's physical status by assigning numerical values (0–2) to each of five criteria: heart rate, respiratory effort, muscle tone, response to stimulation, and skin color; a score of ten indicates the best possible condition. Lucille Nicolosi, Elizabeth Harryman, and Janet Kresheck, *Terminology of Communication Disorders* (Baltimore: The Williams & Wilkins Co., 1978), 9.

[8] N. Bayley, "Mental Growth During the First Three Years: An Experimental Study of 61 Children by Repeated Tests," *Genetic Psychology Monographs* 14 (1933), 1–92; N. Bayley, "On the Growth of Intelligence," *American Psychologist* 10 (1955), 805–818.

efficients proved to be intellectually advanced over infants with low vitality. Her subsequent report on the same group of children at a later age reaffirmed earlier conclusions of the superior intelligence of the motorically active group.

The positive effects of a nutritional and health care program on language development of preschool and school-age children have been reported in many journals. In a contrast study of "chronically deprived children" and children with high socioeconomic status, for example, the effects of a nutritional, health care, and educational program on the perceptual abilities of the chronically deprived were marked.[9] The educational program focused on adequacy of language usage, immediate memory, manual dexterity and motor control, information and vocabulary, quantitative concepts, spatial relations, and logical thinking, with a balance between verbal and non-verbal production. Children were entered at three and a half years and continued through the seventh year. At the end of this four-year program, the gap in cognitive ability between the treated children and a group of privileged children in the same city had narrowed, the effect being greater the younger the children were when they entered the treatment program.

In reflecting on the several hundred children, three to nine years of age, who entered the resident Rockford College Speech Center [10] for speech-language rehabilitation following cleft palate repair, I am sure that a major component in the success of the program (conducted for a quarter century) was the result of the work of the nutrition, nursing, and physical education staffs who succeeded in building the physical index of the youngsters, the majority of whom were "chronically deprived."

Neurophysical Handicaps

A child with major orthopedic handicaps cannot engage in the sensorimotor experiences essential for the emergence and development of oral language. He cannot explore heights, angles, and textures as children normally do. He does not initiate or imitate rhythmic movements; indeed he does not engage in any movement for its own sake as little children frequently like to do. The result is that sensorimotor development is hopelessly impaired, and consequently oral language emerges very late, if at all. If the speech organs are impaired, as is frequently the case in cerebral palsy, the feedback which he receives from his attempts in oral expression

[9] H. McKay and others, "Improving Cognitive Ability in Chronically Deprived Children," *Science* 200(4339) (21 April 1978), 270–278.

[10] The program, although conducted at Rockford College, was funded totally by the Division of Services for Crippled Children, The University of Illinois, Springfield.

is distorted and untrustworthy. Add to these problems the possibility of neural disorganization resulting from gating failures so that sensations, unselected and disorganized, are admitted into the coding process. Children so handicapped can scarcely be expected to develop the perceptual processes needed for the acquisition of oral language. Having taught cerebral-palsied children in three countries, I have shared their struggles to comprehend and to use oral language. I have empathized with their frustration!

Special Sensory Impairments

Special sensory impairments also must be reckoned with in language learning. I noted earlier the effect of distortion of tactile-kinesthesis on the language development of the cerebral-palsied. In another group of children, not cerebral-palsied, the same impairment has been ascribed to a dysfunction of the vestibular mechanism of the inner ear. De Quirós followed fifty-two newborns so affected to school age and found that they were delayed in control of equilibrium, motor development, and *speech acquisition.*[11] Until recently a *conductive hearing deficit* was thought to affect auditory perception only through the diminution of acuity for sounds. Apparently it also affects cerebral function adversely. Katz explains the effect of the dysfunction this way: "Conductive hearing losses are like earplugs in that they restrict the sounds of the environment from stimulating the cochlea, thereby depriving the auditory system of normal activity." [12] The retrocochlear system and the brain both suffer from this deprivation; consequently auditory perception is impaired.

Many children in the Rockford College Speech Center (Rockford, Illinois) were also enrolled in the Reading Clinic. Visuomotor imperception undoubtedly was one factor connecting the two disabilities. We know now that it is particularly significant in the sensorimotor stage of oral language development.[13] Personality is another variable in language learning because it is a part of the human equation in all learning. We omit it at this juncture but will discuss it in the chapters devoted to the teaching program.

---

[11] Julio B. de Quirós, *Neuropsychological Fundamentals in Learning Disabilities,* (San Rafael, Ca.: Academic Therapy Publications, 1978). Julio B. de Quirós, "Vestibular-Proprioceptive Integration: The Influence on Learning and Speech in Children," *Proceedings of the 10th Interamerican Congress of Psychology,* Lima, Peru, April 13–17, 1966, 194–202; Julio B. de Quirós, "Diagnosis of Vestibular Disorders in the Learning Disabled," *J Learning Disabilities* 9(1) (1976), 50–58.

[12] Jack Katz, "The Effects of Conductive Hearing Loss on Auditory Function," *Asha* 20(10) (October 1978), 879–886.

[13] Anne L. Dean, "The Structure of Imagery," *Child Development* 47(4) (1976), 949–958.

HALLMARK 1: PERCEPTUAL-SEMANTIC DEVELOPMENT

> "Take care of the sense," the Duchess said,
> "and the sounds will take care of themselves."

We tend to teach as if the adult's "sense," his interpretation of a "happening," is also the child's understanding. "He must see what we see." Rarely is it so. He perceives the happening in terms of his interactions with his social and physical environment. In language learning the adult's interpretation is far less important than the child's interactional creative response to the happening.

Intelligence and Perception: Synonymous Terms

If intelligence and perception are not equivalent in meaning, they are so closely related as to have common major constituents. Percepts, like intelligence, develop with the child's *awareness* of the sensorimotor events in his immediate environment, with his *experiences and relations* with objects and events around him and with his *eagerness and intent to respond* to these events and experiences. Language is the construct of intelligence.[14] It is the code by which he links his perceptual relationships and his associations resulting from these events. The code may be only a prosodic or verbal cue which others have attached to the events but it carries meaning.

Some Early Signs of Perceptual Development

Fitting New Percepts into Schemata

According to Kagan's theory [15] of intelligence, the baby at three months, perhaps earlier, reduces a novel situation to a predictable familiar one, thus fitting it into his schema of the world. In Piaget's words, the baby actively constructs his world by assimilating its elements into his already-formed behavioral schemes.[16] If he cannot fit the stimulus pattern into the functional image of his environment, he either reacts defensively (crying or withdrawal) or he removes it from his ken; it does not exist. The schemata become his bundle of perceptions and as the bundle grows,

---

[14] Piaget, "Piaget's Theory," 706.

[15] Jerome Kagan, "Do Infants Think?" *Scientific American* 226(3) (March 1972), 74–82.

[16] J. Piaget and B. Inhelder, *L'image Mentale Chez L'enfant* (Paris: Presses Universitaires de France, 1966).

intelligence advances. All infants respond to *persons* and *objects* first, later to *actions* or *events*. There is a high mortality rate for these events because they depend on contextual recognition and the child may not be able to fit them into the contextual frame, the schema. Furthermore comprehension is global, partial, and inexact at this early age. The response may be in the form of nonvocal signs of satisfaction, annoyance, pleasure, anger, or in oral babble with emotional overtones. It is, however, rudimentary communication. Now if a child fits very few objects, persons, or events into his perceptual world and evinces little response, we are worried. The possibility of developmental lag looms large. Here is a mother who reports that her four-month-old baby reacts only to musical sounds by crying; he does not distinguish his mother's voice from other voices of neighborhood callers. The mother reports that he is a "good baby"; he is content "to lie for hours blinking at the ceiling." Unfortunately these are negative signs of perceptual-semantic development.

Object Permanence

In the period, nine to fifteen months, the child begins to comprehend in a global "fuzzy" manner such pleasantries as his father's arrival, although he understands it only with the aid of the mother's prosodic (melodic), gestural and environmental cues. More complex communications—requests, questions, commands—are often misinterpreted. As the boundaries of the percept become more definite, however, the baby begins to respond actively to "objects" (*doggie, ball, car*) in his immediate environment. Soon they will possess permanence, achieved partly by linkage of action words with the "object:" *go-go, all gone, bow-wow,* etc. To be sure, he has been building hypotheses about persons and objects from early infancy *but* the sensorimotor percept was always present in his immediate environment. Such percepts came and went as the object or person passed out of his immediate ken. Now he has the ability to reconstruct sensorimotor knowledge about them although they are not immediately present and, what is more significant, to retain this knowledge. He can use the percept "apart from himself" and apart from the actual presence of the persons, objects, or events. This is the precursor to symbolic thinking, a tremendous boon both to comprehension and to the embryonic efforts in oral expression.

Sensory Organization

Another sign of perceptual development is the child's ability to organize his sensorimotor experiences quickly so that he "perceives as a whole and nothing first." This is called syncretistic perception. Can he put together in a single package what he sees, hears, or feels (via tactile-kinesthetic feedback) and get meaning from the combination? For example, Davie, a one-year-old, is in his highchair in the kitchen when he hears the sound and feels the vibration of the garage door as it rumbles upward; he laughs, flails arms and legs, looks at the kitchen door, tries to get out of his chair and calls something that sounds a bit like "da-da." He is employing his sensorimotor channels—tactile-kinesthetic, auditory, and visual—in his effort to comprehend and to communicate the percept. Note that the auditory "track" is not the only channel. The tactile-kinesthetic channels may be as important as the auditory in perception.[17]

Symbolic Play

A question we always ask mothers of children who are approaching thirty months of age is this: Does the baby use his toys symbolically in play? For example, does he line up blocks and push them about as a toy train? Will he make a horn out of a paper cup and pretend he is talking to someone on the telephone? We also ask parents for other evidence of constructive acts employing imagination. We watched the reaction of two children about the same age in a playpen when a visitor threw his hat into the pen. One child grabbed it, put it on his head and then laughed hilariously when it covered his eyes. He took it off and tried to place it on the head of his cousin. The baby screamed and attempted to get out of the pen. We have watched the imaginative baby pretend to "light" a pencil stub and then blow it out. He makes the toy puppy bark (with sound effects) by pulling on his jaw. He simulates driving the family car with the front bar of his stroller. Imagination is a good index of perceptual-semantic development.

Abstraction and Perceptual-Semantic Growth

You will remember that the first percepts of the infant were global, general, and undefined. In succeeding months the young child perceives relationships between objects and pictures, and between pictures, objects, and words. These relationships refine and enrich the global concept, but they are generally in terms of the concrete, here-and-now experiences. To the extent that he distinguishes among objects, pictures, and concrete experiences as *same* or *different* (which ones go together, which ones do not), he is also engaging in an elementary abstraction process. His com-

---

[17] A.M. Liberman and others, "A Motor Theory of Speech Perception," *Proceedings of the Speech Communications Seminar* (Stockholm: Royal Institute of Technology, 1963).

prehension of oral language pertaining to the percept is also syncretistic in that he first uses words, either meaningful or jargon, to designate general classes of objects, or persons, or events. So all men are *da-da;* all women, *ma-ma;* all toys, *ba-ba.* Then as he perceives relationships and, even more importantly, likenesses and differences, he distinguishes more specific cues from the general sink of stimuli. In other words, he distinguishes *figure from ground,* salient central features which are separate and distinct from their surrounding background.

Interaction of Comprehension and Expression

The schemata into which the baby must fit his percepts undoubtedly precede his attempts to respond orally to them—but not by much. If comprehension (perception) and expression do not go hand in hand, certainly they develop in a mutual interaction. Almost immediately the response to a global percept takes the form of random vocalization, babbling, and intonational jargon accompanying bodily gestures. Although jargon is regarded as prelinguistic communication, it contains few of the phonemes or morphemes to be carried over into oral language. It will be replaced by true syllabic strings, the *syntagma,* a prosodic string of syllables bearing meaning. Thought patterns facilitate oral expression; oral expression helps to build the percept, the thought. So language builds on the developing perceptual repertoire and, in turn, shapes it.

Much research has gone into the young child's comprehension of single sounds yet we know that the child does not learn to comprehend the meaning of oral language that way. Valuable as such research may be for later assessments of articulation, the ability to distinguish sounds is no index of the perception of meaning.[18] In learning to speak Russian, for example, I would be hard put to it today to distinguish between the sounds [ш] and [щ] in isolation although they contribute to my comprehension of the words карандáш [karənda], (pencil); and бóрш [bɔhʃtʃ], (borshch). We cannot learn to perceive meaning sound by sound because speech comprehension is based on what happens between sounds, between words, between phrases. These transitional cues involving intonational changes of time, pitch, and intensity are true perception markers. The baby must learn to comprehend the meaning of the syllable strings before he can imitate even a few syllables of the sequence he hears.

[18]E.D. Schubert, "The Role of Auditory Perception in Language Processing," *Reading, Perception and Language,* eds. D.D. Duane and M.B. Rawson (Baltimore: York Press, Inc., 1975), 107–116.

Prosodic Imitation of Syllable Strings

The baby depends largely upon the melody patterns in his immediate environment to aid him both in the perception of what he hears and feels (tactile-kinesthesis) and in the rudimentary expression of his oral response. He selects the dominant or key syllables and generally mixes them in with jargon sound strings to complete the melody pattern. They are generally parts of words, morphemes, which have been said with unusual stress or pitch change. He enjoys saying them over and over. Sometimes he imitates quite spontaneously an entire prosodic pattern of his elders, although the results may be unintelligible if one attempted to "slice" the pattern into words. Generally the melody pattern is a good imitation of adult prosody, but there may be only one morpheme (the meaningful part of a word) or one complete stressed word which appears usually in the middle or at the end of the expression. Prosodic utterance is a very good sign of interaction between the child and his environment, rather than an action within himself.[19] He directs the "message" with deliberate intention toward other people, not to himself. The oral expression may be very inaccurate, but it is pragmatic. Prosodic utterance, imitative though it may be, is a good sign of perceptual-semantic development for another reason. The child may not understand all that he says, but in the act of saying he perceives more fully the meaning. Often he may not know the meaning, even of the stressed words he puts in the middle or at the end of "the message." Little children love to repeat the melodic string: "Ride a cock-horse to Banbury Cross," for example, and are completely undisturbed by the fact that they haven't the slightest knowledge of a cock-horse or where Banbury Cross might be. Oh, one three-year-old, Jody, "allowed as how" it was the place where Christ died but the other members of the class did not seem to be at all interested in pursuing the matter. Eventually the act of oral expression refines the global percept, sharpens its boundaries, and the syllable strings (syntagmas) are more intelligible in the prosodic sequence. The melody pattern dominates the expression; it must be preserved. Ellen, now three years of age, is hooked on melody. If she does not know the right word, she invariably inserts a fictitious one—something beginning with the phoneme /m/: *mim* or *mimba* or *mimbababa,* presumably for the sake of preserving the prosodic sequence.

[19] H.H. Eveloff, "Some Cognitive and Affective Aspects of Early Language Development," *Child Development* 42(6) (December 1971), 1895–1907; J.F. Miller and D.E. Yoder, *An Ontogenetic Language Teaching Strategy for Retarded Children.* (Paper presented for *NICHD Conference on Language Intervention with the Mentally Retarded,* Chula Vista, Wisconsin Dells, Wisconsin, June 1973.)

The Lexicon in Perceptual-Semantic Development

We can assess a child's perceptual-semantic growth only by what he produces, and the aspect of production in which we now are interested is the development of useful, meaningful words. Out of the syllable strings in the prosodic pattern, words emerge. They are generally elicited in response to objects, pictures, persons, and events. They are stressed words and are accompanied by vigorous gestures, or it may be only a single word, but it is part of a *speech act*. In the period, fifteen to twenty-four months, aspects of the content of the words will remain unstable for some time, but eventually they will enrich the percept. Then perception and meaningful oral expression will forge ahead together. They have bivalent bonds.

Holophrastic Expression

Can a single word express a percept, an idea? Certainly we adults employ single words in that way. The key is the melody pattern, the intonational contours to be found within the single word.[20] We say "apple?"; "now!"; "mine?" and our interlocutor knows exactly what we mean. By the incorporation of the melody pattern within the single word, we indicate an underlying structure of demand, interrogation, request, or simple assertion. *A single word functioning as a phrase or sentence and expressing a percept is called a holophrase.*[21] Contrary to general belief "first words" frequently are not holophrases and contribute little to perceptual development. Many mothers of language-retarded children have reported that "first words" emerged about the usual time in the developmental process (always twelve months it seems), and then no new words developed until the baby was two years old. The fifteenth word is a much better index of language acquisition. It is fairly certain to be a holophrase, communicating by its intonational contour, a percept, fuzzy and ambiguous though it may be. Also contrary to the general belief about beginning utterances, holophrases do not consist solely of nouns. In the first expressions of many children, holophrases are verbs of motion (*of action*), and are more significant than nouns in language development. As more complex communication develops, the child will use several

[20] John Dore, "Holophrases, Speech Acts and Language Universals," *J Child Language* 2(1) (April 1975), 21–40.

[21] The single word, Greenfield contends, is not related to an underlying *sentence* but to "an underlying, cognitive-perceptual-action structure."—Patricia Greenfield, "How Much Is One Word?" *J Child Language* 5(2) (June 1978), 347.

grammatical forms in addition to substantives: verbs, adjectives, indefinite pronouns, prepositions, and negatives. Note the nonsubstantive forms in Jason's speech at fifteen months: *hot; piti* (pretty); *more; all-gone; that; no-go; yum-yum* (good); *go-go; up; off.*

Word-Labels, Word Order, and Structure

As syllable strings within a prosodic frame or "envelope" become meaningful utterances, so the word strings which follow may not yet reflect any syntactic rule but they will have relational significance and hence communicate meaning. They have been constructed out of the child's actions and interactions with objects, persons, and events in his environment. They have pragmatic intent and enrich the percept. They have word order *but without respect to syntax.* Structure is a recognition of logical relationship. The average child two to three years of age knows no syntactic rules yet he is aware of the relation of agent and/or action, possessor and/or possessed, or location words for an action although he may not make use of his knowledge. He understands operator and action words, but he often uses them inexactly and in stereotyped fashion. *More* becomes an inexact stereotype in such expressions commanding action as *more car, more bye-bye, more swing. Shoe off* is fairly exact, but *Tim off* (meaning go away) is understood only by accompanying gestures. Note that many of his utterances are commands or requests. With much gesture and bodily movement—pointing, pulling, pushing— he commands or requests: "put table" (put it on the table); "sit there"; "pull it"; "look TV"; "sock lost?"; "Dolly seep" (put dolly to sleep). Somewhat later, two and a half to three and a half years of age, the child orally places the agent, the initiator of the action, before the word for the corresponding action but again his action verbs—*want, need, see*— are often inexact and stereotyped. He does not *need* "bye-bye," but since *go* is not yet in his vocabulary, he says "I *need* bye-bye." The word order, however, is based on prosody and elementary logic is proof that the child is organizing his percepts. Nouns and pronouns are coming into his talk and although he does not recognize them as subject or object, he puts them in order. Brown concludes that *word order* is the clearest evidence that the child has *semantic intentions,* a cumulative semantic complexity that predicts and determines order.[22] Developing logical word sequences beyond the use of substantives is a marker to which the teacher must attend.

[22] R. Brown, *A First Language* (Cambridge, Mass.: Harvard University Press, 1973), 408; M. Lahey, "Use of Prosody and Syntactic Markers in Children's Comprehension of Spoken Sentences," *J Speech Hearing Research* 17(4) (December 1974), 656–668.

Aaron, a five-year-old child, consistently exhibits unusual word order in his communication although he has many functor words. I know, for example, what he *means* when he says, "Me no school go Saturday" or "Me go buy candy more," but the confusion in word order puzzles me. Unless Aaron develops a more conventional framework or structure for his communication, I suspect that perceptual-semantic growth will suffer. It is a negative sign in language development. Heed the sign, Teacher!

Some children are retarded in developing word strings. They persist in the use of *single word labels* that represent isolated identifications without holophrastic implications. With some children this practice indicates a failure to advance in their interactions with others and with their environment. With other children it may result from the overemphasis by parents and teachers on meaningless word labeling. A common practice is to teach children to name in repetitive fashion persons, places, and things. They seem to have but one question to ask the child: "What's this" or "Who's this?" Dead questions deserve dead words in answer. And they are dead! They are not holophrastic responses.

Another highly questionable teaching method is the introduction in word strings of lexical elements that are not ones holding meaning for the child. Words first take on meaning according to the sensory modalities with which the little child has had some experience. In playing with toys at this stage, he responds to the motokinesthetic modality, rather than to vision, taction, audition, gustation, or olfaction. He attends to action, and action involves the use of verb phrases. Action involves, moreover, the facial expression, gestural accompaniment, and the total bodily movement pattern. So babies perceive objects by what can be *done* with them, by action. In preschool the object does not call, for example, for a *big* ball or *red* ball. It is what is done with the ball that matters in perceptual-semantic development. Four children are playing a game. Jimmie threw the ball over the fence into the weeds. They can't find it. Do you ask, "Was it a big ball?" "A red ball?" Hardly. You ask, "What did you lose, your ball?"

Overextension of Word Meaning

Percepts may be developing so rapidly that his repertoire of words to express the idea cannot keep pace. So the baby does what every traveler does when he attempts to communicate with his limited vocabulary in the language of the foreign country; he overextends the meaning. To the baby, all women are *mommy;* all children, *baby;* all four-legged animals are *bow-wows.* Some children will designate an object or person by an act pertaining to the stimulus. "Cookie" has remained the name of our housekeeper because when our granddaughter appeared in the kitchen, the housekeeper inquired of the baby: "Cookie?" Older children will use a nonsense word as a pivot from which they will sally forth into verbalizing, but the pivot means nothing though it always seems to occur in the same fixed position. This practice is not limited to little children. In teen-agers and adults it usually indicates fuzzy percepts and meager vocabularies. How many times has the teen-ager in your household begun sentences with *Hey?* It's *Hey, Man; Hey, a big deal;* or *Hey—hype!* (or *hyper*)? How many times has your adult friend responded to every remark with *well, really* or *right* or *dig it?* Overextension is promising *in babies.* The child is motivated to communicate and in his eagerness latches on to any word that might give him what he wants. The reverse process, underextension of meaning, may be a good or bad prognostic sign. In one group of children it may reflect limited perception and slow development; in another group, a desire for exactness. Amy (twenty months), for example, said *hot* for objects (dish, stove, and so on), but the weather was never *hot;* it was warm or sunny. She was a facile imitator!

Once past their third birthdays, the Davies and Jodies, Jasons and Amys are no longer babies equipped with fuzzy schemata and primitive lexicons, dependent entirely upon sensorimotor experiences and elementary relationships of their experiences in a limited environment. No longer are they uttering syntagmas or holophrases mixed with jargon. They have full-fledged melodic phrases or sentences, three or four words in length—words that may be overextended in meaning but which are sharp tools of intervention. They are children, not babies, breaking into a world of doing, of imagining, of acting upon their environment, and thereby changing it. As one mother remarked about her four-year-old, "He's barreling down the street under his own steam." One hopes he is barreling along in perceptual-semantic maturation.

Developing Perceptual-Semantic Skills (Three to Five Years)

As the child's world expands—from crib to house to front yard—so do his perceptual-semantic relations with that world. He is exploring, walking, reaching, falling, laughing, crying, and, as Mark Twain said, "brim full of lawless activity."

Synthesis of Gestural and Oral Language

The child's gesture language becomes more exact, more closely related to his oral expression. He also tries voice changes reflecting connotations of feeling. Melody appears in his vocal demands. He cajoles Mommy with

"Me go too." He coos plaintively, "Poor Dolly." He says with unmistakable emphasis: "NO beddy-bye!" Moreover his oral responses no longer are limited to the person, object, or event in his immediate range of vision. He "talks" about people he saw yesterday, about the swings in the park where he will go tomorrow. Although he does not use the future tense, he thinks in the future—an excellent sign of development. Percepts and semantic systems develop together although we can expect comprehension to be slightly ahead of expression. As a result he often uses language, the meaning of which he does not fully understand although he expects others to understand it. But as he reaches his fourth birthday, he employs phrases and/or sentences that express meaning more exactly and in accord with general usage. Word order takes on more conventional patterns although it is still largely determined by the prosodic components of oral language and the child's semantic intentions.

Among language-retarded children, gesture language often takes the place of the spoken word, far beyond the time when oral and gestural language should be conjoined. One summer I spent nearly a week deciphering the meaning of a repeated series of gestures of a four-year-old linguistically handicapped boy in a resident speech center. The child would stand on a chair, look out a window, put an imaginary cigarette in his mouth, and blow rings of smoke. The action, I belatedly realized, was a symbol for his father. The child was homesick and wanted us to fetch his father. The staff agreed to counter all gestures with "Tell me, please" and a reward for oral "telling." It worked. Some linguistically handicapped children will telescope the telling into three words: subject-verb-object and then will follow the utterance with elaborate pantomime in order to express the idea more fully.

Developing Abstraction Skills

When the average child is in his fourth year, perceptual-semantic development accelerates. He begins to abstract meanings, not only from current happenings, but also from past events. This level of abstraction is characterized by *a reorganization of perceptual schemata, by subordination, and by interpretive discrimination.* He now reckons with such new dimensions of the percept as time and space and the exercise of a higher order of recall. An example that comes immediately to mind is the subtest of three commissions in the Stanford-Binet Intelligence Scale (IV-6): "Here is a pencil. I want you to put it on the chair. Then I want you to shut the door; and then bring me the box which you see over there."

The Wh- Questions

Communication, the outward manifestation of perceptual-semantic growth, now moves into high gear. The child will ask questions to delineate more sharply both his comprehension and expression. The questions generally emerge in this order: *what?*, *where?*, *why?*, and *when?* [23] That *who?* and *whose?* are not among the questions most frequently asked at this early stage is not strange. The child is much more interested in securing reasons for action and building inferences and generalizations than in identifying persons or possessions. The questions must be answered. When I offered this advice to a young mother, she replied, "But you have never been locked up with the measles and two incessant questioners for a long weekend, have you?" True. Often the child will repeat the answer in echolalic fashion because he is not quite able to match the words with the meaning. He does not, for example, understand all temporal percepts, particularly those pertaining to the future. So when Mother answers, "We'll do it *tomorrow,*" he repeats the whole sentence. At a later stage of development, echolalic utterance occurs for a different purpose when a child, not knowing how to respond to another's utterance, repeats it in an effort to comprehend it or keep up his end of the dialogue. [24]

Growth in Vocabulary

It goes almost without saying that as percepts grow, vocabularies and the range of choice from the child's lexicon increase. Some researchers suggest that acceleration in vocabulary begins at two years. From my study and observation of children, the true spurt in word combinations (phrase linking) occurs later—some time after his third birthday. It is also the period for the average child in which we observe conscious imitation and a measure of assurance in oral expression. Children learn many new words about this time, words from all grammatical classes, and usually marshall them in a form adults understand. Some may even show ingenuity in constructing lexical forms. A friend reports that she asked two three-year-olds why they were scurrying around the room wiping tables with Kleenex. "We're undusting," one replied.

Can we predict the rate of perceptual-semantic development by an increase in vocabulary? The answer depends entirely on the quality of the

[23] J. Wilcox, Jeanne and L.B. Leonard, "Experimental Acquisition of Wh-Questions in Language Disordered Children," *J Speech Hearing Research* 21(2) (June 1978), 220–239.
[24] W.H. Fay, "On the Basis of Autistic Echolalia," *J Communication Disorders* 2 (1969), 38–47.

vocabulary and its *contextual use*. Word count, frequently used in language studies, is of little value in assessment. A child—and this is also true of some adults—may have thousands of useless words, words that are of little significance in developing meaningful percepts. The child may be able to produce words in the appropriate syntactic and lexical categories, but they may be feeble instruments in the communication of meaning. A qualitative appraisal of the contextual use of words in relation to his needs is the only true measure of vocabulary.

Increasing Complexity of the Semantic System

Three quasi-semantic processes that appear in this period are also indices of growth: the coordination of simple sentences, the use of modifiers, and elementary embedding of phrases and clauses. Traditionally they are associated with syntactical development. We believe that they are clear expressions of semantic function and memory span. When the child puts together two simple sentences, he establishes a propositional relation, a semantic perception. Ann, four years of age, told me about her first ballet lesson: "I do this and then I do that," she said. "Awful hard," she added as she demonstrates "intricate" footwork. I gave her an ice cream cone in appreciation. "No," she said, "you have some *and* I have some," as she offered me the first "lick." While trying to persuade my granddaughter of three and a half years to go to bed, I said, "I don't feel well; I'm going to bed." Her reply was solicitous: "*You* go to bed and *I* call the dokker (doctor)." Modifiers, one would surmise, would add to sentence complexity and hence increase the difficulty in comprehension and recall. Adjectival modifiers, however, seem to enhance both meaning and emotional overlay and hence comprehension and recall. Williams and Cairns report that "The young prince rescued the beautiful princess" was not psycholinguistically more complex than "The prince rescued the princess." [25]

Embedding, considered from the semantic point of view, is any process that places a proposition in a particular semantic role within another proposition. Certainly it entails the ability to perceive semantic as well as linguistic relationships in two actions. Children's first efforts to embed a phrase usually take the form of tacking on or adding to the main clause. "You buy candy 'cause I'm good?' 'asked Tommy. "When I go to the store," answered Mommy. "Mommy go store now—'fore it snows," pleaded Tommy. The use of tense is often faulty, but the child perceives the subordination of one idea to another. Ann, not satisfied with my re-

[25] F. Williams and H. Cairns, "Linguistic Performance," *Normal Aspects of Speech Hearing and Language,* eds., F. Minifie, T. Hixon, and F. Williams (Englewood Cliffs, N.J.: Prentice-Hall, Inc., 1973), 461.

fusal to share the ice cream cone, assured me: "When Mommy take me (to the shopping center), I get you one."

Syntax and Perceptual-Semantic Development

Syntax has a place in language learning, but it does not precede nor direct perceptual-semantic development. The converse is probably more correct. As the child perceives meaning, he casts it into a form or structure based mainly on prosodic patterns which in turn, dictate word order. Syntax is the handmaiden of coding and the recall of meaning, not the progenitor. I do not believe that it is necessarily predictive of perceptual growth. As Brown and others have concluded from their research which followed Chomsky's publication, *Syntactic Structures,*[26] the psychological complexity of a sentence, indexed by speed of comprehension, ability to recall, and so on, is not predictable from the grammatical complexity of the sentence in terms of optional transformations.[27] Despite the spate of texts and programs predicated almost solely upon teaching syntactic structures as *the* way to language learning, perceptual-semantic development must be the primal hallmark. The language retardate's chief problem is his inability to organize structures because he does not perceive the meaning clearly. Fortunately the general consensus of scholars now points to perceptual-semantic development as the basic requisite of language learning. In Chapter 6, the third hallmark, syntactic development, is considered in detail.[28]

Continued Environmental Stimulation of Perceptual-Semantic Growth

The clinical language center and the public school speech therapy classes, *as they now are set up,* are not the best places for observing the language children use or for facilitating useful language learning. In fact, they may be the least congenial places. Young children are quickly stimulus-bound, bound to a language which they use only in a clinical setting and are unable to demonstrate in other situations at home or in the community.[29] Language is best observed and learned by teacher and

[26] Chomsky, *Syntactic Structures.*

[27] Brown, *A First Language,* 404–405.

[28] David Crystal defines grammar as the central organizing principle, of which syntax and morphology are subdivisions.—*Child Language, Learning and Linguistics* (London: Edward Arnold, 1976), 26–29.

[29] C. Shewan, "The Language Disordered Child in Relation to Muma's Communication Game: Dump and Play," *J Speech Hearing Disorders* 40(3) (August 1975), 313.

child in activity programs in a class, on the playground, in the cafeteria, in the corridors, in family arguments, and in planning to make something, or how to do something, or whether to do something. Boomsliter sums it up: "Language is the social situation and the physical situation and the past experience and the future purpose—and some sounds too, of course. If all these things are not learned together, they aren't learned at all." [30] Agreed: Language learning is no sit-listen-drill exercise to be practiced on alternate Saturdays during Lent.

Advancing Skills in Perceptual-Semantic Development (The Elementary School Years)

The Changing Nature of the Content of Child Language

The contextual nature of child language is changing rapidly in the school-age child. The illustrations provided by classical theorists and psycholinguists do not fit the psychological reality of today's world. The content and often the *form* are not those used by children advancing in oral language. We need to know the answer to such questions as these: Why does the child talk nonstop about certain subjects and remain silent about others? What are these subjects? What social needs does he have in a society now largely urban which differ radically from suburban or rural society? What are the major referents about which he seems to be eager to know more and more? What are his communicative intentions? Although we have not yet emphasized the form of the language, there is no polarization between form and perceptual-semantics. A balance, of course, must be preserved. What we are saying is that in the hierarchy of oral language, perceptual-semantics occupies the highest position, preceded in time, but not in importance, by prosody. It will determine form or structure as it will phonology.

Building and Producing Percepts in the Operational Stage (Six to Nine Years); Piaget's Theory [31]

Many special language teachers in the public schools follow some modification of Piaget's outline of perceptual skills in their teaching of the

---

[30] P.C. Boomsliter, *Language Capacity and Language Learning.* (Paper presented at seminar, *Schools for the Mentally Retarded,* New York State Department of Mental Hygiene, 1969.)

[31] Hans G. Furth, *Piaget for Teachers* (Englewood Cliffs, N.J.: Prentice-Hall, Inc., 1970); Jean Piaget, *The Language and Thought of the Child* (London: Routledge

language handicapped. In the concrete operational stage, these skills are *classification, causality and sequencing* (seriation). In the stage of formal operations leading to abstractions of a higher order, they include *deduction (causality), permutation,* and *correlation.* One wonders if this is the way the child really develops percepts? Do they match, as someone has asked, "the psychological reality of the child's comprehension?" Or are these perceptual skills, developed by adults, based on the way the adults continue *their* development of thought processes?

The scheme undoubtedly is helpful to teachers, and we shall use the main divisions with modifications and additions. We will not recommend Piaget's methods and materials because we have not found them to be effective in our teaching. Piaget did not design the theory for the perceptual-semantic building of oral language. He made little attempt to consider the pragmatics of a child's percepts and their expression. Therefore he used illustrations and experiments obviously unsuited to the teacher's purpose or the child's interest in developing the percepts he needs and the language he must use in their expression. Yet I have observed scores of children in many different school systems *silently* classifying birds, animals, fish; grouping colors; and distinguishing geometric forms (on the basis of *same* or *different*) hour by hour. The children in a first grade were mentally arranging sticks according to increasing or decreasing size (seriation), but to what purpose? Apparently it did not serve any commanding need of theirs for they said not a word about the exercise. The next step, I suppose, although I did not observe it, was the Piagetian exercise in seriation of mentally discriminating objects, similar in size but of different weights. I have seen children in the second and third grades replicating Piaget's demonstration of conservation (numbers of checkers in rows of different lengths; comparative judgments of the volume of liquid in different sized containers). In another school, children in the third and fourth grades were struggling with *Boehm's Test of Basic Concepts* [32] and Engelmann's *Basic Concept Inventory.*[33] No, the children were not being *tested.* They were silently performing the exercises in a language remediation class. I should not oppose these ideas so vigorously if they had been used as starting points for a discussion or if a single question had been asked as to the *reason* for the operations of causality, classification, or seriation. Neither the substance nor the method was conducive to producing the percepts the child would encounter in daily life or in the language he would use in talking about them.

---

and Kegan Paul, 1959); Piaget, "Piaget's Theory," chap. 9; Barry J. Wadsworth, *Piaget's Theory of Cognitive Development* (New York: D. McKay, 1971).

[32] *Boehm's Test of Basic Concepts* (New York: Psychological Corporation, 1969).

[33] S. Engelmann, *The Basic Concept Inventory* (Chicago: Follett Educational Corporation, 1967).

I repeat: We must teach the oral language that is dynamic and useful to the child, that fills his intentional, social, and informational needs. And the most effective way, I believe, to carry out these purposes is through language activities. Many writers set the materials in the form of tasks. I do not like the sound of the word. Learning should be an *adventure* in which children, under guidance, choose their methods and tools. Would any one of the "tasks" cited in Piaget's demonstrations match the psychological reality or teach the skills of classification, seriation, and causality as effectively as an adventure in baking Halloween cookies? Instead of arranging sticks, how much more productive would have been a carefully planned trip to the supermarket where the children, all of whom had heard the TV ads, would examine boxes of different cereals on the shelf. They would compare the weight, size, and price of the contents and then return to the classroom with sample boxes where they would continue their comparative analysis, including the *quality* of the products. Would they not have created resistance *with reasons* to the lures of cereal commercials on children's TV programs? Would they not have had an exciting adventure in talking about a real subject in practical, useful language? At home, would they tell parents about liquid in different containers or about their knowledge of the "best buy for the money?"

Formal Operational Stage (Nine to Fourteen Years)

When *and if* children advance from the concrete operational stage, they will go on to more formal kinds of reasoning.[34] These also are based on logic, and deal with more complex percepts with a higher level of abstraction. Piaget calls these skills: deduction (causality), permutation, and correlation. Another classification of skills for this stage which I find more intelligible and adaptable to oral language includes *similarities and differences, sequencing,* and *temporal, spatial,* and *causal relations.* Although a single skill may be dominant in a teaching activity, several of these skills undoubtedly will enter into the operation. Most paper and pencil tasks are just that—tasks—dull and ill-adapted to oral language. For instance the task of finding which cow in a picture series has the greater area (space) in which to graze when buildings are added or subtracted, wouldn't "send" many an eight-year-old child, urban or rural, into a

---

[34] "There seems to be almost universal agreement in results of studies done with older adolescents and adults . . . that not all individuals attain the level of formal operation." Edith D. Neimark, "Intellectual Development during Adolescence," chap. 10, *Child Development Research, IV,* ed. Francis D. Horowitz (Chicago: University of Chicago Press, 1975), 577.

speedy operative solution.[35] But if the youngster watches a bulldozer making a new street by cutting into his house lot or a playground in a park, he has several very real problems in area reduction to solve.

Children frequently will follow one activity with a similar one of their own choosing. They liked this puzzle of *sequencing* sounds in *temporal relations.* These were the sounds, not in sequence, which they were to put in sequence in a story: a loud cry, bell ringing, screeching brakes, ambulance siren, loud talk of many voices, quick footsteps, running. Bell ringing, they insisted at first, didn't fit any place in the sequence. Two children finally succeeded; the school bell marked the end of the recess; a child had run into the street after a ball. Mystery solved! They took their own game of sequencing sounds home to try on members of the family. Practice in *sequencing,* combined with *spatial relations* was taught in another activity that I thought was much too difficult for children in the elementary grades. The staff of T.A.L.K prepared a unit on *How We Talk.* They piqued the children's interest with questions: What makes you talk? *How* do you talk? Why don't birds talk? Why can't chimps learn to talk like you? (They saw the film, *Washoe,* a chimpanzee who acquired a human form of communication, sign language.) [36] The children responded with counter questions and with some bizarre answers. So with the aid of Frohse anatomical models of the chest, pharynx, larynx, and head, and great wall charts, the children examined positions, angles, and space relations of the speech machine. They made *papier-maché* models of their own heads. The most difficult problems were perception of spatial relations and proportions in the construction of the tongue in the mouth. I was wrong about the activity; it was a great success! Delighted with their knowledge and proud of their visual aids, the children took every opportunity to demonstrate "how we talk" before other classes and on parents' night. For one hour they knew more than their parents. When I visited that school recently, members of the class reminded me of the great day two years ago when they showed us all how to talk. One cannot be sure of the activity that will pay the highest returns on the investment of one's time and energy.

Children in the third grade are usually initiated into *causal relations* by the request to complete a *because* clause: *Allen bumped into Fran on the stairs; Fran tripped Allen because* . . . . Sometimes the causal relation takes this form: "What happens after lumps of sugar are dissolved in a glass of water?" What earlier connections do these children have with the latter question or even with the former? Do you see any

[35] Wadsworth, *Piaget's Theory of Cognitive Development,* 80–81.
[36] R. Gardner and R. Gardner, "Teaching Sign Language to a Chimpanzee," *Science* 165 (1969), 664–672.

dynamic interaction of the children extending beyond the solution of the problem? Would not both groups be more vitally attuned to solving the problem if Howard would run into the classroom and shout, "Two cars just smashed into each other right at the corner—right here! They went bang! bang! and stuff flew through the air." After the *who, why, where, what* questions, the children would settle into a discussion of the causes of the accident. If they agreed on the cause, they might go further in problem solving and in decision making. How would you have avoided the accident if you had been driving? What should be done at this corner to prevent future accidents? Who should do it? I have seen this incident produced in role playing. It was like Orson Welles' radio production, *War of the Worlds*. Logic and illogic; relevant and irrelevant causes; adequate and inadequate generalizations: all were demonstrated in a single session. The incident brought in all the perceptual skills the children knew at this stage: similarities and differences, sequencing, and temporal, spatial, and causal relations. They did not think of it as a task; it was a talking adventure. Other role-playing situations tell more of the story in a later chapter.

A Step Beyond Formal Operation Stage

Current research in perceptual development relies on skills that transcend Piaget's operations of deduction, permutation, and correlation. Problem solving and decision making are two of these advanced perceptual processes, heavily dependent upon the transformation of information into sophisticated organized schemes and dependent upon memory for its retrieval in oral and written language.[37]

For children in their preteens a helpful and delightful book on perceptual-semantic development is Hayakawa's popular text: *Language in Thought and Action* [38] Since it has long been the text for early morning classes over national educational TV channels, many parents have caught at least parts of the course. We cannot review all the topics. These aphoristic principles may entice young people to read the book in its entirety:

1. The map is never the territory (intensional vs. extensional orientation);
2. One never steps in the same river twice (generalization and transformation);
3. Everything has a name (identification; evaluation);

[37] Neimark, "Intellectual Development During Adolescence," 566–587.
[38] Samuel I. Hayakawa, *Language in Thought and Action* (New York: Harcourt Brace Jovanovich, 1972).

4. Knowing differences reflects the immature mind; similarities, the mature mind;

5. Logic is tested by climbing the ladder of abstraction.
   a. observations, specific examples;
   b. inferences;
   c. generalizations;

6. Problems leading to decisionmaking have more than two sides; they are multioriented.

Oral Production: The Emerging Social Nature of Expression

Oral language, beginning with the teens, is changing in intent and in the form of expression. No longer is the child's only purpose to affect the actions of the listener in order to get what the child wants. As he develops into a highly social being, his language is less commanding, less telling, less threatening. He talks much less about himself, to himself—or to the gerbils. He has something to say to someone and a reason for wanting to say it. Generally his oral language takes the form of a cooperative dialogue in which each speaker's response is controlled not only by the semantic and pragmatic content of the other speaker's previous utterance, but also by his gestures and subtle nonverbal expressions. Speaker and listener are joined in a common purpose, a referent that includes a chain of events extending into time and space.

The form of expression is still dictated more by its communicative function and its social-prosodic context than by any grammar system per se. Because the person perceives the connection both with respect to the whole and its parts, functor words, connector words, must be used. Basically it is the organizational scheme of the percept which forecasts the form in which the idea will be set. He knows before he begins to respond how the sentence is going to move along. He knows the course of the conversation. The inflectional morphemes carrying information relating to number, tense, possession, comparatives, and quantifiers tend to fall into place—if he keeps the organizational scheme or framework of the percept firmly in mind.

The prosodic memory pattern also is helpful in carrying the sentence when memory for a morpheme or word momentarily fails him. Associations surrounding a referent are increasing at such a pace that the child often has difficulty finding the vocabulary to express all that he knows. Just as musical notes attain their full meaning only when heard within a melody, so words attain their full potential only when embedded in context.

The child must practice oral expression, both by overt and subliminal rehearsal and by paraphrasing meaning. As he connects referents by oral means, he expands the total expression of the referent and presses its expressional form into memory. This is often the hardest lesson for the language-retarded child. He may attempt every skill in the book in building percepts, but unless he is willing to practice orally, to paraphrase meanings aloud, and thus to gain some flexibility, some choice in expression; unless he will practice recall and so increase his memory store, he has yet to exercise the most potent weapon in his arsenal.

Appendix A-4[39]

Development of Comprehension and Use of Oral Language, 1–36 Months

Mean Age in Months	Comprehension of Verbal and Expressive Signals	Vocabulary (Mean No. of Words)	Mean Length of Response	Use of Oral Language
1	Responds to sound. Reflex smiling to tactile and kinesthetic stimulation and mother's voice.			*Precursory stage:* Crying sounds that change in pitch; sign of bodily discomfort. Most frequent sound [ŋ]; other vowellike sounds: [ɛ] [æ] [ʌ]
2	Attends readily to speaking voice. Aware of his own sounds.			*Precursory stage:* Babbling begins. Reflex activities associated with breathing, swallowing, hiccoughing produce sounds resembling nasalized front and middle vowels (not true sounds). Coos and gurgles in vocal play.
3	Aware of many visual and auditory stimuli in environment.		2 syllables (non-speech).	*Precursory stage:* Vocalizes feelings of pleasure in response to social stimuli. Makes many vocal noises resembling speech sounds.
4	Motor response to outstretched arms: raises arms to be picked up. Responds to noise and voice by turning. Vocalizes social stimulus.		*Precursory:* repetitive sound chains (4–5 syllables): *ba-ba-ba,* and so on (comfort sign).	*Precursory stage:* Continued babbling. Cry changes with bodily state. Sound vocabulary changes with bodily position: [m], [n], [p], [b]. Vocalizes in self-initiated sound play.

Development of Comprehension and Use of Oral Language, 1–36 Months

Mean Age in Months	Comprehension of Verbal and Expressive Signals	Vocabulary (Mean No. of Words)	Mean Length of Response	Use of Oral Language
5	In absence of visual contact responds to voice by head turning. Responds to angry tone by crying. Responds to pleasant speech by smiling and laughing.			*Precursory stage:* Continued babbling: (a) vocalizes emotional satisfaction; (b) tuning up speech organs, an integrative process. (Imitates his own noises: *oohs, ahs, gurgles, gargles.*)
6	Distinguishes between friendly and angry talk. Listens to his own voice.		Several syllables (prespeech).	*Precursory stage:* Lalling begins. Vocalizes [mɑ] or [mu]. Pleasurable repetition of sounds and syllables. Tries to repeat heard sound-sequences. Uses intonational pattern with jargon speech in "talking to person." Directs sounds and gestures to objects.
7	Pays attention to speech of family. Pays attention to many sights and sounds in environment. Smiles at onlookers. Listens to his own private vocalizations.			*Precursory stage:* Enjoys imitating sound sequences. Vocalizes emotional satisfaction or dissatisfaction.

Age (mo.)			
8	Listens to greetings and other familiar phrases. Eyes and ears alert to all stimuli in immediate environment.		Lallation continues; back vowels now more like speech sounds. Vocalizes syllables: *da, ba, ka.* Vocalizes interjections and recognition. Copies inaccurately intonational contours.
9	Rudimentary comprehension of symbolic gestures and intonation patterns. Action response to verbal request (opens mouth when asked.) Comprehends *no-no, hot,* his name.	3–4 syllables in chain response but varies syllables (*ba-ba-da-da,* and so on).	*Precursory stage:* Echolalia (*da-da*), and so on. Copies melody pattern of familiar phrases: greetings, interjections, etc. Enjoys making lip noises. Tries out variety of pitches. Facial and arm gestures accompany vocalizations.
10	Pays attention to face of speaker. Comprehends *bye-bye;* waves *bye.* Action response to verbal request: "Where's Baby's shoe?"; shakes head *yes, no* to some questions.	Says word-like syllables *ma-ma-ma; da-da-da.*	*Annunciatory stage:* Tries to name familiar object upon seeing it again, namely, bottle (*babo*). Many speech and nonspeech sounds used in random vocalization. Imitates melody of phrase pattern but phonemes inaccurate.
11	Differentiates family and strangers. Understands many action words.	Median age of *first word.*	*Rudimentary language,* largely annunciatory; proclaims biological needs and psychological satisfactions. "Talks" to himself in mirror.

Development of Comprehension and Use of Oral Language, 1–36 Months

Mean Age in Months	Comprehension of Verbal and Expressive Signals	Vocabulary (Mean No. of Words)	Mean Length of Response	Use of Oral Language
12	Understands phrase-wholes, simple grammatical patterns. Responds in action to commands. Enjoys rhymes and simple songs. Understands arrival and departure signals.	5–6 words: *mama, dada, babo* (bottle), *bye-bye*.	1-word sentences.	*Communicative speech begins.* Copies melodic patterns more accurately but in jargon speech.
18	Understands most linguistic units but does not separate sequences into word units. Recognizes names of many familiar objects, persons, pets. Heeds to *here, now.*	50–75 words. Nouns: 50% of vocabulary. Many words made by phonetic reduplication: *da-da; pa-pa; ma-ma; gog-gie; tato* (telephone); *tick-tock; too-too* (toot-toot).	1.5 word-sentence.	Interjectional speech prevails. Begins extension of meaning (*mama* designates any smiling woman). Perceives and imitates stressed segments of speech, pivot words *with modifiers: more car; more milk; more bye-bye;* etc. Particles *off, on* used with nouns. Uses one word for many unrelated things. Repeats syllables or word-sequences in easy manner. Much vocal overflow with little or no phonetic value (laugh, sigh, whisper). Vocal inflection fair; pitch uncontrolled; tends to rise. Communicates by pulling person to show him object, person, situation.

| 24 | Does not understand many specific words but develops "functional equivalents of comprehension." Action response to verbal request (*close door*); sometimes repeats request. | 272 words
Of total response:
nouns: 38.6%
verbs: 21.0%
adverbs: 7.1%
pronouns: 14.6% | *Egocentric speech* prevails but some socialized speech (adapted information and emotional expression) also used.
Extension of meaning develops.
Asks simple questions about own concerns: "Where ball?" "Go bye-bye?"
Expresses emotions massively; attended by clapping, dancing, and so on.
Names or describes object in environment; names one color.
Uses "language of reference": accompanies speech with pointing.
Grammar: Develops word order based on prosodic sequences.
Some improvisations: *doed, goded* (went).
Uses demonstrative pronoun, *this,* accompanied by gesture.
Adjectives and adverbs gaining steadily at expense of interjections. |
| 24 | Distinguishes prepositions *in* and *under.* Listens to simple stories, especially liking those he has heard before. | 1.8 word-sentences. | *Phonology:* All vowels, labial and labioalveolar consonants in sequences, but they are not stabilized.
Telescopes phrases.
Pitch control improved.
Copies prosodic sequences of parents.
Final and medial consonants slighted or omitted. |

145

Development of Comprehension and Use of Oral Language, 1–36 Months

Mean Age in Months	Comprehension of Verbal and Expressive Signals	Vocabulary (Mean No. of Words)	Mean Length of Response	Use of Oral Language
30–36	Comprehension of sentence structure, syllable-sequences, and prosody develops rapidly. Understands: *yes-no; come-go; run-stop; give-take; grasp-release; push-pull.* Comprehends time words. Understands three prepositions. Enjoys rhythmical repetitions of others. Identifies action in pictures. Listens to longer and more varied stories. Understands semantic difference in subject-object by position of noun. (*Show us the car pushing the truck. Now show us the truck pushing the car.*)	446 words	3.1 word-sentences.	Continues *egocentric speech;* talks about himself to himself. Gives full name. *Repetition of heard phrases* more marked than at 24 months; first repetitions to himself. Names five pictures on card. Recites one to two nursery rhymes. Relays telescoped message to another person. *Grammar:* Begins to use question-making sentences. Independent improvisations of syntactic forms: *Look me no* (don't look at me); *stove bite yes* (stove will burn me). Uses demonstrative pronouns *this, that.* Uses two or three prepositions. Uses several verbs; substitutes *needs for wants.* *Phonology:* Much telescoping of words in primitive sentences with medial consonant still slighted. Pronunciation is unstable. Wide variability of pitch but has established firm base.

146

[39] M.F. Berry, *Language Disorders of Children* (Englewood Cliffs, N.J.: Prentice-Hall, Inc.,), 208–210.

REFERENCES

ABRAMOVICH, R. and R. GRUSEC, "Peer Imitation in a Natural Setting," *Child Development,* 49(1) (March 1978), 60–65.

BAYLEY, N., "Mental Growth During the First Three Years: An Experimental Study of 61 Children by Repeated Tests," *Genetic Psychology Monograph* 14 (1933) 1–92.

BAYLEY, N., "On the Growth of Intelligence," *Amer. Psychologist* 10 (1955) 805–818.

BECKWITH, L. and S. THOMPSON, "Recognition of Verbal Labels of Pictured Objects and Events by Thirty-Month Old Infants," *J Speech Hearing Research,* 19(4) (1976), 690–699.

BERNSTEIN, BASIL and DOROTHY HENDERSON, "Social Class Differences in the Relevance of Language to Socialization," *Readings in Child Development and Personality,* 2nd ed., eds. Paul H. Mussen, John Conger, and J. Kagan. New York: Harper and Row, 240–241.

BERRY, MILDRED F., "The Developmental History of Stuttering Children," *J Pediatrics* 12(2) (1938) 215.

BERRY, M.F., *Language Disorders of Children.* Englewood Cliffs, N.J.: Prentice-Hall, Inc., 1969.

BOEHM, A., *Boehm Test of Basic Concepts.* New York: Psychological Corporation, 1969.

BOOMSLITER, P.C., *Language Capacity and Language Learning.* Paper presented at seminar, *Schools for the Mentally Retarded,* New York State Department of Mental Hygiene, 1969.

BOWER, T.B.R., "Repetition in Human Development," *Merrill-Palmer Quarterly* 20(4) (October 1974), 303–318.

BOWERMAN, M., "Systematizing Semantic Knowledge: Changes over Time in the Child's Organization of Meaning," *Child Development,* 49(4) (December 1978), 977–987.

BROWN, R., *A First Language.* Cambridge, Mass.: Harvard University Press, 1973.

CAZDEN, C.B., *Child Language and Education.* New York: Holt, Rinehart and Winston, 1972.

CHOMSKY, NOAM, *Syntactic Structures.* The Hague: Mouton, 1957.

CORRIGAN, R., "Language Development as Related to Stage 6 Object Permanence Development," *J Child Language,* 5(2) (June 1978), 173–190.

CRYSTAL, DAVID, *Child Language, Learning and Linguistics.* London: Edward Arnold, 1976.

DEAN, ANNE L., "The Structure of Imagery," *Child Development* 47(4) (1976), 949–958.

DE QUIRÓS, JULIO B., "Vestibular-Proprioceptive Integration: The Influence on Learning and Speech in Children." *Proceedings of the 10th Interamerican Congress of Psychology.* Lima, Peru, April 13–17, 1966, 194–202.

DE QUIRÓS, JULIO B., "Diagnosis of Vestibular Disorders in the Learning Disabled." *Journal of Learning Disabilities* 9(1) 1976, 50–58.

DE QUIRÓS, JULIO B. and ORLANDO L. SCHRAGER, *Neuropsychological Fundamentals in Learning Disabilities.* San Rafael, Ca.: Academic Therapy Publications, 1978.

DE QUIRÓS, JULIO B. and O. SCHRAGER, "Postural System, Corporal Potentiality, and Language." *Foundations of Language Development,* Vol. 2. New York: Academic Press, Inc., 1975, 297–307.

DORE, JOHN, "Holophrases, Speech Acts and Language Universals," *J Child Language* 2(1) (April 1975) 21–40.

DORE, JOHN, "Children's Illocutionary Acts," *Discourse Production and Comprehension,* ed. R. Freedle. Norwood, N.J.: Ablex, 1977, 227–244.

DORE, JOHN, "What's so Conceptual About the Acquisition of Linguistic Structures?" *J Child Language,* 6(1) (February 1979), 129–138.

ENGELMANN, S., *The Basic Concept Inventory.* Chicago: Follett Educational Corporation, 1967.

EVELOFF, H.H., "Some Cognitive and Affective Aspects of Early Language Development," *Child Development* 42(6) (December 1971), 1895–1907.

FAY, W.H., "On the Basis of Autistic Echolalia," *J Communication Dis* 2 (1969), 38–47.

FLAVELL, J.H., D.R. BEACH, and J.M. CHINSKY, "Spontaneous Verbal Rehearsal in a Memory Task as a Function of Age," *Readings in Child Development and Personality,* 2nd ed., eds. P.H. Mussen, J.J. Conger, and J. Kagan. New York: Harper and Row, 1970.

FURTH, H.G., *Piaget for Teachers.* Englewood Cliffs, N.J.: Prentice-Hall, Inc., 1970.

GREENFIELD, PATRICIA, "How Much is One Word?" *J Child Lang* 5(2) (June 1978), 347.

GREENFIELD, P. and J. SMITH, *The Structure of Communication in Early Language Development.* New York: Academic Press, 1976.

HAYAKAWA, SAMUEL I., *Language in Thought and Action.* New York: Harcourt Brace Jovanovich, 1972.

JOHNSON, J.W. and E.K. SCHOLNICK, "Does Cognitive Development Predict Semantic Integration?" *Child Development,* 50(1) (March 1979), 73–78.

KAGAN, JEROME, "Do Infants Think?" *Scientific American* 226(3) (March 1972), 74–82.

KATZ, JACK, "The Effects of Conductive Hearing Loss on Auditory Function," *Asha* 20(10) (October 1978), 879–886.

LAHEY, M., "Use of Prosody and Syntactic Markers in Children's Comprehension of Spoken Sentences," *J Speech Hearing Research* 17(4) (December 1974), 656–668.

LEONARD, L.B., *Meaning in Child Language.* New York: Grune and Stratton, 1976.

LEONARD, L.B. and others, "Understanding Indirect Requests: An Investigation of Children's Comprehension of Pragmatic Meaning," *J Speech Hearing Research* 21(3) (September 1978), 528–537.

LEONARD, L.B. and others, "Children's Imitation of Lexical Items," *Child Development,* 50(1) (March 1979), 19–27.

LEWIS, B., "Otitis Media and Linguistic Incompetence," *Archives Otolaryngology* 102 (July 1976), 387–390.

LIBERMAN, A.M. and others, "A Motor Theory of Speech Perception." *Proceedings of the Speech Communications Seminar.* Stockholm: Royal Institute of Technology, 1963.

McKAY, H. and others, "Improving Cognitive Ability in Chronically Deprived Children," *Science* 200(4339) (21 April 1978), 270–278.

McLEAN, J.E. and L. SNYDER-MCLEAN. *A Transactional Approach to Early Language Training.* Columbus, Ohio: Chas. E. Merrill, 1978.

MILLER, G.A. and P.M. JOHNSON-LAIRD, *Language and Perception.* Cambridge, Mass.: Harvard University Press, 1976.

MILLER, J.F. and D.E. YODER, *An Ontogenetic Language Teaching Strategy for Retarded Children.* Paper presented for *NICHD Conference on Language Intervention with the Mentally Retarded,* Chula Vista, Wisconsin Dells, Wisconsin, June, 1975.

MINIFIE, F., T. HIXON, and F. WILLIAMS, eds., *Normal Aspects of Speech Hearing and Language.* Englewood Cliffs, N.J.: Prentice-Hall, Inc., 1973.

MOSKOWITZ, B.A., "The Acquisition of Language," *Scientific American* 239(5) (November 1978), 92–109.

NEIMARK, EDITH D., "Intellectual Development During Adolescence," chap. 10, *Child Development Research IV,* ed. F.D. Horowitz. Chicago: The University of Chicago Press, 1975, 541–587.

NICOLICH, L.M., "Beyond Sensorimotor Intelligence: Assessment of Symbolic Maturity Through Analysis of Pretend Play," *Merrill-Palmer Quarterly*, 23(2) (1977), 89–99.

NICOLOSI, L., E. HARRYMAN, and J. KRESHECK, *Terminology of Communication Disorders*. Baltimore: The Williams & Wilkins Co., 1978, 9.

PARKER, F., "Distinctive Features in Speech Pathology: Phonology or Phonemics?" *J. Speech and Hearing Disorders* 41(1) (February 1976) 23–29.

PAULSEN, M.K., J. MAGARY, and G.I. LUBIN, *Piagetian Theory and the Helping Professions*. Los Angeles: Bookstore: University of Southern California, 1976.

PIAGET, JEAN, *The Language and Thought of the Child*. London: Routledge and Kegan Paul, 1959.

PIAGET, JEAN, "Piaget's Theory," *Carmichael's Manual of Child Psychology, I*, 3rd ed., ed. Paul H. Mussen. New York: John Wiley, 1970, 703–733.

PIAGET, JEAN and B. INHELDER, *L'image Mentale Chez L'enfant*. Paris: Presses Universitaires de France, 1966.

PICK, H.L., A.D. PICK, and R.E. KLEIN, "Perceptual Integration in Children." *Advances in Child Development and Behavior, III*, eds. L.P. Lipsitt and C.C. Spiker. New York: Academic Press, 1967, 192–220.

PICK, H.L. and A.D. PICK. "Sensory and Perceptual Development," *Carmichael's Manual of Child Psychology, I*, 3rd ed., ed. P.H. Mussen. New York: John Wiley, 1970.

PRIBRAM, K., *Language of the Brain*. Englewood Cliffs, N.J.: Prentice-Hall, Inc., 1971.

PRUTTING, A., "Process: The Action of Moving Forward Progressively from One Point to Another on the Way to Completion," *J. Speech and Hearing Disorders*, 44(1) (February 1979), 3–30.

SCHIEFELBUSCH, R.L. and L.L. LLOYD, eds. *Language Perspectives—Acquisition, Retardation, and Intervention*. Baltimore: University Park Press, 1974.

SCHUBERT, E.D., "The Role of Auditory Perception in Language Processing," *Reading, Perception and Language*, eds. D.D. Duane and M.B. Rawson. Baltimore: York Press, Inc. 1975, 107–116.

SHEWAN, C., "The Language Disordered Child in Relation to Muma's Communication Game: Dump and Play," *J Speech Hearing Disorders* 40(3) (August 1975), 313.

SNYDER, L.K. and J.E. McLEAN, "Deficient Acquisition Strategies: A Proposed Conceptual Framework for Analyzing Severe Language Deficiency," *American J of Mental Deficiency* 81(4) (1977), 338–349.

SNYDER, L.S., "Communicative and Cognitive Abilities and Disabilities in the Sensorimotor Period," *Merrill-Palmer Quarterly,* 24(3) (July 1978), 161–180.

SNYDER-McLEAN, L. and J.E. McLEAN, "Verbal Information Gathering Strategies: The Child's Use of Language to Acquire Language," *J Speech Hear Disorders* 43(3) (August 1978), 306–325.

WADSWORTH, BARRY J., *Piaget's Theory of Cognitive Development.* New York: D. McKay, 1971.

WEIKART, D.P. and others, *The Cognitively Oriented Curriculum.* Washington, D.C.: Publications Department, National Association for the Education of Young Children, 1971.

WHELDALL, K., "The Influence of Intonational Style on the Young Child's Ability to Understand Sentences: A Research Note on Passives," *British J. Disorders of Communication* 13(2) (October 1978), 147–152.

WILCOX, J., JEANNE and L.B. LEONARD, "Experimental Acquisition of Wh-Questions in Language-Disordered Children," *J Speech Hearing Research* 21(2) (June 1978), 220–239.

WILLIAMS, F. and H. CAIRNS, "Linguistic Performance," *Normal Aspects of Speech Hearing and Language,* eds. F. Minifie, T. Hixon, and F. Williams. Englewood Cliffs, N.J.: Prentice-Hall, Inc., 1973, 461.

chapter 5

HALLMARKS OF ORAL LANGUAGE

Phonatory (Prosodic) and Phonological Development

HALLMARK 2: PHONATORY (PROSODIC) DEVELOPMENT

The intricate electronic schematics
the slide-rule and monster computer
which order your days
are clumsiest nursery playthings
beside
the rhythm of the helix
the balance and order of snowflakes
the complex choreography
of a single cell.

of oral language.

> Excerpt from *Prosody* by Matt Field *AAUP Bulletin*
> 62(1) (April 1976), 42. "of oral language"
> added by M.F. Berry by permission.

Phonatory Development and Prosody: Definitions

Phonatory development applies to voice: its fundamental frequency, intensity, quality, and the duration of its phones (speech sounds).[1] Out of

[1] These terms refer to the acoustic attributes of tones.

the phenomenon of phonation develop the *melody patterns of oral language* called *prosody*. Prosody then is a *phonatory feature* and a *linguistic function* of voice. Since we are concerned with its linguistic function, prosody is the theme of this chapter. It has been said that prosody is perhaps the least understood signaling system of American English and yet may turn out to be decisive in teaching American children, not only to speak their own language, but also to read and write it.

Prosody goes by many names: intonation, stress, rhythm; all are attributes of prosody but are not synonymous with it. Intonation and prosody are frequently used interchangeably. Prosody is closely related to the dynamic properties of vocal tract motion for the contrasts produced in prosodic patterns are due to variations in pitch, loudness, and duration.[2] These variations or contrasting features, according to Crystal,[3] are

1. Variations in pitch that produce *tone* (direction of pitch movement in a syllable) and *pitch range* (pitch changes between stretches of utterance), the whole making up *intonation* or tone groups;

2. *Loudness* which affects single syllables by producing degrees of *stress* or accent;

3. *Duration* that refers to the rate of *utterance;* and

4. *Rhythmic alterations* in speaking which are the result of particular combinations of the basic attributes of *pitch, loudness,* and *duration.*

Others would include in prosodic features only the time pattern of acoustic events, or intonation and stress, designating other attributes—rhythmic alterations, tempo, and loudness—as *paralinguistic* features.[4] Perhaps the simplest definition is the best for our purposes: *Prosody is the melody pattern of language perceived primarily as stress, intonation or rhythm and often defined by one or the other.*[5]

Prosody: A Language Universal

Every language has its own melody patterns, so deeply ingrained in those that speak it that, once learned, they find it difficult to adapt to new

[2] J.L. Flanagan, "The Synthesis of Speech," *Scientific American* 226(2) (February 1972), 48–58; R. Netsell, "Speech Physiology," chap. 6, *Normal Aspects of Speech, Hearing and Language,* eds. F.D. Minifie, T.J. Hixon, F. Williams (Englewood Cliffs, N.J.: Prentice-Hall, Inc., 1973), 224–233.

[3] D. Crystal, *The English Tone of Voice: Essays in Intonation, Prosody and Paralanguage* (London, England: Edward Arnold, 1975), 94–95.

[4] J. Folkins, C.J. Miller, F.D. Minifie, "Rhythm and Syllable Timing in Phrase Level Stress Patterning," *J Speech Hearing Research* 18(4) (December 1975), 739; F.R. Palmer, *Semantics: A New Outline* (New York: Cambridge University Press, 1976).

[5] L. Nicolosi, Elizabeth Harryman, and Janet Krescheck, *Terminology of Communication Disorders* (Baltimore: Williams & Wilkins Co., 1978).

prosodic features. As yet the speech "synthesizer" has not been able to replicate melody patterns of human speech, probably because the machine does not possess the dynamic properties and capabilities of the human vocal tract. And it cannot be made sufficiently flexible to match our neuromuscular adaptations to the changes in bodily state, moods, thoughts, and psychosocial environments.

If one studies a foreign language with the intent of speaking it, he is immediately aware of the universality of prosody. Why do we think foreigners speak their native tongue rapidly? Because they employ a different melody pattern from ours. The first sentence in texts of three foreign languages is "Will you talk a little slower, please?" Why? Probably because adults have stored firm prosodic patterns in memory and cannot accommodate or process new patterns quickly. Sitting on the deck of a ship with a fellow Fulbrighter, bound for Norway, I said that I would like tea instead of coffee, but I did not know how to ask for it in the deck steward's native tongue. Although my friend knew fewer words than I did, she presented my request in English words with a Norwegian melody pattern! "Ja-ha," said the steward taking in the usual long inspiratory sigh. Success! My experience as an adult in learning to speak several foreign languages replicated a child's learning of language. The first requisite, I found, was to perceive and imitate the foreign intonational patterns, the melody patterns of speech. We learned no single words, only phrases cast upon a prosodic frame. The problems of adult Fulbrighters were quite different from those of their children. The children picked up the melodic pattern quickly and in a few months were speaking the foreign tongue fluently while their parents continued to try to ram foreign phrases into American prosodic constraints. The prosody of the native language clung so tightly that the new language was spoken as a dialect. Why did the children succeed? Perhaps because they had not overlearned melodic English patterns or because their sensorimotor feedback mechanisms were still very flexible. In Denmark the Fulbright lecturers and scholars were invited each month to the Fulbright office to converse with a Danish group. The "visits" were not a signal success because the Americans huddled in one corner (like quail in a cold rain) and spoke Danish with English melody patterns; the Danes gathered in another speaking English with Danish melody patterns.

The Bases of Prosody

Possible Genetic Origin

So basic is prosody in language, that some linguistic scholars regard it as a part of nature, a "prefabricated system of temporal variability," inherent in the organism which permits the brain to process the meaning quickly.[6] Bolinger states in support of this view that the "part of language with closest ties to nature is intonation (a major attribute of prosody, if not a synonym in Bolinger's view). The nature to which it connects is the nature of the human organism—its emotional and attitudinal states. . . ." [7] In a series of subsequent studies Bolinger pursues the answer to this question: Does the child come programmed with a prosodic system or only with a special capacity of the brain to learn prosody, or both? In commenting on this question, Bolinger says,

> There is no proof, as yet, that intonation, or a strong predisposition to it, comes packed in our genes; but all indications are that it does. The child reacts to it first and controls it first. Its semantic domain is that of meanings that are most important to very young children—attention-getters, requests, inquiries, complaints—which function alone at first and then become an illocutionary counterpart to words. . . .[8]

The Psychoneural Basis

Prosody may or may not be the direct result of genetic programming, but its roots are in the CNS which, indeed, is genetic. The nervous system itself generates rhythmic patterns which are not the simple following of an external stimulus. The brain is equipped to organize tonal combinations, first because it finds disorder unmanageable. It seeks orderly change. Perhaps the nineteenth-century poet touched truth when he wrote: "The time-beater . . . has no material and external existence, but has its place in the mind, which craves *measure in everything*."[9]

In which hemisphere, major or minor, prosodically patterned tonal sequences are stronger, we do not know. Although discrimination of pitch and intensity as separate tonal attributes may be perceived in the minor hemisphere,[10] the combination of all attributes in prosodic patterning probably is stronger in the major hemisphere.[11]

[6] D.L. Bolinger, "Intonation as a Universal," *Proceedings of the Ninth International Congress of Linguists,* ed. H. Hunt (The Hague: Mouton, 1964), 833–848; B.M. Tingley and G.D. Allen, "Development of Speech Timing Control in Children," *Child Development* 46(1) (March 1975), 186–190.

[7] D.L. Bolinger, "Intonation and 'Nature,' " Burg Wartenstein Symposium No. 74, *Fundamentals of Symbolism* (New York: Wenner-Gren Foundation for Anthropological Research, 1977).

[8] D.L. Bolinger, "Intonation Across Languages," *Universals of Human Language, Vol. 2: Phonology,* ed. Joseph H. Greenberg (Stanford: Stanford University Press, 1978), 514.

[9] M.A. Roth, *Coventry Patmore's Essay on English Metrical Law* (Washington, D.C.: Catholic University of America Press, 1961), 15.

[10] Ann M. Peters, "Language Learning Strategies: Does the Whole Equal the Sum of the Parts?" Paper read at *Child Language Research Forum,* Stanford University, April 4, 1976.

[11] D. Deutsch, "Musical Illusions," *Scientific American* 233(4) (October 1975), 92–104; H. Gordon, "Hemispheric Asymmetry and Musical Performance," *Science* 189(4196) (4 July 1975), 68–69.

The Sensorimotor Basis:
Bodily Movement Patterns

Melody patterns rise out of the rhythmic bodily movements that precede and accompany oral language. These rhythms are an expression of one's sensorimotor potential and are a part of the basic synergic relations of the entire body. The infant exhibits the natural rhythms of bodily movement first in cephalo-caudal waves, then in more discrete postural changes to be succeeded by individuation of rhythmic arm and leg movements. Out of such differentiated phasic movements, postural activity, and tonic facilitation emerge the rhythms of oral expression. These prosodic patterns are the first linguistic system that a baby comprehends and the first that he uses in communication. Bayley and coworkers followed a group of infants from the delivery room through thirteen years of life. They found that those babies who were active from birth, first in cephalo-caudal general movements, then in specialized movements (discovery of hand or foot, response to moving objects, recognition of mother's voice and presence) were also the ones in whom oral language developed early and was clearly superior at thirteen years.[12] Communication, then, must be considered to be an *action,* an expression of one's awareness of and relation to his environment.

An infant, almost from birth, makes rhythmic bodily responses to his immediate environment, for example to the mother's voice. By the third month, he responds, not only bodily but *vocally,* to the melody patterns that he hears and feels. His cooing reflects his comprehension of his relation to his environment. His bodily posture, eye contact, facial expression, and gesture: all are part of the *act* of communication.[13] He will copy the general prosodic wave usually connoting pleasure. As jargon develops (six to eight months), he exhibits adultlike intonation patterns in babbling.[14]

From eighteen to twenty-four months, the prosodic system is refined. Even single word or "single element" utterances seem to have "interpretable intonation contours." [15] Although it may be a single word, the baby has "semantic intentions" far beyond the naming of referents.[16] At no time in this period does he attempt a phoneme-by-phoneme or syllable-

[12] J. Cameron, N. Livson, and N. Bayley, "Infant Vocalizations and Their Relation to Mature Intelligence," *Science* 157 (21 July 1967), 331–333.

[13] D. Ling and A. Ling, "Communication Development in the First Three Years of Life," *J Speech Hearing Research* 17(1) (March 1974), 146–157.

[14] P. Dalton and W.J. Hardcastle, *Disorders of Fluency* (London: Edward Arnold, 1977), 67–68.

[15] J. Dore, "Holophrases, Speech Acts and Language Universals," *J Child Language* 2(1) (April 1975), 21–40.

[16] R. Brown, *A First Language* (Cambridge, Mass.: Harvard University Press, 1973), 151–153.

by-syllable imitation of an adult utterance. Instead, he segments utterance into phraselike chunks, regardless of the intelligibility of the utterance to an adult listener. He does it chiefly by the prosodic features of pitch-direction, stress, and pause.[17] The pattern usually is highly emotional, expressing pain or pleasure. The baby does not yet comprehend the words but he will utter certain syllable strings with unusual stress in melody patterns carrying unmistakable meaning. This is to be expected since parents in speaking to very young children employ strong, often exaggerated, prosodic patterns. In studying two-word utterances of children under the age of two and a half years, Weiman found that they had very strong patterns of "stress" and that semantic relations expressed by children were more important to their stress needs than syntactic category labels: adjective, noun phrase, noun, or verb.[18]

By the time the baby has reached his third birthday, he uses the prosodic system to differentiate between actions, between voices, and between emotional situations. The melody pattern, in short, is still carrying the heavy load in meaning. It is, indeed, essential to comprehension of meaning, to perception. "A terminal fall, for example, shows by its gradience that what counts is how positively through we are; it is possible not just to be finished but to be *finished-finished,* with an extra low pitch at the end of a series of utterances." [19] The sentences now may be considerable in length and although he knows no syntactic rules, he gets along by slipping the words in the proper order into the "prosodic envelope." In the fourth year the prosodic system closely approximates the adult model,—*as the adult speaks to the child* (usually in an exaggerated melody pattern). Articulation and syntax still are very immature. In the fifth year prosody may become less important, yielding a part of its function to syntactic relations and phonology.[20]

Since prosody is tied to body language, its role cannot truly be minimized, I think, at any age. Our colleagues in the speech arts have long been cognizant of this linchpin in oral expression. They regard posture, for example, as the determinant of vocal and articulatory control. They remind us of the synthesis of body and oral language in great actors. It was said of Eleonora Duse, a great tragedienne of the early twentieth century, that when she buttoned her glove, she buttoned it with her whole body, *toute d'une pièce.* I have observed many language-retarded children who cannot walk "all in one piece," children who have confused right-left orienta-

[17] Ruth Weir, *Language in the Crib* (The Hague: Mouton, 1962).

[18] L.A. Weiman, "Stress Patterns of Early Child Language," *J Child Language* 3(2) (1976), 283–286.

[19] Bolinger, "Intonation and 'Nature.' "

[20] R.J. Scholes, "The Role of Grammaticality in the Imitation of Word Strings by Children and Adults," *J Verbal Learning Verbal Behavior* 8 (1969), 225–278.

tion in space, children whose temporal variability in oral language is reflected both in comprehension and expression. Prosody is as closely tied to basic bodily movement patterns as word order and syntax are tied to prosody. It stands as a primary hallmark of language learning.

Functions of Prosody

Organizer of Meaning

The importance of prosody in the perceptual organization of oral language received scant attention from psycholinguists, psychologists, or physical scientists before 1950. And certainly we in speech, hearing, and language sciences have paid almost no attention to it until recently. A Scandinavian neurologist, Monrad-Krohn, was perhaps the first to use the term, prosodic disturbances, in connection with the speech of neurologically handicapped children. Yet perhaps the most significant advance in teaching children with language handicaps has been, not the discovery of distinctive features of phonemes but the *rediscovery* of distinctive features of prosodic systems. I say, rediscovery, for it was Lashley in 1951 [21] who advanced the postulate that rhythmic action, applied to expression, and hierarchical motor organization were highly related concepts. He went on to theorize that rhythmic action might be the natural link between the *perception* and *production* of connected speech. Ten years later at the Stockholm Conference, Liberman enunciated his motor theory of *speech perception*. Motokinesthetic perception, he maintained, is an integral part of language learning. "The perception of speech sound-strings is more closely related to the articulation than to the acoustic stimulus." The articulatory movement patterns signalling transitions are not merely accompaniments of the movements that a speaker must make when he goes from "consonant" to "vowel." "Rather," he concludes, "they are *perceptual cues,* and it is difficult to exaggerate their importance." [22]

Another decade passed before James Martin's landmark study, "Rhythmic (Hierarchical) Versus Serial Structure in Speech and Other Behavior" appeared.[23] Martin contends that rhythm (a significant feature of prosody) is a concept based on motor functioning. These natural movement sequences as produced by the motor system are determined by a variety of

---

[21] K.S. Lashley, "The Problem of Serial Order in Behavior," *Cerebral Mechanisms in Behavior,* ed. L.A. Jeffrees (New York: John Wiley, 1951).

[22] A.M. Liberman and others, "A Motor Theory of Speech Perception," *Proceedings of the Speech Communication Seminar* (Stockholm: Royal Institute of Technology, 1963).

[23] J.G. Martin, "Rhythmic (Hierarchical) Versus Serial Structure in Speech and Other Behavior," *Psychological Review* 79(6) (1972), 487–509.

factors including temporal constraints. The constraints determine the organization of syllable strings both for speaker and listener. The listener cannot perceive or order separate sound elements because his brain is not able to "process" them. The sound input must be patterned on *relative timing,* which is to say, that every sound element along the time dimension is determined relative to the locus of all elements in the sequence, adjacent and nonadjacent. The length of the string of syllables held by rhythmic constraints may be six or seven and is often called the prosodic (melodic) unit or syntagma.[24] This is what other scholars call the "tone groups." [25] Syntagmas, or tone groups, then, will possess a coherent internal structure, a hierarchical organization based upon temporal relations and resulting in rhythmic patterning. Martin sees speaking and listening as dynamically coupled rhythmic activities, instruments of perception. Linguistic information is coded rhythmically into the signal by the speaker and coded out on the same basis by the listener. Although some scholars would not agree,[26] the majority of psycholinguists writing on this subject apparently believe that the temporal constraints imposed by the melody contribute to the organization of the percept. The melody, once begun, has a time trajectory that can be tracked without continuous monitoring so that later elements of the pattern can be *anticipated.* In the words of an old tune from the thirties, "It don't *mean* a thing if it ain't got that *swing.*"

Determinant of Word Perception and Word Order

We all use prosodic cues to aid in the perception of words and in their recall. Of course the most powerful cue to perception is the word itself. We perceive the words we know—perceive them quickly. One English word at a foreign airport amid a jabber of strange tongues immediately attracts our attention. The second most powerful cues to word perception and recall are the prosodic features of stress and rhythm. What do you do when you cannot recall the last name of the person you are about to meet on the street? You "run up" on the name by uttering the first name again and again, thus reinforcing audito-kinesthetic feedback of the way

[24] V.A. Kozhevnikov and L.A. Chistovich, *Speech: Articulation and Perception* (Washington, D.C.: Joint Publications Research Service, 1965).

[25] P. Lieberman, *Intonation, Perception and Language* (Cambridge, Mass.: The M.I.T. Press, 1967), 104ff; G. Branigan, "Some Reasons Why Successive Word Utterances are Not," *J. Child Language* 6(3) (October 1979), 411–421.

[26] Lahey states: ". . . prosody may play a role in language learning by pointing out the major lexical items upon which to apply an order strategy, and not as a device signalling relationships." Margaret Lahey, "Use of Prosody and Syntactic Markers in Children's Comprehension of Spoken Sentences," *J Speech and Hearing Research* 17(4) (December 1974), 664.

the name rolls along in a prosodic sequence. A two-year-old child may be able to stretch one word over an intonational frame and so make it a complete speech act. Although it does not have the structure of the sentence, it has the meaning.

In recent studies of adult prosody, "reiterant speech" (speech obtained when the same syllable, /mɑ/, is substituted for every syllable of a meaningful sentence) was perceived by its prosodic pattern. Even trisyllabic adjective noun phrases were comprehended by patterns of stress and rhythm.[27]

Little children not only use the melody patterns of language by which to comprehend the meaning of words; they also use the melody to dictate the *form* of their expression, the word order. The word string, conforming to an *order*, must fit into the prosodic envelope. Crystal thinks that the function of intonation is similar to the use of punctuation in writing, yet it is far more complex than punctuation. "It is more basic, I think, than syntax in the determination of word order, phrase order. Indeed it *governs* syntax."[28] Lenneberg calls the prosodic features the "underlying pulse" which carries the form and the idea along. He concludes that it is an indispensable ingredient in much the same way as a figure may only be recognized against a ground.[29] In terms of prosody, we conclude that both the word meaning and word order (presyntactic structure) must be contained within the prosodic frame.

Prosodic Control over Grammar

We cannot specify the extent to which melody patterns stimulate the development of grammar. Certainly intonational segmentation of the constituents of an utterance must precede syntactic development. It would be difficult, in fact, for the child to induce a syntactic pattern without it. Linguists agree that intonation gets a foothold in syntax, but as one has added, "the foothold is with one foot; the other one is back there doing its primitive dance."[30] The very act of fitting syllables and words into a prosodic contour must help to determine the grammar (morphology and syntax). Perhaps children use only certain prosodic features in expressing grammatic-semantic relationships. Five-year-olds, for example, will use emphatic stress to change the grammatic role of pronouns. They also will

---

[27] L.H. Nakatani and J.A. Schaffer, "Hearing 'Words' Without Words: Prosodic Cues for Word Perception," *J Acoustical Society America* 63(1) (January 1978), 234–245.

[28] D. Crystal, *Psycholinguistics* (Baltimore: Penguin, 1971), 133.

[29] E.H. Lenneberg, *Biological Foundations of Language* (New York: John Wiley, 1967), 212.

[30] Bolinger, "Intonation as a Universal."

use stress and intonational changes to change an order strategy. Some authorities hold that older children learn grammar without reference to prosodic features.[31] I do not subscribe to this view if for no other reason than that prosody is inextricably linked with the affective meaning. To be sure, I have observed "older children" six- and seven-year-olds, using syntactic markers and generally using them accurately. They may have done so, however, without conscious knowledge of the syntactic-prosodic relationships. My contention is that grammar as a linguistic feature has little reference to the *reality of language learning,* at least for little children. The prosodic attribute of stress, for example, may and does determine semantic relations more effectively than such adult syntactic category labels as adjective, noun phrase, noun, or verb.[32] Certainly intonation can always be manipulated independently of the syntax or grammatical class. The meaning of a declarative sentence, for example, may be clear although the intonational curve rises at the end. It is conceivable that children learn to comprehend and use structured language by other means than by the rules of grammar.

The Role of Phonemes

I have placed the function of prosody in phonemic development last because children pay little attention to phonemes per se, at least in the early stages of language learning. Later, much later, when they are aware of the need to fit the utterance more exactly into prosodic constraints— prosodic segments modeled by adults or one's peers, they may pay greater attention to certain features of phonemic production. Speech is neither perceived nor expressed phoneme by phoneme.[33] That prosody can play a role in phonemic production in child language is evident in the recital of rhymes. I have observed children, six years and older, who will omit or distort the phonemes /l/, /ʃ/, and /θ/ in free conversation but when they must follow the intonational contours prescribed in a rhyme said in choric style, these phonemes are no longer omitted or noticeably distorted. The temporal sequencing dominates the phonemic form to such an extent that the child *perceives* the correct production of the phoneme. Other examples in which the prosodic system guides the phonemic form come to mind. One cannot omit the sibilant /s/ in *stop,* for example, as some

[31] Lahey, "Use of Prosody and Syntactic Markers in Children's Comprehension of Spoken Sentences," 664.

[32] L.A. Weiman, "Stress Patterns of Early Child Language," *J Child Language* 3(2) (1976), 283–286.

[33] Earl D. Schubert, "The Role of Auditory Perception in Language Processing," *Reading, Perception and Language,* eds. D.D. Duane and M.B. Rawson (Baltimore: York Press, Inc., 1975), 97–130.

little children are wont to do, without violating the entire melody pattern. The aspirated character of plosive consonants [p], [b], [t], [d], [k], [g] must change with the position of the consonant in the word or phrase and hence alter temporal relations. Note the difference in duration and degree of aspiration of the plosive [t] in *hot, stop, hotcakes.* In the substitution of velar consonants [k] [g] for lingual-alveolar sounds [t] and [d], the temporal factor again operates to correct the substitution. If prosodic features dominate the utterance, it is very difficult to omit an entire unstressed syllable or several syllables. This is a common practice particularly among language-retarded children. As they are able to fit phonemic combinations into the prosodic frame, productive skill increases which, in turn, facilitates perceptive skill.[34]

Prosody as a language universal is a fascinating hallmark still incompletely understood and undervalued in language learning. It may well be a genetically determined trait manifested in the sensorimotor organization of our nervous systems. As I have said, intonation, stress, and rhythm may be thought of as attributes, or features, of the melody patterns of oral language. But by whatever prosodic feature you approach it, you will mark its force on perceptual organization, word perception, and word order, on structure and to some extent, on formal grammar. When we really understand its importance and its role, perhaps we will learn how to teach it and the order in which the very young must learn it: first. We must teach our children to perceive and execute the melody patterns of oral expression characteristic of the community and of the best in the culture of which they are a part. "The mind craves measure in everything."

HALLMARK 3: PHONOLOGICAL DEVELOPMENT

Phonology and Phonological Development of Child Language

Phonology has been defined as the study of the sounds of a language, as the consideration of each phoneme in the light of the part it plays in the structure of speech forms. This definition meets the requisites of the theoretical and scientific study of the subject: phonology. It is neither an analytical nor descriptive definition of the *phonological development* of language as it occurs in children. The difference between the two is great. The special language teacher is not primarily concerned with the phoneme per se for it has no meaning. She must be concerned with meaningful units of oral language, both in its perception and production. Perhaps this phase of scientific development of sounds should be called *phonemics,* not

[34] D. Ingram, *Phonological Disability in Children* (London: Edward Arnold, 1976), 24–25.

phonology. As a historical approach and an evolutionary process in linguistic studies, it provides a valuable background in teaching. She will have little occasion to teach the production of the isolated phoneme, but phonemics will help her in understanding the problems of some language-retarded children. We shall consider the subject within that framework.

The Evolution of Phonology:
Phones and Phonemes

Phoneticians, the first speech scientists, focused on the *phone,* a speech sound to be measured physiologically and acoustically. Phones make up phonetic units which form the basis of vowel and consonantal charts derived from the International Phonetic Alphabet. Charts of phones are designed according to the manner and place of articulation. The I.P.A. provides a symbol for each speech sound, or phone, and every sound is represented only by that symbol. Phones are marked by brackets; [p] and [b], for example, are twin sounds, both bi-labials, and except for voicing, produced in essentially the same manner. Phoneticians gradually came to recognize that the I.P.A. symbols did not always represent one sound, that features of its production varied with its position in the syllable, word, and phrase. Moreover the tonal characteristics of sounds—pitch, intensity, quality and duration—were altered further in accordance with their position in the continuum of speech. Modifying marks were introduced to indicate nasalization; fronting, elevation, and depression of the tongue, and so on. They could not represent, however, all phonemic changes in the flow of speech. Phoneticians proceeded to advocate the phonemic theory of speech sounds.

Phonemic Theory of Speech Sounds

Phoneticians recognized that no sound in the speech stream always was produced in one fixed position. The process of coarticulation, or assimilation, alters sounds according to their position in the syllable, word, or phrase. [Tables 5-1 and 5-2] Varying muscle tensions in the organs of speech, general physical conditions, moods, emotions, and social conventions also alter the phonetic characteristics of sounds. Recognizing the shortcomings of this theory of fixed position, phoneticians developed the concept of the *phoneme,* a "bundle of relevant sound features . . . a class of sounds, actualized or realized in a different way in any given position" in the total utterance.[35] So the [p] phone in *pit, spit,* and *slip* now becomes a family of sounds and therefore is represented by the phoneme /p/

---

[35] Mario Pei, *Glossary of Linguistic Terminology* (New York: Columbia University Press, 1966), 200.

TABLE 5-1   The Phonemic Chart

Vowels; Vowel-type sounds:
  glides & diphthongs   *Consonants*

/i/	he	/ʜ/	hoe	/l/	lit	/f/	fie
/ɪ/	is	/w/	would	/r/	rit	/v/	vie
/ɛ/	met	/j/	yell	/n/	nit	/p/	pie
/æ/	at	/eɪ/	late	/m/	mit	/b/	by
/ɑ(ɪ)/	my	/ɔɪ/	boy	/ŋ/	tang	/ʃ/	shy
/ɑ/	father's	/ju/	you	/s/	sit	/ʒ/	rouge
		/oʊ/	throw	/z/	zee		
/u/	who	/aɪ/	my	/θ/	thigh		
/ʊ/	would	/ɜ/	bird	/ð/	thy		
/o(ʊ)/	throw	/ɚ/	murmur	/t/	tie		
/ɔ/	water	/ʌ/	cup	/d/	die		
/ɒ/	on	/ə/	sofa				
/ɑ/	father						

(marked with a slash). It is governed by phonological rules which determine the change in the features without the necessity of modifying signs. For example, front vowels following velar consonants will produce a forward velar shift. With continued research on the features of phonemes, phoneticians attempted to set the phoneme in a broader frame. It became an abstract sound unit conveying semantic differences; it possessed "psychological elements" of the language code. They tried to invest the phoneme with substance by association with words but in itself the phoneme was "semantically empty." [36]

The Order of Phonemic Development

Jakobson [37] was among the first to declare that babies do not normally learn individual sounds as single articulatory adjustments. Instead, he claimed, they employ contrastive articulations. Extreme contrastive adjustments, for example, are present in *pa*, that is, a consonant with maximal closure is followed by a vowel with a maximum degree of oral aperture. Although the baby at first might babble single sounds, always vowellike representations, they bear little resemblance to his later vowel repertoire. These early cries and babble sounds might have had certain features of the vowels /ɑ/, /æ/, /ɛ/, and /ə/, but they were not distinctive features. In this

[36] Roger Brown, *Social Psychology* (New York: The Free Press, 1965), 247.
[37] R. Jakobson, *Child Language, Aphasia, and Phonological Universals* (The Hague: Mouton, 1968).

TABLE 5–2   TABLE OF PHONEMIC DEVELOPMENT *

Phonemes and Phoneme-Blends

3 years	Vowels: /i/ɪ/e/ɛ/æ/a/ɒ/ɔ/ʊ/u/ Diphthongs: /ju/eɪ/aɪ/oʊ/ɔɪ/ Consonants: /m/n/-ŋ/p/t/k-/-k-/b-/-b-/d-/-d-/g-/-g-/f/ Double-consonant blends: /ŋk/
3.5	Consonants: /-s-/-z-/r/j-/-j-/ Double-consonant blends: /-rk/-ks/-mp/-pt/-rm/-mr/-nr/-br/-dr/-gr/-sm/
4 years	Consonants: /-k-/-b/-d/-g/s-/ʃ-/-/-ʃ/-v-/j/r-/-r-/l-/-t-/ Double-consonant blends: /pl-/pr-/tr-/tw-/kl-/kr-/kw-/bl-/br-/dr-/gl-/sk-/sm-/sn-/st-/ /-lp/-rt/-ft/-lt/-fr/ Triple-consonant blends: /-mpt/-mps/
4.5	Consonants: /-s-/-ʃ-/č/ Double-consonant blends: /gr-/fr-/-lf/
5 years	Consonants: /-ʝ-/ Double-consonant blends: /gr-/fr-/-lf/ Triple-consonant blends: /str-/-mbr/
6 years	Consonants: /-t-/-θ-/-ð/v-/-v/ /-lk/-rb/-rg/-rθ/-nt/-nd/θr-/-pl/-kl/-bl/-gl/-fl/-rʝ/-sl/ Triple-consonant blends: /skw-/-str/-rst/-ŋkl/-ŋgl/-ntθ/-rč/
7 years	Consonants: /-ð-/-ð/z-/-z/ Double-consonant blends: /θr-/ʃr-/sl-/sw-/-lz/-zm/-lθ/-sk /-st/-ʝd/ Triple-consonant blends: /skr-/spl-/spr-/-kst/-skr/
8 years	Consonants: /-ʒ-/ʒ/ Double-consonant blends: /-kt/-tr/-sp/

* If no position is marked, phoneme is present in all positions.
Sources: Ingram, *Phonological Disability in Children,* 10–50. E.K. Sanders, "When Are Speech Sounds Learned?" *J Speech Hearing Disorders* 37(1) (February 1972), 55–63. M.C. Templin, "Certain Language Skills in Children." *Child Welfare Monograph 26.* (Minneapolis, University of Minnesota Press, 1957, 51.

prelinguistic stage, some consonantal combinations appeared, but they were poorly defined in quality.[38] The babbling stage is important, if for no other reason than because it is proof of the integrity of the sensorimotor system. Hearing-handicapped babies may begin to babble and then give it up because they experience no feedback. The point to be made here is that babble sounds do not make up the child's later repertoire of speech sounds.

Jakobson [39] bases the order of the developing phonemic system on contrastive articulatory positions which call for reciprocal muscle action. Working from this premise he enumerates the following schedule of the appearance of phonemes:

1. First phonemic combinations are oral-nasal, labio-dental, and continuant-stop.

2. Vowel-consonant contrasts are probably the earliest combinations.

3. Continuant-stop contrasts /m/ vs. /p/ also appear in an early sequence.

4. The contrast between low and high vowels /ɑ:/ vs. /i:/ will appear before a front vs. back contrasting vowel /i:/ vs. /u:/.

5. Contrasts in place of articulation precede contrasts in voicing.

6. Consonants usually appear earlier in the initial position than in the medial or final position.

7. Consonantal blends appear late in the developmental sequence (*pl, kr, tr,* and so on).

8. Stops and nasals precede such affricates as /č/ and /ɟ/ in appearance.

Several specific schedules of the acquisition of phoneme and phoneme combinations by children from three to eight years of age were based on studies of small populations. Hence, Templin's extensive study of the phonemic development of 480 children represented a signal advance in phonological knowledge.[40] [See Table 5-2] The study has been criticized for its mode and number of elicitations and for its failure to take account of individual variance. Yet its final reliability has not been challenged successfully.

Distinctive Feature Theory of Phonemic Development

A significant alteration in phonemic theory occurred when sounds no longer were described as integers but as possessing distinctive features belonging to a class of sounds. The theory developed principally as an off-

[38] M.M. Lewis, *Infant Speech* (New York: Harcourt, Brace Jovanovich, 1936), 24–36.

[39] Jakobson, *Child Language.*

[40] Mildred C. Templin, "Certain Language Skills in Children," *Child Welfare Monograph No. 26* (Minneapolis: University of Minnesota Press, 1957), 51.

shoot of the work of Chomsky and Halle [41] and has been called generative phonology. A more accurate term is generative phonemics. It rests on the assumption that phonemes may be perceived by their several distinctive articulatory features: vocal, strident, nasal, coronal, lateral, and so on. These are features which a sound holds in common with others in a group or class of sounds. When a child perceives, comprehends thoroughly, a distinctive feature or basic element in one phoneme of a class—voice, stridency, nasality, and so on—presumably he transfers this knowledge to other sounds possessing the same feature. Let us say that a child has perceived the distinctive feature of nasality of the phoneme /m/, he then should be able, with monitoring, to extend the feature to all English nasals: /m/, /n/ and /ŋ/. "A feature is taken from an established set and combined with another feature to establish a new feature set." [42] Table 5-3, which follows, is based on Chomsky and Halle's paradigm of distinctive features. [43]

Four serious weaknesses are apparent in the distinctive feature theory of phonemic development.

1. Each feature is assigned values of (+) and (−), that is, the feature is totally present or totally absent in the phoneme. Obviously this is not the case with many phonemes in the speech stream. /æ/ and /i/ are rarely free of some degree of nasality in connected speech; /t/ and /d/ may be noncoronal in some syllables or words although theoretically from the phonetician's point of view, they are always coronal.

2. The assumption that a "set of well-defined distinctive features" of each phoneme is always present in its *production* is invalid. An English speaker interprets /v/ as a fricative; a Spaniard, as a stop; a Persian, as a semivowel. [44]

3. A third weakness is its lack of neurological support. How can the nervous system code the distinctive features of single phonemes? The continuum of speech is far too rapid for the nervous system to perceive single phonemes, much less the distinctive features of a single phoneme. Coding must take place, not with single sounds or phonemes or with features of phonemes, but in much larger swaths, in syllables and in syllable sequences, words, and phrases. Moreover, in these speech units distinctive features change in intensity, duration, and quality according to the position of the phoneme in the syllable, word, or phrase. Consequently the feature in an

---

[41] N. Chomsky and M. Halle, *The Sound Patterns of English* (New York: Harper and Row, 1968).

[42] S. Singh, *Distinctive Features: Theory and Validation* (Baltimore: University Park Press, 1976).

[43] Chomsky and Halle, *The Sound Patterns of English.*

[44] F. Parker, "Distinctive Features in Speech Pathology: Phonology or Phonemics?" *J Speech Hearing Disorders* 41(1) (February 1976), 27.

TABLE 5-3 Distinctive Features of English Phonemes*

	i	ɪ	e	ɛ	æ	a	a	u	ʊ	o	ɔ	c	j	w	h	l	r	m	n	ŋ	p	b	t	d	k	g	f	v	θ	ð	s	z	ʒ	č	c	ĵ
vocalic	+	+	+	+	+	+	+	+	+	+	+	+	−	−	−	+	+	−	−	−	−	−	−	−	−	−	−	−	−	−	−	−	−	−	−	−
consonantal	−	−	−	−	−	−	−	−	−	−	−	−	−	−	−	+	+	+	+	+	+	+	+	+	+	+	+	+	+	+	+	+	+	+	+	+
lateral																+	−	−	−	−	−	−	−	−	−	−	−	−	−	−	−	−	−	−	−	−
high	+	+	−	−	−	−	−	+	+	−	−	−	+	+	−	−	−	−	−	+	−	−	−	−	+	+	−	−	−	−	−	−	+	+	+	+
back	−	−	−	−	−	−	+	+	+	+	+	+	−	+	−	−	−	−	−	+	−	−	−	−	+	+	−	−	−	−	−	−	−	−	−	−
low	−	−	−	−	+	+	+	−	−	−	+	−	−	−	+																					
anterior																+	+	+	+	−	+	+	+	+	−	−	+	+	+	+	+	+	−	−	−	−
coronal																+	+	−	+	−	−	−	+	+	−	−	−	−	+	+	+	+	+	+	+	+
round	−	−	−	−	−	−	−	+	+	+	+	−	−	+	−																					
tense	+	−	+	−	−	+	+	+	−	+	−	−																								
voice																+	+	+	+	+	−	+	−	+	−	+	−	+	−	+	−	+	+	−	−	+
continuant													+	+	+	+	+	−	−	−	−	−	−	−	−	−	+	+	+	+	+	+	+	−	+	−
nasal																		+	+	+	−	−	−	−	−	−	−	−	−	−	−	−	−	−	−	−
strident																					−	−	−	−	−	−	+	+	−	−	+	+	+	+	+	+

* Adapted from Chomsky, N. and Halle, M., *The Sound Pattern of English*. New York: Harper and Row, 1968. 176–177.

168

isolated phoneme cannot possess the same characteristics that it does in the syllable, or word, or phrase.

4. A fourth qualification of the distinctive feature theory is the relation of appearance of phonemes to the complexity of the distinctive features. If complexity is the rule, then vowels should be first in appearance, followed by the bi-labial phonemes /m/, /p/, /b/, and the lingua-alveolar plosives /t/, /d/; then fricatives or stridents /s/, /z/, /ʃ/, /ʒ/, /f/, /v/; and finally the affiricates /č/ and /ɟ/). By the seventh year, the child is supposed to have mastered all these phonemes and in the prescribed order. Jakobson, you will remember, concluded that vowels appeared only in contrastive positions with consonants. Journals including both the order and the time of completion of the phonetic inventory show wide variance among children.[45]

The Morpheme and Phonological Development

The morpheme is the legitimate child of *phonological development,* for it represents *the minimal unit of language that has meaning.* Two types of meaning are implicit in the term: morpheme. *Lexical meaning relates to words, word formatives, and vocabulary; grammatical or structural meaning indicates tense, possession, plurals,* and so on. For example, *sing, start,* and *box* are free, or lexical morphemes because they mean something standing alone; *ing, s, 's, es, ed,* and so on representing tense, plurals, possession are bound or grammatical morphemes. From the linguist's view, morphemes make up the building blocks of language design. From the teacher's view of the child's operation the morpheme does not satisfy her needs. It does not comprehend *the continuum of the living language.* Even a word perceived and produced as a prosodically patterned holophrastic expression serves the child's early language needs somewhat more effectively. Later he learns words, not singly but in their relationship in the phrase. In perceiving and producing utterances communicating ideas and feelings, little people employ strings of syllables in prosodic frames paying due attention to the free morpheme by prosodic emphasis. This *communication unit* is known as the *syntagma.*[46] For us engaged in teaching oral language development or its remediation, this is the linchpin. It consists of a group of six or seven syllables *communicating meaning to a listener.* One is concerned, not with single sounds—phones, phonemes,

[45] A.J. Compton, "Generative Studies of Children's Phonological Disorders: Clinical Ramifications," *Normal and Deficient Child Language,* eds. D.M. Morehead and A.E. Morehead (Baltimore: University Park Press, 1976), 87; E.M. Prather, D.L. Hedrick, and C.A. Kern, "Articulation Development in Children Aged Two to Four Years," *J Speech Hearing Disorders* 40(2) (May 1975), 179–191.

[46] Kozhevnikov and Chistovich, *Speech: Articulation and Perception.*

morphemes—but with the interrelation of *units of sounds,* forming words and phrases. Many years ago a pioneer in phonology said,

> It is apparent that the phonemic system cannot be constituted without reference to the syllable and its factors, and to the train of syllables which furnish a varying context for the syllables with their factors. . . . "Position," which has come to play so large a part for logistic phonemics in defining the phoneme, can only be position in relation to the phonemic phrase of the syllable train; especially position at the limits of the phrase; or position in relation to the dominant stress of the phrase; or position between syllables . . . or position within the syllable . . . or position in relation to the factors of the syllable in the compound consonant; all assume the fundamental unit of the syllable.[47]

If the syllable "train" is the key to phonological development from the linguistic view, then phonic and phonemic production might be called a prephonological system. With the evolution of the morpheme or syllable, syllable strings, words, and phrases, the child is coming into a phonological system in which relationships among all components of oral language —morphemes, syntagmas, words, and phrases— become meaningful components of perception and production.

Role of Imitation in Phonological Development

The weight that one gives to *imitation of adult language* in the development of a phonological system may be considerable or insignificant. Certainly it is not derived wholly from the language of adults, although some would claim that the child's system is the result of his imperfect perception of the adult system. If the system *is* a copy, it is much more likely to be a spontaneous imitation of other children, of his peers. But the phonological system generally is more than a copy if the child has intellectual ability. He adds to imitation his creative or generative imprint. He may add to the faulty perception of morphemic combinations of others, but he also makes his own creation, colored by physiological and psychological characteristics and by the kinds of feedback responses he desires. The child constructs a phonological system "in his own image."

Practices of Children in Developing Phonological Units

These practices are based on observations of groups of children endowed with average intelligence. They cannot be called general principles because children reach phonological competence by many roads. A single anecdotal diary of a brilliant child's phonological development, a child I

---

[47] R.H. Stetson, *Bases of Phonology* (Oberlin, Ohio: Oberlin College, 1945), 25–26.

know well, includes few of these practices. Undoubtedly there are additional practices which we have not considered sufficiently general to include here. The ones we have included have sound neurophysiological bases. Two major objectives seem to direct children in engaging in them: pleasurable response and economy of effort.

1. Children enjoy phonemic reduplication, and this is the beginning of repetition of sound combinations, precursor to syllable strings. They engage in the practice because it provides both internal and external pleasurable feedback. The early warblings, *ba-ba, ma-ma, da-da,* turn into semantic intentions and enjoyable reinforcement. The pleasure of rhymes and songs with repetitive syllable sequences is experienced even by adults.

2. The phonemes and phonemic combinations most frequently used and substituted in syntagmas, words, and phrases are those with a low energy index.[48] Phonemic clusters requiring a high energy index appear later in the developmental sequence.

3. Following the practice of economy of effort, children produce syllables or morphemes according to the ease in combining phonemic features. They will insert or alter certain features of phonemes that are similar in place or manner of production. It is easier, isn't it, to say [sʌmpθɪŋ] (something), much easier from the production standpoint than [sʌmθɪŋ].

4. Unstressed syllables are deleted for several reasons, in addition to economy of effort: One-syllable words may not be perceived clearly because the sensorimotor equipment is not sufficiently adept to handle more than the cue words. And the initial, unstressed one-syllable words which are most frequently omitted are not essential to meaning.[49]

5. Voiceless phonemes frequently become voiced in connected speech. Tensions of the vocal apparatus, particularly of the laryngeal and oral pharynx, may be caused by a desire to be heard or by the fact that emphasis can be more easily applied by voice than by aspirated plosives. So a three-year-old said, "Don hid my do." (Don't hit my toe.)

6. Phonemic clusters become a single sound largely because the sensorimotor integration and physical production of two or more phonemes in a cluster are too difficult. Even adults have problems with such clusters as *sl* in sleep; *skr* in screw; *sm* in smooth; *pl* in please; *mp* in pump; *ŋg* in finger.

Consideration of Teaching Practices in Phonological Development

What to teach and how to teach it? These are questions facing every teacher in a field that is filled with theories often supported by the flimsiest

[48] M. Parnell and J.D. Amerman, "Subjective Evaluation of Articulatory Effort," *J Speech Hearing Research* 20(4) (December 1977), 644–652.

[49] David Ingram, "Phonological Rules in Young Children," *J Child Language* 1(1) (May 1974), 49–64.

substructure of data. I begin with a negative: *The sound in isolation,* if it is to be taught at all, should not be taught in the early stages of phonological learning. Since children neither perceive nor produce phonological units by extracting phonemes one at a time, from the syllable, word, or phrase, it cannot be considered a valid practice. Someone has suggested that teaching sounds in isolation is like plucking a petal one at a time, declaring that it is a rose, and ending up with something that certainly is not a rose. In fact one can rule the rose out of existence, assuming that there was one to begin with. The problem, as every teacher knows, is to put the sounds together again in a meaningful unit, the smallest of which is the morpheme. A phone or phoneme, you will remember, is empty of meaning. Later, much later, in the teaching term we may have to attend to the accurate perception and production of certain difficult combinations of phonemes in syntagmas, words, and phrases. We must remind ourselves frequently, however, that we are not engaged in "articulation therapy" although we may have linguistically handicapped children whose language problems involve articulation. I reiterate this injunction because teachers are prone to begin teaching the language retarded with a unit on "articulation."

Phonological development is dependent on *linguistic constraints* put upon it by the other hallmarks of language. Linguistic constraints apply to coarticulation, prosody, syntax, and vocabulary. They act as constraints on phonological patterns, fitting syllable or syntagma strings within prosodic boundaries, developing verb forms that must go into the syntactic frame, and so on. Consequently these constraints operate both to enhance accurate production of phoneme clusters and to increase comprehension of the listener.[50] Herein lies the chief reason for delaying training in discrimination and production of phoneme clusters until the constraints are operative in contextual utterance.

The ability to perceive and produce syllable clusters in the speech continuum is determined, in part, by the child's *neurophysiological equipment.* Teachers must gauge the maturation level of this equipment and know ways to improve it. Some children can *discriminate* these clusters, but they seldom or never *produce* them correctly.[51] A review of the factors interfering with normal neurophysiological integration will help you to understand and compensate for this problem. Does the child have the neuromotor equipment essential for this task of *production?* Is the reciprocal

[50] P.B. Hoffman, G.H. Schuckers, and D.L. Ratusnik, "Contextual-Coarticulatory Inconsistency of /r/ Misarticulation," *J Speech Hearing Research* 20(4) (December 1977), 631–643.

[51] R.L. Shelton and A.R. Johnson, "Delayed Judgment Speech-Sound Discrimination and /r/ or /s/ Articulation Status and Improvement," *J Speech Hearing Research* 20(4) (December 1977), 704–717.

innervation of muscle patterns sufficiently fast to synchronize the respiratory, phonatory, and articulatory synergies? How effective is auditory and especially tactile-kinesthetic-motor feedback? Basically the child's ability to produce phonemic sequences accurately is derived from a sensorimotor index exhibited first in general body rhythms (body language), gesture, melody, articulatory flexibility, and so on (see Chapter 2). Perhaps the best clue to his production potential is reflected in his ability to imitate *total patterns of communication.* If the child can learn to imitate the melody, bodily movements, facial expression associated with syllable clusters of the syntagma or word, he probably has the sensorimotor equipment for the rapid fire of speech. Sessions stimulating active and total modeling will be more effective than hours devoted to listening for speech sounds.[52]

All children are profoundly influenced by the *psychosocial environment* of the classroom. This is particularly so when the emphasis is on phonological development. Is it because much of the teaching will be concerned with production, with "the way he talks?" For many children it becomes an implicit criticism of the person, of his sociolinguistic status. It takes courage, for example, to imitate models of phonological sequencing if the pattern does not accord with the child's sociolinguistic background. It is up to the teaching staff to create the environment and institute the strategies which are most effective in encouraging the children in phonological development. You may want to read again Chapter 3, *Neuro-Psychosocial Substrates of Oral Language.*

No test of articulation will go far toward an analysis of a deviant phonological system. To ask a child to imitate a series of key words and phrases cannot result in an accurate exposition of the child's phonological system. What one needs is a complete sampling of the spontaneous speech of the child, the language of free play with his peers or of activity-centered conversation. It should be recorded in a place far away from a clinic-oriented atmosphere and over a span of time

Remediation of the phonological system should be an on going part of the ontogenic oral language program. (Chapter 8.) To repeat, the phonological deviations really cannot be taught as something apart from the phonatory, perceptual-semantic, or grammatic aspects. In an earlier text I referred to the total learning operation as a "complex, interlocking system." If it is necessary to plan a direct attack on a specific phonological deviation, the analysis of the child's speech should reveal the aberrant

[52] W.H. Moore, J. Burkey, and C. Adams, "The Effects of Stimulability on the Articulation of /s/ Relative to Cluster and Word Frequency of Occurrence," *J Speech Hearing Research* 19(3) (September 1976), 458–466; M. Elbert and L.V. McReynolds," "An Experimental Analysis of Misarticulating Children's Generalization," *J Speech Hearing Research* 21(1) (March 1978), 136–150.

rule which he uses and probably applies with deadly consistency in syllables, words, and phrases. Perceptual and production training in prosodic utterance strings (not sounds), reinforcement, modeling, and extensive practice in spontaneous oral production should bring success.

Deviant Phonologies in Children's Oral Language

Articulation as a Language Deficit

"Simple artic!" This is the last line of the evaluation summary, I daresay, on thousands of reports of children with phonological problems. Apparently articulatory deficits have become so simple that public school "clinicians" now have delegated the task to "communication aides" or "para-professionals" whose employment is funded by federal grants.[53] I grant that the remediation of some articulatory deficits, the immature production of a single phoneme, may be achieved without a professional aide, indeed without any intervention by any person. Maturation will probably correct the erring sound by the time the child has reached the third grade. But this is not the case with articulatory problems that are inherent in a deviant phonological system.[54] They are language problems and cannot be separated in our teaching from the perceptual-semantic, phonatory, and syntactic hallmarks of linguistic development.

Deviations as a Dimension of Time

The most common phonological deviations probably are very similar to those that appear in the normal speech development of children. The difference is their persistence in time. A child, not quite three years old, asking to be carried through deep grass, shifted the phonetically related glides, [l] and [r] into [w] when she said [ðə wɪtə wæbɪt wə baɪ maɪ wɪtə wɛgz]; *The little rabbit will bite my little legs;* but at four years this phonological deviation was no longer present. The nervous system, mediating perception and production, had matured. If it had persisted beyond the sixth year, it would have been a true phonological deviation requiring intervention. Other principal deviations that children ordinarily

[53] D.J. Alvord, "Innovation in Speech Therapy: A Cost Effective Program," *Exceptional Children* 43(8) (May 1977), 520–525; V. Abraham, "Parents as Articulation Therapists," *Illinois Speech Hearing J* 10(3) (May 1977), 19–22.

[54] E. Pollock and N. Rees, "Disorders of Articulation: Some Clinical Applications of Distinctive Feature Theory," *J Speech Hearing Disorders* 37(4) (November 1972), 451–461.

will remedy as the nervous system matures are the reduction of consonant clusters (usually to one member), the deletion of final consonant combinations, the transformation of fricatives into stops, and liquids into glides [r] and [j]. The deviations, while they exist, however, are not irregular; they are a part of a rule-operated system. The child applies the rule evenly, albeit it is the wrong rule.[55] With maturation, the problem is usually solved.

Persistence of Atypical Phonological System

Other deviations may be unique and represent major phonological disorders that are not the result of immature or delayed development. Ingram says of this group,

> . . . the phonologies of these children are systematic. They show the use of sounds to contrast the meanings of words, and they use a variety of phonological processes to simplify the production of words . . . they sometimes use processes that are not commonly or widely used by normal children . . . (They) may use simplifying processes that the normal child often need not resort to, e.g., the stopping of liquids . . . Certain processes tend to *persist,* eventually co-occurring with those more characteristic of older children's speech.[56]

Neurophysical and Anatomic Deficits Affecting Phonology

Another class of deviations are still more pronounced. They may stem from the neurophysiological inability of the child to produce the phonological units in the normal speech continuum. The primary causes of this disability may be a CNS injury as in cerebral palsy; anatomical abnormalities as in cleft palate; temporal coding anomalies reflected in deficits in the neuromotor equipment necessary to produce phonemic clusters *within a time frame;* [57] or psychoemotional disturbances blocking perceptual-motor integration of language.

Children handicapped by neurological deficits, either congenital or adventitious in origin, may be able to elicit a motor engram for production. What they cannot do is target properly on the accurate *perception* of the utterance. Consequently there is a mismatch. A kind of phonemic-seman-

---

[55] L.V. McReynolds and K. Huston, "A Distinctive Feature Analysis of Children's Misarticulations," *J Speech Hearing Disorders* 36(2) (May 1971), 155–166.

[56] Ingram, *Phonological Disability in Children,* 129.

[57] P. Tallal, "Rapid Auditory Processing in Normal and Disordered Language Development," *J Speech Hearing Research* 19(3) (September 1976), 561–571.

tic confusion prevails; it may be caused by faulty auditory-haptic integration in temporoparietal areas of the cortex or in subcortical areas that represent nonetheless a high organizational level of linguistic processing. Another deficit may come from a mismatch in timing in the neuromotor system which produces untoward effects in prosody, coarticulation, and assimilation. Each phoneme in the phonological unit is produced as if it stood in isolation. Tongue configurations, atypical release patterns, prolonged duration of certain phonemes, and other factors contribute to bizarre expression.[58]

It is important to keep in mind the evolution of the phonological system, from phone to phoneme to morpheme. But in the phonological development in the child, the *unit of communication* is the *syntagma* which governs both perception and production of syllable clusters having meaning. We have noted too that deviant phonological development, confused and chaotic as it may seem, also operates by rules. The deviant rules may be deeply ingrained in the system because of imperception, incapability of production of the accepted system, or because of integrative failure with the other hallmarks of oral language.

REFERENCES

ABRAVANEL, E., and others, "Action Imitation: The Early Phase of Infancy," *Child Development,* 47(4) (1976), 1032–1044.

ALBERT, M.L., R.W. SPARKS, and N.A. HELM, "Melodic Intonation Therapy for Aphasia," *Archives Neurology* 29(2) (1973), 130–131.

ALLEN, MARIAM, *Dance of Language.* Portola Valley, Cal.: Richards Institute of Music Education and Research, 1974.

ALVORD, D.J., "Innovation in Speech Therapy: A Cost Effective Program," *Exceptional Children* 43(8) (May 1977), 520–525.

BERLIN, C.I., "On Melodic Intonation Therapy for Aphasia by R.W. Sparks and A.L. Holland," *J Speech Hearing Disorders* 41(3) (August 1976), 298–300.

BERRY, M.F. *Language Disorders of Children,* chap. 2. Englewood Cliffs, N.J.: Prentice-Hall, Inc., 1969.

BLOOM, L., *Selected Readings in Language Development.* New York: John Wiley, 1977.

BLOOM, L. and MARGARET LAHEY, *Language Development and Language Disorders.* New York: John Wiley, 1978.

BOLINGER, D.L., "Intonation as a Universal," *Proceedings of the Ninth*

---

[58] H. Walsh, "On Certain Practical Inadequacies of Distinctive Features Systems," *J Speech Hearing Disorders* 39(1) (February 1974), 32–43.

International Congress of Linguists, ed. H.G. Lunt. The Hague: Mouton, 1964.

BOLINGER, D.L., "Intonation and 'Nature.' " Burg Wartenstein Symposium No. 74, *Fundamentals of Symbolism.* New York: Wenner-Gren Foundation for Anthropological Research, 1977.

BOLINGER, D.L., "Intonation Across Languages." *Universals of Human Language, Vol. 2: Phonology,* ed. Joseph H. Greenberg. Stanford: Stanford University Press, 1978.

BOOMSLITER, P.C., W. CREEL, and G.S. HASTINGS, JR., "Perception and English Poetic Meter," *PMLA* 88(2) (March 1973), 200–206.

BRAINE, M., "The Acquisition of Language in Infant and Child," *The Learning of Language,* ed. C. Reed. Englewood Cliffs, N.J.: Prentice-Hall, Inc., 1971.

BREARLEY, MOLLY, ed., "Movement: Action Feeling and Thought," chap. 5, *The Teaching of Young Children.* New York. Schocken Books, 1970.

BROWN, ROGER, *Social Psychology.* New York: The Free Press, 1965.

BROWN, R., *A First Language.* Cambridge, Mass.: Harvard University Press, 1973.

CAMERON, J., N. LIVSON, and N. BAYLEY, "Infant Vocalizations and Their Relation to Mature Intelligence," *Science* 157 (July 21, 1967) 331–333.

CHOMSKY, N. and M. HALLE, *The Sound Patterns of English.* New York: Harper and Row, 1968.

COMPTON, A.J., "Generative Studies of Children's Phonological Disorders: Clinical Ramifications," *Normal and Deficient Child Language,* eds. D.M. Morehead and A.E. Morehead. Baltimore: University Park Press, 1976, 61–98.

COSTELLO, J. and J. ONSTINE, "The Modification of Multiple Articulation Errors Based on Distinctive Feature Theory," *J Speech Hearing Disorders* 41(2) (May 1976), 199–215.

CRAMBLITT, N.S. and G.M. SIEGEL, "The Verbal Environment of a Language-Impaired Child," *J Speech and Hearing Disorders* 42(4) (November 1977), 474–482.

CROCKER, J.R., "A Phonological Model of Children's Articulation Competence," *J Speech Hearing Disorders* 34(3) (August 1969) 203–213.

CRYSTAL, D., *Linguistics.* New York: Penguin, 1971.

CRYSTAL, D., *The English Tone of Voice: Essays in Intonation, Prosody and Paralanguage.* London: Edward Arnold, 1975.

DALTON, K., *Music for Wonder.* San Francisco: Renna-White Associates, 1976.

DALTON, P. and W.J. HARDCASTLE, *Disorders of Fluency.* London: Edward Arnold, 1977.

DE QUIRÓS, JULIO B., "Vestibular-Proprioceptive Integration: The Influence on Learning and Speech in Children," Proceedings of the 10th Interamerican Congress of Psychology. Lima, Peru, April 13–17, 1966, 194–202.

DE QUIRÓS, J.B. and O. SCHRAGER, "Postural System, Corporal Potentiality, and Language," *Foundations of Language Development,* Vol. 2. New York: Academic Press, Inc., 1975, 297–307.

DE QUIRÓS, JULIO, "Diagnosis of Vestibular Disorders in the Learning Disabled," *J Learning Disabilities* 9(1) 1976, 50–58.

DE QUIRÓS, JULIO B., "Significance of Some Therapies on Posture and Learning," *Academic Therapy,* 11(3) 1976, 261–270.

DEUTSCH, D., "Musical Illusions," *Scientific American* 233(4) (October 1975), 92–104.

DORE, J., "Holophrases, Speech Acts and Language Universals," *J Child Language* 2(1) (April 1975), 21–40.

ELBERT, M. and L.V. McREYNOLDS, "An Experimental Analysis of Misarticulating Children's Generalization," *J Speech Hearing Research* 21(1) (March 1978), 136–150.

FLANAGAN, J.L., "The Synthesis of Speech," *Scientific American* 226(2) (February 1972), 48–58.

FOLKINS, J.W., C.J. MILLER, and F.D. MINIFIE, "Rhythm and Syllable Timing in Phrase Level Stress Patterning," *J Speech Hearing Research* 18(4) (December 1975), 739–753.

FROMKIN, V. and R. RODMAN, *An Introduction to Language,* 2nd ed. New York: Holt, Rinehart and Winston, 1978.

GOODGLASS, H. and others, "Some Linguistic Structures in the Speech of a Broca's Aphasic," *Cortex* 8(2) (June 1972), 191–212.

GORDON, H., "Hemispheric Asymmetry and Musical Performance," *Science* 189(4196) (4 July 1975), 68–69.

GRUNWELL, P., "The Phonological Analysis of Articulation Disorder," *British J Disorders Communication* 10(1) (April 1975), 31–42.

HOFFMAN, P.B., G.H. SCHUCKERS, and D.L. RATUSNIK, "Contextual-Coarticulatory Inconsistency of /r/ Misarticulation," *J Speech Hearing Research* 20(4) (December 1977), 631–643.

INGRAM, D., "Phonological Rules in Young Children," *J Child Language* 1(1) (May 1974), 49–64.

INGRAM, D., *Phonological Disability in Children.* London: Edward Arnold, 1976.

JAKOBSON, R., *Child Language, Aphasia, and Phonological Universals.* The Hague: Mouton, 1968.

KAGAN, J. and others, "Infant Antecedents of Cognitive Functioning: A Longitudinal Study," *Child Development,* 49(4) (December 1978), 1005–1023.

KNAFLE, JUNE D., "Children's Discrimination of Rhyme," *J Speech Hearing Research* 17(3) (September 1974), 367–372.

KONORSKI, J., *Integrative Activity of the Brain.* Chicago: University of Chicago Press, 1967.

KOZHEVNIKOV, V. and L. CHISTOVICH, *Speech: Articulation and Perception.* English translated from the Russian. Washington, D.C.: Joint Publications Research Service, U.S. Dept. of Commerce, 1965.

LACKNER, J.R. and K.B. LEVINE, "Speech Production: Evidence for Syntactically and Phonologically Determined Units," *Percept. Psychophys.* 17(1) (1975), 107–113.

LAHEY, MARGARET, "Use of Prosody and Syntactic Markers in Children's Comprehension of Spoken Stentences," *J Speech Hearing Research* 17(4) (December 1974), 656–667.

LASHLEY, K.S., "The Problem of Serial Order in Behavior," *Cerebral Mechanisms in Behavior,* ed. L.A. Jeffress. New York: John Wiley, 1951.

LENNEBERG, E.H., *Biological Foundations of Language.* New York: John Wiley, 1967.

LEON, P.R., G. FAURE and A. RIGAULT, *Prosodic Feature Analysis.* Ottawa: Marcel Didier (Canada) LTEE, 1970.

LEONARD, L.B., *Meaning in Child Language.* New York: Grune and Stratton, 1976.

LEWIS, M.M., *Infant Speech.* New York: Harcourt Brace Jovanovich, 1936.

LIBERMAN, A.M. and others, "A Motor Theory of Speech Perception," *Proceedings of the Speech Communication Seminar.* Stockholm: Royal Institute of Technology, 1963.

LIEBERMAN, P., *Intonation, Perception and Language.* Cambridge, Mass.: The M.I.T. Press, 1967.

LING, D. and A. LING, "Communication Development in the First Three Years of Life," *J. Speech Hearing Research* 17(1) (March 1974) 146–157.

LUND, NANCY L. and JUDITH F. DUCHAN, "Phonological Analysis: A Multifaceted Approach," *British J Disorders of Communication* 13(2) (October 1978), 119–126.

LYONS, JOHN, *Semantics, I.* London: Cambridge University Press, 1977.

MARTIN, J.G., "Rhythmic (Hierarchical) Versus Serial Structure in Speech and Other Behavior," *Psychological Review* 79(6) (1972), 487–509.

McHUGHES, JANET LARSEN, "The Poesis of Space: Prosodic Structures in Concrete Poetry," *Quarterly J Speech* 63 (April 1977), 167–179.

McREYNOLDS, L.V. and K. HUSTON, "A Distinctive Feature Analysis of Children's Misarticulations," *J Speech and Hearing Disorders* 36(2) (May 1971), 155–166.

MENYUK, PAULA, "The Role of Distinctive Features in Children's Acquisition of Phonology," *Studies of Child Language Development,* eds. C.A. Ferguson and D. Slobin. New York: Holt, Rinehart and Winston, 1973. 49–52.

MINIFIE, F., F. DARLEY, and D. SHERMAN, "Temporal Reliability of Seven Language Measures," *J Speech Hearing Research* 6 (1963), 139–148.

MOORE, W.H., J. BURKEY, and C. ADAMS, "The Effects of Stimulability on the Articulation of /s/ Relative to Cluster and Word Frequency of Occurrence," *J Speech Hearing Research* 19(3) (September 1976), 458–466.

MUMA, JOHN R., *Language Handbook.* Englewood Cliffs, N.J.: Prentice-Hall, Inc., 1978.

NAKATANI, L.H. and J.A. SCHAFFER, "Hearing 'Words' Without Words: Prosodic Cues for Word Perception," *J Acoustical Society America* 63 (1) (January 1978), 234–245.

NETSELL, R., "Speech Physiology," chap. 6, *Normal Aspects of Speech, Hearing and Language,* eds. F.D. Minifie, T.J. Hixon, and F. Williams. Englewood Cliffs, N.J.: Prentice-Hall, Inc., 1973.

NICOLOSI, L., ELIZABETH HARRYMAN, and JANET KRESCHECK, *Terminology of Communication Disorders.* Baltimore: Williams & Wilkins, 1978.

PALMER, F.R., *Semantics: A New Outline.* New York: Cambridge University Press, 1976.

PANAGOS, J., M. KELLEHER, and R. KLICH, "Effects of Syntactic and Phonological Complexity of Children's Misarticulations," *Illinois Speech Hearing J* 11(2) (February 1978), 1–3.

PARKER, F., "Distinctive Features in Speech Pathology: Phonology or Phonemics?" *J Speech Hearing Disorders* 41(1) (February 1976), 23–39.

PARNELL, M. and J.D. AMERMAN, "Subjective Evaluation of Articulatory Effort," *J Speech Hearing Research* 20(4) (December 1977), 644–652.

PEI, MARIO, *Glossary of Linguistic Terminology.* New York: Columbia University Press, 1966.

PETERS, ANN M., "Language Learning Strategies: Does the Whole Equal the Sum of the Parts?" Paper read at *Child Language Research Forum,* Stanford University, April 4, 1976.

PIAGET, J., *The Language and Thought of the Child.* London: Routledge and Kegan Paul, 1959.

PICK, ANNE D. and others, "Young Children's Knowledge of Word Structure," *Child Development* 49(3) (September 1978), 669–680.

POLLOCK, E. and N. REES, "Disorders of Articulation: Some Clinical Applications of Distinctive Feature Theory," *J Speech Hearing Disorders* 37(4) (November 1972), 451–461.

PRATHER, E.M., D.L. HEDRICK, and C.A. KERN, "Articulation Development in Children Aged Two to Four Years," *J Speech Hear Dis* 40(2) (May 1975), 179–191.

REES, N.S., "Bases of Decision in Language Training," *J Speech Hearing Disorders* 37(3) (1972), 283–304.

ROTH, M.A., *Coventry Patmore's Essay on English Metrical Law.* Washington, D.C.: Catholic University of America Press, 1961.

SANDERS, E.K., "When Are Speech Sounds Learned?" *J Speech Hearing Disorders* 37(1) (February 1972), 55–63.

SCHOLES, R.J., "The Role of Grammaticality in the Imitation of Word Strings by Children and Adults," *J Verbal Learning Verbal Behavior* 8 (1969), 225–278.

SCHUBERT, EARL D., "The Role of Auditory Perception in Language Processing," *Reading, Perception and Language,* eds. D.D. Duane and M.B. Rawson. Baltimore: York Press, Inc., 1975.

SHELTON, R.L. and A.F. JOHNSON, "Delayed Judgment Speech-Sound Discrimination and /r/ or /s/ Articulation Status and Improvement," *J Speech Hearing Research* 20(4) (December 1977), 704–717.

SINGH, S., *Distinctive Features: Theory and Validation.* Baltimore: University Park Press, 1976.

SPARKS, R., N. HELMS, and M. ALBERT, "Aphasia Rehabilitation from Melodic Intonation Therapy," *Cortex* 10 (1974), 303–316.

SPARKS, R.W. and A.L. HOLLAND, "Method: Melodic Intonation Therapy for Aphasia," *J Speech Hearing Disorders* 41(3) (August 1976), 287–297.

STETSON, R.H., *Bases of Phonology.* Oberlin, Ohio: Oberlin College, 1945.

TALLAL, P., "Rapid Auditory Processing in Normal and Disordered Language Development," *J Speech Hearing Research* 19(3) (September 1976), 561–571.

TEMPLIN, M.C., "Certain Language Skills in Children," *Child Welfare Monograph* 26, Minneapolis: University of Minnesota Press, 1957.

TINGLEY, B.M. and G.D. ALLEN, "Development of Speech Timing Control in Children," *Child Development* 46(1) (March 1975), 186–190.

VALLANCIEN, B. and B. GAUTHERON, "Speech Melody and Articulatory Melody," *Folia Phoniatrica* 26 (1974), 265–274.

WADSWORTH, B.J., *Piaget's Theory of Cognitive Development*. New York: D. McKay, 1971.

WALSH, H., "On Certain Practical Inadequacies of Distinctive Feature Systems," *J Speech Hearing Disorders* 39(1) (February 1974), 32–43.

WEIMAN, L.A., "Stress Patterns of Early Child Language," *J Child Language* 3(2) (1976), 283–286.

WEIR, RUTH, *Language in the Crib*. The Hague: Mouton, 1962.

WHITAKER, H.A., *On the Representation of Language in the Human Brain*. Alberta, Canada: Linguistic Research, Inc., 1971.

WINITZ, H., *Articulatory Acquisition and Behavior*. Englewood Cliffs, N.J.: Prentice-Hall, Inc., 1969.

WINITZ, H., "Articulation Disorders: From Prescription to Description," *J Speech Hearing Disorders* 42(2) (May 1977), 143–147.

ZERN, DAVID and AMIE LOU TAYLOR, "Rhythmic Behavior in the Hierarchy of Responses of Preschool Children," *Merrill-Palmer Quarterly* 19(2) (April 1973), 137–145.

chapter 6

HALLMARKS OF ORAL LANGUAGE
Syntactic Development

HALLMARK 4: SYNTACTIC DEVELOPMENT

> Ignorant people think it's the noise which
> fighting cats make that is so aggravating,
> but it ain't so; it's the sickening grammar
> they use.
>
> Mark Twain

Basic Considerations

Theories and the Practice

Theories of syntactical development have not been included in this discussion. Complete texts on the structure of language are available. I leave the theories of generative grammar, linguistic competence and performance, and grammatical transformations to the linguist. The linguist's laboratory and his materials serve a purpose different from ours in many respects. We have tried to sort out the syntactical knowledge that is applicable to our teaching.

The linguist may find that "Grammar is all" for him. Well and good, but, in my experience, teaching the structural development of oral language by application of rules has not been effective in terms of time or target. Despite the insistence of linguists on structural rules, I doubt that one can find two identical sentences produced by competent speakers of any language. Moreover linguists do their work on immaculate prose.[1] Such prose consists of grammatically correct sentences with nouns, verbs, and other parts of speech in their proper places. Our classroom, however, is not a linguistics laboratory. We are concerned with children's oral language, not adult language. More significantly, we teach language-retarded children, about whom theoreticians in linguistics have little first-hand knowledge and certainly limited teaching experience.

Structure of Child and Adult Speech

If we should follow the precepts of the theoreticians in teaching, we would employ a structure that few actually use, for people do not naturally speak in sentences. Most of us realize this in an intuitive way, but I suspect that few appreciate just how untidy normal conversations really are. In the boarding lounge of a Portland airport on a recent Sunday afternoon in June, I was surrounded by a party of six adults returning from a wedding reception. I taped their spirited forty-five-minute conversation. In this "normal human conversation" there were two complete sentences! Another observer recorded the conversation of two typists who were solving an equipment-assembly problem. Not one grammatically correct sentence appeared in the entire protocol; yet "the information got through," and the members completed their task successfully in less than the average time.[2] Adults do not speak in complete sentences, and the majority could not pass a test on the rules of grammar.[3] My teacher friends speak acceptable conversational English, but they cannot give an example of the conditional present tense. As for the plural possessive or the proper use of the pronoun in the objective case (how many times have you heard college graduates say "for him *and I?*"), they might be able to cite the rule, but they rarely apply it in speaking. Undoubtedly my friends are able to write English with a degree of accuracy, but written English and spoken English are miles apart. Certainly teachers should understand the rules of grammar. My belief, however, is that rules are of little use in teaching oral language at any age. Neither do I support the common claim of linguists that syntactic development is

[1] A. Ortony, "Language Isn't for People: On Applying Theoretical Linguistics to Practical Problems," *Review Educational Research* 45 (1975), 485–504.

[2] A. Chapanis, "Interactive Human Communication," *Scientific American* 232(3) (March 1975), 36–50.

[3] L.J. Sanders, "The Comprehension of Certain Syntactic Structures by Adults," *J Speech Hearing Research* 14(4) (December 1971), 739–745.

essentially complete by the age of five years.[4] Like all aspects of language learning, one rarely "reaches criterion" in his lifetime. So let the linguist stick to his last. We have quite a different concern: teaching children to comprehend and use oral language.

The Subordination of Syntax in Early Language Learning

Our reasons for placing knowledge of structure in a secondary role are based on our teaching experience, observation of other programs, and on the psychology of learning.

1. Perceptual-semantic development, we maintain, occupies prime time in order of development and importance. The child's primary purpose is to express semantic intention. His "earliest patterned speech is not organized in terms of knowledge of grammatical categories, but in terms of more fundamental coordinations of conceptual meanings with phonetic (and rhythmic) outputs." [5] This finding is supported by other studies, that is, that perceptual development, rather than knowledge of particular syntactic structures, is the key to language development at this early stage.[6] In fact, the child manifests minimum use of syntactic information in the early stages of language acquisition. As percepts become less fuzzy and the motivation and reward of communicating more intense, an embryonic framework emerges in child language, but it is not a true syntactic framework. Both in comprehension and expression, *word order* governs all at this early level.[7] And semantic intention and meaning, in turn, govern the word order. Theoretically syntactic development may present a neat construct which children supposedly follow. In practice they pay greater attention to the semantic and pragmatic intentions they want to convey. This is not to

[4] F.S. Kessel, "The Role of Syntax in Children's Comprehension from Ages Six to Twelve," *Monographs of the Society for Research in Child Development* 35(6) (September 1970), 54.

[5] J. Dore and others, "Transitional Phenomena in Early Language Acquisition," *J Child Language* 3(1) (February 1976), 13–28; P.A. deVilliers and J. deVilliers, "Early Judgments of Semantic and Syntactic Acceptability by Children," *J Psycho-Linguistic Research* 1(4) (1972), 299–310.

[6] R.S. Prawat and H. Jones, "A Longitudinal Study of Language Development in Children at Different Levels of Cognitive Development," *Merrill-Palmer Quarterly* 23(2) (April 1977), 118; H. Strohner and K.E. Nelson, "The Young Child's Development of Sentence Comprehension: Influence of Event Probability, Nonverbal Context, Syntactic Form, and Strategies," *Child Development* 45(3) (September 1974), 567–576.

[7] M.D. Braine, "Children's First Word Combinations," *Monographs Society Research Child Development* 41(1) (1976), 90–93; R.S. Chapman and L.L. Kohn, "Comprehensive Strategies in Two and Three Year Olds: Animate Agents or Probable Events?" *J Speech Hearing Research* 21(4) (December 1978), 746–761.

say that a kind of structure is not present in beginning oral language. Even the one-word sentence has structural status. In a one-word sentence, the agent often is followed by a gesture indicating the object. The object is linked semantically with the agent. And as semantic relations are observed in two- and three-word sentences, they likewise have structural status, but their structure also is derived from word order.[8] Some scholars argue that the subordination of grammar to semantic relations obtains only in the initial steps in language learning. Does it ever occupy first place in the use of oral language? Asking directions in a service station in a Maine village, I understood the boy's response, "It's up yonder piece." His purpose was to communicate and with the aid of gestures, his meaning was clear. Perhaps by the age of seven or eight years, the child's knowledge of rules of structure may assist the understanding of semantic relations, but it is clearly secondary to it. In my experience with "older" children, six to ten years old, systematic training in semantic relations within and between linguistic units is far more productive (and exciting) than training in a "preposition deficit." [9]

2. Another reason for subordinating syntax to other hallmarks of language learning is that little children are not motivated to "make sentences." It is not an enjoyable adventure for five- or even eight-year-olds because both the form and function are foreign to the child's pragmatic needs. I have observed innumerable classes in oral language development in which sentence making was the target. The classes were dull, dull as dishwater. The sentences seemed to be "baked," stifling the kind of creativity that is needed for a child to be fully at home with an *action*. The passive voice is an illustration of a new form and a new function, but will the five-year-old learn to *use* it from this lesson?: "Ask the child which picture shows *The milk was eaten by the cat. The door was closed by Janet. The boy was chased by the girl.*" Does he need to learn it? From a rhetorical standpoint, the active voice is much to be preferred in all types of communication. As DeVito remarks, "the little words introduced by passive transformation . . . increase the *lexical redundancy.*" [10] Certainly this is not the goal the language teacher has in mind. Few adults pepper their speech with passives. The tag question usually is another early target in sentence making. Why bother the child with the complex apparatus of the tag questions when *right?* or *huh?* achieve the same purpose, even in

---

[8] P.M. Greenfield and J.H. Smith, *The Structure of Communication in Early Language Development* (New York: Academic Press, 1976), 67.

[9] L.V. McReynolds, "Application of Systematic Procedures in Clinical Environments," chapter 7 *Developing Systematic Procedures for Training Children's Language,* ed. L.V. McReynolds, *Asha Monographs* No. 18, August 1974.

[10] J.A. DeVito, "Some Psycholinguistic Aspects of Active and Passive Sentences," *Quarterly J Speech* 55(4) (December 1969), 401–404.

adult language? If the child uses the simple declarative and imperative with the tag-end question, is it not intelligible?

3. A third reason for eliminating formal lessons in syntactical development is that the transfer of such learning to language use in the home or on the playground is minimal, particularly when it is taught in a clinic-oriented environment. Like the ninth glass of lemonade, appetite for that kind of learning declines in inverse ratio. When I praised a youngster for his success as he was leaving such a class, he responded, "Geez, that's not the way I really talk." I am reminded of a noted stuttering comedian who bemoaned the fact that he had learned to say, "Peter Piper picked a peck of pickled peppers," but he found very few occasions when he could use it.

Secondary Factors Contributing to Syntactic Development

The evolution of linguistic structure depends primarily on perceptual-semantic development and cannot be separated from it or from the primary precursor of both: intellectual capacity. Neither can syntax be taught except as it becomes "part and parcel" of perceptual-semantic development. In other words, structural relationships are based on semantic percepts, and until a child has the semantic percept, until he is aware of the meaning, he cannot correct the grammar in an ungrammatical sentence. It is in this perspective that we discuss factors which contribute to perceptual-semantic development but which are particular aids in the acquisition of syntax.

Among these secondary, but strong, contributory factors are: 1. the child's ability to imitate spontaneously the speech he hears in his environment; 2. socioenvironmental influences; and 3. neurophysiological determinants.

Imitation

Before the age two and a half to three years, the child is not aware of the fact that he is imitating his elders, sibs, or other children. The degree to which he evinces spontaneous imitation of the melody pattern at this stage will depend on auditory and tactile-kinesthetic-motor feedback. If his sensorimotor system is developing very slowly, judged by other patterns of behavioral adjustment, he will show little inclination to copy any melody patterns. The child with good sensorimotor equipment, on the other hand, imitates in toto the melodic phrase or sentence, sometimes repeating words with unusual emphasis. These words generally become cue words to understanding. The melodic pattern determines the structural order. Although we call this imitation spontaneous, it rarely occurs at the immediate time or in the immediate situation. Some time after the event, perhaps in his bed, the child will "rehearse" the phrase or sentence in its prosodic envelope.

The extent to which he engages in spontaneous imitation, immediate or delayed, will be dictated by his comprehension of the vocabulary, his familiarity with a new, but *not too new* structure, and by the length of utterance which must be within his memory span.[11] That the most likely imitation occurs when the pattern is known, but is quite new, agrees with Kagan's observation that only the *relatively new* stimulus, that which can be fitted into some hypothesis the child already has, will be attended to. To the absolutely new he reacts defensively; the old familiar stimuli he disregards.

In the succeeding stages of syntactic development, imitation, although present, is rarely the result of elicited or directive imitation ("Now say what I say."). Mothers of children in the third year report that although they encourage spontaneous imitation, they find elicited imitation to be unsuccessful and, hence, they seldom employ it.[12] I am sure that my colleagues have had a similar experience: When a child is told, "Say it like this," he usually will not do so. He either makes up his own phrases or sentences—or he is silent. Later, away from other children and from teachers, he may try to rehearse various ways in which to "say it."

When children reach kindergarten age, they frequently imitate each other's verbalization exactly when talking together but seldom do so when talking to adults. It is, of course, spontaneous imitation. This, it seems to me, is further confirmation of the fact that "older" children, five to eight years, learn language more quickly from other children than from adults.[13] Spontaneous imitation serves several purposes. Some children repeat the utterance because they are seeking further information; that is, they are unsure of the meaning; they repeat it to understand it more fully. Others repeat the sentence with an altered prosodic pattern in order to test a change in meaning; others turn the utterance into a question. In short, imitation has a pragmatic purpose. Some children rarely resort to imitation because the speech that they hear in the home or school is highly directive and subjective; it does not stimulate imitative responses.[14]

[11] P.L. Dale, *Language Development* (Chicago: Holt, Rinehart and Winston, 1976), 116.

[12] D. Ling and A. Ling, "Communication Development in the First Three Years of Life," *J Speech Hearing Research* 17(1) (March 1974), 146–159.

[13] J.B. Gleason, "Code Switching in Children's Language," *Cognitive Development and the Acquisition of Language,* ed. T.E. Moore (New York: Academic Press, 1973).

[14] J.P. Folger and R.S. Chapman, "A Pragmatic Analysis of Spontaneous Imitation," *J Child Language* 5(1) (February 1978), 25–38; L.K. Synder-McLean and J.S. Mc-

The extent to which elicited imitation or modeling is effective with linguistically retarded children is moot. Even if the child learned and remembered fifty or a hundred sentences by this method, he would not generate and remember other sentences from this core. Furthermore imitation or modeling is rigid because it is imposed upon the child. It is not his creation, and the sentences are unrelated to the event that cause *his* language behavior. On the other hand, imitation may be a very useful technique in initiating communication with nonverbal children. "The establishment of a tendency to imitate and an initial vocal or verbal repertoire might be the first step in producing communicative, if not yet linguistic, behavior." [15]

Socioenvironmental Influences

It goes almost without the saying that the child's interactions with the people in his immediate environment—their actions, habits of speech, and educational and cultural standards—will affect his language development, either positively or negatively. Interaction, however, is a two-way street, and we are not certain of the effect of the adult's action on the child. Does the mother interact physically and verbally with the child, even as early as one month after his birth? Is her interaction consistent or erratic? As the child develops, does the mother nurture understanding and oral response by using very simple sentences, repeating important parts and accompanying them with repetitive gestures? Does she stimulate the child's motivation to respond by picture books, by reading stories aloud? Does she engage in language play with the child?

We also do not know all the factors within the child's make-up which determine the vigor and extent of his or her interaction. Many investigations have gone forward, but no "final report" has been filed. Paucity of experience and its correlate, lack of motivation, have been postulated. Inner-city children, we are told, receive lower scores on all tests of morphology and syntax.[16] Immediately we must ask: What scores derived from what tests? Did the inner-city children use a dialect which was acceptable and well developed by other standards than those used in tests employing middle-class white standards? Consider the ghetto child's psychological reaction to such tests, indeed his feeling of alienation from

---

Lean, "Verbal Information Gathering Strategies: The Child's Use of Language to Acquire Language," *J Speech Hearing Disorders* 43(3) (August 1978), 306–325.

[15] N.S. Rees, "Imitation and Language Development: Issues and Clinical Implications," *J Speech Hearing Disorders* 40 (August 1975), 339–350.

[16] M. Lively-Weiss, and D.E. Koller, "Selected Language Characteristics of Middle-Class and Inner-City Children," *J Communication Disorders* 6 (1973), 293–302.

all learning when he is made to feel that his language, dialectal or bilingual, is not to be used in school. The effects of one's environment on structure cannot be assessed with any surety. One suspects, but cannot prove, that the structure of our speech, more than any other single dimension of language, reflects our immediate environment.[17]

Neurophysiological Determinants

We know that neurophysical disabilities, and particularly those associated with the speech and hearing processes, can and do retard the development of oral language. The child with a central or peripheral hearing handicap, the cerebral-palsied child with sensorimotor disabilities affecting tactile-kinesthetic-motor and auditory feedback, the child handicapped by cleft palate: all may suffer from peripheral and/or central neurophysical handicaps impairing oral language development. We are puzzled particularly by the language retardation of the child handicapped by cleft palate because it does not seem to be related directly to the anatomic anomaly. The possibility of an associated deficiency in the sensorimotor innervation of the facial muscles has been suggested. Having taught hundreds of these children in a resident speech center, I would add that these children talk less and hence have limited experience in the perception and expression of oral language. We have no valid measure of haptic perceptual abilities. Tests of oral stereognosis, although interesting, tell us little about these sensory modalities. The field of auditory perception is replete with theories, research data, and measures. Their validity when applied to the speech continuum is yet to be established. A review of Chapter 2 will provide you with a more detailed discussion of the neurophysical basis of these language disabilities.

Practices in Teaching Syntactic Development

Dependence on Other Hallmarks

If teaching is to be effective, syntax cannot be taught as a separate unit. Structures must be taught in conjunction with their perceptual-semantic correlates.[18] In fact, the *form* of an utterance may be dictated

---

[17] I. Holdstein and J.F. Borus, "Kibbutz and City Children: A Comparative Study of Syntactic and Articulatory Abilities," *J Speech Hearing Disorders* 41(1) (February 1976), 10–15.

[18] "In many ways the acquisition of a language resembles the formation of a percept. In both language acquisition and perception there is a preliminary analytic phase, during which general properties are worked out, followed by a constructive phase, during which details are elaborated."—D. McNeill, *The Acquisition of Language* (New York: Harper and Row, 1970), 3.

more by its communication function and its sociophysical context than by any grammar system per se.[19] The child's generation of the structure follows, does not precede, the meaning and cannot be separated from it. So we do not believe in teaching exercises in "making sentences." The linguistic forms which the child uses will depend on his perceptual-semantic and prosodic growth; and this, in turn, depends upon many factors in his language environment. Thinking follows a plan, and it is the projection of this plan in verbalization which determines the structure. The syntactic forms that appear early in a child's oral language are the result of the child's intellectual advance.

Current Teaching Practices

Predication vs. the noun phrase.   Little children generally are taught first to name objects, persons, pets; then colors, numbers, pieces of clothing. The popular and endless exercise beginning "This is a _____" really tells us little, if anything, about performative language and the pragmatic intentions of the child. Perception is translated into action which demands predication. Hence, if the child wants to express action—and he generally does—he must use verbs, not isolated nouns. Verbs truly constitute "the real motor behind the critically important process of predication." [20] The normal *performative language* of a little child reflects action involving motion verbs and verbs showing change of location, aided always by bodily gestures. By contrast, the act of naming tells us little about the child's pragmatic intentions in communication. Naming exercises, in many instances in my observation, actually have stultified intellectual and language development. My inclination in such situations has been to cry out, "But what does he say *about* the puppy, *about* Pojo, *about* Snoopy? Tell me more! Run with him! Jump with him! Then he will remember his name." I did not cry out; another deck of picture cards is brought out; another thirty minutes of "This is a _____."

Prepositions.   Even less important in the determination of structural relations are prepositions, although they seem to constitute the major part of language training in many teaching programs. The great emphasis put on prepositions seems completely disproportionate to their significance. They are, in fact, a minor syntactic category. As Roger Brown writes, little children "generally do not use prepositions, conjunctions,

---

[19] Snyder-McLean and McLean, "Verbal Information," 306–325.
[20] A.M. Liberman, I.G. Mattingly, and M.T. Turvey, "Language Codes and Memory Codes," *Coding Processes in Human Memory,* eds. A.W. Melton and E. Martin (Washington, D.C.: V.H. Winston & Sons, 1972), 338.

articles or auxiliary verbs." [21] And older children will use them as they learn that structural relationships are in themselves semantic percepts. The prepositions, *in, on, up, down,* for example, have meaning only as it accrues to them in the context of the utterance. Suppose that the child wants to communicate the time of an action, action ongoing or completed, or his concept of possession and other relational percepts. The context in which he does it must be real, not contrived, expressed in his words and in the terms in which he construes reality. In short, the child will express semantic functions relative to his experience and environment, employing the proper structural relationship *when he understands that relation.* [22] Exercises in the use of prepositions, divorced from the child's reality, his language environment and his language needs are busy work, a time waster.

Learning rules of grammar vs. logical relationships. What I have said about exercises on prepositions applies to teaching rules of grammar in general. Rules are semantically empty. What you, the teacher, must motivate is the child's understanding, not of a rule, but of the logical relationships to be comprehended or expressed. In short, the child will express semantic functions *relative to the pragmatic needs in his world,* employing the proper structural relationship when he understands that relation. Language teachers frequently judge the "older" child's syntactical development by his use of complex sentences. In some respects it tells us more about a child's total language development than any other aspect of syntactical development. Why? Because it reflects his perceptual-semantic knowledge, not only of logical relationships demanding coordination and subordination, but also of semantic, phonatory, and phonological values. The mechanics, from the syntactic point of view, is called *embedding,* that is, the inclusion of one sentence as a grammatical constituent of another sentence, whether the constituent be subject, object, verb complement, or some sort of adverbial or adjectival modification. From the view of logical relationship, it places a proposition in a particular *semantic role* within another proposition. Your objective, as the special language teacher, is to develop those entities and relationships in situations which are a part of the child's world.

The use of evaluation measures as teaching guides. Lest we be misunderstood at the outset, let us make clear that the tests we are about to discuss are *not* to be used as tests. Since no test of syntax takes into

[21] Roger Brown, *A First Language:* The Early Stages (Cambridge, Mass.: Harvard University Press, 1973), 75.
[22] R. Brown, "Language: The System and Its Acquisition," chap. 6 *Social Psychology* (New York: The Free Press, 1965), 294.

consideration the perceptual-semantic base of syntactic development, a score is meaningless. What we *are* suggesting is that language teachers take advantage of the research on the progression of structural forms in language development. She should incorporate these structures in the materials she has gathered, materials adapted to the needs and interests of the children she is teaching. The *Berry-Talbott Developmental Guide to the Comprehension of Grammar* can be used in this way.[23] No score is possible; no age equivalent can be found. The Guide includes the features of English grammar most commonly understood and used by a child in the lower grades of the public schools (K–3). These features are: a.) the third person singular of the verb; b.) the progressive and past tense of the verb; c.) plural of nouns; d.) comparative and superlative forms of the adjective; e.) negative transformations; f.) possessives of the noun; and g.) five prepositions. We have not included the use of the passive voice because we can find little verification of its use in our study of the oral language by children, even among adolescents. As a result of using this Guide with dyslexic children, Vogel comments that it was a source of "useful information for the clinician or language therapist." [24]

The fallibility of objective tests as tests. In view of the popular demand for objective test results, perhaps I should document more completely my reservations with respect to them and why I use them, not as tests, but as materials for teaching. I know that school administrators still are demanding that language teachers in the public schools report percentage or age-equivalent scores for all children in special language programs. Many teachers know that scores are meaningless, but they have a tendency to respond to the pressures from administrators and crediting authorities, those "pedagogical plainsmen" who are so obsessed with norms and averages that they shovel off peaks of excellence to make plains of uniformities.[25] Only recently have language educators questioned the validity of objective tests and particularly of tests of syntax. Their action might seem to be heretical, for textbooks have been written and volumes of research published in which syntactic competence has been regarded as the only true measure of language learning. It is, we were told, the "word and the way."

We question both the premise and the validity of the test scores. Why? Because, as we have said in the opening paragraph of this section, the semantic correlates of the grammatical classes being assessed are not a

---

[23] The *Berry-Talbott Developmental Guide to the Comprehension of Grammar,* 1977. (Published and distributed by Mildred F. Berry, 4332 Pine Crest Road, Rockford, Illinois 61107.)

[24] S.A. Vogel, *Syntactic Abilities in Normal and Dyslexic Children* (Baltimore: University Park Press, 1975), 70–71.

[25] D. Wolfle, "Pedagogical Plainsmen," *Science* 199(4331) (February 24, 1978), 843.

part of the test. Children employ structures to serve particular uses in communication. The perceptual-semantic percepts rising from pragmatic intentions, which children express, simply are not present in the syntactic test batteries now in use. The structural forms are there, but the language and the ideas are foreign to the children. Developmental scoring tests, for example, are particularly vulnerable in this respect because, 1.) they have been constructed from the language used in formal "clinical" or class situations; and 2.) because the sample of sentences is too small.[26] But even if 175 sentences were required for reliability instead of the fifty sentences, even if norms had been established after testing sizable groups of children with varying socioeconomic backgrounds (which was not the case), even if the sentence making were carried on in a completely natural, unstructured, nonclinical situation, the test would still suffer because it does not deal with the children's perceptual-semantic correlates of structure. The sentences are not relevant to their pragmatic needs of communication. They are, in fact, new, both in form and function, and hence unfamiliar. Some children will respond to new forms that express old functions or new functions that are first expressed by old forms, but they will be silent when called upon to express new functions in new forms. Here is an example of a test for four-year-olds embracing both *new forms and new functions*. It is a pictured story with the accompanying narrative:

> This is the police station.
> Those are police cars.
> Here is a man. See him.
> He wears a big star on his coat.
> He drives the police car.
> He is a policeman.
> Who is he?

Target response: He is the policeman.

Would a child in a beginning language development group respond to the question by saying, "He is the policeman"? Here is a taped report of a group of preschoolers who have just returned from a visit to a police

---

[26] B.J. Hellner, *The Temporal Reliability of the 50-Sentence Language Sample.* (Unpublished Master's Thesis, Illinois State University, August 1974); M.R. Johnson and J.B. Tomblin, "The Reliability of Developmental Sentence Scoring as a Function of Sample Size," *J Speech Hearing Research* 18(2) (June 1975), 372–380; T.M. Longhurst and J.J. File, "A Comparison of Development Sentence Scores from Head Start Children Collected in Four Conditions, *Language Speech and Hearing Services in Schools* 8(1) (January 1977), 54–64.

station. The teacher asked two questions of the group; the first: "What did you (dja) see?" "Peesmans," said one. "Uh-uh," said Joe shaking his head, "two bu cars" (blue cars), and he held up first one and then two fingers. "And we seed peesmans, lots of'm," proffered Billy. "Big hats," said another, gesturing to show size. The teacher returned to the earlier comment: "Who? two policemen?" "Naw, fwee (three) peesmans," Billy insisted, holding up three fingers. The teacher did not pursue the irregular plural, the past tense, or the phonemic distortions: $/\theta/$, $/r/$, and $/l/$. She did continue the question of numbers, a concept for which they were ready. Three months later, the same group of preschoolers visited the local airport. Here are some "sentences" from a taped report: "We seen two mans n̩ (in a?) big airp(l)ane," whereupon another child broke in with scornful intonation, "Big? Not big! Daddy f(l)yed (on) big, big p(l)ane; this (one at the airport) wi-a [lɪtl] p(l)ane." After vivid simulations of the noisy take-off, still another child exclaimed, "Fwyed high up—way-wayup (in the) (s)ky." The teacher later repeated several times in talking about the trip the structures, "we saw" and "two men." Some youngsters changed *mans* to *men* but continued to say *seen,* instead of *saw,* probably because it was regular usage in their environment. The teacher did not try to correct other irregular forms but played a game with flying toy planes in order to strengthen the consonant clusters: *fl* and *pl.* Contrast these utterances with the earlier example of a formal lesson. The conversations at the police station and airport strike me as the real language of children communicating their semantic intentions and feelings in a real situation. The structure has its semantic correlates. Objective test materials, by contrast, seem to be semantically empty exercises.

As long as one understands that knowledge of the forms of syntax—tense, plural, possessive, negative, and so on—is only one element of its development, he might use developmental test *schedules* as rough guides to *progression* in this element. But certainly the schedules cannot be used as the major criteria by which to appraise a child's growing competence in syntax.

Beyond Syntactic Forms:
More Fundamental Considerations

Earlier in this chapter we discussed considerations which transcend the forms of oral language. Before we go to more specific steps in structural development, let us review some general principles which pertain to children's learning of language structure.

Syntactic development is *not a continuous incremental process* with today's accomplishment becoming part of tomorrow's competence. Like all learning, learning of structure often proceeds at an uneven pace—and sometimes there is retrogression. The assumption that as a child gets older and progressively bigger, he also gets progressively better at any kind of perceptual, intellectual, or motor task is an assumption, unsupported by fact.[27] Teachers should be prepared for these uneven increments of progress among children. In some instances children will not advance in the knowledge and use of personal pronouns, verb tense (present, past), or functors (the little words) for several months and then quite perceptibly will forge ahead. With other linguistically deviant children, the acquisition lag is consistent.

The syntactic forms that children use at any stage of development—morpheme or syllable strings, one-word "sentences," phrases, and sentences employing negatives, wh-questions, auxiliary verbs, or relative clauses—any of these forms is significant in syntactic development only *when its use is considered in relation to pragmatic functions, perceptual-semantic factors, and the social environment.* Children have to understand the syntax of the phrase or sentence in terms of its perceptual-semantic correlates and its relations with the whole utterance, or they will not use it. This interrogative sentence appears in a formal test for children in kindergarten: *Why didn't the girl sit down?* In the first place the average kindergartner would find the structure too complex for immediate comprehension and repetition. Secondly the context is completely alien: A picture of strangely garbed people in an unfamiliar setting and situation. Finally the child would not use such a structure at this level of learning.

Is *sentence length* or *complexity* the critical measure of growth? One is inclined to regard longer and longer sentences as a favorable sign of syntactic development in early child language. But as we know from our experience both with children and adults, a sentence can go on and on like a roller towel, communicating nothing.

Many linguists have regarded the mean length of utterance (MLU) as the most valid measure of development in early child language.[28] Obviously sentence length does increase with age but not in any strict linear relation. We also have found it difficult to know how to measure the sentence length of children's utterances. You teachers have studied tapes of the speech of preschool and kindergarten children so you know how difficult it is to identify when a sentence *is,* in truth, a sentence or where a sentence begins and ends. Furthermore many human variables enter into

---

[27] T.G.R. Bower, "Repetitive Processes in Child Development," *Scientific American* 235(5) (November 1976), 38–47.

[28] Brown, *A First Language,* 53–55.

the question of sentence length. The speech style of ethnic groups, of dialect areas; the social and educational backgrounds of parents; the socioeconomic status of the child's community: all are factors affecting the length of utterance.[29] And even more important is the fact that the length of a sentence is little indication of the effective use of structure in communicating meaning. If we were forced to take a single measuring stick, I suppose that sentence complexity would tell us more about a child's *perception* of the meaning of structure and its semantic relations than any other single aspect of syntactic development. Sentence complexity implies a knowledge of these semantic values and also of prosodic constraints which affect structure. As vocabulary and comprehension of syntax grow, the child generally will find more ways of "saying it." The resulting complex sentence is a sign of facility in the use of language. A problem, yet unsolved, is to find a common basis for judgment of degrees of sentence complexity. In other words, what factors determine that one sentence is more complex than another sentence? [30] You who teach these children are the ones to solve the problem.

We must pay particular attention to the child who *begins late* with a few single words and then *continues these one-word responses* for months. The persistence in naming, the use of a few nouns for eight months to a year after onset, is an unfavorable prognostic sign. Unfortunately neither parents nor teachers seem to understand that a child must be motivated to communicate an action or interaction. Naming objects, people, pets, and so on rarely contributes to action and interaction.

Time and tense, which theoretically should be concordant, often cannot be equated. The forms of the copula, *to be,* for example, may not relate to time in communication. No time element, for example, is present in "there are," "it is," and so on; yet they are forms frequently taught in the very early stages of sentence making.

We must guard ourselves against using adult language as a model for child speakers. My three-year-old friend, Gille, said, "Yours, that no ice cream. This my ice cream—good!" Gille is not a poor speaker of adult language; she is a good speaker of child language.

Developing Your Teaching Guides
to Structural Development

In the course of the first six weeks of exploratory teaching, you will want, 1.) to develop a base level of syntactic development both in the com-

---

[29] F. Minifie, F. Darley and D. Sherman, "Temporal Reliability of Seven Language Measures," *J Speech Hearing Research* 6(1) (March 1963), 139–148.

[30] D. Crystal, P. Fletcher, and M. Garman, *The Grammatical Analysis of Language Disability* (London: Edward Arnold, 1976), 27.

prehension and use of structural language in your group; and 2.) to identify the primary problems of children who exhibit a lag in structural development. In realizing these purposes, you will need to keep a chronicle of the structures which each child regularly uses in connected speech, structures which express true perceptual-semantic relations. The second purpose, the identification and appraisal of linguistic deviations, is not so readily accomplished. A complex of factors, ill-defined and ambiguous, is frequently associated with deviant structure.

What means will you use to secure this information? Certainly you will not use a screening test! It will only lead you to a squirrel track and up a tree. Here are three better ways:

1. Assemble extensive taped samples of connected speech of your children in varied speech events. Depending on the developmental level of the group, the speech events may include directive speech (requests, commands, and instructions); role play (playing house, cleaning, baking, and so on); make-believe experiences (original drama, replication of a TV program, or construction experiences such as making a walkie-talkie system, picture taking, slide and/or film making, gardening) "special day" parties (greetings, social talk, particular duties calling for speech), and so on. In selecting speech events, I find that commercially packaged materials are generally of little help for the reason that they do not fit the current interests, the socioeconomic environment, or the level of development of the children. Conservation may seem a very advanced topic for third graders; yet I know that in one language class, it produced a long and animated series of exchanges about recycling paper and containers and in another class, a very exciting discussion about solar heating which was followed by a visit to a solar home. I cannot vouch for the accuracy of this story, but it illustrates a point which I have stressed throughout the book: Two second-graders who were standing on the school playground during recess saw a jet fly over. "Look at that," said one lad, "it's a B747." "No, a 727," said the other. "You can tell by its tail engines." "You're right," the first youngster conceded. "Not going more than 600 m.p.h. either because it didn't break the sound barrier." On this point they both agreed. "Geez, what a friction drag on those planes travelling at that speed!" the second boy said. At this point the bell called the children back into the classroom. The first boy turned to the second. "There's the bell," he sighed. "Let's go back in and finish stringing those darn beads."

2. Collate the replies from your letters to parents (see PR, *Parents Respond,* Appendix A–8 for examples) in which you have asked them to note or tape dinner table or TV conversations, arguments, jokes, riddles, and so on and to report words, phrases, and sentences which the child habitually uses at home.

3. Enlist the cooperation of your colleagues in supplying you with frequent notes on the actual phrases, sentence fragments, and sentences which your children use in the other classes, on the playground, in the lunch room, and so forth.

Questions for You, the Teacher

This series of questions, based on the principles discussed earlier in this chapter, should assist you in the discovery of the base syntactic level of your group and the children who exhibit a definite linguistic lag:

1. Perceptual-semantic correlates of syntax

   a. Does the base level of the child's structural development match or is it below his perceptual-semantic development?
   b. Does he comprehend the perceptual-semantic relations in the structure he uses?
   c. Does the structure aid or hinder him in the expression of his semantic intentions and pragmatic needs?
   d. Is he able to make his semantic and pragmatic intentions clear to others only with the aid of gestural language?

2. Environmental influences

   a. Is the child's linguistic style a copy of the linguistic style of the adults in his environment?

      1) Does he imitate spontaneously the prosodic and syntactic patterns of parents and peers in his language environment?
      2) Are faulty atypical syntactic structures, sentence fragments, verb forms, use of pronouns, and so on characteristic of the ethnic and/or socioeducational environment in which he lives?
      3) Are the motivation and rewards of structured communication present in his home environment?
      4) Does he generate new structures, not present in his environment?

3. Syntactic use at the preschool level

   a. Does he generally use word order, a presyntactic structure, to communicate meaning? Are such utterances always aided by gestural language?
   b. Does the phrase or sentence fragment fit within the prosodic frame?
   c. Do word order and the prosodic pattern carry the semantic relations he wishes to convey?
   d. Does the child make spontaneous corrections in word order as evidenced by revisions and false starts?
   e. Do communicative intent, prosody, and body language carry the meaning when structural relations are faulty?
   f. Does he use nouns or noun phrases exclusively to express meaning?

g. Does he communicate only in one-word "sentences"?

h. Does the word order express clearly agent-verb-(action)-object?

i. Does he use verb phrases other than *want to, need to, have to* in order to express semantic intent?

j. Does he ask *what* and *when* questions by attaching a tag-end word (*huh, o.k., right?*) to a declarative statement?

k. Does he occasionally or regularly use the functors *in* and *on?*

4. Syntactic use from kindergarten through second grade

a. Does the kindergartner extend the verbs in common usage (*fall down, play with, hang up, pick up, sit down, stand up, cut out, run away*) to new instances, new experiences?

b. Does he use different forms for the question?

c. Are demand and negation more frequent responses than questions and explanations?

d. Does a word have but one meaning or can the child expand the meaning of a word to adapt it to different uses?

e. Can he extend the phrase, the clause, when pressed by his peers?

f. Does the kindergartner connect sentences with the conjunctions *and, so, because,* thus expressing a true conjunctive relationship, especially in narrative speech? (*I went with Daddy and he buyed me a lollypop.*)

g. Does the child use immediate and spontaneous imitation in order

1) to comprehend and remember the sentence structure and learn to use critical parts of the sentence structure?

2) to continue the dialogue in order to secure more information?

3) to let the other speaker know that he understands the utterance? He is not engaging in simple imitation in (2) and (3).[31]

h. Is his knowledge of vocabulary and forms sufficiently extensive to permit variety in the use of words and structure; that is, can he comprehend and "say it" in different ways?

i. Does he generate new structures which are not used in his environment but which he needs from a pragmatic standpoint?

j. Has he progressed from the simple coordinate sentence linked by the conjunction *and* to other connective forms producing *when, because, what,* or *if?*

k. In working with his peers in new experiences, particularly those which call for making and doing (constructive tasks such as holiday decorations, poster exhibits, reporting new experiences outside the classroom, devising new instruments, and so on), is there a notable advance in the child's use of structured speech with some variety in structure?

l. Has he succeeded in sentence transformations, particularly of *what, when, where* and *why* questions?

m. Does he employ complex sentences indicating causality, conditionality, or antithesis? Does he use *because, if, what, so, until?* ("What would you do if you lost your bus fare just as the bus stopped for you?")

n. Has he mastered the use of present, past, and future tenses?

---

[31] E.O. Keenan, "Making it Last: Repetition in Children's Discourse," *Child Discourse*, eds. S. Ervin-Tripp and C. Mitchell Kernan (New York: Academic Press, 1977), 126–129.

o. Is he skillful in embedding phrases and clauses or does he use the same forms over and over, producing a stereotyped speech?

p. Does he use a limited set of structures, reflecting perceptual deficits in comprehension of syntactic structures and their relations?

q. Does he understand the semantic relations in and between syntactic forms? (Noun phrases, verb phrases, prepositional phrases and clauses, compound sentences, interrogative sentences, negative sentences, and so forth.)

r. Is his oral expression fairly grammatical with respect to tense (present, past, future); pluralization of nouns; agreement of subject and verb in number; use of the possessive; comparative and superlative degrees; and use of the auxiliary verb?

REFERENCES

The Berry-Talbott Developmental Guide to the Comprehension of Grammar, 1977. (Published and distributed by M.F. Berry, 4332 Pine Crest Rd., Rockford, Ill. 61107.)

BOHANNON, J.N., "The Relationship Between Syntax Discrimination and Sentence Imitation in Children," *Child Development* 46(2) (June 1975), 444–451.

BOWER, T.G.R., "Repetitive Processes in Child Development," *Scientific American,* 235(5) (November 1976), 38–47.

BOWERMAN, M.F., "Discussion Summary—Development of Concepts Underlying Language," *Language Perspectives—Acquisition, Retardation, and Intervention,* eds., F.L. Schiefelbusch, and L.L. Lloyd, Baltimore: University Park Press, 1974, 191–210.

BOWERMAN, M., "Semantic Factors in the Acquisition of Rules for Word Use and Sentence Construction," *Normal and Deficient Language,* eds. D.M. Morehead and A.E. Morehead. Baltimore: University Park Press, 1976, 99–180.

BRAINE, M.D., "Children's First Word Combinations," *Monographs Society Research Child Development,* 41(1) (1976), 90–93.

BROWN, ROGER, "Language: The System and Its Acquisition," chap. 6, *Social Psychology.* New York: The Free Press, 1965.

BROWN, ROGER, *A First Language: The Early Stages.* Cambridge, Mass.: Harvard University Press, 1973.

BRUNER, J.S., "The Ontogenesis of Speech Acts," *J Child Language* 2(1) (April 1975), 1–19.

BURTON, D., *Language and Learning: Investigations and Interpretations.* Cambridge, Mass.: Harvard Educational Review Reprint Series No. 7, 1972.

CAZDEN, C.B., "The Acquisition of Noun and Verb Inflections," *Child Development,* 39(2) (1968), 433–448.

CAZDEN, C.B., *Child Language and Education.* New York: Holt, Rinehart and Winston, 1972.

CHAPANIS, A., "Interactive Human Communication," *Scientific American,* 232(3) (March 1975), 36–50.

CHAPMAN, R.S. and L.L. KOHN, "Comprehension Strategies in Two and Three Year Olds: Animate Agents or Probable Events?" *J Speech Hearing Research,* 21(4) (December 1978), 746–761.

CLARK, E.V., "Strategies for Communicating," *Child Development,* 49(4) (December 1978), 953–960.

COLE, P. and J.L. MORGAN, eds., *Syntax and Semantics, Vol. 3, Speech Acts.* New York: Academic Press, 1975.

CROMER, R.F., "Receptive Language in the Mentally Retarded: Processes and Diagnostic Distinctions," chap. 9, *Language Perspectives—Acquisition, Retardation, and Intervention,* eds. R.L. Schiefelbusch and L.L. Lloyd. Baltimore: University Park Press, 1974.

CRYSTAL, D., P. FLETCHER, and M. GORMAN, *The Grammatical Analysis of Language Disability.* London: Edward Arnold, 1976.

DALE, P.L., *Language Development.* Chicago: Holt, Rinehart and Winston, 1976.

DEVILLIERS, P.A. and J. DEVILLIERS, "Early Judgments of Semantic and Syntactic Acceptability by Children," *J Psycho-Linguistic Research,* 1(4) (1972), 299–310.

DEVITO, J.A., "Some Psycholinguistic Aspects of Active and Passive Sentences," *Quarterly J Speech,* 55(4) (December 1969), 401–404.

DORE, J. and others, "Transitional Phenomena in Early Language Acquisitions," *J Child Language,* 3(1) (February 1976), 13–28.

FERGUSON, C.A. and D.I. SLOBIN, eds., *Studies of Child Language Development.* New York: Holt, Rinehart and Winston, 1973.

FOELLINGER, D.B. and T. TRABASSO, "Seeing, Hearing and Doing: A Developmental Study of Memory for Action," *Child Development,* 48(4) (December 1977), 1482–1489.

FOLGER, J.P. and R.S. CHAPMAN, "A Pragmatic Analysis of Spontaneous Imitation," *J Child Language,* 5(1) (February 1978), 25–38.

GLEASON, J.B., "Code Switching in Children's Language," *Cognitive Development and the Acquisition of Language,* ed. T.E. Moore. New York: Academic Press, 1973.

GREEN, M.G., "Structure and Sequence in Children's Concepts of Chance and Probability," *Child Development,* 49(4) (December 1978), 1045–1053.

GREENFIELD, P.M. and J.H. SMITH, *The Structure of Communication in Early Language Development.* New York: Academic Press, 1976.

HELLNER, B.J., *The Temporal Reliability of the 50-Sentence Language Sample.* Unpublished Master's Thesis, Illinois State University, August 1974.

HOLDSTEIN, I. and J.F. BORUS, "Kubbutz and City Children: A Comparative Study of Syntactic and Articulatory Abilities," *J Speech Hearing Disorders* 41(1) (February 1976), 10–15.

HUNT, K.W., "Syntactic Maturity in School Children and Adults," *Monographs of the Society for Research in Child Development,* 35(1) (February 1970), 55–61.

INGRAM, D., "Developing Systematic Procedures for Training Children's Language," *Amer Speech Hear Assoc Monog* 18 (August 1974), 5–14.

JOHNSON, M.R. and J.B. TOMBLIN, "The Reliability of Developmental Sentence Scoring as a Function of Sample Size," *J Speech Hear Res,* 18(2) (June 1975), 372–380.

KEENAN, E.O., "Making it Last: Repetition in Children's Discourse," *Child Discourse,* eds. S. Ervin-Tripp and C. Mitchell Kernan. New York: Academic Press, 1977, 126–129.

KESSEL, F.S., "The Role of Syntax in Children's Comprehension from Ages Six to Twelve," *Monographs of the Society for Research in Child Development,* 35(6) (September 1970), 1–95.

KOENIGSKNECHT, R.A. and P. FRIEDMAN, "Syntax Development in Boys and Girls," *Child Development,* 47(4) (1976), 1109–1115.

KRAUSS, R.M. and S. GLUCKSBERG, "Social and Nonsocial Speech," *Scientific American,* 236(2) (February 1977), 100–105.

LAVATELLI, C.S., ed., *Language Training in Early Childhood Education.* Urbana, Illinois: University of Illinois Press, 1972.

LEWIS, M.M., *How Children Learn to Speak.* London: Harrap, 1957.

LIBERMAN, A.M., I.G. MATTINGLY, and M.T. TURVEY, "Language Codes and Memory Codes," *Coding Processes in Human Memory,* eds. A.W. Melton and E. Martin. Washington, D.C.: V.H. Winston & Sons, 1972.

LING, D. and A. LING, "Communication Development in the First Three Years of Life," *J Speech Hearing Research* 17(1) (March 1974), 146–159.

LIVELY-WEISS, M. and D.E. KOLLER, "Selected Language Characteristics of Middle-Class and Inner-City Children," *J Communication Disorders* 6 (1973), 293–302.

LONGHURST, T.M. and J.J. FILE, "A Comparison of Developmental Sentence Scores from Head Start Children Collected in Four Conditions," *Language Speech and Hearing Service in Schools,* 8(1) (January 1977), 54–64.

LOVE, J.M. and C. PARKER-ROBINSON, "Children's Imitation of Grammatical and Ungrammatical Sentences," *Child Development,* 43(2) (June 1972), 310–319.

MCLEAN, J.E. and L.E. SNYDER-MCLEAN, *A Transactional Approach to Early Language Training.* Columbus, Ohio: Chas. E. Merrill, 1978.

MCNEILL, D., *The Acquisition of Language.* New York: Harper and Row, 1970, 3.

MARSLEN-WILSON, W., "Committee on Cognition and Communication," *Science,* 189(4198) (18 July 1975), 226–227.

MENYUK, P., "Sentences Children Use," *Research Monograph 52.* Cambridge, Mass.: M.I.T. Press, 1969.

MENYUK, P. and P.L. LOONEY, "A Problem of Language Disorder: Length vs. Structure," *J Speech Hearing Research,* 15(2) (June 1972), 264–279.

MINIFIE, F., F. DARLEY and D. SHERMAN, "Temporal Reliability of Seven Language Measures," *J Speech Hearing Research,* 6(1) (March 1963), 139–148.

MONSEES, E.K., *Structured Language for Children With Special Language Learning Problems.* Washington, D.C.: Children's Hearing and Speech Center, 1972.

MUNSINGER, H. and A. DOUGLAS, "The Syntactic Abilities of Identical Twins, Fraternal Twins, and Their Siblings," *Child Development,* 47 (1976), 40–50.

NELSON, C., "Structure and Strategy in Learning to Talk," *Monographs of the Society for Research Child Development,* 38(1,2) (1973).

ORTONY, A., "Language Isn't for People: On Applying Theoretical Linguistics to Practical Problems," *Rev Educ Res,* 45 (1975), 485–504.

POPOVICH, L., "On the Nature of Elicited Imitation and Its Role in Language Assessment," *J Child Com Dis,* 2(2) (Fall-Winter 1978), 66–75.

PRAWAT, R.S. and H. JONES, "A Longitudinal Study of Language Development in Children at Different Levels of Cognitive Development," *Merrill-Palmer Quarterly,* 23(2) (April 1977), 115–120.

RAMER, A.L., "Syntactic Styles in Emerging Language," *J Child Language,* 3(1) (February 1976), 49–62.

REES, N.S., "Imitation and Language Development: Issues and Clinical Implications," *J Speech Hearing Disorders,* 40 (August 1975), 339–350.

SANDERS, L.J., "The Comprehension of Certain Syntactic Structures by Adults," *J Speech Hearing Research,* 14(4) (December 1971), 739–745.

SCHIEFELBUSCH, R.L., *Language of the Mentally Retarded.* Baltimore: University Park Press, 1972.

SHRINER, T.H. and R.G. DANILOFF, "The Relationship Between Articulatory Deficits and Syntax in Speech Defective Children," *J Speech Hearing Research,* 12 (June 1969), 319–325.

SNYDER-MCLEAN, L. and J. MCLEAN, "Verbal Information Gathering Strategies: The Child's Use of Language to Acquire Language," *J Speech Hearing Disorders,* 43(3) (August 1978), 306–325.

STROHNER, H. and K.E. NELSON, "The Young Child's Development of Sentence Comprehension: Influence of Event Probability, Nonverbal Context, Syntactic Form and Strategies," *Child Development,* 45(3) (September 1974), 567–576.

VOGEL, S.A., *Syntactic Abilities in Normal and Dyslexic Children.* Baltimore: University Park Press, 1975.

WEAVER, K.S. and K.F. RUDER, "The Effect of the Gestural Prompt on Syntax Training," *J Speech Hearing Disorders,* 43(4) (November 1978), 513–523.

WHELDALL, K., "The Influence of Intonational Style on the Young Child's Ability to Understand Sentences: A Research Note on Passives," *British J Disorders Communication,* 13(2) (October 1978), 147–152.

WIIG, E.H. and E.M. SEMEL, *Language Disabilities in Children and Adolescents.* Columbus, Ohio: Chas. E. Merrill, 1976.

WILCOX, M.J. and L.B. LEONARD, "Experimental Acquisition of Wh-Questions in Language-Disordered Children," *J Speech Hearing Research,* 21(2) (June 1978), 220–239.

WILSON, M.S., *Syntax Remediation.* Cambridge, Mass.: Educators Publishing Service, Inc., 1977.

WOLFLE, D., "Pedagogical Plainsmen," *Science,* 199(4331) (24 February 1978), 843.

chapter 7

POSITIVE MARKERS
OF PROGRESS IN
LANGUAGE ACQUISITION

INTRODUCTION

This chapter should be a useful reference for teachers. We shall discuss stage by stage, the positive and negative signs of language acquisition. They should serve as markers by which teachers can peg the child's progress and identify signs of retardation at each stage.

We have set these markers or signs in four stages of language learning, recognizing at once, however, that neither stages nor markers within each stage are exact. We have delimited the following stages: (1) Emerging Language; (2) Early Intermediate; (3) Later Intermediate; and (4) Continuing Education in Oral Language. Of course there is no perceptible transition from one stage to the next. The signs or markers of progress within the three stages are also rough approximations. For obvious reasons we have no markers for Stage 4; education has no terminal point. Children vary, for example, in their acquisition of language as the cultural, ethnic and socioeconomic environments in which they live vary. The rate of acquisition also will vary according to sex. Boys usually remain longer in the first stage of emerging language and also have relatively more difficulty in acquiring higher levels of linguistic comprehension-expression.[1] Neither do all children acquire oral language in the same way. Although this may

[1] A.L. Ramer, "Syntactic Styles in Emerging Language," *J Child Language* 3(1) (February 1976), 49–62.

be rare in the experience of others, I have known children whose earliest speech was a two-word phrase that expressed clear semantic intentions. The single occurrence, however, of a sentence in a child's speech is no proof of any knowledge of syntax. Structures, like percepts, are most unstable and depend on use. Phrases and sentences come and go, not to reappear, perhaps, for several months. The most unstable period of sentence construction occurs when the child must use such functor words as conjunctions and auxiliary verbs.

STAGE 1: BEGINNING ORAL LANGUAGE

Phonatory Markers: Action Percepts; Prosody

Action percepts develop first from a child's "hypotheses," about persons, things, and happenings in his environment and from his motivation to intervene in his environment. His intervention will be conditioned at this stage by his perception of the situation and by his use of body language, out of which prosody, the language melody develops. Secondly, as he comprehends the categories of action: agent, action, object, or the recipient of action, location, possession, and so on, he will follow an embryonic order or form in morphemic combinations or words. In speaking of this embryonic structure, Bruner explains, the "primitive categories of grammar refer to actions (demanding verbs), carried out by agents and having effects of particular kinds in particular places." [2] In the very early period of speech action, let us say fifteen to eighteen months, the baby is developing rapidly in his ability to investigate objects and happenings around him and also to place his relations with other people in the scheme of things about which he verbalizes. Bradley's first word at one year was *see,* followed at fifteen months by *some* (*I want some*), *down; up* (*I want to get down; want up*). In the action-interaction of daily life, he gradually learns to differentiate perceptually among the producers and the receivers of action. Because of the child's need to interact, the verb phrase generally develops before the noun phrase. As I pointed out in the preceding chapter, the prevailing practice, nonetheless, is to teach naming, identification of objects, forgetting that the child is more interested in comprehending and expressing *actions* relating to the object, person, or event. In my view, this practice of dealing with nouns exclusively deters the child's progress.

Some writers identify this early marker of the one-word "sentence" as holophrastic. The meaning of the single word can be interpreted, however, only in union with the action and interaction of others in the child's en-

---

[2] J.S. Bruner, "The Ontogenesis of Speech Acts," *J Child Language* 2(1) (April 1975), 1–19.

vironment. His actions, consisting both of gross bodily movements and gestures, will assist him in signaling his intentions and his wish to share attention with others or to carry out an "operation" with others. Frequently the child repeats the word several times in order to show emotional reinforcement and accompanies it in the same perseverative way with bodily gestures. So he says *more-more, go-go* ("pushing" toward the record player after it has stopped), *no-no don't* (holding onto his shoe that Daddy is taking off).

Action Percepts and Attention-Focus

In this stage of action and interaction, the common focus of attention of parent and child seems to be essential to comprehension. It is an eye-to-eye relationship, a communicative bond directing attention and held together by physical gestures—body, eyes, and hands. Perceptual discontinuity producing a loss in attentional focus is apparent in several groups of people, but it is most pronounced in the child retardate and in the aged. In both groups the individual seems to be unable to follow the sequence of interaction and consequently the attention-focus is lost altogether. Aged people, troubled by the deterioration of focus, often remark that they are not centering upon the same object, situation, or reference as others and, hence, "lose the connection." The retarded child says, "I didn't know you meant *that*" although *that* is the most immediate and most recent reference. A daughter visiting her father, a distinguished professor, often reports that they will discuss a play, but when she asks if he would like to see it again, he frequently replies, "What?" If he attends a reception, he is so completely confused by the diverse threads of conversation that he can make no sense of any of it. He grasps Ariadne's ball of yarn, but he cannot make his way out of the mental labyrinth.

Prosody is the second marker closely associated with perceptual-semantic development, action percepts, and presyntactic form. It, too, stems from general bodily and vocal rhythms, for prosody is built on action and interaction. The first melodic patterns may be jargonistic responses to the baby's environment and then gradually he may introduce recognizable morphemes to be followed by single action words in the intonational or prosodic envelope. He may intermingle the few words he has with sound strings that resemble words. It is difficult to fill the prosodic envelope with single syllable words in order to preserve a basic melody pattern so frequently he makes them into two or three syllable combinations: *bye-bye, beddie-bye, night-night, da-da-da,* and so on. A string of *da-da-das,* however, may never develop into a "first word"; it may be only random vocalization enjoyable to the child because of its haptic-motor feedback. *First words are significant only if they are uttered in response to an action event, a response of intervention, or a response with semantic intent.* A single word can become a "sentence" and when assisted by facial and bodily gestures, may be a true directive in meaning. *Hot* (referring to stove or television cabinet) is such a word. Action verbs similarly may be used alone. In fact, they are more important than nouns at this stage because they enable the child to intervene in his environment in order to control it. In the early stages of language learning, a baby comprehends meaning largely through his interpretations of the prosodic pattern. *"Bye-bye?"* or *"Baby bye-bye?"* the mother asks. The baby is filled with hope mixed with delight. It is a highly emotional, but also propositional, situation. *Bye Daddy? Bye, Daddy! My truck? My truck!* The same phrase can bear different meanings.

Can this single word or "holophrastic" sentence have structure? By its intonational or prosodic pattern, can it indicate an internal form? I think it can and does. Through intonational changes the baby indicates agent, recipient, possessor, and vocative. He clearly uses prosody as a structural marker. So, although he has a very limited vocabulary consisting of *dada, tata, mamma, goggie, too-too, go-go* [doʊ -doʊ], *bang-bang, bye-bye* (waving), *open* [oʊ p], *blow* [boʊ] (your nose), *no-no, mo(r)e* [mɔr], *make* [meɪ], *stay* [teɪ], he has many one-word sentences of communication.[3]

Emergence of Word Order (Presyntax)

As percepts become less fuzzy and the motivation and reward of communicating more intense, an embryonic framework emerges in the child's communication, but it is not a full blown syntactic framework. *Word order,* determined by the child's semantic intention, action percepts, and prosody, becomes the binder for communication at this early sensorimotor level as he engages in two- and three-word "sentences."[4] It also reflects the child's perception of word order in the input language. These noun phrases have a meaning relationship but no true syntactic relationship. In general the child seems to learn a fair batch of phrases clustered about one constant or key word. At first the word order is monotonously the same: *more milk, more bye-bye, more go-go,* or *Mommy-go, bow-*

[3] M.M. Lewis, *How Children Learn to Speak* (London: Harrap, 1957), 80–83.

[4] M.D.S. Braine, "Children's First Word Combinations," *Monograph Society Research Child Development* 41(1) (Serial No. 164) (April 1976), 90–93; S. Chapman and J.F. Miller, "Word Order in Early Two and Three Word Utterances: Does Production Precede Comprehension?" *J Speech Hearing Research* 18(2) (June 1975), 355–371.

wow-go (go away). Unlike the first single word directives, these phrases or morphemic strings bear some resemblance to the *adult melody* or intonational pattern. The prosodic pattern itself has come to set up definite expectancies in the child, and the child not only comprehends the intention in this pattern but also learns to produce it intentionally.[5] These adult-like phrases, however, do not generate new phrases and are not formula-making. Nevertheless they are extremely useful as directives. As he attends to the action percepts and melody patterns of parent and sib talk, he expands or modifies his expressions to conform to those adult positional patterns and the rhythmic constraints which accompany them. And as his hypotheses and intentions about his world gradually become more complex, he verbalizes more and more in accordance with a rhythmic pattern that he seems to "absorb" and internalize from the "special people" around him.

Stage 1. Positive Markers of Beginning Language Development [6]

Teachers of the very young child might peg progress by these steps:

1. The child interacts with "special" people and pets in his environment. He sees, hears, feels them; he is responsive to them. He imitates spontaneously the melody patterns of family talk.

2. He imitates spontaneously morphemes, words, or parts of phrases in family talk associated with familiar activities. The imitation may be immediate or delayed.

3. He produces single word "sentences," announcing or communicating actions related to himself, other "special" people, objects, food, and so on in his immediate environment. His purpose is pragmatic. The one-word sentence has semantic intent and prosodic reinforcement.

4. He uses bodily action and gestures with single-word sentences in order to amplify semantic intention.

5. He will proceed to two- or three-word phrases with meaning relationship based on word order and melody patterns but without true syntactic relation.

6. Sometimes he will utter word strings with semantic intent but without syntactic relation.

7. As pragmatic intention grows, the child will formulate utterances expressing semantic relationships, observing prosodic constraints, and reflecting an embryonic syntactic structure.

8. The child's earliest patterned speech is not organized in terms of knowl-

---

[5] Bruner, "The Ontogenesis of Speech Acts," 1–19.

[6] Appendix A-4 contains a schedule of language development, one month to three years.

edge of grammatical categories but in terms of more fundamental syntheses of perceptual meanings with phonological and rhythmic outputs.[7]

Stage 1. Early Signs of Linguistic Retardation

Among the significant behavioral signs characteristic of some language retardates are the following:

1. Lack of awareness of or reaction to his immediate environment. He makes little effort to intervene in his environment to satisfy his wants or to take part in nonverbal communication with parent or peers.

2. Delay in onset of gestural language or prosodic patterning of sound strings.

3. Apparent lack of comprehension of simple directives: *no-no, hot,* and so on. Early comprehension is the key to early communication.[8]

4. Development of meaningful interactions with others is limited. The communicative use of body language and manual gestures is limited even in emotional situations.

5. Failure to progress beyond the one- or two-word vocabulary for six months after an initially delayed onset. This silent period generally is predictive of retarded language development unless illness or other trauma has intervened.

6. Comprehension and use of such a primary linguistic structure as agent-action or action-object are delayed. These are the usual patterns of the two-word sentence.

7. At three years these children make no attempt to use such hypothesis-testing questions as *where?* or *what?*

8. Failure to respond by elicited or spontaneous imitation of familiar talk of parent or peers.

9. Extension of word-naming far beyond the normal stage of one-word sentences. He tries to make the word stand for much more than it does. If a child in preschool continues to name people and objects in his environment or reproduces visual situations by single words without prosodic emphasis, he should be enrolled in your program.

STAGE 2: EARLY INTERMEDIATE STAGE OF LANGUAGE DEVELOPMENT

Expansion of Interaction

Two- and three-word pre-sentences now emerge in the child's speech.[9] He enters what might be called the groping stage of oral language. He

---

[7] J. Dore and others, "Transitional Phenomena in Early Language Acquisition," *J Child Language* 3(1) (February 1976), 13–28.

[8] C. Nelson, "Structure and Strategy in Learning to Talk," *Monograph Society for Research Child Development* 38(1, 2) Serial No. 149 (February–April 1973), 81–83.

[9] M. Bowerman, "Semantic Factors in the Acquisition of Rules for Word Use and Sentence Construction," *Normal and Deficient Language* eds. D.M. Morehead and A.E. Morehead (Baltimore: University Park Press, 1976), 100.

needs something beyond word order to express his hypotheses and his activities, and most importantly to use language in interaction, mediating social control. At this early sensorimotor level of development, word order may continue to be the dominant guide, but the two- and three-word combinations are not meaningless word strings. The word order is regular, expresses semantic intent, and implies a syntactic relationship.[10] The child knows no rules specifying the position of the words in a phrase, but *agent* will generally precede *action,* and the *object* of the action will follow the verb. This skill reflects the child's response to a growing need to interact with his world, to use language as a social mediator. As Krauss and Glucksberg comment, "The social use of language depends as much on that knowledge as it does on knowledge of language itself." [11]

Prosody and Syntactic Relations

The child's intent and meaning, however, are determined by something more than word order. The difference between *Mommy bye-bye* and *bye-bye Mommy* or *Daddy car* and *car Daddy,* one understands because of the constraints of the prosodic or melodic pattern. The child comes to this achievement not by rule or rote. He does not try to replicate all the steps and glides of adult prosody. Quite unconsciously he absorbs by haptic feedback the distinctive melodic patterns connoting command (imperative), negation, yes-no answers to questions, designation, and location. It is truly his sensitivity to body language, reported through feedback, that will determine the facility with which he fits the words into the prosodic contour. Such a sensitivity heightens as his attention to the melody of parent and sib talk increases. The sentence may consist only of two words, but if it is shaped by prosody and accompanied by the appropriate bodily movement and gesture, he can communicate his semantic intentions. He will use certain "operator words" over and over, but the meaning of the operator word changes with the melodic pattern. He may say *more milk?* but often it is *MORE milk!* (On the double please.) *All gone* may express satisfaction and delight as the child turns the porridge bowl upside down, or it may connote amazement and inquiry as the thumb "disappears" from Daddy's hand. *Dolly dress* at one time means possession; at another time the baby wants help to put the dress on Dolly. Similarly he can negate with *no water* indicating that water in the bottle is "all gone" or refuse the offer of water. He can show location of Mommy

[10] J.N. Bohannon, "The Relationship Between Syntax Discrimination and Sentence Imitation in Children," *Child Development* 46(2) (June 1975), 444–451; M.D. Braine, "Children's First Word Combinations."

[11] R.M. Krauss and S. Glucksberg, "Social and Nonsocial Speech," *Scientific American* 236(2) (February 1977), 105.

with *here Mommy* or location of an object with the same words. Certainly the child is not aware of structure at this stage. He is aware of melody and he uses it to differentiate meaning.

Constituents of the Early Sentence

These early sentences are not abbreviated versions of adult sentences because adult models have related knowledge, based on past experiences which are reflected in the structure. Rather these are the child's creations about the "here and now," and they are the best he can make from his limited experience and from his knowledge of vocabulary. The child may employ only three words in these units of expression, but if they form one intonational pattern in which meaning can be determined by the relation among the words, the structure is inherently syntactic.

The Order of Development

Syntactic forms will vary in developmental order as the language environment varies. It will be dictated first by the repetitive phrases that children hear. Under the aegis of parents, nouns (naming) and noun phrases will first appear, but they are not the most significant syntactic forms. As the child develops, his percepts translated into action will demand *predication;* this is the earliest syntactic form of importance. Syntactic development takes this general progression at this stage: 1.) action verbs and verb phrases; 2.) three-word sentences (subject-verb-object); 3.) sentence types: declarative, yes-no questions, wh-questions, negations, imperatives, directives, and occasionally true compound sentences. We shall illustrate only the more important steps in developing *elementary syntactic forms.*

The three-word sentence generally consists of a verb phrase and noun phrase or two nouns and a verb. (Mary go home.) The forms of the copula, *to be,* are not in the child's syntactic repertoire so he says: *This* (is) *not ice cream; I* (am) *not crying; Joe* (was) *not eating that.* He makes a few verbs, such as *need* and *make,* express many kinds of action. So by his third birthday he has gone beyond *no goggie* (doggie), *me play,* and so on to such three-word expressions as *Me need bye-bye; me need cookie;* or *me need fow* (flower), (quickly pulling off the blossom), in which *need* is used instead of *want.* Or he uses *make* in the sense of producing action. He entreats or commands Mommy: Make it big; make loon (balloon) fly; or he announces: *Me make it* (block tower). He expresses negation by adding a negative word (*no* or *not*) to an affirmative statement: *No look me; Kim no fall; no play* (with) *that.* Few children before the third year use any of the following structures: prepositions (*in, on, under*); conjunctions (*and, but, or*); articles (*a, the*), auxiliary verbs (*has, have, did*); copular verbs (*am, is, are, was, were*); or inflectional endings to indicate the plural or past or progressive tenses (*walked, walking*). That the child, three years old, still depends heavily on word order for comprehension can be ascertained easily by mixing the word order in a short story, a kind of Donald Duck game. It will not "make sense" to him.[12]

The Sentence and Free-Wheeling Syntax

By the time the child has reached his fourth birthday or before, he usually has learned how to put together a four-word declarative sentence denoting agent-action-object-location. As someone has said, he has assumed the awful burden of the sentence which he will be rid of as an adult. And in emotionally fraught situations he will add adverbs and an occasional adjective. *"Me take Dolly home,"* said Debbie, and when Mother remonstrated that it was not her doll, Debbie clutched the doll with both arms and with a vigorous nod of her head, shouted, *"Me take Dolly home NOW* (with) *me!"* On another occasion, she put her cereal dish on the floor and later reported, *"Bad doggie, he ated it all up."* When she excitedly reported an immediate happening, she strung sentences together without conjunctions: *Kitty jump; smash go lamp* (with sound effects); *Kitty hidded* (in? under?) *cupboard; me runned.*

The Wh-Question and Perceptual-Semantic Progress

It has been said that the wh-question is indicative of a surge of semantic growth, an authentic forecast of language development. I believe this to be true, for I have seen a child's world virtually explode both in ideas and in their expression in the third year. At the beginning of the third year they are somewhat embryonic: *Where my shoe? What you do? Daddy home? Me no go?* A year later he may still be asking for yes-no answers, but he is also demanding longer answers to his questions, answers which extend his referents about things and actions and which frequently require cause-effect reasoning. He imitates most easily and spontaneously the semantic wh-questions, *what* and *where,* omitting unfamiliar structures and words. The form is not yet perfect although the wh-word usually appears in the initial position in the sentence. He makes no inversion in the negative

[12] J.M. Love and C. Parker-Robinson, "Children's Imitation of Grammatical and Ungrammatical Sentences," *Child Development* 43(2) (June 1972), 310–319.

question. The auxiliary verb is often missing and if it is present, he may mark tense on both auxiliary and main verb. Here are illustrations of these practices: *Why do that?* (to his mother putting on the turn-signal of the car) (missing auxiliary); *Why Kitty can't stand up?* (no inversion); *Look what you made me did!* (double marking of tense). At this stage the child usually expresses the number by inflecting the subject-noun, not by inflecting the verb.

The *tag question* often appears in place of the acceptable form and may remain in the child's speech for a long time. *You don' cry Mommy, huh?* (Mommy is pretending.) *I want ride trike, huh? Jay falled down, right?* The tag takes the place of the direct and more complex form involving *linguistic transformation and expansion.* In fact, I see no reason why teachers should struggle with the complex apparatus of the tag question when *right* or *huh* seems to serve the purpose even with nonhandicapped adults.

Sentence Expansion

It is doubtful if children at this level and age respond well to intentional expansion of the sentence by mothers and teachers. As Cazden says, expansion by interpolation demands little of the child. Since he has been understood he feels no need to respond to the goading of expansion.[13] This kind of teaching, in my experience, has been ineffective, not only because expansion demands little of the child and is not used by mothers,[14] but also because the kinds of expansion are not useful at this stage. The child, three to four years of age, really does not find it necessary to distinguish between a *yellow apple* and a *red apple* or a *big balloon* and a *little balloon.* These are artificial expansions because they do not develop from the pragmatic needs of the child or from familiar situations in his environment. He would not remember: *I go store SO* (in order to) *I can buy candy.* He makes his meaning clear when he says, *Me* (I) *go store. Me* (I) *need* (want) *candy.*

Isomorphic Observations

Normal language development at this stage is not static although there may be "holding periods" in oral expression. At this juncture he may be making great strides in comprehension and developing new or revising

[13] C.B. Cazden, *Child Language and Education* (New York: Holt, Rinehart and Winston, 1972), 118–122.

[14] D. Ling and A. Ling, "Communication Development in the First Three Years of Life," *J Speech Hearing Research* 17(1) (March 1974), 146–159.

present "schema" of his world for which he must learn new vocabulary, new structures, and "get his tongue around" unusual phonemic clusters. Shortly he will be in the free-wheeling stage in which he will experiment with many forms of oral expression. There is an on-line interaction among the semantic, structural, and prosodic levels of sentence making. As prosodic development was isomorphic with perceptual-semantic growth, so are they both now isomorphic with specific aspects of syntactic development, and all are based on action and interaction. If we put the matter in reverse order, the ability to classify in action, to embed action patterns one within the other, to contract syntactic relationships between parts of sentences on the basis of action: these developmental sign posts of sentence construction emerge as a result of prosodic and perceptual-semantic growth.[15] Hannah, in this age group, uses structures that no adult has ever uttered. For example, she imitates no one when she regularizes the past tense in strong verbs and the plural of a few nouns. Melodically and logically, *goed, sitted, runned, sleeped* and *mans, mouses, tooths,* and *foots* strengthen her expression.

Stage 2. Positive Markers of Early Intermediate Stage of Language Development

Teachers at the kindergarten level will find these markers of progress useful.

1. Perceptual-semantic growth, now accelerated by burgeoning environmental stimuli, will produce many new, some unusual words, word forms, and inflections. Because of his interest in people, places, and things, he peppers his speech with questions. Strong semantic intentions also induce him to experiment with new lexical forms, new rhythmic patterns, new grammatical features. He creates, rather than imitates, language.

2. These environmental stimuli now demand knowledge and use of forms for the acts of asserting (declaration); requesting information or action (question); denying (the negative although the transformation is often faulty); and commanding or warning (the imperative).

3. Prosodic patterns often are extreme, caused in part by imitation of the parents' talk *to them* and in part, by a desire for emphasis in order to command the situation. Consequently the child often generalizes his or her rule for the past tense in order to achieve emphasis (goed-ed; didded, and so on).

4. Vocabulary is growing rapidly although the child may not understand or pronounce the words correctly. Such spatio-temporal terms as *over-under* or *top-bottom* are often used incorrectly. He rejects the multiple-meaning word, for no word can have two meanings at this stage.

[15] W. Marslen-Wilson, "Committee on Cognition and Communication," *Science* 189(4198) (18 July 1975), 226–227.

5. Although phonological development is proceeding on schedule, the child seems to pay little conscious attention to phonology. Phoneme clusters may be reduced and weak syllables deleted occasionally; yet he maintains a meaningful prosodic pattern. He has generally mastered the plosive consonants [p], [b], [t], [d], [k] and [g]; the nasal consonants [m], [n], and [ŋ], except in the final position for which he substitutes [n] as most adults do; the glides [l], [w], [j] and [h]; and some fricative consonants, usually [f]; [θ], and [ʃ].

6. He employs the true compound sentence rarely although he conjoins noun phrases and verb phrases with *and* or *but*. ("Two cars; zookie-bang, bang! and the police come.")

Stage 2. Signs of Linguistic Retardation in Early Intermediate Stage

It is probably true that many children with a linguistic lag follow the same general course of language learning as nonretardates, *but at a slower pace*. Such a statement implies that eventually the laggards will "catch up" if, early on, proper interventional strategies are instituted. The problem is not so easily solved. Some children indeed will "catch up;" others may find oral communication a handicap throughout their lives. The extent to which they are able to overcome these behavioral manifestations of linguistic retardation may distinguish between the two groups:

1. Perceptual-semantic retardation. The child retardate generally shows little curiosity about his environment or about oral communication as a means of controlling that environment. He is not exploratory or eager to investigate or participate in experiences, verbal or nonverbal. He makes monosyllabic answers to questions. He initiates few *where* or *what* questions which are semantic in nature. He uses neither *why* nor *who* questions. He has sensorimotor experiences in and out of the classroom, but he does not "tie together different experiences, interpret them," and talk about them.[16] He does not link and interpret what he sees, hears, tastes, or feels in a meaningful way!

2. If body language is noncoordinated, the finer movement patterns basic to prosody probably also will be deficient. The resulting rigidity is reflected in stereotyped oral and gestural expression.

3. Both vocabulary and structural forms are limited. Sentences are short and unvaried in structure, partly because the child has limited recall and partly because he is reluctant to experiment with forms of expression. "He knows only one way to say it." As Morehead and Ingram state, ". . . deviant children appear to be significantly restricted in their ability to develop and select grammatical and semantic features which allow existent new major lexical categories to be assigned to larger sets of syntactic frames."[17] The child still follows word

[16] D.P. Weikart and others, *The Cognitively Oriented Curriculum* (Washington, D.C.: National Association for Education of Young Children, 1971), 57.

[17] D.M. Morehead and D. Ingram, "The Development of Base Syntax in Normal and Linguistically Deviant Children," *J Speech Hearing Research* 16(3) (September 1973), 343.

order constraints rather than true syntactic constraints.[18] To teach sentence structure by "rule and rote" will only exaggerate the rigid language habits he already has adopted. Because he has a meager vocabulary he overgeneralizes the lexemes he has; that is, he uses one word to designate several referents. He no longer calls all small animals *kitty,* but *thing* may refer to any object or event.

4. The limited speech he possesses is frequently unintelligible because he reduces consonant clusters, deletes many weak syllables, and substitutes velar (back) consonants for front sounds: [geɪkɪŋ] for [teɪkɪŋ]; [gʌk] for [dʌk], and so on. If he reduces the rate of speaking in order to be understood, he further distorts the prosodic pattern.

5. The child does not imitate spontaneously the speech of others, and the results of elicited imitation of modeled utterances even with familiar stimuli and materials are meager. Pronounced prosodic reinforcement, however, tends to increase his retention.

STAGE 3: LATER INTERMEDIATE STAGE OF LANGUAGE ACQUISITION

Learning by Rule Evaluated

As children approach the sixth year, or perhaps somewhat later, girls are generally advancing more rapidly than boys.[19] Are they, both boys and girls, learning language by rules? Certainly neither sex is consciously learning abstract rules. The average child is able to perceive syntactic relations in subject and object noun phrases and verb phrases although he is not aware of the rules themselves.[20] Comprehension of meaning comes before expression, and he still—and always will—comprehend meaning first by the order of words in a prosodic slot and secondarily by the syntactic relations implicit in the order. As new stimuli, new experiences come into his ken, he extends unconsciously his knowledge of syntactic relations because he must express complexities of new concepts of time, space order, and relationships. He does not verbalize about a rule.[21]

As the child moves into the seventh year, he uses the proper number, verb tense, and suffixes with increasing regularity. He constructs sentences

[18] Ramer, "Syntactic Styles in Emerging Language," 46–62.

[19] R.A. Koenigsknecht and P. Friedman, "Syntax Development in Boys and Girls," *Child Development* 47(4) (1976), 1109–1115; Ramer, "Syntactic Style in Emerging Language," 49–62.

[20] L.V. McReynolds and D.L. Engmann, "An Experimental Analysis of the Relationship of Subject and Object Noun Phrases," *Developing Systematic Procedures for Training Children's Language,* ed. L.V. McReynolds, *ASHA* Monographs Number 18 *American Speech Hearing Association,* Washington, D.C. (August 1974), 30–46.

[21] J.G. deVilliers and P.A. deVilliers, "Competence and Performance in Child Language: Are Children Really Competent to Judge?" *J Child Language* 1(1) (May 1974), 11–22.

he has not learned from others, or he may join by subordination two or more whole utterances which others have spoken.[22] In general their speech will reflect the following advances in syntax: (1) sentence modification by pronouns, auxiliary verbs, plurals, conjunctions, and inflections (number and tense); (2) the use of the possessive; (3) elaborations and expansions; and (4) transformations involving the interrogative, possessive, relative noun, and relative clause. Understanding the meaning however, is basic to syntactic use.

Sentence Structure: Length, Transformation, Complexity, Degree

Sentences are growing longer, but length will depend largely upon his memory of word units and their logical relations. Functor words are coming in rapidly although he is not always using them accurately; frequently he omits them. *I go with my Daddy,* for example, now appears more frequently than *I go by my Daddy. Give it me* is still more common than *give it to me.* He has known how to use the imperative for a long time. Now he often transforms the declarative into an interrogative form. Indeed he can go both ways; he can transform his questions into a negative or positive declarative form. So he will change *I can go too* to *Can I go too?* and finally to *Why can't I go too?*

Complexity

Grammatical expressions of intention or meanings that are expressed by prefixes or prepositions may still be difficult. It is much easier for him to use endings or suffixes.

Some "sentences" are simply run-on utterances linked by [ænə] at this level although the parts may not be temporally or causally connected. They are not complex sentences. If the child understands sequencing, however, he probably will use the true compound sentence. In reporting an exciting event to Mother, Ann (seven years old) said, "I just ran out and there comes the fire truck. Two guys *pull* out a long hose and another guy was there (hydrant) and he put it together." She is less likely to conjoin two proper nouns or a noun and a pronoun. Generally she says, *Tom played Monopoly and I played too;* rarely does she say, *Tom and I played Monopoly.* If Ann *perceives* cause-effect relations, as a result of her knowledge of classification and categorization, she may join sentences in other ways than by *and;* she could use such connector words as *because, to* (in order to), *while, when,* and so on.

---

[22] C.F. Hockett, "The Origin of Speech," *Scientific American* 203 (September 1960), 94.

Embedding one sentence within another sentence increases its complexity. Success in embedding depends again on the child's perceptual-semantic development, for it presupposes knowledge of subordination and coordination and of the syntactic relations essential for their expression. The child may "embed" single words or phrases within simple subject-predicate sentences. *"Go school now? No?,"* Jamie asked when he was five years old. Now at six, he embeds the negative: *"I don't go* (to) *school now."* Or instead of simply combining two sentences, he now embeds one in the other as a relative clause. At five years, the child would probably have said: "Give me that pencil. I want to write." Now, at six or seven years, he may say, "I want to write with your pencil." (You have a pencil. I want to write with it.) There are syntactical and phonological errors in the following conversation, but embedding is present: "You made me falled down," says Jason. "Naw, Joee who's runnin' away did it (but) I didn't." He often omits the relative pronouns, *who, which, what,* or interchanges them. *Whom* is simply not employed. But why should we expect the six-year-old to use the relative pronoun properly? Apparently it is beyond the understanding of adults.

Use of Degree

Expressions of difference in quantity appear quite regularly in the superlative, less frequently in the comparative inflection. Children regularly say, *I want the biggest ice cream cone* although there are only two. *I'm the biggest,* Jack says, when he challenges his brother; occasionally he may say, *I'm bigger than you* (are). Six-year-olds seldom, if ever, employ the adverbial comparative or superlative, *more* or *most. Terribler, terriblest; awfuler* and *awfulest* are heard regularly at this intermediate stage. Occasionally a six-year-old substitutes *badder* and *gooder* respectively for the highly irregular adjectives *worse* and *better* although he usually says *worst* and *best.*

In summary, we may say that the average child at this stage speaks grammatically—on *occasion.* He employs changes in tense, number, articles, prepositions, conjunctions, and pronouns—but he does so in a most unstable and erratic fashion. In certain situations and with certain words and structures, he is quite accurate. Like adults, he sometimes uses such expressions in informal conversations as *I come and I see this guy* and *he say to me.* Like many adults, he often uses the loose, run-on sentence instead of subordination and true coordination although he can demonstrate their use. Under the aegis principally of his own perceptual abilities, less so under the stimulation and imitation of the verbal patterns of his peers, he communicates meaning.

Stage 3. Later Intermediate Stage:
Positive Signs of Language Development

1. Perceptual development leaps ahead. The child is now giving and asking for information on all fronts. A portion of his oral expression is still egocentric —talking to himself, for himself, about himself—yet he also has a fair perception of his relation to others and to his world. As he responds to this wider range of sensorimotor stimuli, thinking and oral expression become less syncretistic (perception of the whole without analysis). Under the goad of intellectual operations, he must find new words and structures to express his percepts. His percepts extend to spatial (relative size, dimensions, and so on) and temporal order (days, time, seasons, and so on); to classification or categorization of actors and actions according to subgroups (sports, animals, domestic tasks, professions, machinery); and to interpretive relationships in terms of appearance, class and use (similarity and difference) and logic. The qualitative and quantitative lexical development is quite phenomenal.

2. He uses many new words quite correctly in the noun class, not always so in the verb class. His success in the accurate use of other word classes declines in this order: adjectives, pronouns, and adverbs.

3. He generally makes appropriate morphological modifications in present, past, and future tense, in adjectival comparative and superlative degrees (bigger-biggest; hotter-hottest), and in the pluralization of nouns. He is not proficient in agreement in number of subject and verb. He employs simple, compound and, to a limited degree, complex sentences in spontaneous conversation. His social environment largely dictates his use of personal pronouns.[23]

4. Gestures are generally indicative or emphatic in nature but at this level, they have become more subtle, more skillfully coordinated with total body language and with semantic intent.

5. Prosodic and gestural patterns reinforce each other in verbal expression, and both promote syntactic and morphological expansions. In fitting the syntactic elements—phrase, clause, sentence—into prosodic envelopes, he closely simulates adult prosody.

6. The accurate production of /r/ and /s/, and in some cases, /l/, /č/ and for these phonemes, phonological development is fairly complete.
/ʝ/ is yet to be learned or at least incorporated in spontaneous speech. Except

7. He does not consciously imitate linguistic forms set forth by the teacher in the classroom or clinic-oriented center, or by adults in the home.[24] On the other hand, he frequently and spontaneously imitates the verbalization of his peers when talking together.[25]

---

[23] M.F. Bowerman, "Discussion Summary—Development of Concepts Underlying Language," *Language Perspectives—Acquisition, Retardation, and Intervention,* eds. R.L. Schiefelbusch and L.L. Lloyd. (Baltimore: University Park Press, 1974), 207.

[24] L.B. Leonard, "Modeling as a Clinical Procedure in Language Training," *Language Speech Hearing Services in Schools* 4(2) (April 1975), 72–85; N.S. Rees, "Imitation and Language Development: Issues and Clinical Implications," *J Speech Hearing Disorders* 40(3) (August 1975), 339–350.

[25] J.B. Gleason, "Code Switching in Children's Language," *Cognitive Development and the Acquisition of Language,* ed. T.E. Moore (New York: Academic Press, 1973).

Stage 3. Signs of Linguistic Retardation
in Later Intermediate Stage

Earlier in this chapter, I disagreed with the view that "the major differences between normal and linguistically deviant children. . . are found in the onset and acquisition time necessary for learning base syntax and the use of aspects of that system once acquired, for producing major lexical items in a variety of utterance." [26] I reiterate my view that linguistic handicaps are not simply the result of a time lag; they are, to a significant degree, the result of a perceptual-semantic deficit resulting in an atypical linguistic system. Many children whom I have taught are now adults, and although they learned a basic linguistic system as children, they still reflect limitations in structural and lexical variety, vocabulary, and phonological proficiency. They do not approach the average adult standard in oral language; yet their achievements in nonverbal tasks in some instances indicate average mental ability. They continue to be handicapped by linguistic deviations.

What are some signs of deviant language development at this late intermediate stage?

1. If the perceptual-semantic level is in deficit, the syntactic level of language behavior, standing in a hierarchical relation, also will be deficient.[27] Among the causes of the primary deficit are mental retardation; inability to code verbal input at the normal rate as a result of reduced perception of one or both modalities, auditory and haptic, or of temporal confusion among neuronal assemblies mediating several modalities. (See Chapter 2.)

2. As sequellae to perceptual problems, knowledge of syntactic relations and the employment of transformation, embedding, and complexity and variety in sentence structure will be realized at a much slower rate. Such sentence elaborations as clausal constructions and prepositional phrases will be meager. In terms of meaning units, however, the limited elaborations they employ will be a better measure of linguistic advance than sentence length.[28] These children probably will always talk less—but will they always talk less well? Not all.[29]

[26] Morehead and Ingram, "The Development of Base Syntax in Normal and Linguistically Deviant Children," 222–223.

[27] D.M. Aram and J.E. Nation, "Patterns of Language Behavior in Children with Developmental Language Disorders," *J Speech Hearing Research* 18(2) (June 1975), 229–241.

[28] K.W. Hunt, "Syntactic Maturity in School Children and Adults," *Monograph Society for Research Child Development* 35(1) (February 1970), 55–61.

[29] D. Ingram, "Developing Systematic Procedures for Training Children's Language," *American Speech Hearing Association Monograph* 18 (August 1974), 5–14; P.

3. A short memory span limits experimentation or practice in a variety of sentence forms.[30] These children feel a certain safety in the elementary patterns of short, active-declarative and imperative sentences. These are structures they can remember and hence will use to the exclusion of all other forms. Certainly they will not remember the passive form because they must rely heavily upon the prompting of the noun phrase for the cue to meaning.

Another observation associated directly with memory span is that these children are poor "rehearsers," either overtly or semi-overtly. In terms of recall of structure, phonemic sequence, and vocabulary, rehearsal is inestimable in value.[31]

Because they cannot recall the order of sequencing, their sentences are frequently incomplete or interrupted by such fillers as *now you see, well-a, like this,* and *I mean.*

4. Prosody may not provide its usual aid to syntax and phonology because the melody patterns are often rigid, broken, and distorted. Prosodic distortions and the deletion of unstressed syllables occur together. Atypical prosodic patterns may be the cause, rather than the result, of syllable deletion.

5. The children with deviant phonological development have their greatest articulatory problems with the phonemes /s/, /r/, /ʃ/, /ʒ/, /θ/, /ð/, /č/, /ɟ/, and /v/. Perception should facilitate production, and conversely if these children can learn to *produce* these phonemes, that action should improve their perception of distinctive features of these phonemes.

6. If a child engages in spontaneous imitation, he frequently imitates inconsequential utterances, rather than meaningful and purposive speech.

7. Because these children are restricted to certain sentence-types, they find permutations a difficult process. They cannot freely transform an interrogative sentence into a declarative statement; a positive into a negative form. "Stevie, you must give a tally back to me," said Miss Beckie. Stevie responded: "Stevie you give tally back—No!"

8. Agreement of subject and verb in number and the form of the past tense in third person singular (*he come* and *he say*) are often inaccurate —but have you listened to the free speech of adults in the supermarket? They also make these errors.

Menyuk and P.L. Looney, "A Problem of Language Disorder: Length vs. Structure," *J Speech Hearing Research* 15(2) (June 1972), 264–279; D.J. Sharf, "Some Relationships between Measures of Early Language Development," *J Speech Hearing Disorders* 37(1) (February 1972), 64–74.

[30] T.H. Shriner and R.G. Daniloff, "The Relationship between Articulatory Deficits and Syntax in Speech Defective Children, *J Speech Hearing Research* 12 (June 1969), 319–325.

[31] B.A. Kennedy and D.J. Miller, "Persistent Use of Verbal Rehearsal as a Function of Information About Its Value," *Child Development* 47(2) (June 1976), 566–569.

STAGE 4: CONTINUING EDUCATION STAGE: PRIORITY OF THE MAJOR HALLMARK, PERCEPTUAL-SEMANTIC DEVELOPMENT, IN LANGUAGE LEARNING

Oral language development cannot be "finished" at a certain age like the reading of a book at a certain time. The major emphases are the same whether the children are in the third grade or sixth grade. The all-important linguistic need of these children is education in the perceptual-semantics of oral language. Let me remind you once again, however, that perception goes far beyond the recognition of stimuli, far beyond the description or interpretation of a single idea or event. It encompasses and links past and present ideas and events in a perceptual whole. Semantics, likewise, signifies more than the meaning of a word. It signifies meanings of words in a context, words fitted together like pieces of mosaic, word groups united by their position in a perceptual field.[32] Upon the growth of perceptual-semantics depend syntactic relations, the complexity and variety of structural forms, the acquisition of adult prosodic patterns, and articulatory proficiency. In turn, perceptual-semantic growth is dependent upon the psychological attributes of motivation, attention, and memory (Chapter 3). And all substrates of oral language, in the final analysis, are dependent on the integrity of neurointegrative mechanisms (Chapter 2).

Extracts from the journal of a child, Sandy, who suffered a cerebral accident will illustrate these interdependencies. (The full journal summary may be found in *Language Disorders of Children* by M.F. Berry, Englewood Cliffs, N.J.: Prentice-Hall, Inc., 1969, 328–336.) Sandy was nine years old when he fell from a haymow to a cement platform, incurring a crushing injury to the left occipital-parietal-temporal areas of the cortex (Chapter 2). All perceptual-motor modalities associated with the comprehension-use of language were impaired. Whereas he had been a star student previous to the accident, he now found it difficult to attend and impossible to retain materials on which he had worked hour after hour. He made so many errors in reading (now at the second-grade level), particularly in the recognition of nouns, that the story was incomprehensible. He was unaware of his errors and made no spontaneous corrections. He was unable to retain visuomotor percepts of the letter-order in words so spelling became anathema. The loss in visual perception was evident in his inability to distinguish figure from ground. Auditory comprehension likewise was impaired. In elicted imitation of sentences, *lecture* became *electric chair, skill* was *skip,* and so on. Sandy often said words that resembled the sound of the word he should have used: *Ofaker (October),*

[32] G.A. Miller and P.N. Johnson-Laird, *Language and Perception* (Cambridge, Mass.: Harvard University Press, 1976), 238.

edel (*elbow*), *shubble* (*shoulder*), *burf* (*purse*). If apraxia were defined, as I believe it should be, as a *sensorimotor,* not a *motor* impairment, then these words might be called symptomatic of apraxia. Sandy had grave problems in structure. "I may go fishing on Sunday" turned into "I got to fish." To the question, "What's the thing for you to do when you are on your way to school and notice that you are in danger of being late?", Sandy said, "We get that when we got snow and got. . ." Memory cannot be considered apart from perception. In Sandy's case it meant the loss of what the word sequence looked like (visual memory); what it sounded like (auditory memory); and what it felt like (tactile-kinesthetic or prosodic memory). I can hear it now, his poignant cry of frustration: "I knew it once but now I can't remember it."

In the next chapter we shall discuss the teaching of perceptual-semantic skills. The lacunae in our knowledge are extensive.

REFERENCES

ARAM, D.M. and J.E. NATION, "Patterns of Language Behavior in Children With Developmental Language Disorders," *J Speech Hearing Research,* 18(2) (June 1975), 229–241.

BOHANNON, J.N., "The Relationship Between Syntax Discrimination and Sentence Imitation in Children," *Child Development,* 46(2) (June 1975), 444–451.

BOWERMAN, M.F., "Semantic Factors in the Acquisition of Rules for Word derlying Language," *Language Perspectives—Acquisition, Retardation, and Intervention,* eds. F.L. Schiefelbusch and L.L. Lloyd. Baltimore: University Park Press, 1974, 191–210.

BOWERMAN, M.F., "Semantic Factors in the Acquisition of Rules for Word Use and Sentence Construction," *Normal and Deficient Language,* eds. D.M. Morehead and A.E. Morehead. Baltimore: University Park Press, 1976, 99–180.

BRAINE, M.D.S., "Children's First Word Combinations," *Monographs Society Research Child Development,* 41(1) (Serial no. 164, April 1976), 90–93.

BRUNER, J.S., "The Ontogenesis of Speech Acts," *J Child Lang,* 2(1) (April 1975), 1–19.

CAIRNS, H.S. and J.R. HSU, "Who, Why, When, and How: A Development Study," *J. Child Language,* 5(3) (October 1978), 477–488.

CARROLL, J.B., *Words, Meanings and Concepts.* Cambridge, Mass.: Harvard Educational Review Reprint Series No. 7, 1972.

CAZDEN, C.B., *Child Language and Education.* New York: Holt, Rinehart and Winston, 1972.

CHAPMAN, R.S. and J.F. MILLER, "Word Order in Early Two and Three Word Utterances: Does Production Precede Comprehension?" *J Speech Hearing Research,* 18(2) (June 1975), 355–371.

COKER, P.L., "Syntactic and Semantic Factors in the Acquisition of *Before* and *After,*" *J Child Language,* 3(2) (June 1978), 261–278.

deVILLIERS, J.G. and P.A. deVILLIERS, "Competence and Performance in Child Language: Are Children Really Competent to Judge?" *J Child Language,* 1(1) (May 1974), 11–22.

DORE, J. and others, "Transitional Phenomena in Early Language Acquisition," *J Child Language,* 3(1) (February 1976), 13–28.

ERVIN-TRIPP, S. and C. MITCHELL-KERNAN, *Child Discourse,* New York: Academic Press, 1977.

FURTH, H.G., *Piaget for Teachers.* Englewood Cliffs, N.J.: Prentice-Hall, Inc., 1970.

GLEASON, J.B., "Code Switching in Children's Language," *Cognitive Development and the Acquisition of Language,* ed. T.E. Moore. New York: Academic Press, 1973.

HOCKETT, C.F., "The Origin of Speech," *Scientific American,* 203 (September 1960), 94.

HUNT, K.W., "Syntactic Maturity in School Children and Adults," *Monographs Society for Research Child Development,* 35(1) (February 1970), 55–61.

INGRAM, D., "Developing Systematic Procedures for Training Children's Language," *American Speech Hearing Association Monographs* 18 (August 1974), 5–14.

KENNEDY, B.A. and D.J. MILLER, "Persistent Use of Verbal Rehearsal as a Function of Information About Its Value," *Child Development,* 47(2) (June 1976), 566–569.

KOENIGSNECHT, R.A. and P. FRIEDMAN, "Syntax Development in Boys and Girls," *Child Development,* 47(4) (1976), 1109–1115.

KRAUSS, R.M. and S. GLUCKSBERG, "Social and Nonsocial Speech," *Scientific American,* 236(2) (February 1977), 100–105.

LEONARD, L.B., "Modeling as a Clinical Procedure in Language Training," *Language Speech Hearing Service in Schools,* 4(2) (April 1975), 72–85.

LEWIS, M.M., *How Children Learn to Speak.* London: Harrap, 1957.

LING, D. and A. LING, "Communication Development in the First Three Years of Life," *J Speech Hearing Research,* 17(1) (March 1974), 146–159.

LOVE, J.M. and C. PARKER-ROBINSON, "Children's Imitation of Grammatical and Ungrammatical Sentences," *Child Development,* 43(2) (June 1972), 310–319.

LYONS, J., *Semantics, I, II*. London: Cambridge University Press, 1977.

MCREYNOLDS, L.V. and D.L. ENGMANN, "An Experimental Analysis of the Relationship of Subject and Object Noun Phrases," *Developing Systematic Procedures for Training Children's Language*, ed. L.V. McReynolds. ASHA Monographs Number 18 *American Speech Hearing Association* (August 1974), 30–46.

MARSLEN-WILSON, W., "Committee on Cognition and Communication," *Science*, 189(4198) (18 July 1975), 226–227.

MENYUK, P. and P.L. LOONEY, "A Problem of Language Disorder: Length vs. Structure," *J. Speech Hearing Research*, 15(2) (June 1972), 264–279.

MILLER, G.A. and P.N. JOHNSON-LAIRD, *Language and Perception*. Cambridge, Mass.: Harvard University Press, 1976.

MOREHEAD, D. and D. INGRAM, "The Development of Base Syntax in Normal and Linguistically Deviant Children," *Normal and Deficient Child Language*, eds. D. Morehead and A.E. Morehead. Baltimore: University Park Press, 1976, 209–238.

NELSON, C., "Structure and Strategy in Learning to Talk," *Monograph Society for Research Child Development*, 38(1, 2) (1973).

PIAGET, J. and B. INHELDER, *The Psychology of the Child*. New York: Basic Books, 1969.

RAMER, A.L., "Syntactic Styles in Emerging Language," *J. Child Language*, 3(1) (February 1976), 49–62.

REES, N.S., "Imitation and Language Development: Issues and Clinical Implications," *J Speech Hearing Disorders*, 40(3) (August 1975), 339–350.

SCHLESINGER, I.M., "The Role of Cognitive Development and Linguistic Input in Language Acquisition," *J Child Language*, 4(2) (June 1977), 153–169.

SHARF, D.J., "Some Relationships between Measures of Early Language Development," *J Speech Hearing Disorders*, 37(1) (February 1972), 64–74.

SHRINER, T.H. and R.G. DANILOFF, "The Relationship between Articulatory Deficits and Syntax in Speech Defective Children," *J Speech Hearing Research*, 12 (June 1969), 319–325.

WEBB, R.A., M.E. OLIVERI, and L. O'KEEFE, "Investigations of the Meaning of 'Different' in the Language of Young Children," *Child Development*, 45(4) (December 1974), 984–992.

WEIKART, D.P. and others, *The Cognitively Oriented Curriculum*. Washington, D.C.: National Association for Education of Young Children, 1971.

chapter 8

A GLOBAL-ONTOGENIC
TEACHING PROGRAM

INTRODUCTION

And gladly wolde he lerne and gladly teche.

Prologue, *Canterbury Tales*

If you are looking for a cookbook of skills, devices, or structured materials to be used in rigid sequence, this chapter is not for you. Packaged programs are commercially available. Undoubtedly they assist the ill-prepared "clinicians" to become "operational," but, as someone has commented, they have little if any lasting effects.[1] Special language teachers will find them a feeble crutch producing a dependency that stifles the creative and halts challenging thought.

In this chapter we shall develop a program, ontogenic and global in approach, pragmatic and situational in its substance. Examples suggesting how to approach each skill will be offered liberally at every juncture. Teachers should regard them as illustrative, not prescriptive. Rightly used, they will serve as a stimulus to the teacher who must extend and adapt plans and materials to meet the needs and interests of the children in her

---

[1] C. Cazden, *Programs for Promoting Language Skills in Early Childhood* (Panel discussion at the Convention of the National Association for the Education of Young Children. Boston, 1970).

class. Needs? Do they need oral language development? Or language re-habilitation? Or language enrichment? The children's interests? They will reflect the social and cultural environment of the community. The basics are presented here; the adaptations must be made by the teacher.

BASIC CONCEPTS AND TERMS

The title of this chapter suggests the underlying philosophy and direction of the program. The concepts implicit in the title, however, merit further explanation.

Global

A global approach does not mean "teaching the whole child," a be-labored idea at its best. It does mean teaching all facets of language, linguistic and paralinguistic, in an interlocking relationship. The dominant profile is perception, and out of it comes perceptual-semantic development (comprehension-expression of meaning); phonation (prosodic, or melodic and gestural, development); structure (morphological and syntactic development or grammar); and phonology (sound patterns and systems). In emphasizing here their relations to the master hallmark, perceptual-semantic development, we are also expressing our reservations with respect to the ways each hallmark is presently taught.

These linguistic features or lineaments are not to be taught as separate entities and in tandem fashion. As they emerge from the fabric of perceptual-semantics, so must they be returned as part of its warp and woof. The aspects of *phonation*—prosody, body language, and gesture—for example, are sometimes called paralinguistic features yet, if one considers the total speech act, they are true linguistic features.[2] The term prosody, or melody, subsumes such features as rhythm, intonation, stress patterns, and voice quality and is intimately related to true paralinguistic features: emotional states, personality, social identity, and so on.[3] Phonatory developmental features also emerge from the common perceptual base: awareness and discrimination of visual, tactile-kinesthetic-motor, and auditory sensations. They are baby's first communicative mode. He comprehends and responds to the prosodic and gestural features of oral language before he comprehends the meanings of words or the form of the phrase. Phonation is a fundamental linguistic feature.

Grammar (morphology and syntax) is not "all" there is to language

---

[2] John Lyons, *Semantics I* (London: Cambridge University Press, 1977), 61.

[3] D. Crystal, *The English Tone of Voice* (London: Edward Arnold, 1975), 2–3.

learning. Grammar is but one facet locked into the comprehension-expression of language. Grammar cannot be taught economically or successfully as a thing apart from other linguistic features. "She can teach me grammar," said an eight-year-old boy "but it's hers, not mine." Neither can the *phonological system* be regarded as the primary goal of language learning, although there are many in the public schools at present who hold this view. It is a part of the perceptual-semantic hierarchy and hence cannot be taught by drills on single sounds or phonemes. Proof of the inefficacy of such procedures has been given in preceding chapters. Suffice it to say here that the child does not comprehend and use sounds singly any more than an adult comprehends and pronounces a word immediately when it is spelled for him. The "binder" is meaning.[4]

Ontogenic

The developmental or ontogenic order refers to the natural order of the growth of language from birth to adulthood, from nonverbal to verbal communication. Nonverbal signals are gestural and prosodic. A six-week-old baby forms a hypothesis about an object, situation, or event. If he can fit it into the scheme of his "world" of percepts, he usually responds in body language and/or prosodic patterns. Long before he can talk, the baby is a communicator, with pragmatic needs, feelings, and expectations which he wants to convey to others. Between fourteen and eighteen months, he will express meaning in prosodic patterns—sound strings producing few identifiable words but, nonetheless, oral patterns unmistakable in their communicative intent. He comprehends and expresses meaning by the melodic pattern. Syllable or morpheme strings intermingled with jargon make up a prosodic pattern. Still later the phrase, dictated by word order, is slipped into the prosodic envelope. Out of word order will come, as a process in development, the knowledge and use of structure. He has learned no rules but he has perceived and sometimes imitated spontaneously acceptable phrase and sentence patterns. He likes the feedback so much that he repeats them over and over. In the same way he has advanced from unintelligible syllabic utterances characterized by phonemic and functor deletions to articulate meaningful speech (Chapter 4).

So much for a skeletal review of the development of expression but what about the natural order of growth in input language, the number and

[4] W.A. Wickelgren, "Phonetic Coding and Serial Order," *Handbook of Perception: Vol. VII: Language and Speech,* eds. E.C. Carterette and M.P. Friedman (New York: Academic Press, 1976), chap. 7, 250; E.D. Schubert, "The Role of Auditory Perception in Language Processing," *Reading, Perception and Language,* eds. D.D. Duane and M.B. Rawson (Baltimore: York Press, 1975), 107–109.

kinds of hypotheses (organized schemas) he develops of the world around him? He develops them best, we believe, in experiences, events, and situations which extend, but are not strange to, his world. The purpose is plain. The child interprets the meaning of the new experience or situation by modifying or extending the hypotheses in his repertoire or by forming new ones (Chapter 4). The number of his hypotheses will depend on the quality of his sensorial environment, for at this stage the child's learning is largely on the sensorimotor level. That is, he must have experiences with movement, shape and size, taste, sound, and texture. The way things feel and *function* (make it go!), space and direction, sequences in time: these are sensorimotor interchanges between him and the world of sights, sounds, and feelings. He is the agent, the active "intervener" in his environment and from it he gains a rudimentary knowledge, "guesses," about the world and how it works. We recognize that situational learning, or learning by sensorimotor experience, is the first stage; we also know that it is basic to the later developmental stages: significant, concrete situations or events and finally symbolic experiences resulting in propositional thinking.

Situational teaching stems from the premise that children will learn to talk when they have something to talk about and *that something* must be of prime interest to them. Linguistically handicapped children generally talk very little. A primary aim in the first year of school, therefore, is sheer volume of spontaneous talk. We will not elicit this kind of talk by demanding carefully constructed sentences. In my view no child delayed in language development is going to be motivated to talk spontaneously by "clinic-bound exercises." Since "spontaneous talking is usually the ultimate goal of language training," as Hubbell has stated in a recent article,[5] it behooves all of us to encourage verbal interaction about experiences that truly matter in the child's world. We know that when the child is associating with his peers in a stimulating environment, he is motivated to talk more, to experiment with new words, and to perceive the patterning and articulation of oral expression by the *act* of talking.

Pragmatic factors are foremost in this kind of learning. Oral language is best taught in the context of use in the child's environment. Here is a child, Joey, who has proffered few verbal comments in the first month; he has depended largely on gestural language. Now he is "working" with others on the operation of a toy machine. Finally he asks, "Why you turn it that way?" (to set the gears). The teacher does not correct the form of the question, but a peer quite spontaneously says, "Why do I turn it that way? Because . . . Because . . . you see . . ." Now the teacher may reinforce the correct form of a question by introducing other questions with the

[5] R.D. Hubbell, "On Facilitating Spontaneous Talking in Young Children," *J Speech Hearing Disorders* 42(2) (May 1977), 217.

same form. In no sense is it an exercise in grammar to be memorized out of context. The phrases or sentences identify, describe, or interpret a specific situation; the form becomes a part of the child's oral style and his ideas. In situational teaching we do not present exercises in grammar; we do not teach syntax and morphology as separate entities divorced from the speech event. Nor do we develop a unit on phonation, articulation, or vocal expression. This does not mean that the program is without organization. Each hallmark has "its day," a period of primary emphasis, but all other hallmarks necessarily must be involved in the teaching. We would not, in fact we could not, teach phonatory development as a speech event, for example, without the assistance of other linguistic skills.

Another example or two may describe more extensively the nature and organization of situational language teaching. This is a self-contained classroom of kindergartners, all in need of oral language development. In the week preceding the opening of school, the parents (one or both) have taken an orientation course (two hours each day for four days) in which their responsibilities for home teaching are outlined. Many parents, especially among the disadvantaged, fail to realize that learning is not the sole responsibility of the public school. Children can and must learn at home. The parents receive a notebook that contains the trilateral contract (parents, child, teachers); a profile of their child's needs based on preliminary assessment; sections for assignments; materials; forms that will contain teachers' reports of progress; and "PR pages" (*Parents Respond* to questions). A list of inexpensive children's books to purchase for the home is also included. The loose-leaf notebook also contains the teaching syllabus that the teachers in the class will use. If no teacher aides are provided for this class, parents are urged to volunteer for service on specific days of each month. This, too, must be included in the contract. Fear of failure to "measure up" is a great deterrent in the success of a parent volunteer program. Active encouragement and lessening of this fear usually result in eager parent participation. The teacher may be in luck and receive an unexpected bonus: the discovery of a parent skilled in art, crafts, music, or some other field. The section *PR* (*Parents Respond*) (examples in Appendix A–8) contains forms which will be sent home from time to time seeking advice from the parent. The request for "advice" acts as a further guarantee of parental participation.

THE LANGUAGE-LEARNING ENVIRONMENT

Language development does not take place by direct attack on its hallmarks. Neither does it take place in a vacuum. It is a social phenomenon reflecting such paralinguistic features as the emotional status, personality, social identity, and so forth. Children may quite suddenly accelerate, perceptibly slacken, or arrest their learning altogether because of these features which are not a part of language but which exert an important influence over its acquisition. The shaping of these features owes much, for better or worse, to the environment and the people in that environment.

The Physical Environment of the "Language Clinic" or "Speech Center"

The environment must provide sensorial enrichment conducive to learning. In the medical and educational institutions that I have observed or in which I have taught for a long stretch, I have found little opportunity for appropriate stimuli—sight, hearing, taction, kinesthesis—to pierce the gloomy or sterile confines of the "speech clinic" cubicles. From recent studies we have supporting evidence that sensory enrichment stimulates cortical development at least in rats.[6] And if the brains of rats and men are similar in function, as Herrick proclaimed a half-century ago,[7] we suggest that sensory enrichment will also act to increase cortical development in young children. Why is the environment of "clinics," either in hospital or educational centers, a deterrent to language learning? Because they lack both physical space and the proper atmosphere. Moreover, the child regards "clinic-bound" language as something apart from the oral language he needs in daily life. He reserves what he learns in the clinic *for* the clinic.[8]

Social Stimulation and Pleasurable Reinforcement

The motivating factors in the learning environment will vary in form with the community, but the common aim is satisfying personal exchanges, both oral and nonoral. They extend to the people outside the family circle, to the neighborhood. Body contact, gesture language, laughter, games, ball-romps: all communicate meaning just as words do. Children need and thrive on these stimuli. Language is most easily learned in association with one's peers. It is the teachers' concern to innovate and

[6] R.A. Cummins, P.J. Livesay, and J.M. Evans, "A Developmental Theory of Environmental Enrichment," *Science* 197(4304) (12 August 1977), 692–694.

[7] C.J. Herrick, *Brains of Rats and Men,* 3rd ed. (Chicago: University of Chicago Press, 1963).

[8] C. Shewan, "The Language Disordered Child in Relation to Muma's 'Communication Game: Dump and Play'," *J Speech Hearing Disorders* 40(3) (August 1975), 313.

promote the activities, the experiences, in and out of the classroom which stimulate children to comprehend and express meanings and feelings which can be understood by others. We stress the need for fun, for pleasure, in a language-learning environment because all too frequently the child has heard only the language of crisis. The language of crisis is one of estrangement, not communication; of censorship, not information. Optimal learning occurs when the child finds it an enjoyable adventure, a highly motivated activity for which oral communication is an essential tool.

What activities? What situations? They must be the activities and situations which motivate him so that he is eager to know and to tell others what he knows. Where does one find these situations in which the child best observes, comprehends, and learns language? *In planning to make something, how to do something, or whether to do something,* we create these situations. For a time these situations may be centered in the classroom. Sooner or later, however, the child will also observe and learn language on the playground, in the cafeteria, in the corridors. Teachers must appropriate these theaters of action. Playing the game of kick-ball, four squares, or hopscotch; making red jello hearts for Valentine's Day; planning the Christmas party luncheon in the cafeteria; making posters for the "stop litter" campaign; snow-sculpture contests: all can be language situations on which teachers can capitalize.

The Home Environment

The need for an environment conducive to learning is the reason for placing parents at the hub of our teaching plans. That is why we enter into orientation courses and contractual relations with parents before we begin to teach their children. We conduct the orientation sessions as round table discussions in which views on diet, sleep, quiet time, TV control, guidance in one-parent families, and home discipline are shared. No real consensus probably is reached; yet parents begin to sense in the discussion a commonality of purpose and a sense of "belonging."

Emotional Climate

The emotional climate of the home is extremely important because it exerts a powerful influence on oral language growth. Miller and Johnson-Laird suggest that feeling may be considered a "perceptual predicate" in that "our feelings are a special class of perception of inner states." [9] We know that the 21-month-old child, "securely attached" affectively to Mother uses more language than children "insecurely attached." Insecur-

---

[9] G.A. Miller and P.N. Johnson-Laird, *Language and Perception* (Cambridge, Mass.: The Belknap Press of Harvard University Press, 1976), 111.

ity not only can produce a language lag and retardation; it also induces an emotional instability adversely affecting communication. Because these children cannot analyze (perceive) their internal feelings, they are frustrated and will veer from one extreme to the other very quickly and without obvious cause. Here is a summary of data extracted from reports about an older child, Lennie, who until he was ten years of age, belonged to no one. The reports are from the psychologist, language diagnostician, and Lennie's language teachers.

Lennie was nearly nine years old when he entered an oral language development improvement program in a self-contained classroom. Both the language diagnostician and the psychologist repeatedly emphasized the child's dysrhythmia, his repetitions, false starts, fillers, and reformulations when talking to his peers or teachers. The interesting contrast was his verbal play with puppets; he assumed various roles, changed his voice to suit the characters he was portraying, and although the speech was not always intelligible, his prosodic patterns were typical of normal conversation. But when he was pressed to engage in speech events with his peers or teachers, scanning speech and linguistic confusion returned. He would attempt complex sentences when pressed to do so but the sentence "would fall apart" before its ending. Here are two examples: "Can I fix you eat?" (Can I fix you something to eat?) "Well, we was goin' an' Jerry said—well you know how he talks—he said—well it was kinda funny . . ." The psychologist reported that Lennie seemed unable to shut out interferences, internal and external, which interrupted coding. Following these failures in communication, he would invariably engage in verbal play. The teaching team agreed with the consultants that it was indeed a retreat from psychological reality.

Several factors were thought to contribute to Lennie's linguistic retardation, but judging by later reports, the chief factor was an environment which provided no security. It was unstable and nonmotivating, serving only to diminish the person. At two years he was described by the social worker as malnourished and neglected. From the age of five he had been in and out of foster homes, rejected, and then reclaimed by an unstable mother. The death of one parent and desertion by another left him completely without ties. A subsequent report by his teachers made note of further retreats into a nonreal world. But in his tenth year the environment changed. Lennie had a stable home and school environment with understanding foster parents and teachers and two fast friends in his class. He made giant strides in learning. The last sentence in the report (made when Lennie was eleven years old) is exciting: "His verbal skills have begun to match his high performance skills in nonverbal situations."

Prescriptions for the establishment and control of the proper emotional climate cannot be set down. The aim is to encourage social attitudes of "feeling in," of empathy toward family and playmates. To that end, acts of kindness and of love should occur each day. How much love? How many demonstration acts? We would like to find the measure that produces the optimum effect on learning, but emotion will not be subjected to such controls. We do know that toxic levels of love can be a positive deterrent to learning. Parenting, particularly of the handicapped, demands a judicious mixture of serious concern and humor, of loving and laughing. Humor, after all, reflects a sense of perspective about life.

The Learning Set in the Home

Attentional behaviors are a critical problem for many language-handicapped children. (See Chapter 3 for information on the neurological and psychological bases of attention.) They seem to be especially difficult for children in economically disadvantaged families. Weikart and others note from their observation of disadvantaged preschoolers that "the child flits from one activity to another without really concentrating on any particular one. . ." [10] Parents can help to increase the child's attention span in several ways. Rather than engaging the child in one-shot games, word drills, or puzzles, the parents should encourage him to participate in a *sustained activity,* in a situation or operation. When interest grows in an experience or sustained activity, breathing, pulse, and extraneous motor activity will slow down. In such a positive, sustained, interactive environment, even hyperactive children develop audiomotor and haptic-motor skills which are needed for language learning.

Parents can also encourage sustained attention by motivating and modeling an active listening "set." As the child listens to himself and to others, he can be made aware of his own internal dialogues (self-initiated feedback). As he plays, constructs (by connecting shoe boxes), and "destructs" a train, a very young child will "think out loud" about the operation. A kindergartner will talk about his plane as he constructs and flies it to the moon. The child also must be encouraged to listen *actively* to others. And you are one of those "others" who must listen *actively* to him. As he "talks" to you, you show your genuine interest by responding with eye contact, facial expression, and gesture language. Television programs rarely provide anything except passive listening; and this can be done with a disengaged brain. If parents will exercise selection, both in program and time on TV-radio, and if they, the parents, motivate feedback and recall by their own modeling of the proper attentional behavior, these media may provide a small modicum of learning experience. If, on the other hand, the TV "operates" from morning to night with or without listeners, the child will also disregard it. But if he does not hear the telephone, your call to him, or the children playing across the street, you can be sure that he is actively listening and, in intense moments, making subvocal movements. Children who have learned at home to listen actively to themselves and to others are achieving a readiness for learning.

[10] D.P. Weikart and others, *The Cognitively Oriented Curriculum* (Urbana, Ill.: University of Illinois, 1971), 65. (Available through Publications Dept., National Association for the Education of Young Children, 1834 Connecticut Ave., Washington, D.C. 20009.)

Children build language out of their sensorimotor experiences. A deterrent to attentional behavior at every socioeconomic level is not the lack of sensorimotor experiences. The misfortune is that they make so little use of those with educational value. Their real deprivation is not sensory but cultural. In every environment parents can find stimulating sensorimotor experiences which will motivate the child to participate in the resulting speech events. Unfortunately the verbal interactions which children hear all too frequently—demands, commands, ventings of feelings, and expressions of wants, delivered in overloud, high-pitched tones—rarely motivate them in the use of language. It frequently does the opposite; it produces a negative attitude toward oral expression.

The home in the beginning is the child's laboratory for practice in oral language. The practice can occur without sitting down and having "lessons." It can occur while Mother is in the kitchen cooking. (Look, how I mix the cake! Help me stir it. Whoops! You dropped the spoon! Are you going to lick the bowl?) It can happen when she is washing dishes or setting the table, when Daddy washes the car or is repairing a toy. The child's spontaneous imitation of the mother's speech, however, may not be completely intelligible; it may be only an imitation of the key words. And these key words will probably be the action units, the verbs (or the nouns transformed into verbs) because they are the carriers of meaning for him. Although mothers are tempted to emphasize a collection of names of persons, objects, and so on, nouns really are not the child's first requisite in terms of use; verbs are. Nouns, to be sure, are joined with verbs and modifiers in meaningful phrases, but they are not useful standing alone. Moreover, as I have stated before, situational language experiences involve *semantic relationships* in which action at this juncture in the child's learning is the key factor. Language learning can be fun, even for the language-retarded child, if parents make it a part of the ongoing activities in the household. After the child enters school, many learning experiences can be continued at home as the children and family talk together at the supper table about school experiences. The child's language notebook, *My Journal,* often becomes a cooperative venture for the whole family. The child's talk is never penalized, verbally or nonverbally. Even his qualified successes must be rewarded.

Extension of Language Learning
beyond the Home

The home does not stop at the front door. It extends into the neighborhood, the school, and the whole community. And situational learning of oral language should go the same route. Parents, teachers, and neighborhood friends can find ways to extend these language-learning experiences *if* they are made aware of opportunities. Andy, five years of age and moderately retarded in oral language, had a single experience which will illustrate how many people cooperated in such an extension. The great event was the circus which Andy had attended with his parents. Immediately upon coming home, he ran to the neighborhood playground intent on telling his friends all about it, particularly about the antics of the clown. It was not connected speech, but he used all his communicative resources—action phrases, interjections, and gestural language—to represent the clown. The children asked, "Where does he get those funny clothes? The shoes with the turned-up toes? How does he paint his face?" Andy repeatedly said: "Me goed circus," but when his peers chimed in with "*I went* to the circus" and "We went too," Andy did not correct his sentence. But a few days later when a peer used the past tense of *go,* Andy also used *went,* but in a slightly different context. This kind of semi-conscious modeling tells us that Andy has engaged in active listening and that in particular contexts, he will use the proper tense. This example also supports the thesis that developing structure is not dependent on prior teaching in basic construction.[11] The circus excitement and talk continues. Andy's sister brings home an animated clown book which Andy takes to school so that all the children in class may see it. The team teachers alter their teaching plans. Within the week a clown from *The Shrine Jesters,* a local organization, appears at school to tell the class more about clowns. The children, wearing clown hats, circle the room walking, pantomiming, and talking like clowns. It is exciting; it is fun! It is a learning experience in oral language that began in the home and was continued in the school.

Teacher-Parent Relationships

Parents are people too and, hence, call for understanding by teachers. The association will be enhanced if the teacher understands that her job is neither to denigrate the child's abilities nor to withhold information about him to his parents. She accentuates the positive but does not hide the negative. All too frequently both parents and child reflect discouragement and defeat when they enter the program. The teacher's initial purpose must be to increase the confidence of parents in their child. She must be sensitive, too, to the cultural background of parents, to their wish to be proud of themselves and their children. As the teacher knows what it means to be a real person, so she must also know what it means for the other fellow to be a real person too. In the first year at least—and perhaps always—it is well to cultivate the habit of suspending judgments about

---

[11] L.B. Leonard, "A Preliminary View of Generalization in Language Training," *J Speech Hearing Disorders* 39(4) (November 1974), 429–436.

parental attitudes. Certainly the teacher will do nothing to undermine the status of the parent in the child's eyes. Her purpose is to build the status both of parents and child. This cannot be done if the teacher holds the popular misconception that all children with language handicaps are mentally retarded or that children with cultural-linguistic differences are inferior, or that the oral language standard of minority cultures is substandard.

Finally teachers and parents together will agree upon short-term and long-term goals. The programming activities must be geared to a mutual understanding by all parties of the child's needs and potentialities for accomplishment. Realistically the child's wagon may have to be hitched to a lower star.

In the orientation sessions Andy's parents have had a preview of the role the family will take as "helpers" for Andy, their language-disadvantaged child. On the first day of school, Andy is completing the preface of his language journal, a giant scrapbook. Someone must help him mount the pictures of his father, mother, sister, and baby brother, putting Andy, of course, in the center. His mother prints the names above the pictures. In the succeeding days Andy will talk about his family in terms of their *actions,* what Mom does, where Daddy goes to work, and "big" sister's project in Brownies (Girl Scouts). With proper encouragement, he will also talk about the happenings at school. Parents will find out more about these learning events through the leaflet, *PR* (*Parents Respond.* See examples in Appendix A-8). It is their invitation to become involved in the language education of their child.

Teachers in language seminars and workshops frequently tell me that parents of children in their classes will not cooperate. "They are poor and uneducated," they tell me. If the motivations and attitudes you communicate to them are adequate, the majority of parents, poor or wealthy, will cooperate. I remember the mother (with a three-year-old in a go-cart) who walked ten blocks, three days a week to our Center so that her six-year-old son, Warren, could attend the summer program. It was a long, hot summer. When I suggested that the Center could provide a bus ticket for Warren, she said, "But this is my only chance to go some place—nice. I like it here." It can be an ego-boosting experience for child and parent.

Cooperation of Special Language Teachers with Classroom Teachers

Although a distinguished colleague once questioned the status of our profession when "in bed with Special Ed," the relationship should prove to be beneficial if it is based on mutual understanding of the goals, methods, and materials of both parties. Intergroup cooperation among teachers is imperative yet sometimes it is difficult to come by. Workshops in which teachers with advanced study in childhood education, special education, and learning disabilities interchange ideas with the special language teachers have helped to promote a measure of cooperation, mutual understanding, and trust. Special language teachers report that they may be able to gain ready acceptance of their teaching goals and materials but find certain attitudes toward them difficult to overcome. The notion still persists that the special language teacher does not belong in the classroom because, as a "clinician," she knows little about elementary education. Unfortunately both the title, "clinician" and university curricular requirements in former years have given credence to this idea. Another misconception is that the special language teacher is prepared only in oral expression. Since her field embraces both the comprehension and expression of language, she must be prepared in all aspects of language learning.

Professional and Nonprofessional Aides

The special language teacher must take advantage of the resources both within and outside the school. Among staff members who have given inestimable help in a program I know well are the health and nutritional specialists. The nutritionist initiated the "hot" breakfast for a language class with the cooperation of the parent group because she found that two-thirds of the class were poorly nourished. It was the health educator who took spot checks on the home environment, eliciting information from the children on sleep time, meal time, watching TV, and so on and then talked to the parents at their monthly meeting about the home schedule.

Another helper was the physical education teacher who provided assistance in identifying children who needed help in rhythmics and motor skills. But rather than dealing only with these children, the physical education teacher taught the whole class while giving extra time and encouragement to those who needed it. It was not long before this teacher was searching for speech materials to accompany the rhythmic activities.

Civic organizations, particularly in the arts, can furnish several kinds of help if they are invited to participate *when the program is being planned.* A nationally recognized program *Arts for the Handicapped* is largely the result of the energizing force of a single person who enlisted the help of other agencies to implement her program, *Camp Sunshine.* Read *Icarus and Other Flights.*[12] Folk dance organizations, music clubs, little theater

[12] M. Perrone, *Icarus and Other Flights at Camp Sunshine.* (The publication is a joint project of The National Committee, Arts for the Handicapped, and Camp Sunshine, Rockford Park District, Rockford, Ill. The National Committee, Arts for the Handicapped, 1701 K St., N. W. Washington, D.C. 20006.)

associations, and arts councils all have provided teachers, materials, costumes, and so on for classes in language development. In the Ethnic Festival Week, celebrated in one particular community, Spanish, Scandinavian, and Italian leaders in drama, music, and folk dancing made signal contributions to the self-contained classes in language learning. This activity was not a diversion, a "spot project"; it was a language-learning experience fitted into Unit I, our first teaching division. Community participation is good for the children, for the program, and for the community itself.

Special Talents of the Special Language Teacher

I suppose no teacher worth her salt is an "ordinary" teacher, but special teachers dealing with the most important attribute of man, oral communication, must be extraordinary. Every generation throws up a few great teachers, and among them must be teachers of oral language.

What special qualifications must she meet in addition to mastery of the subject, its methodology, and strategies? Perhaps I can describe a language teacher, "Miss Madeleine," whom I have known and observed in this kind of classroom for many years. Her four- and five-year-old children call her "Mi-Mad." Miss Madeleine has been educated in the liberal arts and sciences. She is knowledgeable in the neurobiology of language, psycholinguistics, and the psychology of human relations; hence she is able to discuss findings and problems with doctors, school psychologists, nurses, administrators, parents, and her colleagues in the classroom. In no sense is she a speech technician possessing certain skills although she knows techniques and strategies. She has long since demolished the wall built up by her predecessors. She has shed isolation for a partnership with the "regular" classroom teachers.

Miss Madeleine possesses the *personal qualities* that commend her to people of all ages. She is attractive at forty-five years of age, well-groomed, and entirely outgoing and likeable. She laughs easily, particularly at herself. And although she has a merry heart "which doeth good like a medicine," she enters into the problems of her children and their parents with sympathy, understanding, and above all, with a high sense of integrity.

Miss Madeleine has *purpose*. She has a plan for her children because she knows that children cannot tolerate chaos or indifference, that nothing destroys the learning climate faster than disorganization. She would not ask, "What do you want to do today?" for she knows the usual response: "Nuthin." She may alter schedules and plans to suit the needs of her children and to make use of the day's events. She will capitalize, for example, on unexpected, unplanned opportunities in order to achieve specific goals.

She agrees with Gibbons and colleagues that "stray thoughts, sudden insights, meandering digressions and other unpredicted events constantly ruffle the smoothness of the instructional dialogue. In most classrooms . . . the path of educational progress could be more easily traced by a butterfly than by a bullet." [13] Nonetheless the butterfly finally locates the nectar; Miss Madeleine will draw the children back to the master scheme.

She is a woman of *indefatigable energy.* The funds are cut so she must "scrounge" for materials. A church gives her an upright piano. The Rotary Club provides her with funds for electronic equipment: radio, record player, TV, and so forth. The parents decorate the windows of her spacious, but bleak, quarters with gay curtains. An artist friend brightens the walls with murals geared to children's interests. The city traction company provides a bus and driver for special trips. *SOURCE,* a volunteer clearance house for educational personnel, schedules programs celebrating Veteran's Day, Santa Lucia Fest (Swedish), Martin Luther King Day, and the Mexican Feast of Our Lady of Guadalupe. Miss M. also has taken her program to the media. She is an able speaker before civic and professional organizations. In short, she has called on many community resources in the city to help her. Although teachers generally have been selling at a discount, the "Speech Lady" in this community exceeds market price.

You who work in megalopolis will say that it can't be done in your setting. I suspect, however, that every one of you could discover, very close to you, a neighborhood, a minicenter for support *if* you "went out to look." To be sure it takes endurance and the ability to bear frustrations courageously—but it can be done.

Miss Madeleine is *creative. Every* teacher can be creative if all materials are in the cupboards of her room. The cupboards were bare when Miss Madeleine began. The "bones" of the sociodrama came from the staff; the "meat," from the children. Having no "props," Miss M. used a single symbol to represent the character or action. A paper hat made a scarecrow; a cap, a clown; a towel-tube was a dog; a velvet muff, a kitty; cereal boxes made up a train; its tunnels were plastic bottles. Children accept symbolic representation easily. Things stand for other things as very shortly letters, numbers, and sounds will also stand for objects, people, and experiences, and still later, as they will stand for theories, facts, and ideas.[14]

---

[13] J.F. Gibbons, W.R. Kicheloe, and K.S. Dawn, "Tutored Videotape Instruction: A New Use of Electronics Media in Education," *Science* 195(4283) (18 March 1977), 1139–1146.

[14] L.M. Nicholich, "Beyond Sensorimotor Intelligence: Assessment of Symbolic Maturity Through Analysis of Pretend Play," *Merrill-Palmer Quarterly* 23(2) (1977), 89–99.

The Children: Initial Adjustments
and Learning Activities

Who are these children retarded in oral language? Many are faceless; they have no real sense of self-identity; they do not really know who they are. Some have become silent because their attempts at communication brought only criticism or abuse. Others are resentful, aggressive, or emotionally disturbed. It is the business of the teacher to show them how to break out of their silent or unhappy worlds, how to communicate more effectively either nonverbally or verbally. In the first months of teaching certain immediate goals should be implemented which will encourage these children to make the break.

1. *Help each child to adjust psychologically and emotionally* by
   a. showing acceptance of him, getting close to him, hugging him, patting his head, admiring his shirt;
   b. encouraging nonverbal, satisfying, and pleasurable interchange in the class (social skills);
   c. reinforcing immediately even his qualified successes in communication;
   d. giving him tasks, simple commissions which increase his sense of identity and of belonging to the group;
   e. developing in him a self-image of which he can be proud (I am I and nobody else!);
   f. "turning him on," by motivating him to try to communicate experiences. Devise lifelike experiences in the classroom, experiences in which he is eager to communicate. The key words are security, identity, belonging, and motivation.
2. *Motivate the children to accept you as you accept them.*
   a. "I'm O.K.: You're O.K." [15] They will accept you if you are the same each day, if they can depend on you. They will accept other children if you show your acceptance of all children.
   b. Children must feel that they are equal participants in the plan. You as teacher will not do something *to* them or *for* them but *with* them.
3. *Increase the sheer volume of "talk" in the classroom.* Surround the children with an atmosphere of pleasurable communication. Teach them how to settle differences with friendly gestures or words, not with fists.
4. *Make the child the center of his own teaching, his own behavior modification.* When he feels responsible for his own learning, he will move ahead without your urging. In one classroom I observed this schedule:
   a. The day began with the children in a circle for the planning session. They told or demonstrated what they were planning to do.
   b. The "work-time" session followed.
   c. An evaluation session ended the period. The children came into the circle again to tell what they did, how it worked out, and to receive

[15] T.A. Harris, *I'm O.K.: You're O.K.: A Practical Guide to Transactional Analysis* (New York: Harper and Row, 1967).

suggestions and praise. The "older" group (six to nine years) was encouraged to engage in autocriticism.[16]

5. *Motivating and learning activities* include the following:
   a. Children are responsible for duties in the classroom. They work in pairs
      1) in care of feeding of tropical fish;
      2) posting and clearing the calendar bulletin board;
      3) serving the breakfast or snack;
      4) tracking the litter bugs;
      5) returning toys, costumes, and equipment to cupboards.
   b. Each week two children are chosen to select a book from the room, school, or public library for the story telling (or reading) hours. If a holiday is near, they will look for a book pertaining to it. First and second grade children may be encouraged to make line drawings of the main character or of a single scene portraying action.
   c. They form a "Shutter-Snappers Club." The camera serves several purposes: It gives the child
      1) a means of discovering himself and his world through the lens;
      2) practice in ordering or categorizing things and people, putting together those which belong together in the picture;
      3) knowledge in focusing and concentrating on a single perception;
      4) a "surrogate" of reality for initiating conversation. The Shutter-Snappers Club has proven to be the best single motivator we have found for little children. In the third week of school, each child was provided with a box camera (gift of Kamera Kraft) but film only for 12 shots. The tykes quickly realized the artistic limitations of their equipment and snapped only those scenes that were important to them. They became quite firm about what they wanted and didn't want; self-confidence swelled with each flick of the flash bulb. Previously uncommunicative children were eager to discuss their new photographic careers. The first pictures on each film were taken of the camera "owner" by the teacher. "Why, that's me!" the child shouted in glee. Ego boost and achievement go hand in hand.[17]

UNIT 1: TEACHING ORAL LANGUAGE WITH EMPHASIS ON PROSODY AND PHONOLOGY

Prosodic Education in Language Delay and Language Disorders

Some language teachers have recognized the importance of prosody in teaching language handicapped children but they have not developed an organized, well targeted program. Certain aspects of prosodic therapy, however, have been employed in the language rehabilitation of adult

[16] Weikart and others, *The Cognitively Oriented Curriculum,* 65–69.

[17] "Instamatic Therapy," *Human Behavior, II* (February 1973), 30; D.W. Naiman, "Picture Perfect," *Teaching Exceptional Children* 9(2) (Winter 1977), 36–38.

aphasics since a Norwegian neurologist first called attention to its importance in oral language.[18] Within this decade, scholars in adult aphasia have paid increasing attention to prosodic education because they have found that (1) melodic, rather than grammatical, characteristics of function words may account for their retention or loss [19] and (2) melodic patterns are often retained despite severe cerebral trauma affecting all other facets of language. The most specific contribution on melodic intonation therapy by Sparks and Holland presents a series of four levels to be employed in teaching the adult aphasic. In their program the aphasic engages in tasks of intoning melody patterns accompanied by handtapped rhythms, imitating the clinician's intoned utterance, responding to the clinician's intoned utterance, imitating appropriate intoned responses, and initiating independent rhythmic responses or free speech.[20]

Yves Chesni [21] reporting on the disrupted prosody in Parkinson's syndrome contended that when the patient was unable to perceive and execute prosodic patterns, "inner language" also suffered. Chesni believed that when cortical and subcortical areas integrating and projecting prosodic or melody features were damaged, comprehension and hence "inner language" was impaired. Parkinsonism was not simply a *motor speech disorder;* it was a *language disorder* affecting both perception and expression.

Prosodic training for children delayed in language development is earning an established place in public schools where such programs as *T.A.L.K.*[22] have won state and national recognition by educational authorities. The self-contained classroom in which children with *language disorders* are taught is less prevalent. In an earlier text, *Language Disorders of Children* (Prentice-Hall, Inc., 1969), I presented the "case for prosody." Prosodic training is best adapted to group education, and hence speech and language centers associated with medical clinics rarely have

---

[18] G.A. Monrad-Krohn, "The Prosodic Quality of Speech and Its Disorders," *Acta Psychiatrica Neurologica* 22(3–4) (1947), 255–260.

[19] H. Goodglass and others, "Some Linguistic Structures in the Speech of a Broca's Aphasic," *Cortex* 8(2) (June 1972), 191–213.

[20] M.L. Albert, R.W. Sparks, and N.A. Helm, "Melodic Intonation Therapy for Aphasia," *Archives, Neurology* 29(2) (1973), 130–131; R.W. Sparks and A.L. Holland, "Method: Melodic Intonation Therapy for Aphasia," *J Speech Hearing Disorders* 41(3) (August 1976), 287–297; R. Sparks, N. Helms, and M. Albert, "Aphasia Rehabilitation from Melodic Intonation Therapy," *Cortex* 10 (1974), 303–316; H. Goodglass and others, "Some Linguistic Structures in the Speech of a Broca's Aphasic," 191– 212; C.I. Berlin, "On: Melodic Intonation Therapy for Aphasia by R.W. Sparks and A.L. Holland," *J Speech Hearing Disorders* 41(3) (August 1976), 298–300.

[21] Y. Chesni, "La Parole Intérieure," *Confinia Neurologica* 23 (1963), 192.

[22] T.A.L.K. (Teaching Activities for Language Knowledge), an instructional program designed to improve children's oral language skills (Rockford, Ill.: Rockford Public School District 205 Approved by Education Division, H.E.W., as an "Exemplary Educational Program," (July 1979).

either space or organization to carry on this kind of program. The hospital cubicle is ill-fitted for such a program.

One group of language-handicapped children whose prosody has been the subject of research for almost a century is the deaf. In her book, *Dance of Language,*[23] Mariam Allen presents "materials, methods and ideas" which she has found "particularly effective in using musical experience games to help deaf children feel and produce the language rhythms of English." She finds the approach effective even with the very young because "the child fits syllables and words into intonational patterns and rhythmic tracks which he has mastered previously." [24] Employing the rationale of "language rhythm families," the child, having "learned to move rhythmically to one of the basic patterns," uses it "to help him develop correct speech and language patterns." [25] Similar publications on prosodic language training (initiated through music) are *Music for Wonder* (*Early Childhood Language Book*) by Sister Kathleen Dalton; [26] and *Music for Special Children* by Dorothy Gilles.[27]

Cluttering, traditionally treated as a motor-speech disorder, is by its description and symptoms a rhythmic disorder of oral language. It may be a genetic disorder with neurological manifestations. Cluttering is symptomatic of disturbances in the perception of oral language and is probably caused either by deficits or fluctuations in the sensorimotor integration mediating oral expression.[28] The child clutterer, in my observation, usually begins speech well and then is subject to articulatory breakdowns, excessive rate, syllable repetitions and erratic rhythms. The result is an alteration of prosody, meaning, and intelligibility. Someone has described it, "speed-tumbled speech." When one asks the child clutterer what happened, he may say that he could not remember, he could not attend, he could not find the words, his tongue "got stuck," or everyone in his family "talks the same way."

Peter at six and a half years has all the earmarks of a clutterer, although there is little indication of cluttered speech in the record before he was five years of age. Here are some extracts from studies of his language development beginning with his entrance (at thirty-two months) in a hospital clinic for delayed speech. The clinician reported that Peter had "no speech" at thirty-two months although his mother insisted that he had a

[23] Mariam Allen, *Dance of Language* (Portola Valley, Cal.: Richards Institute of Music Education and Research, 1974); Mariam Allen, "Music is Her School for the Deaf," *San Francisco Sunday Examiner and Chronicle,* June 8, 1975.

[24] Mariam Allen, *Dance of Language,* 3.

[25] Ibid., 6–7.

[26] K. Dalton, *Music for Wonder* (San Francisco: Renna-White Associates, 1976).

[27] Dorothy Gilles, *Music for Special Children* (Edwardsville, Ill.: D. Gilles, 1976).

[28] D. Weiss, *Cluttering* (Englewood Cliffs, N.J.: Prentice-Hall, Inc., 1964); P. Dalton and W.J. Hardcastle, *Disorders of Fluency* (London: Edward Arnold, 1977).

few two-word "commands" by that time. At four years he did not refer to himself by his name or by *me*. At *five years,* the school psychologist noted a "serious lag in perceptual-motor skills, gross and fine motor incoordination, fleeting attention span, and a complete lack of interaction with people, toys, etc." He sedulously avoided any physical or eye contact with others. He could not or would not answer simple yes-no questions.

Now Peter is six and a half years old and has been in a language diagnostic teaching program for six weeks. From the staff report it is clear that his oral language is completely dysrhythmic: "He makes false starts, often pauses long in the middle of a phrase, slurs certain syllables, prolongs others, transposes phonemes and words in sentences. He seems to have great difficulty in formulating sentences. When asked a question requiring a direct answer he generally goes into a rambling discourse, characterized by increasing loudness in voice, agitated movements, perseveration and articulatory disintegration." When under strict monitoring by the staff, however, his behavior changes markedly. His voice and manner are quiet, and if visual input is added to auditory, he gets along quite well in perceiving and executing melody patterns. The staff is encouraged by his response to prosodic training although they realize that they are dealing with the external manifestations of what may be deeper and more serious problems. Language deviations are rarely simple, rarely amenable to single-pronged attack. Consequently the staff is helping Peter in the integration not only of haptic-motor but also of audiomotor and visuomotor skills. The child's emotional problems are probably the result, not the cause, of his language disability; yet they also must be dealt with. But the main thrust of the teaching at this juncture is on the prosodic patterns of oral language.

Why Prosody Is the First Unit in Teaching

In Chapters 2, 3, 4 and 5 we have presented the bases of this approach, both from the standpoint of ontogenic development and of logic. In review and summary here are our reasons for this teaching order.

1. Prosody is a psychoneuromotor phenomenon expressed in general and discrete movement patterns. In nonhandicapped children, these movement patterns are synergic in nature and constitute a complex of movements involving the speech instrument and the entire body. It follows then that motor learning is a precursor of prosody and a reinforcer of prosodic utterance. Linguistically handicapped children often appear to be normal in gross motor skill but lack the fine gradations of tension and relaxation which accompany normal posture and movement. All stimuli either are translated into bodily movement patterns sharing "equal time and force" or they result in a summation of small units

that cannot produce a smooth fluid performance. These nonselective responses of the perceptual-motor systems are often called soft neurological signs because their pathology cannot be established. They are nonetheless atypical, affect the prosodic base, and must be reckoned with in teaching children handicapped in oral language. The best way, we believe, to teach prosodic patterns is through sensorimotor learning with particular stress on the audiomotor and haptic-motor modalities in the perception of prosodic patterns of oral language.[29]

2. Prosodic patterning is an inherent neural response to successive auditory and haptic stimuli. The primal nature of rhythmic patterning is evident in the way we unconsciously pattern repeated sounds. The clickety-clickety-clickety of train wheels crossing joints in a track very quickly turns to an alternation of twos: clickety-click, clickety-CLICK, clickety-CLICK or to a more complex pattern (but still of twos): clickety-CLICK, clickety-CLACK; clickety-CLICK, clickety-CLACK. More familiar to a child is the tick of a clock. It first seems to say tick-tick-tick-tick, then tick-tock, tick-tock; and finally tick-TOCK, tick-TOCK, tick-TOCK. Neither the train wheels nor the clock change, but auditory perception changes their rhythm and stress. Depending on the severity of the hearing loss, the audio-handicapped child may have to rely on haptic (tactile-kinesthetic) stimuli in prosodic perception. That it can be achieved is attested to by numerous reports of teachers of the hearing-handicapped. One teacher wrote:

> A hearing baby comes out with no words but with a rhythmic melodic flow which is babbling; then he puts the words into that track . . . We're trying to teach the acoustically handicapped child an internal way of monitoring his own speech . . . We don't know why, but when these children make music inside themselves, somehow it works.[30]

3. Perception markers are basically prosodic in nature, involving, not the single phoneme, but a string of syllables, five to seven in number.[31] It follows that we must know the distinctive features, not of the sound, but of the syllable and syllable strings. In other words, a single sound is never single or isolated in the dynamics of the speech continuum.[32]

4. Prosodic patterning carries the heavy information, phonologic and structure loads in ordinary connected speech. Both syntax (or early word order) and semantics ride on the denominator of rhythmic patterns of sound and syllable sequences, and these sequences are an important part of phonological development.[33] In the speech of the language-retarded child, for example, the functor

---

[29] D.D. Hammill and N.R. Bartel, *Teaching Children With Learning and Behavior Problems* (Boston: Allyn and Bacon, 1975), 229–230; K.P. DePauw, "Enhancing the Sensory Integration of Aphasic Students," *J Learning Disorders* 11(3) (March 1978), 142–146.

[30] Mariam Allen, "Music is Her School for the Deaf."

[31] V.A. Kozhevnikova and L.A. Chistovich, *Speech Articulation and Perception.* (Moscow-Leningrad, trans. by National-Technical Information Services, U.S. Dept. of Commerce, Springfield, Va., 1965.)

[32] S.G. Fletcher, "Time-by-Count Measurement of Diadochokinetic Syllable Rate," *J Speech Hearing Research* 15(4) (December 1972), 763–770.

[33] An obstacle in "communicating with computers by voice" is that the computer may generate a string of words but in order to give meaning to the string, the correct

words determining structure are frequently omitted. Goodglass and others conclude that here again prosodic, rather than the grammatical, characteristics of function words determine whether they are lost or retained in ungrammatical speech.[34] Foreign or dialectal speech affords another example of the importance of prosody. As long as prosodic or original timing relationships between accented syllables are preserved, we are quite insensitive, I note, to phonemic distortions produced by foreign or dialectal variation. If this is true, then children should be taught to perceive and execute the rhythms of oral expression characteristic of the community in which they live before articulatory problems are attacked.[35]

Phonology and Phonation (Prosody) Conjoined in Teaching

The reader by this time is familiar with my position that the phonological features of oral language should not be separated at this stage of learning from prosodic or melodic patterns. Phonemic clusters, phrases, and sentences must be perceived and fitted into the "prosodic envelope." They are indeed bound by prosody, the speech flow of sound. In this chapter every utterance, rhyme, or story will reinforce the significant features of sounds and sound combinations which make up the phonological system. Our belief is that children learn the distinctive features of each class of phonemes more easily and speedily when they are an integral part of the production of language. Because prosodic patterning demands practice in *production,* the two can be taught together. If special attention must be given to certain phonemes or phonemic clusters, the language teacher will cull them, concentrate on the perception-production of their distinctive features, and return them to their place in the text.

Some phonological deviations, however, may be so severe as to require unusual strategies and resources. Indeed in the teaching of Sandra, six years old, we went beyond phonological and prosodic methods. The rhythm of Sandra's speech was distorted, but a greater problem was her perceptual deficit in phoneme sequencing. She employed so many idio-

---

stress, pitch, and timing of words in the speech output must be obtained and this can only be done by a syntactic analysis.—A.L. Robinson, "Communicating With Computers by Voice," *Science* 203(4382) (23 February 1979), 734–736.

[34] Goodglass and others, "Some Linguistic Structures in the Speech of a Broca's Aphasic," 191–212.

[35] D. Bolinger, "Intonation is a Universal," *Proceedings of the Ninth International Congress of Linguists,* ed. H.G. Lunt (The Hague: Mouton, 1964), 833–848; D. Ling and A.H. Ling, "Communication Development in the First Three Years of Life," *J Speech Hearing Research* 17(1) (March 1974), 146–157; J.D. MacDonald and others, *An Experimental Parent-Assisted Language Program for Preschool Retarded Children.* (The Nisonger Center, 1580 Cannon Drive, The Ohio State University, Columbus, Ohio, 43210, 1974.)

syncratic combinations that her speech was unintelligible. She learned new combinations by employing these phonemes, but she did not drop the deviant ones that she had learned earlier. The result was a chaotic phonological system. For example, when a *nonnasal* consonantal phoneme began a word in which a nasal appeared later, she also nasalized the first consonant. She said *ning* for *thing; nen* for *ken* (*I ken* (can) *do it); nin* for *win,* and so on. We intensified the prosodic training in her group because we thought that we then would be able to interpret her meaning by the melody pattern. So the children "read the music" of the phrase or line (on the chalk board); they hummed the phrase; they used helping hand gestures. During the six months' period of prosodic and phonological reinforcement, Sandra also had the assistance of the itinerant speech therapist. She provided intensive training in auditory perception, placement of the articulators, feature analysis, and reinforcement of syllable strings. Intelligibility did improve, but it was not enough. Finally we sought the help of the classroom teacher who was teaching Sandra to read. The training in visual-auditory recognition of symbol sequences on the page and in auditory feedback in reading aloud made "all the difference" between success and failure.

Teaching Language Without Words
(Body Language; Gestural Language)

In preceding chapters (2 and 5) we have presented the theoretical bases and the specific need for training in neuromotor coordination involving the entire body. We have pointed out again and again that the prosodic patterns of oral language rise out of such differentiated phasic movements as postural activities and tonic facilitation. These patterns, of which speech movements are a part, must be experienced as an entity, not as a summation of small units. Here are the children who do not walk "all in one piece"; who cannot skip, who lose their balance and trip over objects they do not see; who stumble up steps because they do not sense, tactile-kinesthetically or visually, the height of the riser; who exhibit motor impersistence or disintegration both in gross and fine motor activities, such as speech. These are children who are terror stricken when they are asked to put on a blindfold before hopping ten paces on one foot. Are these the manifestations of the "awkward child" syndrome? They also may be the manifestations of a mild cerebral palsy, a genetic deficit affecting cerebral dominance, or a mild mental retardation. And these are children who are linguistically handicapped. It is interesting to note that special language teachers assisting in L.D. classrooms for the *learning disabled* report that the great majority of their students profit by perceptual-motor training which begins with body language. The dividends are reflected both in prosody and in articulation. With the participation of the team: classroom, physical education, and language teachers and, often, parent aides (see examples in *Parents Respond,* Appendix A-8), successes will outnumber failures. The sequence of activities in teaching silent language which we outline here is clearly suggestive, entirely flexible. In many of these activities in learning language, both silent and oral, tape and disc records will provide excellent background rhythms for marching, dancing, pantomime, rhymes, finger plays, choric verse, and so on. Here are a few titles: *Ease on Down the Road* (The Wiz, Atlantic Recording Company); *Peace Train* in Cat Stevens' Greatest Hits (A and M Records); *Beat the Drum* in *Happy Time Records* (Pickwick International, Inc. L.I.C.N.Y.); *The Lion Sleeps Tonight* (Atlantic Records); *Magic To Do* (Pippin, Motown Records).

1. *Movement patterns involving posture, motion, balance, locomotion and action sequences,* such as the following:
   a. Walking, hopping, skipping; jumping rope, tripping down the stairs; walking down the stairs to the beat of a drum;
   b. turning the body from side to side;
   c. balancing on one foot while swinging the other;
   d. marching and dancing to the beat of the drum or cadenced music;
   e. pantomiming the movement patterns of favorite animals: rabbit, squirrel, rooster, monkey, kangaroo, or elephant;
   f. moving as the toy soldier which can be wound up, and then stopping slowly when the clock runs down;
   g. walking as a spaceman arriving on a planet with little or no gravity.

2. *In training children in pivoting and directional movements, those children whose movements are indecisive, confused, or reversed should be paired with their more able peers.* Remember that many linguistically handicapped children, even at nine years, have not established cerebral dominance. One might begin with these verbal directions: "Swing right-swing left; now swing all the way around. Rock: heel-toe; toe-heel, with one foot, then with both feet; step forward on left foot; shift weight to forward foot; now forward on the right foot," and so on. "Jump this way, now that way; four steps forward, then turn left; four steps, then to the right." and so forth.

3. *The next step which we would take is to teach pantomimic response to speech and other situations employing skillful coordination of sequential movement.* This step in language learning is more difficult. Here the children are responding, not with others, but alone. The sequences are more complex, sometimes more subtle, portraying an emotional response. Moreover they now are responding in action to situations which they encounter in their daily life— situations most closely associated with their language behavior at home and in school. They must listen actively to the directive or description in order to perceive completely and to respond accurately. Motivation, attention, and memory now are increasingly important in the learning process. A child will usually be successful with such verbal directives as these: *You are a major league pitcher going into the wind-up for a curve ball; you are the drum major in a marching*

band; you bank the shot twenty feet away from the basket. But when the response must have emotional coloring, as does all genuine communication, he may have difficulty. Yet unless children can perceive and communicate feelings, the interchange has little pragmatic value. Here is a list of directives for little children which seems simple but is not:

a. *Wave to your friend across the street as if to tell him some exciting news;*

b. *Make a fist in anger* ("I'd like to beat up on you.");

c. *A driver is about to run a stop light; you, the policeman, shout STOP;*

d. *Everyone, Do you hear? PLEASE sit down!;*

e. *Listen! Do you hear her bark?* These directives are not simple because they are emotional; they require subtle bodily movements, fine hand gestures, facial expression, and eye contact. Older children can be engaged in a situation requiring a chain of responses; this is a single example: *You hear an airplane. Where is it? It sounds close. There it is: right overhead! It swoops even lower! Is it in trouble? Will it make it over the trees? No! Terrible! Terrible!* The language retardate needs practice outside the classroom. Time for another *PR* (*Parents Respond*) to be sent home. Examples in Appendix A-8.

Teaching Melody Patterning in Verse and Speech

In earlier chapters, I have documented the position that we comprehend meaning in large part through the melody of language. Once having learned to communicate, not only meanings but feelings in rhythmic language *without words,* the child with a linguistic lag is better able to translate the rhythms of body language into verbal expression. One way to determine the influence of melody on comprehension is to tape a series of questions using the normal inflections, timing, and intonation, and then to record the response time of the youngsters to these questions. Some time later, prepare another tape of the same questions employing distorted melody patterns and again play the game with the children. You will want to compare both speed and accuracy with their earlier responses.

The melody of speech probably can be taught in many ways. We approach it first through rhymes, finger plays, and chants; then choric verse, drama, and stories. The advantages of this approach for linguistically handicapped children are several. They do not have to formulate word order and structure, but as they memorize the material for interpretation, the act of repetition establishes syntactic and morphological patterns. They are free from the "burden" of the pragmatics and structure of daily dialogue. They are stimulated in imagination, creativeness, and the perception and expression of heightened meaning. The vast body of children's literature becomes a treasure house to be exploited in the cause of language acquisition.

1. *Movement Patterns in Time with Rhymes, Chants, Verse.* Finger plays and rhymes such as, *Skipping Is Fun, Stretch Away Up High, Hickory, Dickory, Dock, The Little Turtle,* and *Hands Up* are well suited to the needs of beginners. Slightly older children enjoy pantomiming more complex movement patterns of chants, games, and sports. For example, the children pantomime the action as leaders of the group alternate in chanting (with heavy stress): *The Mulberry Bush; The Wheels on the Bus Go Round and Round; Merry-Go-Round* or *The Squirrel.* As the children become familiar with the lines, repeated over and over, they will spontaneously join their peer leaders in saying the lines as they act them. I have seen even the silent, faceless child yield to social pressure and join in. Titles of books containing rhymes, chants, choric verse, finger plays, and singing-chanting games for different age groups may be found in Appendix B-8.

2. *Moving on to the Melody Patterns of Choric Verse, Minidrama and Stories.* The majority of language-handicapped children take to choric verse. And they have reasons. They are not alone. If they get the melody and basic gestural patterns, they can follow along despite morphophonemic distortions. They also have the help of their peers in *maintaining* the melody; and the melodic pattern in turn heightens their perception of such phonological processes as syllable structure and stress, normal assimilation in sound sequences, and so on. Choric verse also makes demands on their attention span, alertness in timing, and memory. The repetition of lines resulting in overlearning is particularly valuable for the slow learner, a practice he must acquire. The child must be motivated to help himself in this learning process. Almost any poem or story employing dominant and repetitive rhythms of speech and suggestive of lively movement patterns can be adapted for choric production. A child may have a single line to say over and over, or the group as a whole may say such a rhyme as, *Hickety-Tickety Bumble Bee. Can you say your name to me?* and one child answers, *Ma-ry, Ma-ry.*[36] This preschool group also has a game chant: *Liddley, Liddley, Liddley, Lee. Throw the ball please to me.* Older children (six to nine years) like antiphonal speaking with two or three part choruses as in *The Big Clock, Sometimes, Go Wind* and *What in the World.* (Collections of verse suitable for choric production are found in Appendix B-8.)

Prosodic and phonological development is still our main goal in the production of minidramas, role playing, and puppet plays, but now they are associated with and based on other more complex skills. The child must have accurate perception of the character he is to create or reproduce. He must talk like, walk like, act like, be like the character he is portraying. He must make up appropriate lines while paying attention to word order and syntax; he must produce appropriate melody patterns with bodily action suited to the word. Since the line or lines may be said in chorus with other children, as in *Chicken Little,* he must remember the word order and the prosodic pattern exactly: "Chicken Little, The sky is

[36] M.H. Richards, *The Child in Depth* (Portola Valley, Cal.: Richards Institute of Music Education and Research, 1969), 31.

falling; we must go to tell the King." He must also exercise unusual imagination in the use of props, sometimes constructing hand or stick puppets as aids (with the help of his parents). Interestingly enough, children prefer nonrealistic props. They will use tables as houses or bridges, twigs as fishing poles, cereal boxes hitched together as trains, and so on.[37] Fairy tales, such as *Goldilocks and the Three Bears, Three Billy Goats Gruff, The Ginger Bread Man,* and *Chicken Little* are excellent for this purpose. Children also enjoy making up pursuit stories or ghost stories which call for changing rhythmic movement patterns and for highly melodic utterance. *The Bear Hunt* was made up by a group of five- and six-year-old children in a special language class. In Appendix B–8 you will find collections of children's stories which may be told and retold or adapted for plays, role playing, and puppet drama. Thus children's literature builds the natural bridge between learning to perceive and express the thoughts and feelings of others and learning to perceive and express the child's own ideas and feelings in daily life.

From the Prosodic Language of Others to the Child's Own: Prosodic Speech

By this time the child probably has incorporated the melody patterns he has acquired into his own speech. By this time the special language teacher also knows the kinds of speech situations in which children are most frequently engaged and which will be interpreted mainly by their prosodic connotations. They are situations involving themselves. They are highly personal and hence are dominated by their feelings about themselves, their actions, and interactions with others. Their purpose is pragmatic; children use language with the intent to intervene in their environment.

Speech situations exemplary of these actions and interactions, in which feelings and hence prosodic utterance dominate, concern a.) emotional responses (anger, fear, happiness, discomfort); b.) directives; c.) announcements of special skills or achievements and; d.) purely social interchange. You will remember that in recounting my experiences in a cleft palate center, one of my goals was to change those faceless children into lively, expressive persons. Could I teach them to express effectively in action and words: "Ooh—it's cold in here—shivery!"; "I know what's in that box— Yum-Yum!"; "Ouch! You're stepping on my toe"; or "I like you—I DO!"

---

[37] G. Gregg, "Fantasy Training Tips," *Psychology Today* 8(9) (February 1975), 36; A. McGovern, *Too Much Noise* (New York: Scholastic Book Service, 1967); M.E. Martignoni, *The Illustrated Treasury of Children's Literature* (New York: Grosset and Dunlap, 1955).

They did not take very well to these emotional exchanges; they were better in the use of the directive. Probably bcause the children had observed speech situations in which the following directives were used, the actions and words seemed less contrived: "Gimme that: it's mine"; "Money please" (school bus driver rubs thumb over finger tips); "Go over there; he's at the corner now"; "Will you both come here, please?" (finger signaling approach). The *Gourmet Girls and Guys* who announced, demonstrated, and produced the "world's best pizza" exchanged highly prosodic utterance with the class. There is much to teach in social talk which should involve subtle expression and interpretation of prosodic speech, but we rarely take the chance to teach it. A class of youngsters mentally and linguistically impaired were in a good social situation, a unit in table manners. Its purpose—or so I thought—was to teach social interchange. But the special language teacher concentrated on the use of the present and past tense! The basics of social talk, they were not learning. They evinced little intent, meaning, or feeling in their laconic phrases. They had no eye contact with the listeners; even *hi* and *bye, please* and *thank you* were empty, drab—as the walls of the room. The lack of prosodic overtones was equalled only by the teacher's ironic remark: "You certainly have good manners."

In all these speech situations, perceptual-semantic skills have been demonstrated on an elementary level, both by listener and speaker. So for little children, the outline of the teaching program including perceptual-semantic skills is now complete. For "older" children, six to ten years of age, especially handicapped by perceptual-semantic problems, a discussion of the formal organization of the strategies by which individuals learn to perceive and express meanings and feelings through oral language is in order.

UNIT 2: TEACHING ORAL LANGUAGE WITH EMPHASIS ON PERCEPTUAL-SEMANTIC SKILLS

It is the happy accident when we are understood.

William James

Meanings-Percepts

We have hyphenated the term, perceptual-semantics, because we believe that perception and semantics have common roots. Indeed, semantic categories are determined by the same relations that determine the character of human perception and thought. Linguistic knowledge results from the association between contextual meanings expressed in words and percepts.[38] A stumbling block to success in our present teaching is that we tend to treat perceptual development only as an information gathering and analytic processing of "facts." We have forgotten that *feelings,* a special class of perceptions of inner states, cannot be excluded from the comprehension or use of language.[39] In instructing children in perceptual-semantic skills, all too often we talk and teach as if the children were computers, information-processing systems, completely dispassionate and divorced from the *act* of communication. They are not; they engage in dialogue; they express and respond to interactions, attitudes, and feelings which interpenetrate other perceptual-semantic filiates; the computer can do none of these things. It follows then that in your teaching you will want to stress those skills which will best help the children in your class to comprehend and participate in these interactions and to engage in such practical, contextual uses of language as social interchange; requests, instructions, and intentions; question-answer seeking; and problem solving leading to decision making. The pragmatic approach is the realistic approach to learning.

Situational or *experiential learning* should not suggest that the child is learning by osmosis. The goals, organization, materials, and procedures are carefully worked out although they may be subject to change without notice when events necessitate change. The emphasis is on action. The child, for example, does not engage in passive listening. He observes actively, using both feedback and feedforward as he moves on beyond the use of ordered context to contextual improvisation or association. The situations or experiences, as you will remember from Chapter 4 cannot be entirely new or entirely strange; yet they must be sufficiently new and exciting in order to motivate the children. Children must be motivated to discover ideas and their relationships and *to talk about them.* These ideas must be couched in an appropriate vocabulary and in a structural and prosodic form which best expresses the relation. If the melody is deviant or the word order confused, obviously the idea will be obscured. Further along in this chapter, we suggest experiences that might be exciting and somewhat novel for your community of children. Undoubtedly you will take them *as suggestions* and will make adaptations and additions. The most effective situations will be those capitalizing on events in your own community. At this moment in our community, the conversation in and out of the classroom concerns the great fire in which a renowned shop, filled with irreplaceable treasures, burned to the ground. A group of lan-

[38] J. Deese, "Semantics: Categorization and Meaning," *Handbook of Perception VII,* eds. E.C. Carterette and M.P. Friedman (New York: Academic Press, 1976), 266, 291.
[39] Miller and Johnson-Laird, *Language and Perception,* 109–112.

guage-retarded youngsters (third through fourth grade level) brought in rumors of arson, break-in, a burning cigarette left behind by an employee, and so on. The special language teacher immediately seized upon the event to teach the conditional proposition: "Suppose that _____." Following a description of the happening (in sequence) by two boys who had gone to the scene of the fire and a free discussion of the rumors, these questions were posted on the chalk board:

a. Suppose you were walking by the shop on the night of the fire and noticed some boys running down the alley behind the building. What would you think? What would you do?

b. If you were driving by the shop and saw what looked like smoke coming from a waste bin by the back door, what is the first thing you would do? the second?

c. If while you were in the restaurant section of the shop, someone shouted "Fire" and people began to run to the exit door, what would you do first, second, third?

Two primary perceptual-semantic skills are apparent: temporal sequencing and the conditional proposition. In *Parents Respond* (Appendix A–8), you will find an example of extension into the home of the conditional proposition.

Learning Perceptual-Semantic Skills through Situational Teaching

These skills have been implicit in all hallmarks of language learning. Prosodic training involves the perception of the relationship of ideas and the form necessary to express such relationships. The idea, moreover, must have a structural frame, a frame dictated by prosodic constraints. And just as prosody must be perceived, so children must perceive, must comprehend, structures which will communicate their ideas and feelings. Children, we think, comprehend and use perceptual-semantic strategies most easily, not by formal exercises in prosody, grammar, and phonology, but *by doing things,* and by *talking about what they are doing as they do them* or *about what they have done.* In short, they perceive the totality of the language act, all in a single context. Such a program demands that the child perceive and use language in an activity or situation of immediate interest to him. He is, he must be, an active participant, for the relationships involved in these skills can only be established as the skills are linked with him, with his activity. This is what we mean by situational or experiential learning.

Questionable Practices in Teaching
Perceptual-Semantic Skills

In Chapter 6 we did not recommend the direct head-on attack on structure, per se, because we believe that this kind of teaching imposes formal, rather than useful, organization on language materials.[40] Instead we tried to show how such syntactic features as tense, class, and sentence length and complexity can be taught as a part of perceptual-semantic development.

Vocabulary Building

Just as we have presented no formal exercises in grammar, so we have not included vocabulary drills or tests based upon *The Dolch List, Gates First Five Hundred Words Vocabulary List,* or any other list a child "should know." A child's early language does not or should not consist in a collection of words, in naming things, or persons, or events. To communicate meaning even at the simplest level, he must express relationships in his environment. Naming, identification, will not do it. The simplest form of infantile expression concerns relations in action, and such action usually involves both verb phrases and noun phrases. It involves, moreover, the facial expression, the gestural accompaniment, and the total bodily movement pattern. Elizabeth, four years old, changes the words and the word order quite spontaneously if the relationship, generally consisting of her solution to a "need" situation, must be made clearer.[41] She often repeats part of her mother's question, the better to understand it. These efforts are evidence of her semantic development.

A vocabulary test is scarcely a valid index of semantic development. We regard vocabulary, not as an entity to be dealt with separately or formally, but as part of a total operational scheme. To be sure, we motivate children to use words which express the idea accurately, but we do not remove the words from the context or ask the child to imitate the expression of others. Vocabulary training is profitable only when it is based on the associative strength among words in a meaningful sequence. The word must become a part of a semantic unit *if it is to be remembered and used.* I have observed the teaching of color names, animal names, food names, toy names: all without any attempt to make them part and parcel of the

---

[40] E. Hatch, "Language Teaching and Language Learning," *Handbook of Perception, VII,* eds. E.C. Carterette and M. P. Friedman (New York: Academic Press, 1976), 69.

[41] T. Gallagher, "Revision Behaviors in the Speech of Normal Children," *J Speech Hearing Research* 20(2) (June 1977), 303–318.

child's life situation. Unfortunately, memory is generally measured by the number of digits or words a child can recall. Since such tests demand recall of isolated items, dissociated from the child's experiences and the perceptual complex in memory storage, they cannot be considered reliable indices, even of vocabulary knowledge. The study of antonyms and synonyms, likewise, is a sterile exercise unless the child can use them in spontaneous speech.

Artificial Combination of Attributes

In language learning in live situations, children acquire new percepts based on parts or wholes of previous percepts. In the spate of "learning packets" now on the market, I find a complete reliance on strange, completely artificial combinations of attributes, instead of those logical combinations based on previously learned experiential percepts. Even standardized tests of perception employ artificial combinations of attributes based on conjunctive, rather than relational, aspects of perception. Most of them are clearly foreign to a child's interests; yet they are used in teaching. Can any child find great excitement or adventure in placing the red circle in the blue square? Is he learning anything when he locates three yellow triangles of the same size? Moreover, such test materials rely on visual stimuli whereas the child's percepts are verbal. And because they are visual materials, the learning exercises are carried on in silence. In thirty-minute exercises of visual matching or classifying which I have observed recently in several schools, no teacher asked the child: "*Why* did you put these together?" or "*Why* did you take this one out of the group?" In short, *how* does he relate the perceptual units involved in a task? Aren't these the questions, the answers to which truly measure his perceptual ability?

Dichotomy between Comprehension and Expression

Training in the strategies of comprehension should not be separated from those employed in oral production. The reason for the dichotomy is understandable. Scholars and teachers in our field have taken their direction from psycholinguists who have shown little interest in the *expressive functions* of language. As teachers, we must be equally interested in comprehension and expression if we are to succeed. Practice strengthens all links in the comprehension-expression of the perceptual-semantic chain: prosody (phonation), syntax, and phonology. As I have said before, comprehension-expression might well be written as one term for it has bivalent bonds. When children begin the first grade, all verbal activities—

speaking, reading, and writing—should be employed to amplify percepts, facilitate oral production, and enhance recall.

Teaching Elementary Organizational Processes of Perceptual-Semantic Growth

In this section we shall be concerned with teaching those processes of thought and expression which are organizational. We must not forget, however, that pragmatic and attitudinal factors have a pervasive role in these organizational processes. They are highly variable constituents, imprecise in exposition, and dependent on the child's psychoemotional behavior and environment (Chapter 3).

Basically a child must have an understanding of himself and his world which enables him to place himself in time and space and to order or classify objects and events in such a way that they fit into his hypotheses about his world. In order to develop his hypotheses, the child must expand relationships in an organized, systematic way. We know that these elementary organizational processes are not mutually exclusive, psychological operations. The divisions are artificial yet useful in that one is able to implement teaching-learning goals more easily. We know also that they are not all-inclusive. Indeed there may be other organizational processes even more important than those we have culled. We have chosen these because we have found them to be related to actual learning and use in children and because they are most frequently in deficit in linguistically handicapped children. They are (1) *Identifying a Referent;* (2) *Categorizing* (classification); (3) *Sequencing* (seriation), and (4) *Problem Solving.* We can best explain the meaning of each process by providing examples of its use in perceptual-semantic development in classroom activities.

Identifying a Referent

The referent is defined as the object, event, or abstraction that is pointed to by oral or other symbolic signals. Referencing is an act creating meaningful representation of the person and his environment; it *relates* representations to each other. Hence it means more than naming, more than a categorical label. Language teachers have been wont to bury children in labeling ("what is this?") instead of proceeding to relationships in word groups which, in turn, result in a syntactical and prosodic union. Referencing, in short, is the act of establishing relationship and depends for its semantic intent upon our knowledge and immediate experience. Put more simply, a word, phrase, or a sentence means what it means only by virtue of its use in *expressing* a relationship. The single word, *ball,* means little to a child except as he relates the word to its properties of *bouncing and rolling.* A *clock,* likewise, has the auditory attributes of *tick-tock. Cup* will be functionally related to *drink, ring* to *bell, shake* to *rattle.*

Place relationships.   When a child begins to ask questions, he wants to learn more relationships to the referent. The answers generally represent three types of relationships: (a) place, (b) use, and (c) behavior. Here are examples of *place relationships:* Four preschoolers are assembling the pieces to complete the manikin's head. "Where does this piece go? That's wrong; that ear doesn't go on that side." The kindergarten group examines a papier-maché mock-up of a zoo on the front table. "I know," exclaims one child, "it's a zoo!" "Yes," confirms the teacher. "Now let us all decide what animals should go in this zoo." From the toy animal box, Jeff selects a calf and places it in the den with a bear. "No, no," the children protest, "it doesn't belong there." Then ensues a discussion of wild and domesticated animals although none of the children actually can define the place relationship. They know what belongs in the category but are unable to explain *why* it belongs there. The older children (seven to nine years) are engaged in identifying relations as they pertain to cities, people, and events. The teacher introduces the subject: "Here is a map of your state, Illinois. You're going to travel to Springfield. When I say, Springfield, do you think of someone who once lived there? When did he live there? (long time ago? last year?) Why would you want to go there? How would you go from your town to Springfield? Show us on this big map." (A large, simplified map of the state has been posted.)

Use relationships.   Use relationships is the common taxonomic means of identifying the referent in all cultures.[42] Our earliest definitions are in terms of function or use. Where or how you would use the object generally is answered according to place, time, manner, or body part. Children respond, for example, to such a guessing game as "I'm thinking of something – – – –
that you find in _____ (place),
that you use this way _____ (manner)
that you use when _____ (time)
that you move with _____ (body part)."
Guessing games can be expanded in many ways—by verbal description, action patterns demonstrating use, role playing, dramatizations, and so on.

Behavior relationships.   Behavior relationships are very early signs of identifying reference and hence perceptual-semantic development. Allan, a

[42] L.A. Abramyan, "On the Role of Verbal Instructions in the Direction of Voluntary Movements in Children," *Institute for Comparative Human Development* 1(4) (October 1977), 5.

six-month-old baby, hears his mother's voice and immediately responds with a squirming body and waving arms. At two years he hears the garage door going up and excitedly says, "Da-da!" At four years he is in your preschool. Allan's coat is found on the floor in the hall. "Whose is this?" you ask. "Mine," Allan shouts. It is his because he identifies it by color and size. He can prove possession by showing the name tag. He depends on visual perception. At five or six years, the relationship expressing the identifying reference becomes more complex, more elusive, less exact. Often he must depend on the auditory attributes of perception. They are more difficult than visual at this stage because he has had more practice in visual discrimination. If you wish to test the ability of a group of six- or seven-year-old children to perceive the auditory referent, engage them in the "Who says?" game. The leader asks, "Who says:—'Good morning, children;' 'How are you feeling today? better?'; 'Tickets, please!'; 'Wash your hands before dinner'; 'You may cross the street now'; 'Here's a letter for you!'; 'The plane is now loading on Concourse K.'" An older group of children finds that several possible behavior relationships may be attached to the referent. They are quite willing to examine all the possibilities in such questions as these: "What would you do if—(a) you saw a very little child run into the street? (b) you damaged the gear shift while riding your friend's ten-speed bike? (c) gas (for cars) was rationed, and you did not live near a bus stop? (d) oil or gas was no longer available for home heating?"

The double referent.   Riddles and cartoons provide an endless source of the double referent in word meanings. For the first time, perhaps, children become curious about words and their double meanings. A riddle will extend the word in divergent ways. The illustrated riddle books, I am told, are best sellers in children's books. Apparently they incite more original riddle making. (See book list in Appendix B-8).

Identifying a critical referent in a complex of possible referents.   This perceptual-semantic skill poses a frequent perceptual problem among children with severe language handicaps. Why does that five-year-old always attend to the mouse in the corner but miss the centrum, the place where the action is? Why does the eight-year-old tell insignificant details of the story he has read but fail to sketch the main plot? Or why does the mental retardate attempt to repeat every sentence in the short story but is unable to tell the class in a single sentence what the story is about? Children must learn how to choose from all the possible referents the one critical to the percept. They must focus only on those elements that are central to the meaning of the picture, the event, the idea—to the "figure upon a ground" which stands out, separated from all the nonessential or insignificant details.

One activity that nearly always meets with success in giving children practice in discerning the centrum, or critical referent, is the use of familiar comic characters or the humorous cartoon. In the preschool a child may appear "made up" as a comic figure from cartoons or as a character in a children's TV program: Bozo the Clown, Kermit the Frog, The Cookie Monster, Snoopy, or Big Bird. After the child has left the group, the children agree upon one item (clothing, speech, or favorite expression) that gave them the referent, the key to identification. Older children tackle the humorous cartoons. To do so, they must identify and connect humorous relationships in incongruous events or situations. The bizarre events of a child's cartoon, for example, usually belong to a single uncomplicated theme. The children are to tell in a single sentence why the cartoon is funny. A prize for the best single-sentence interpretation is awarded. The brain-storming session follows: Why was it the best? The answers probably will identify those children who are having difficulty in finding the critical referent.

Categorizing

Perhaps the very heart of all organizing processes for language is categorization. If we have no general catalog by which we classify people, new events, or new issues, our thinking becomes confused, in limbo. For perceptual-semantic development to progress, the mind must hit on a format, a design, some plan of categorization. The brain cannot store hundreds of disparate sensorimotor impulses in a network or neuronal assembly unless they fall into a pattern with which it already has had experience. When a child continues to label beyond his developmental age, failing to show any relationships among the labels or names, special instruction in oral language development is essential. Some strategies of categorization we can explain. Others are as elusive as thought itself. Some children will use taxonomic organization; all toys are grouped together; all furniture; all foods. Others will go beyond the class and group according to function. Super and his colleagues [43] discuss categorizing by adults. In arranging clothes, for example, for temporary storage, the organization will be taxonomic in part, functional in part: Everyday clothes are kept in a bureau with all socks together in one drawer, all shirts together in another, and so on. But tennis clothes, for example, including tennis shorts, athletic socks, and the like are all kept together in the same place; they are stored according to a single functional use. Children early on classify and talk in terms of

[43] C.M. Super, S. Harkness, and L.M. Baldwin, "Category Behavior in Natural Ecologies and in Cognitive Tests," *Institute for Comparative Development,* Rockefeller University Press 1(4) (October 1977), 5.

use or action. What can you *do* with it? What is it *used* for? These are their queries.

Class inclusion and exclusion. An elementary strategy employed in categorization is class inclusion and exclusion. Those elements of the percept that are not closely tied to the class in which the experience falls must be excluded. In simpler rhetoric, the conflicting elements of the percept are thrown out. Teaching young children this strategy has focused frequently on dull taxonomic grouping. The child is told, for example, to find all the blue blocks, all red blocks, and so on. Would it not serve the child better if he were stimulated to categorize according to *use?* Find all the blocks that must "make" the base of the tower, all the blocks for the middle, the top, the spire, and so on? Other examples are (a) Four butterflies and two squirrels: Are there more butterflies than squirrels? Why? (b) Five apples and three crayons: Are there more things to eat? Why? (c) Six cats and four cows: Are there more animals than cats? Sneaky!

Better evidence of young children's perceptual development is their ability to exclude the unreal from the real and hence from the class. They enjoy stories and verse, many of which deal with fantasy or a mixture of fantasy and reality. *The Tale of Peter Rabbit* by Beatrix Potter is such a one. In determining what belongs in the class, they make distinctions between what is real and what is unreal. They go from magic to logic. They have read the stories of *The Talking Turtle, Stuart Little,* or played roles in the dramatization of *Chicken Little.* They know, however, that Timmy Turtle, Stuart Little (mouse), Henny Penny, and Peter Rabbit—whatever their human traits are—do not communicate in oral language. The experience of class inclusion and exclusion extends far beyond naming. The referent embraces the attributes, the activity related to, or closely associated with the object, the person, or the event.

Class inclusion is used regularly in nonanalytical communication. "Everyone's going, Mom," pleads the youngster. "People who take Geritol every day enjoy good health," the TV advertiser assures us. Not *some,* not *several,* not *three* but *all* people. It is the old semantic error of *allness.* Children must learn early how to descend the ladder of abstraction, how to go from the general to the specific, and vice versa, if they are to progress rapidly in perceptual-semantic growth.

Differences and similarities. Differences take priority over similarities in categorization at any age although we have no sound psychological explanation for it. It has been suggested that there is more information in negative than in positive instances in the early stages of perceptual-semantic development. A three-month-old baby will use defensive tactics to shut out those stimuli and percepts which he cannot fit into his schema, his organization of the world about him. He evinces some flexibility, accommodating those stimuli that are slightly different but rejecting completely those entirely new. The scheme may be nebulous and somewhat ambiguous yet, it is a hypothesis insuring his safety and based largely on the exclusion of differences—differences in objects, events, or people. Children four to six years of age find it easy to tell you "what it is not." They will always "find the one that doesn't belong" more easily than those "that belong together." They will reject the bathtub placed in the kitchen, but they are very unsure of success when they are asked to make an independent selection of all pieces of furniture that belong in a kitchen. Even at very high perceptual-semantic levels, people or nations rarely find in two seemingly divergent proposals factors that are similar and hence provide a common ground. To find likeness in diversity underlies creative thinking.

The real task in categorization is to find the *relations* among similarities and differences. Again comes the question: *Why* are they alike? *Why* are they different? In the language classroom the equivalent rhetorical categories are comparison and contrast. Relationship for children, four to six years of age, is generally expressed by use. "You can use both spoons and forks for eating." In employing categorization in situations, events, or stories, older children frequently will draw upon their memory bank for previous experiences which they believe to be similar. Sometimes they may be so far afield as to compare "oranges with orangutans." But, if they are developing perceptive skills, they will correct the error in time. Teachers are tempted, I think, to spend a disproportionate amount of time on categorization. It is important, but it is an initial, not a final, process in building perceptual-semantic hierarchies. Frequently it becomes a simplistic and final operation instead of a stepping stone. And what concerns me even more is the common practice of making categorization a silent exercise in sorting and analysis when it should entail a lively oral discussion. In verbalizing about the category or class, a child must place groups of words in a framework, that is, in a semantic-syntactic relationship. He cannot relate events—class picnics and museum visits, for example—without making use of appropriate word groups, prepositions, and connectives in putting the "items" together that belong together. So the meaning which he communicates is educed from the words he uses in labeling the object or event and in the syntactic form which "labels" the relation.[44]

Categorization skills will be learned more quickly if they are reinforced at home and through class excursions into the community. In your bulletin, *PR* (*Parents Respond*) (examples in Appendix A-8), you will suggest ways in which they, the parents, can reinforce the skill of categorization in connection with activities in which the whole family participates.

---

[44] I.M. Schlesinger, "The Role of Cognitive Development and Linguistic Input in Language Acquisition," *J Child Language* 4(2) (June 1977), 159.

(See Appendix C-8 for suggested materials.) You will also want to enlist their cooperation in finding pictures of fruits and vegetables which the child will put in his journal in preparation for his trip with the class to the supermarket. The children (six to seven years old) have listed (with the help of their teachers) the fruits and vegetables that they think will be in the market at this time of year. One group is to buy only fresh fruits; the other, fresh vegetables. When they return from the trip, they will have other categorizations to make: those similar in price per pound must be put together; those which can be prepared in the same way for eating are grouped, and so on. The question that will stump them all is this: Why is this a vegetable? a fruit? Children often know categories without understanding the basis of the categorization. Funds for the expedition? Remember your community resources!

Children with perceptual problems are inclined to stop with obvious categorizations of likenesses and differences. They have to be challenged to answer this question in every situation: What things, what events, what ideas may be truly related, actually may belong together? This is a true benchmark of perceptual-semantic growth, that is, the ability to discover new relationships from old ones, "to extend the connections." If the story, *Very Tall Mouse and Very Short Mouse* [45] is read to your language-handicapped youngsters of kindergarten age, will they find the relationships from the difference in greetings? Here is an excerpt: Tall Mouse: "Hello Birds"; Short Mouse: "Hello Bugs"; Tall Mouse: "Hello Rain Drops"; Short Mouse: "Hello Puddles." Why would the tall mouse see the birds; and the short mouse, the bugs? Then comes the chance to extend the connections. What birds? What bugs? Do some bugs fly? Such line-a-page picture stories or cartoon sequences as the Charlie Brown stories and cartoons afford excellent studies in new relationships based upon likenesses and differences.

For the older group, categorization provides the opportunity to develop *semantic relations* through vocabulary building. Knowledge of semantic relations, of extended word meanings, requires a perceptual skill far beyond that for words used as *referents* or labels. Basic differences exist between the referential aspect and the relational aspect of word meaning.[46] In the case of the language retardate the acquisition of relational terms seems to lag far behind the acquisition of referential terms. He will need your individual attention and home cooperation if he is to jump this hurdle. Discussion of terms used in a TV educational program immediately after the family has watched it is a good starting point. In your classroom

[45] A. Lobel, *Mouse Tales* (New York: Harper and Row, 1972).
[46] M.D. Smith, "The Acquisition of Word Meaning: An Introduction," *Child Development* 49(4) (December 1978), 950–951; J.M. Anglin, "From Reference to Meaning," *Child Development* 49(4) (December 1978), 969–976.

synonym and antonym games, multiple meaning word games, and puns are good learning tools. Children at this age (seven to ten years) will also make use of simple analogies or with aid from the staff, will try their hand at figurative categorization: similes and metaphors. ("He charged into the ring like a giant bulldozer," John said.) But if you do not help them to extend the semantic relations they have acquired to other contexts, little of any value has been learned. Since these children now "can read," you have an excellent chance to cooperate with the reading teacher in extending their knowledge of perceptual-semantic skills both in reading and speaking.

Sequencing (Seriation)

At this juncture in the program the children have learned how to find and express syntactic and semantic relationships in identifying a referent and in categorizing and relating objects, persons, and events. In the process they probably have acquired some knowledge, too, of sequencing. Initially this skill is approached by two principal routes: *temporal relations* and *spatial relations* (distance, size, position).

Temporal relations.   Because one must identify the links in an action, temporal relations are basic to clarity of thought. Those links prompt such time organizers as *yesterday, today, tomorrow; before and after; first, next, last.* Questions basic to any temporal sequence follow this order: *What* has happened? What is happening *now?* What comes *next?* that is, what *will* happen? Little children, however, generally ask the so-called "narrow question" in their daily dialogue: "How many times a day do you feed the guppies?" Or, "How long does it take to bake fudge brownies?" But in cartoon sequences, stories, and happenings, they must deal with broader questions of time intervals, time sequences, duration of time, and so on. These are questions which enable the child to relate a series of events in order of occurrence. They call for factual, predictable answers. But even broader questions, *why, how, where,* will go beyond these questions of time; they demand interpretation based on inference and the qualities of the experience. In a series of scrambled picture cards of a birthday party, for example, one might ask: Why do you think these children are not going to school? Are they walking fast or slowly? Why are they walking fast? What are they celebrating? Whose birthday is it? Why do you think so? What are they singing? Is the singing loud or soft?

Forward and reverse sequencing.   Generally preschool and kindergarten children use forward sequencing in time almost entirely. They do not reflect so much on what *has* happened as on what *will* happen next. Learning to anticipate and express what comes next not only is essential in sequencing, but it also reinforces the links in memory. The very young do not sequence events either in forward or reverse order. A three-year-old boy is riding his trike; he hits a log, falls off, scrapes his knee, cries, and runs home to Mother for medical attention. As a result, Mother usually hears three stories about three different boys. The child has yet to learn forward sequencing. When he is four years old, he probably will respond correctly to the question, "How old will you be on your next birthday?" He now is able to engage in "what next?" games. He understands the rudiments of forward sequencing.

Reverse sequencing, thinking and talking about what *has* happened, is harder. What did you do yesterday? the day before yesterday? the day before that? These questions demand specific and orderly recall. The child must identify the name of the day, ordering within the day, and so on. A group of older language-retarded children, nine to twelve years of age, were dealing with forms of energy, a unit in social science. In oral reports on the immediate history (why are we interested in conserving energy today?), they were able to employ reverse sequencing for the immediate past, but when they were asked later to go further back in an orderly way, they could not do it. (See Appendices C-8 and D-8 for reference materials and ideas.) The mental retardate, the child who has suffered neurological deficit or insult (Chapter 2), and the emotionally disturbed will need extra time and special attention if they are to comprehend and use sequencing. (A review of the sections on attention and memory in Chapter 3 will be helpful here.)

We use temporal sequencing in almost every phase of daily life so it is not difficult to find learning situations. The majority of kindergartners can recount the daily routine of getting ready for school: toileting, brushing teeth, showering, breakfast, school books and lunch bag, outdoor wear, bus. The linguistically handicapped frequently have trouble either because such a routine has not been established or because they do not remember the order. I asked the mother of Donna, a five-year-old autistic child, if Donna unzipped and removed her coat when she came home from the Center. "No," she said, "she may play for two hours without removing either her coat or scarf." "She will wear her PJs all day if I allowed it." Was Donna not aware of temperature changes? Or was it a part of her retreat from reality? She felt no compulsion to remove her coat or her PJs, yet she had other compulsive routines such as smelling the food before she ate it, the crayons before she used them, and the doll before she played with it. Our success in teaching sequencing in this case was not spectacular. We had better luck with a ten-year-old boy who had special perceptual problems. He told his classroom teacher, "Now I know how to tell a story." Incidents occur daily that prompt the children to recite sequential actions and set them in memory. The fire alarm sounds in the school; a tree falls directly in front of the school bus during a windstorm; smoke is billowing up from a building close by the school; two cars collide at the corner; the hockey game ended in a fight: All involve sequencing.

For little children, *The Norman Rockwell Poster Book* [47] is excellent for picture reading, an activity that tests the child's ability to perceive the order of present events and to infer from them future events. Here are some questions which were raised as the children "read" (interpreted) a picture, *The Runaway:* (a) *What* has the little boy done?; (b) *Where* are the policeman and the boy now?; (c) *What* are they going to do there (lunch counter)?; (d) *Why* is the little boy looking at the policeman?; (e) *What* will they eat?; (f) *Where* will they go next?; (g) And then— *what?* (See Appendix C-8 for additional suggestions.) In a self-contained classroom for a language-handicapped group (eight to eleven years), the children were engaged in discussing and making two visual representations (mock-ups) of the seasons, one in Milwaukee, the other in Brazilia. Sequencing went far beyond the order and time of the seasons to include comparative changes in temperature, precipitation, and vegetation. Here was an opportunity to give special attention to those children who were still having trouble in sorting out the critical referents and categorizations and in recalling from their own experience the relevant associations with each season.

Space relations (distance, size, shape, position). Earlier in this program the child has had experience with space relations in perceptual-semantic comprehension and expression. Beginning with perception of his body orientation in space, he then demonstrated his perceptual knowledge of position, movement, and gesture in oral production. This synthesis of comprehension and expression of language is an early and primary target in language learning. Spatial relations is a difficult perceptual-semantic skill at any age. The prepositions *in, above, below, beside,* and *near* correspond, as Carroll has said, to relations in spatial position in a surprisingly complex and subtle way.[48] Consequently children will try several different connectives to make meaning clear. "Where is the Children's Farm?" asks a child. "Near Macktown Park," replies his friend. A third child shakes his head, "Uh-uh, it's next to the Fish Hatchery."

Space relations in sequencing are comprehended and used in various ways. In terms of distance we formulate such expressions as *far away, closer, nearby,* or *near* and *far.* When we come to space modifiers such

[47] M.F. Fox, ed., *Norman Rockwell* (New York: Harry N. Abrams, Inc., 1970).
[48] J.B. Carroll, *Words, Meanings and Concepts* (Cambridge, Mass.: Harvard Educational Review Reprint Series No. 7, 1972), 130.

antithetical expressions as *full-empty* and *many-few,* are traditionally stressed in the classroom. Space modifiers, however, are not always antithetical in the speech of these children. Many of them will use such modifiers as *nearly, almost full, but not many, half of it, not quite so much,* and so on. In teaching we do not introduce exercises in which sentences containing these words are to be repeated again and again. Instead team teachers, aides, and volunteers devise situations or experiences in which the child will need to employ these expressions of space relations in order to make his meaning clear. He will hear these expressions again and again from his peers. *It's six blocks away; you go one mile before you turn; I live near the school.* In certain sections of the country, short distances are expressed in time, as for example, *It's just a ten-minute walk from here.* Shortly after the beginning of the school year, six-year-old children in this program were rehearsing directions to the cafeteria where they would shortly go each day for their noon-day meal. "Is it near the Teachers' Lounge?" asks one child. "How far to the blue corridor?" "Do we turn right or left there?" Meantime the camera buffs or shutter-snappers in the advanced class are taking a neighborhood walk (with aides and volunteers). They are estimating the distance from each scene to be photographed so that optimal focus and clarity are achieved.

Space relations essential to sequencing also comprehend perception of *size, shape,* or *position.* Learning experiences in these areas may be difficult and necessarily prolonged for the child with perceptual-motor disorganization or deficit (Chapters 2,7). Certainly in planning tasks or experiences to further his comprehension of size, shape, or position, only those requiring verbalization should be used. Unfortunately in present practice, they seem to be silent sessions of sorting blocks, fitting various shapes and sizes in form boards, puzzles, or picture card games. Their transfer value to language learning is questionable. Here are two examples in which children are not sitting, but are engaging actively in learning-talking experiences: (a) The children are decorating the classroom for their Christmas party. The questions in some instances are purely rhetorical, but they are aids to their perceptions and expressions of size, shape, and position. "How high on the door should we hang the wreath?" "Wait, that isn't in the center, is it? That looks crooked to me," (from the child whose unstable reference system, both horizontally and vertically is one evidence of his perceptual problem). "The sheep are too far away from the shepherd (in the nativity scene); let's change it." "How long is the shepherd's stick (staff)?" "Print the letters, *Merry Christmas,* so they slant the same way." "This one (shepherd) goes next"; "Why?" "Because he's shorter." (b) It is late November; the class is an older group of language-retarded children. It is agreed that all will watch the Macy Christmas parade on television and describe one figure in the parade on the following Monday: Tolkien's dragon (The Hobbit); the talking bear, the two-story giraffe. In the *PR* (*Parents Respond*) report, the family is invited to participate in the program by helping the child to take pictures (instant camera) or to make line drawings of favorite characters. After each child describes his chosen figure, the questions come fast: "Really now, how big is the dragon?" "Could you put him in a bar? a silo?" "Is he taller than our school?" "How did these monsters get through the Holland tunnel?" "I didn't see the talking bear; was he there? Where was he in the parade?" "Right next to," "behind," or "in front of?" This is the most bothersome sequencing question of all! Other illustrative learning experiences are listed or described in Appendix C-8.

Problem Solving and Decision Making

What Robert Frost once wrote may be true:

> We dance round in a ring and suppose,
> But the Secret sits in the middle and knows.

The Secret Sits by Robert Frost [49]

But I hardly think so. In this discussion of problem solving leading to decision making, the perceptual-semantic skills involved will take us far beyond supposition. Although Piaget and others [50] do not believe that the six-year-old child is ready to exercise those thought processes used in problem solving, experience suggests an opposite conclusion. Any mother who has responded to the thousand "why" questions of five-six—or nine-year olds locked in by a winter storm on a long weekend knows that even the youngest is engaged in some kind of elementary problem solving. The *why* questions may bring *because* answers (causal relation), or they may be questions requiring answers of motivation or justification. Problem solving in the home may be less definitely programmed than in your classroom or language center; that may be the chief difference. Admittedly the skills involved in problem solving are somewhat complex, more abstract. Logical relations based on inductive or deductive reasoning must be established between cause and effect; true correlations between acts, events, and/or experiences must be made; generalizations must be based upon a sufficient number of *relevant,* supporting examples. And precedent to the

[49] L. Frost Ballantine, ed., *The Poetry of Robert Frost* (New York: Holt, Rinehart and Winston, 1967).
[50] J. Piaget, *The Language and Thought of the Child* (London: Routledge and Kegan Paul, 1959), 77–126.

establishment of these relationships, children have had to master the elementary skills we have just discussed.

In contrast to the usual treatment of perceptual skills in which the child engages in a nonverbal task in response to the teacher's directive,[51] our purpose as with the earlier skills must be to link problem-solving skills with semantic growth. The target, in short, is to teach the child to comprehend and use oral language in solving problems associated with situations or experiences in the context of his environment. He must be able to perceive and verbalize the relationships inherent in these problems or experiences. Smilansky believes that disadvantaged children do not lack these experiences. Rather they are unable to tie together, to *relate* different experiences, to interpret them, to synthesize and utilize them in problem-solving situations.[52] This is true of the majority of language-handicapped children, whatever the cause.

Children can provoke discussion by posing such a simple *Why* question as "Why was Eldora (a professional aide) late in arriving at school this morning?" and then by formulating the answers: Because her car wouldn't start; because she overslept (her alarm failed); because she had to go back home for her costume for the play. But they can be stumped completely by this question: Birds can fly; why can't I? Problem solving can become more complex; it can reach a higher level because the situation includes, not one, but a complex of interrelated problems. Here is such a situation: It is Good Friday, and the children are coloring Easter eggs. Some questions the children pose and try to answer are "My purple is not as dark as Joan's; why?" "Why is an egg hard after it has been boiled?" "How do you make steam?" and the final question posed by a five-year-old lad, a question which even the language teacher seemed unable to answer: "Why you not call it Bad Friday?"

Children develop generalizations usually by citing specific examples instead of using formal inductive-deductive reasoning. A teaching team introduced the subject of energy conservation to a class of language-handicapped youngsters (five and six years old). Despite the reservations of other consultants, the children took to the topic: *You Can Help Too: Save Water, Light, Heat.* They had previously watched a series of cartoons on a TV program on conservation. With the aid of parents, the letters which made up the title were extracted from magazine ads and put in the children's journals. Then in a brainstorming session and with the help of a team teacher, the children told all the ways they could save: "Turn off the

---

[51] C. Bereiter and S. Engelmann, *Teaching Disadvantaged Children in the Preschool* (Englewood Cliffs, N.J.: Prentice-Hall, Inc., 1966); S. Engelmann, *Basic Concept* Inventory (Chicago: Follett Educational Corporation, 1967).

[52] S. Smilansky, *The Effects of Sociodramatic Play in Disadvantaged Pre-School Children* (New York: John Wiley, 1968).

faucet; switch the TV and the light off when you leave the playroom or family room; set the thermostat at 65 degrees and wear a sweater; puddle the water in the wash bowl; wash the dishes in the sink, not in the dishwasher." There was disagreement on some items. Some items were not very important; some were irrelevant. Almost all children wanted to save water by taking fewer baths! Everyone wanted the list to be put in his journal as proof of success!

Encouraged by their success, the team subsequently introduced the subject of energy, its conservation and alternate sources, to an older group of children handicapped by cerebral palsy and oral language problems resulting probably from CNS deficits. This time they had allies in the social and physical science teachers and the reading and art teachers. Their aim was to introduce the children to problem solving on a more advanced scale. They narrowed the topic to alternate sources of heating the home. They read stories about wind, solar, and atomic energy; they visited a reactor plant in an adjoining county. They drew windmills, homes with sharply slanted roofs to contain solar slabs, and woodburning stoves for homes. They tried to figure the effect of heat-conserving clothing, but that was too difficult. They prepared simple outlines of talks using organizational strategies. The Energy Fair, in which parents gave great assistance, was the climax of their program. The children presided at the energy booth in their "specialty." And they talked! No, not always using successfully the strategies they had learned, not always intelligibly, certainly not always with prosodic utterance or good sentence form. But the social dynamics of their communication compensated for their shortcomings. They were intent on informing, entertaining, or persuading others. They were interacting, aware of the ideas and feelings of others. They were engaged in an exciting adventure. (Outlines of other learning adventures employing perceptual-semantic strategies are contained in Appendix C–8.)

MISSIVE TO MY READERS

My friends who teach or are preparing to teach children handicapped in oral communication: What you find in this book is what you asked for. It represents the sum and substance of the seminars, summer sessions, and workshops in which you and I have participated during the last fifteen years. In large part it is *your* book. You will find your ideas and your experiences in its pages. Now, the pages finally within covers, does it all seem too great a task for you? I hope not. It does not mean a drastic alteration in your philosophy, for you already have accepted fundamental changes in thinking about language handicaps of children. *Implementation* of your ideas is now the challenge. It may mean changes in your teaching program, a new organization, new cooperative agencies, new responsibilities extending into the community. Public Law 94-142 has aided you tremendously in mandating new programs. Of one fact I am convinced: You and I hold in common the belief that we are educators, confident that oral communication is essential to "the way and the life," and that our teaching will help these handicapped children to find the way. My successors, I salute you!

REFERENCES

ABRAMYAN, L.A., "On the Role of Verbal Instructions in the Direction of Voluntary Movements in Children," *Institute for Comparative Human Development,* 1(4) (October 1977). 1–7.

ALBERT, M.L., R.W. SPARKS, and N.A. HELM, "Melodic Intonation Therapy for Aphasia," *Archives Neurology,* 29(2) (1973), 130–131.

ALLEN, MARIAM, *Dance of Language.* Portola Valley, Cal.: Richards Institute of Music Education and Research, 1974.

ALLEN, MARIAM, "Music is Her School for the Deaf," *San Francisco Sunday Examiner and Chronicle,* June 8, 1975.

ANGLIN, J.M., "From Reference to Meaning," *Child Development,* 49(4) (December 1978), 969–976.

ARNDT, W.B. and others, "Identification and Description of Homogeneous Sub-Groups within a Sample of Misarticulating Children," *J Speech Hearing Research* 20(2) (June 1977), 263–292.

BEREITER, C. and S. ENGELMANN, *Teaching Disadvantaged Children in the Preschool.* Englewood Cliffs, N.J.: Prentice-Hall, Inc., 1966.

BERLIN, C.I., "On: Melodic Intonation Therapy for Aphasia by R.W. Sparks and A.L. Holland," *J Speech Hearing Disorders* 41(3) (August 1976), 298–300.

BLOOM, L. and M. LAHEY, *Language Development and Language Disorders.* Chap. 19. New York: John Wiley, 1978.

BOLINGER, D. "Intonation is a Universal," *Proceedings of the Ninth International Congress of Linguists,* ed. H.G. Hunt. The Hague: Mouton, 1964, 833–848.

CARROLL, J.B., *Words, Meanings and Concepts.* Cambridge, Mass.: Harvard Educational Review Reprint Series No. 7, 1972, 130.

CAZDEN, C., *Programs for Promoting Language Skills in Early Childhood.* Panel discussion at the Convention of the National Association for the Education of Young Children, Boston, 1970.

CHESNI, Y., "La Parole Intérieure," *Confinia Neurologica,* 23 (1963), 192.

CLARK, E., "Strategies for Communicating," *Child Development,* 49(4) (December 1978), 953–959.

COMETA, M.S. and M.E. ESON, "Logical Operations and Metaphor Interpretation: A Piagetian Model," *Child Development,* 49(3) (September 1978), 649–659.

CONTA, M.M. and M. REARDON, *Feelings between Friends.* Milwaukee: Advanced Learning Concepts, 1974.

CRATTY, B.J., *Remedial Motor Activity for Children.* Philadelphia: Lea and Febiger, 1978, 140–184.

CRYSTAL, D., *The English Tone of Voice.* London: Edward Arnold, 1975.

CUMMINS, R.A., P.J. LIVESEY, and J.M. EVANS, "A Developmental Theory of Environmental Enrichment," *Science,* 197(4304) (12 August 1977), 692–694.

CYR, D., "The Snapshooter Camera," *Arts and Activities,* 83(2) (March 1978), 42–44.

DALTON, K., *Music for Wonder.* San Francisco: Renna-White Associates, 1976.

DALTON, P. and W.J. HARDCASTLE, *Disorders of Fluency.* London: Edward Arnold, 1977.

DEESE, J., "Semantics: Categorization and Meaning," chap. 8. *Handbook of Perception, VII,* eds. E.C. Carterette and M.P. Friedman. New York: Academic Press, 1976.

DEPAUW, K.P., "Enhancing the Sensory Integration of Aphasic Students," *J Learning Disorders* 11(3) (March 1978), 142–146.

DEVILLIERS, P.A. and J.G. DEVILLIERS, "Early Judgments of Semantic and Syntactic Acceptability by Children," *J Psycholinguistic Research,* 1(4) (1972), 299–310.

FLETCHER, S.G., "Time-by-Count Measurement of Diadochokinetic Syllable Rate," *J Speech Hearing Research,* 15(4) (December 1972), 763–770.

FOWLES, B. and M. GLANZ, "Competence and Talent in Verbal Riddle Comprehension," *J Child Language,* 4(3) (October 1977), 433, 452.

GALLAGHER, T., "Revision Behaviors in the Speech of Normal Children," *J Speech Hearing Research,* 20(2) (June 1977), 303–318.

GIBBONS, J.F., W.R. KICHNELOE, and K.S. DAWN, "Tutored Videotape Instruction: A New Use of Electronics Media in Education," *Science,* 195(4283) (18 March 1977), 1139–1146.

GILLES, DOROTHY, *Music for Special Children.* Edwardsville, Ill.: D. Gilles, 1976.

GIORDANO, G., "Convergent Research on Language and Teaching Reading," *Exceptional Children,* 44(8) (May 1978), 604–611.

GOODGLASS, H.J. and others, "Some Linguistic Structures in the Speech of a Broca's Aphasic," *Cortex* 8(2) (June 1972), 191–213.

GREGG, G., "Fantasy Training Tips," *Psychology Today,* 8(9) (February 1975), 36.

HAMMILL, D.D. and N.R. BARTEL, *Teaching Children with Learning and Behavior Problems.* Boston: Allyn and Bacon, 1975, 229–230.

HARRIS, T.A., *I'm O.K.: You're O.K.: A Practical Guide to Transactional Analysis.* New York: Harper and Row, 1967.

HATCH, E., "Language Teaching and Language Learning," chap. 11, *Handbook of Perception, VII,* eds. E.C. Carterette and M.P. Friedman. New York: Academic Press, 1976.

HERRICK, C.J., *Brains of Rats and Men,* 3rd ed. Chicago: University of Chicago Press, 1963.

HUBBELL, R.D., "On Facilitating Spontaneous Talking in Young Children," *J Speech Hearing Disorders,* 42(2) (May 1977), 216–231.

IRWIN, E.C., N.E. BAKER-FLYNN, and L.A. BLOOM, "Fantasy, Play and Language: Expressive Therapy with Communication Handicapped Children," *J Childhood Communication Disorders,* 1(2) (Fall-Winter 1976), 99–115.

KOZHEVNIKOVA, V.A. and L.A. CHISTOVICH, *Speech Articulation and Perception.* Moscow-Leningrad, trans. by National-Technical Information Services, U.S. Dept. of Commerce, Springfield, Va., 1965.

LEONARD, L.B., "A Preliminary View of Generalization in Language Training," *J Speech Hearing Disorders,* 39(4) (November 1974), 429–436.

LEONARD, L.B. and others, "Nonstandardized Approaches to the Assessment of Language Behaviors," *Asha,* 20(5) (May 1978), 371–379.

LING, D. and A.H. LING, "Communication Development in the First Three Years of Life," *J Speech Hearing Research,* 17(1) (March 1974), 146–157.

LYONS, J., *Semantics, 1.* London: Cambridge University Press, 1977, 61.

MACDONALD, J.D. and others, *An Experimental Parent-Assisted Language Program for Preschool Retarded Children.* The Nisonger Center, 1580 Cannon Dr., The Ohio State University, Columbus, Ohio, 43210, 1974.

MCGOVERN, A., *Too Much Noise.* New York: Scholastic Book Service, 1967.

MCLEAN, J.E., D.E. YODER, and R.L. SCHIEFELBUSCH, eds., *Language Intervention with the Retarded.* Baltimore: University Park Press, 1972.

MARTIGNONI, M.E., *The Illustrated Treasury of Children's Literature.* New York: Grosset and Dunlap, 1955.

MILLER, G.A., *Language and Communication.* New York: McGraw-Hill, 1951.

MILLER, G.A. and P.N. JOHNSON-LAIRD, *Language and Perception.* Cambridge, Mass.: The Belknap Press of Harvard University Press, 1976.

MONRAD-KROHN, "The Prosodic Quality of Speech and its Disorders," *Acta Psychiatrica Neurologica,* 22(3–4) (1947), 255–260.

MUMA, J.R., *Language Handbook.* Englewood Cliffs, N.J.: Prentice-Hall, Inc., 1978.

NAIMAN, D.W., "Picture Perfect," *Teaching Exceptional Children,"* 9(2) (Winter 1977), 36–38.

NICHOLICH, L.M., "Beyond Sensorimotor Intelligence: Assessment of Symbolic Maturity through Analysis of Pretend Play," *Merrill-Palmer Quarterly,* 23(2) (1977), 89–99.

PARRILL-BURNSTEIN, M., "Teaching Kindergarten Children to Solve Problems: An Information-Processing Approach," *Child Development,* 49 (3) (September 1978), 700–706.

PERRONE, M., *Icarus and Other Flights at Camp Sunshine.* The National Committee, Arts for the Handicapped, Washington, D.C.

PIAGET, J., *The Language and Thought of the Child.* London: Routledge and Kegan Paul, 1959, 77–126.

RATNER, N. and J. BRUNER, "Games, Social Exchange and the Acquisition of Language," *J. Child Language,* 5(3) (October 1978), 391–402.

RICHARDS, M.H., *The Child in Depth.* Portola Valley, Cal.: Richards Institute of Music Education and Research, 1969.

SCHLESINGER, I.M., "The Role of Cognitive Development and Linguistic Input in Language Acquisition," *J Child Language,* 4(2) (June 1977), 159.

SCHUBERT, E.D., "The Role of Auditory Perception in Language Processing," *Reading, Perception and Language,* eds. D.D. Duane and M.B. Rawson. Baltimore: York Press, 1975.

SHEWAN, C., "The Language Disordered Child in Relation to Muma's 'Communication Game: Dump and Play,' " *J Speech Hearing Disorders,* 40(3) (August 1975), 310–315.

SMILANSKY, S., *The Effects of Sociodramatic Play in Disadvantaged Pre-School Children.* New York: John Wiley, 1968.

SMITH, M.D., "The Acquisition of Word Meaning: An Introduction," *Child Development,* 49(4) (December 1978), 950–951.

SPARKS, R. and A.L. HOLLAND, "Method: Melodic Intonation Therapy for Aphasia," *J Speech Hearing Disorders* 41(3) (August 1976), 287–297.

SPARKS, R., N. HELMS, and M. ALBERT, "Aphasia Rehabilitation from Melodic Intonation Therapy," *Cortex,* 10 (1974), 303–316.

SUPER, C.M., S. HARKNESS, and L.M. BALDWIN, "Category Behavior in Natural Ecologies and in Cognitive Tests," *Institute for Comparative Development,* Rockefeller University Press, 1(4) (October 1977), 4–7.

T.A.L.K., Rockford, Ill. *Rockford Public School District* 205, Approved by Education Division, H.E.W. as an "Exemplary Educational Program," (July 1979).

TONKOVA-YAMPOL'SKAYA, R.V., "Development of Speech Intonation in Infants during the First Two Years of Life," *Studies of Child Language Development,* eds. C.A. Ferguson and D.I. Slobin. New York: Holt, Rinehart and Winston, Inc., 1973.

WACHS, T.D., "Utilization of a Piagetian Approach in the Investigation of Early Experience Effects: A Research Strategy and Some Illustrative Data," *Merrill-Palmer Quarterly,* 22(1) (1976), 11–30.

WEIKART, D.P. and others, *The Cognitively Oriented Curriculum.* Urbana, Ill., University of Illinois, 1971.

WEISS, D., *Cluttering.* Englewood Cliffs, N.J.: Prentice-Hall, Inc., 1964.

WICKELGREN, W.A., "Phonetic Coding and Serial Order." *Handbook of Perception, VII: Language and Speech,* eds., E.C. Carterette and M.P. Friedman. New York: Academic Press, 1976.

WIIG, E.H. and E.M. SEMEL, "Comprehension of Linguistic Concepts Requiring Logical Operations by Learning-Disabled Children," *J Speech Hearing Research,* 16 (1973), 627–636.

———, "Development of Comprehension of Logico-Grammatical Sentences By Grade School Children," *Perceptual Motor Skills,* 38 (1974), 171–176.

WILCOX, M.J. and L.B. LEONARD, "Experimental Acquisition of Wh-Questions in Language-Disordered Children," *J Speech Hearing Research,* 21(2) (June 1978), 220–239.

Appendix A-8

We have been practicing "body language" for some time---

I. So your child will show you how well he can perform the following feats.

(please fill in the blanks on his achievement.)

    1. Walk to the beat of a drum (or hands). Good____Fair____

    2. Skip (to the barber shop) Good____Fair____

    3. Skip rope. Good____Fair____

    4. Hop on one foot across the room. Good____Fair____

    5. Hop on two feet like a rabbit. Good____Fair____

II. Did you show your child how to bat a baseball? Can he do it? Yes____No____

III. Did Daddy or Brother play kickball with him? Yes____No____

Parents Respond
Progress Report

We are getting ready for our first "play,"
<u>Chicken Little</u>. The children have talked
about and shown the way the "characters"
in this playet walk, hop, skip, or run;
how the birds and animals talk. Let him show
you how well he can do the following:

1. Waddle like a goose. Good____Fair ____

2. Strut like a rooster. Good____Fair____

3. Follow the leader in running fast,
   slowly; turning while running to
   right; to left. Good ____ Fair ____

4. Bird and animal imitations: Chee-
   chee! Quack-quack-quack! Gobble-
   gobble! Cluck-cluck! Good___ Fair____

5 Line practice: "The sky is falling."
  "We're going to tell the king."
  Good ____ Fair_____

      ****

Can you help him to make a hand or stick
puppet representing a bird or animal?

TABLE TALK
WHAT THINGS CAN YOU DO WITHOUT?

Was Ralph Waldo Emerson right when he said: "Things are in the saddle and ride mankind?"

In your child's regular classroom they have read about the great American writer, Henry Thoreau, who, for two years (1852-1854) lived a hermit's life at Walden Pond, Mass. Thoreau, feeling he was a slave to things, wanted to prove that he could live happily without so many possessions by simplying his life.

Now in our special language class these children have talked about Thoreau's ideas. What things could they do without? Each child was asked to list those things in his home that he would hate to part with. After class discussion, he crossed off those possessions that he honestly could do without.

At home around the supper table, your child will read his list. Will you decide together which things on the list are not essential to the way you live? Give your child plenty of time to explain why he kept or struck off certain items. Tomorrow he will tell us what happened at home during your table talk.

Mother or Father: Please return this section in the envelope.

Was it fun--this lesson in thinking? _____

Were his reasons good ones for keeping certain items? _____

Once he had begun a sentence, did the family allow him to finish it? _____; Or did they break in? _____

What item provoked the most discussion? _____

Did he enjoy talking? _____

Did he look at you as he talked? _____ Was his voice lively? __

How did the family react to his talk? Encouraged him?_____
Laughed at him? _____

Did everyone get into the discussion? Yes_____ No____

1. Did your child enjoy his pantomime of Superman? _____

2. Who helped him find the costume_____

3. Record parts of your conversation with him at the table about the exper-ience. Does he use eye contact in talking at the table?_____

4. How many members of your family are at the table?____ How many younger?____ Older?_____

5. Does he now use more bodily action and facial expression in talking at home?_____

6. What new language activity did you try this week that we could all try?_____

7. What activities does the child like best? Playing with other children? Story read to him? Repairing his trike?_____
_____

8. Has his spontaneous speech increased in amount at home?_____ In neighborhood play?_____

9. Do you have materials (books, costumes, construction materials, etc.) that can be used in language development?_____
_____

282

Appendix B-8

CHILDREN'S STORIES, CHANTS AND FINGER PLAYS, RHYMES, POEMS AND CHORIC VERSE AND RIDDLES

Chants and Finger Plays (Arranged in order of difficulty, beginning preschool)

SPIER, P., *London Bridge is Falling Down!,* Doubleday, 1971.

MITCHELL, D. and C. BLYTON, *Every Child's Book of Nursery Songs,* Crown Publishers, 1968.

TORREY, M., *Sing Mother Goose,* Dutton, 1946.

BURROUGHS, M., *Did You Feed My Cow?* (Street games, chants, rhymes), Follet Publishing Co., 1969.

RASMUSSEN, C., *Playtime Poems for Tiny Tots,* Vantage Press, 1971.

TASHJIAN, V.A., ed., *Juba This and Juba That,* Little Brown, 1969.

CARLSON, B.W., *Listen! And Help Tell the Story,* Abingdon Press, 1965.

GLAZER, T., *Eye Winker, Tom Tinker, Chin Chopper,* Doubleday, 1973.

ENGLER, L., *Making Puppets Come Alive,* Talinger Publishing Co., 1973.

Riddles

SARNOFF, J. and R. RUFFINS, *Giants Riddle Book,* Scribner, 1977.

THALER, M., *Magic Letter Riddles,* Scholastic Book Services, 1974.

THALER, M., *Riddle Riot,* Scholastic Book Services, 1975.

Rhymes, Poems and Choric Verse

HADER, B. and E. HADER, *Cock-a-Doodle Doo,* Macmillan, 1940.

STEVENSON, R.L., *A Child's Garden of Verses,* Grosset & Dunlap, 1957.

MARTIGNONI, M.E., ed., *The Illustrated Treasury of Children's Literature,* Grosset & Dunlap, 1955.

FRASCONI, A., (adaptation), *The House That Jack Built,* Harcourt Brace Jovanovich, 1959.

MERRIAM, E., *There is No Rhyme for Silver,* Atheneum Press, 1962.

ETS, M.H., *Just Me,* Scholastic Book Services, 1965.

ETS, M.H., *Play With Me,* Viking, 1955.

DE LA MARE, W., *Rhymes and Verses: Collected Poems,* Holt, Rinehart and Winston, 1947.

BISHEN, EDWARD, ed., *Oxford Book of Poetry for Children*, Franklin Watts, 1963.

TIPPETT, J.S., *I Live in a City*, Harper and Row, 1927.

LINDSAY, V., *Golden Whales*, Macmillan, 1948.

MILNE, A.A., *When We Were Very Young*, E.P. Dutton, 1924.

LITTLE, L.J. and E. GREENFIELD, *I Can Do It By Myself*, Crowell, 1978.

MOORE, L., *I Feel the Same Way*, Scholastic Book Services, 1967.

BURGESS, G., *Goops and How to Be Them*, Gelett Burgess, 1928.

SILVERSTEIN, S., *Where the Sidewalk Ends*, Harper and Row, 1974.

FROST, R., *Mountain Interval*, Henry Holt, 1916.

SANDBURG, C., *Complete Poems*, Harcourt Brace Jovanovich, 1950.

BENET, R. and S. BENET, *A Book of Americans*, Holt, Rinehart and Winston, 1933.

ARBUTHNOT, M.H., *Time for Poetry*, Scott Foresman, 1959.

UNTERMEYER, L., ed., *Modern American-British Poetry*, Harcourt Brace Jovanovich, 1942.

Stories

GILBERT, E., *A Cat Story*, Holt, Rinehart and Winston, 1963.

WING, H.R., *What is Big?* Holt, Rinehart and Winston, 1963.

ARUEGO, J., *Look What I Can Do*, Scribner, 1971.

STEIG, W., *Roland and the Minstrel Pig*, Farrar, 1977.

SPIER, P., *Gobble, Growl, Grunt*, Doubleday, 1971.

ALLEN, R., *Zoo Book*, Platt, 1968.

HUTCHINS, P., *Good Night, Owl!* Macmillan, 1972.

AVERILL, E., *Jenny's Birthday Book*, Scribner, 1978.

KEATS, E.J., *The Snowy Day*, Viking, 1963.

BROWN, M. (adaptation), *Once a Mouse*, Scribner, 1962.

WARD, L., *The Biggest Bear*, Houghton Mifflin, 1953.

COHEN, M. *Bee My Valentine*, Greenwillow, 1978.

HOBAN, L., *Mr. Pig and Sonny Too*, Harper and Row, 1977.

BAKER, R., *The Upside-Down Man*, McGraw-Hill, 1977.

POTTER, B., *A Treasury of Peter Rabbit and Other Stories*, Franklin Watts, 1978.

MILNE, A.A., *Winnie the Pooh*, E.P. Dutton, 1957.

LOBEL, A., *Mouse Tales*, Harper and Row, 1972.

MILNE, A.A., *Pooh Bear*, E.P. Dutton, 1926.

MARTIGNONI, M.E., ed., *The Illustrated Treasury of Children's Literature,* Grosset & Dunlap, 1955.

Grimm's Fairy Tales, Macmillan, 1963. (Hansel and Gretel, Little Red Riding Hood, Snow White and the Seven Dwarfs)

JONES, G., *Scandinavian Legends and Folk Tales,* Oxford Press, 1956.

SCARRY, R., *Richard Scarry's Please and Thank You Book,* Random House, 1978.

WABER, B., *Nobody is Perfick,* Scholastic Book Services, 1971.

BAYLOR, D., *The Way to Start a Day,* Scribner, 1978.

AARDEMA, V., *Who's in the Rabbit's House?* Dial, 1977.

BRUNHOFF, J.D., *Babar the King,* Random House, 1937.

WOLF, B., *Adam Smith Goes to School,* Lippincott, 1978.

KEATS, E.J., *The Trip,* Greenwillow, 1978.

SIDEMAN, B.B., ed., *The World's Best Fairy Tales,* Readers Digest Association, 1967. (Three Billy Goats Gruff, Chicken Little)

SCHULZ, C.M., *He's Your Dog, Charlie Brown,* World Publications, 1968.

SCHULZ, C.M., *It's the Easter Beagle,* Random House, 1976.

SCHULZ, C.M., *Snoopy and the Red Baron,* Holt, Rinehart and Winston, 1966.

SCHULZ, C.M., *A Charlie Brown Christmas,* Random House, 1977.

STEIG, W., *Caleb and Kate,* Farrar, Straus and Giroux, 1977.

HADER, B. and E. HADER, *The Big Snow,* Macmillan, 1949.

DALGLIESH, A., *The Thanksgiving Story,* Scribner, 1955.

CONTA, M. and M. REARDON, *Feelings between Friends,* Advanced Learning Concepts (Milwaukee), 1967.

PRAGER, A., *The Surprise Party,* Pantheon Books, 1977.

JOHNSON, H., *Old Fashioned Thanksgiving,* Lippincott, 1974.

GOODALL, J., *The Surprise Picnic,* Atheneum, 1977.

BROAN, M., (tr.) *Cinderella* or *The Little Glass Slipper,* Scribner, 1955.

BRIGGS, W., *The Snowman,* Random House, 1978.

BROWN, M., *Dick Whittington and His Cat,* Scribner, 1951.

ANDERSEN, HANS C., *Fairy Tales,* Oxford Press, 1946. (The Princess and the Pea, Emperor's New Clothes, Ugly Duckling)

THOMPSON, K., *Eloise,* Simon Schuster, 1955.

WHITE, E.B., *Stuart Little,* Harper and Row, 1945.

WHITE, E.B., *Charlotte's Web,* Harper and Row, 1952.

WHITE, E.B., *The Trumpet of the Swan,* Harper and Row, 1970.

ALIKI, *Story of Johnny Appleseed,* Prentice-Hall, Inc., 1963.

THOMAS, D., *A Child's Christmas in Wales,* New Directions, 1969.

LEAF, M., *The Story of Ferdinand,* Viking, 1936.

GRAHAME, K., *The Wind in the Willows,* Scribners, 1966.

SALTEN, F., *Bambi,* Thrushwood Books, 1969.

ASIMOV, I., *ABCs of Space,* Walker, 1969.

STEIG, W., *Tiffky Doofky,* Farrar Strauss and Giroux, 1978.

CARROLL, L., *Alice's Adventures in Wonderland and Through the Looking Glass,* E.P. Dutton, 1965.

The Annotated Mother Goose, Bramhall House, 1962.

HAVILAND, V., *Favorite Fairy Tales Told in Spain,* Little, Brown, 1963.

SPERRY, M., *Scandinavian Stories,* Franklin Watts, 1971.

TRESSELT, A., *What Did You Leave Behind?* Lothrop, 1948.

ALEXANDER, M., "I Sure Am Glad to See You," *Blackboard Bear,* Dial, 1976.

TRESSELT, A., *White Snow, Bright Snow,* Lothrop, 1946.

THURBER, J., *Many Moons,* Harcourt Brace Jovanovich, 1944.

Appendix C-8

IDEAS FOR TEACHING PERCEPTUAL-SEMANTIC SKILLS (In order of progressive difficulty)

1. (Categorization) The Thanksgiving Basket. Two baskets are on a long table. One is filled with tomatoes, apples, oranges, potatoes, grapefruit, carrots, grapes, celery, nuts, lettuce, bananas, and the like. The other basket is empty. Circle A takes out all the vegetables, identifies them by name and places them in the empty basket. Two members of the Circle choose the vegetable they like best and tell the class how to prepare it for eating (always potatoes!). Circle B in turn separates the fruit and vegetables, but this group selects a fruit for preparation for eating. The task of telling *why* it is a vegetable or fruit was too difficult. Children often know categories without understanding the basis of categorization.

2. (Categorization) The Farm. A grass carpet, two feet square, is laid on the floor. A fabricated barn-silo is placed in one corner of the farm. Each child in Circle B selects one animal belonging on the farm. The children excluded bear, deer, rhinoceros, elephant, giraffe, and tiger but when a child reported his mother's "true story" about a deer that came into the town and plunged through the glass window of a furniture store, they decided that sometimes deer might live on a farm. The Story Lady from the Public Library who conducted the half-hour story time each day, chose *Bambi* by Marjorie Kinnan Rawlings for the language class.

3. (Categorization) The Zoo. A fabricated zoo building has been set up with movable units. The children suggested the organization, discussing which animals were neighborly, their space needs, food habits, sleep schedules, liking for children, and rules of the zoo, warning signs, and so on.

4. (Categorization) Free-for-all. A teacher or aide goes around the class touching several children on the top of the head. Before she makes a second round, she asks the class: "What do they all have in common?" "Why are they alike?" (in the same category). Any real likeness must be accepted. (They are all wearing belts; they all have long sleeves; their names all start with *M*.) In the free discussion after the "awards," they all participate in deciding why certain answers were wrong. The children now take charge. Each circle meets to select a "secret category" and continue with the game.

5. (Categorization) Best Match. An aide taps a child and whispers to her to find a partner whose clothes, hair color, height, or first letter of name matches hers. The pair appears before the class and presents a nursery rhyme or verse. They ask the class: "In what way are we alike?" A prize for the first child who identifies the similarity.

6. (Size and Shape) My Dame Has Lost Her Shoe. Two rows of shoes, one of a pair (belonging to children, teachers, aides, and volunteers) are set in random order on the floor at the front of the room. The problem: To match foot to shoe without trying the shoe on the foot. Team A will go "into committee" and come back with a way agreed upon by the team. Then Team B tries out its agreed-upon plan on the row of shoes assigned to it.

7. (Sequencing) Boot Muddle. All boots have been taken from the cubbies (cloakroom cupboards) and mixed up. Team A decided on a plan for organizing the work and chooses three of its members to tell why they are using

this sequence. The team then proceeds to carry it out. Team B has another plan (classifying by color), but it doesn't work. Why didn't it work? A free-for-all discussion ensues.

8. (Critical Referent) A Happening. Selection of large poster pictures (preferably from *The Norman Rockwell Poster Book* [53]) in which action is dominant. Divide the class into "committees" of five. Each group is instructed to look at the picture for four minutes without talking but with the question in mind: "What has happened?" or "What is happening?" Then each committee takes a corner of the room, agrees upon an interpretation of the happening and chooses the child who is to tell the story. When all groups are ready, each leader tells his story. Because the leader represents the group he cannot alter the interpretation. Now comes the brain-storming. Which group had the most accurate interpretation of the happening? Why?

9. (Incongruities) That's weird. Construction or selection of a series of poster pictures presenting incongruities in state or in action. The question to the children is: "What is funny about this picture?"

    a. The girl is putting loaves of bread in the refrigerator to bake.

    b. He is getting the milk from the bathtub.

    c. She is pouring the milk in the basket.

    d. He is putting the telephone in the wastebasket.

    e. Bunches of bananas are hanging from the apple tree. "That's weird," said Jasper, four years of age.

10. (Categorization by Similarities) Noun relationships: In what way are they *alike?*

    a. mouse—cat

    b. boxes—jars

    c. newspaper—magazine

    d. celery—carrots

    e. milk—coke

    f. school—church, or temple, or mosque

11. (The Referent) Part-whole relationships. Now the children must deal with certain cues that refer to a total object or situation. First they must identify the cues accurately and then, by inference, "determine the *whole* from the parts." Polar opposites word game: What it is *not.*

    a. noisy is not ＿＿＿＿＿ (quiet)

    b. wet is not ＿＿＿＿＿ (dry)

    c. go is not ＿＿＿＿＿ (stop)

    d. green is not ＿＿＿＿＿ (red)

    e. long is not ＿＿＿＿＿ (short)

    f. heavy is not ＿＿＿＿＿ (light)

    g. sick is not ＿＿＿＿＿ (well)

[53] M. Schau, ed., *The Norman Rockwell Poster Book* (New York: Watson-Guptill Publications, 1976).

12. (Critical Referent) Matrix puzzles. Before the first set of pictures is presented, the teacher or her aides talk about relationships between colors (black is to white as night is to day), objects, persons, and events. Two pictures which are related in some way are then presented to the children. If they are not able to find the relationship, it is pointed out to them. Then a second set of pictures is presented in which they are to find and express the relationship. Each circle, widely separated from the other circles, may discuss the basis of the relationship before they present their response. In the free discussion session that invariably follows this game, teachers and aides can be of great assistance by providing additional pictured sequences in which the strategy of categorical relationships can be employed.

13. (Sequencing) The children are preparing a play: *Snow White and the Seven Dwarfs.* The leader asks, "Who should be first in the row of dwarfs when we sing our song: 'Heigh-Ho: It's off to work we go?' Who is next? Grumpy, Happy or Bashful? Sneezy? Sleepy? Doc? Then who is next? Who is last? Why should Dopey be last?"

14. (Spatial Relations) Garden Plan. The "advanced" group is in an extended learning experience. They are planning and "planting" a garden of annuals. Team A is to plant dwarf marigolds; Team B, petunias; Team C, snapdragons; Team D, tall zinnias. Several brainstorming sessions occur in the classroom, once the teaching team or its aides have sketched the general plan. "Is the garden square?" "No, it's a half circle." "How big is it?" "Show us pictures of dwarf marigolds, petunias, snapdragons, tall zinnias." "Which is the shortest, the next in height, the next, the highest of all?" "How far apart should marigolds be planted?" "petunias?" "How deep?"

Advance information on the project has been given to parents in a *Parents Respond* report. With the help of the parents and seed catalogs, the children's journal will include pictures or a drawing of the flower that the team is to plant. It will also include a chart of its position in the garden. The mock-up is prepared in the classroom.

15. (Problem Solving) Professional aides (or parents) have contributed rare objects for presentation: an African mask, a bamboo back-scratcher, a Scandinavian pusher (child's utensil used in eating), Chinese chopsticks, and an Alaskan papoose carrier. By categorizing (similarities and differences), sequencing, and so on, the children establish a name, describe its construction, and define its use.

16. Problem Solving. Practical problems demanding practical solutions:

    a. John and Jeff are in danger of being late for school. How can they get to their school room in time? Should they go back home and ask Mother to take them in the car? Go back home and stay there? Take a shorter route, cutting across lots and running fast?

    b. If Jean walks through pools of water on her way home from school, what will happen?

    c. A great box of used Christmas cards came to the class. What should they do with them? Give them to a children's agency? Cut the picture from the card and mount it on construction paper? Select the best or most artistic ones, mount them, and display them in the classroom? Send them to their friends?

    d. What will happen to Angie's cake if she removes it from the oven after thirty minutes when baking time should be forty-five minutes?

e. The tree fell because _____? It was rotten; it was cut down by lumbermen who wanted the wood; the tree had burned in a forest fire.

17. Synthesizing the skills through activities outside the classroom. Here are outlines of three happenings or experiences focused on the use of the four perceptual-semantic skills: identifying a referent, categorizing, sequencing, and problem solving. Two are designed for four- and five-year-olds; one for children six to nine years of age.

I. *The Cookie and Juice Party*

A. Staff: language and classroom teachers; nutritionist (or nurse), mothers
B. Review of stories and rhymes we know about food

    1) Rhymes: Little Tommy Tucker; Pat-a-Cake, Baker's Man; Peas Porridge Hot; Hickety, Pickety, My Black Hen; Jack Sprat; The Queen of Hearts.
    2) Stories: The Cookie Monster; Johnny Cake.
    3) Poems: Milking Time (C. Rossetti); The Sugar-Plum Tree (E. Field); Animal Crackers (C. Morley).

C. Cookies I like best:

    1) Brownies
    2) Sugar cookies
    3) Peanut butter cookies

D. Parents Respond report: The mother prints the recipe for the simplest cookie she makes. Photo or colored sketch of Mom's cookies placed in child's journal.
E. Choosing the cookie the children want to make

    1) Criteria: ease of making, taste, number of ingredients
    2) What ingredients and why? spices, butter, flour, milk, flavoring

F. Making up the shopping list
G. The Market Place: Buying
H. Pre-preparation by the staff and children

    1) Clean hands, plastic aprons, and paper towels.
    2) Assignment of tasks: mixing bowl, utensils, ingredients, cookie tins.
    3) The baking: preheat, setting timer.

I. The Cookie and Juice Party

    1) Oral messages to administrative staff
    2) Serving: What do you say?

II. *Our Spring Garden*

A. Drawing the plot for the spring garden: Design

    1) Names and pictures of flowers (family participation)
    2) Color relationships (why?)

3) Space relationships (why?)
(size, distance between, direction, right-left)

B. Preparation of soil for tulip clusters

1) Tools for gardening
2) Fertilizers (?) (Problem solving)

C. Planting the bulbs

1) Tulips, daffodils, narcissus
2) How deep?
3) Position?
4) How far apart?

D. Winter covers:

1) Snow
2) Marsh grass

E. Spring:

1) Rain
2) When will they show first shoots? (Asking questions, teaching tenses, expanding sentences.)
3) May buds
4) June flowering
5) Photographing the first blooms

F. Helpers:

1) The family (pictures, stories, poems)
2) Visit to garden store
3) The garden club

G. Problem solving in the garden:

1) What would you do?

a. Wrong soil
b. Invaders

1) animals: rabbits, chipmunks, gophers? who? where? why? how many?
2) weeds
3) fungi or plant lice

c. Colors that don't go together
d. Plants that don't go together
e. Sun and shade plants

III. *Other Activity Projects*

A. Party for mothers (social skills)

1) Guest book
2) Punch and cookie servers
3) Program: drama

    a. *Snow White and the Seven Dwarfs*
    b. *Goldilocks and the Three Bears*
    c. *The Princess and the Pea*
    (Drama in which costume includes jewelry: beads, necklaces, bracelets, rings.)

B. Hunt in the woods

  1) Identification and classification of wildflowers, trees, vines, poison plants

  2) Differences and similarities in two flowers

IV. *The Photo Buffs (or Shutter-Snappers).* Experiential learning directed to perceptual-semantic growth (six to nine years)

A. Subject: The Children's Farm (Meadowbrook Farm)
B. Staff: Language and classroom teachers, outdoor education instructor, physical education instructor, clerk from camera shop, director Children's Farm
C. Funding: PR (Parents Respond) Club, civic organizations interested in children

D. Preparation

  1) Map study and drawing of trip
  2) Sketch of buildings: barn, house, machine shed
  3) Learning about the animals: pony, cows, sheep, pigs, rabbits, puppy.
  4) Birds: guinea hens, turkeys, ducks, chickens, geese
  5) Field: hay, corn, straw, wild flowers
  6) PR: Post map and all sketches in child's journal
  7) Pictures of animals, birds, flowers to be posted in child's journal
  8) Learning how to operate a camera (camera shop expert). Instant or conventional camera

    a. Demonstration of parts
    b. Loading the camera
    c. Order of operation: What do you do first? second? next?
    d. Selection of scene for photo: animal feeding, persons, rider on pony, and so on

E. The Happening: Afternoon at Meadowbrook Farm

  1) The bus trip
  2) The tour

    a. Selection of action pictures
    b. Selection of still pictures
    c. Critic's corner: Teachers' aides

F. Brainstorming back in the classroom

  1) Report of shutter-snappers

    a. The best picture: each child selects his best and presents it, telling why it is his best

b. Prize awards
c. Telling:

    1) The most interesting single piece of action
    2) The funniest thing that happened
    3) All the animals you saw on the farm
    4) What would you say if I said:

        You eat them. (eggs, chicken, turkey)
        You play with it. (puppy, rabbit)
        You drink it. (milk)
        You put hay in it. (barn, haymow)
        You ride on it. (pony, tractor)
        You make cloth out of their coats. (sheep)
        It lives in a nest. (bird)
        It lives in the barn in winter. (pony, cow)
        It likes to eat lettuce. (rabbit)

Appendix D-8

TEACHING PERCEPTUAL-SEMANTIC SKILLS IN COOPERATION WITH CLASSROOM TEACHERS

Book List (For children 8–11 years; Social Studies and Science)

GROSS, H.H. and others, *Exploring Our World Regions;* 4th grade. Follett, 1977.

GROSS, H.H. and others, *Exploring Our World; The Americas;* 4th grade. Follett, 1965.

BROWN, G.S., *Your Country and Mine* (Our American Neighbors) 5th grade. Ginn and Co., 1965.

FISCHLER, A.S. and others, *Modern Elementary Science (Animals, Plants and Places); Energy; The Changing Earth;* 4th grade; *Air, Water, Weather; Electricity and Magnetism;* 5th grade. Holt, Rinehart and Winston, 1971. (children 8–11 years—Reading)

WOLFE, D.M., *Enjoying English (Experiences in Speaking, Listening and Writing);* 3rd grade. L.W. Singer Co., 1961.

WOLFE, D.M., *Enjoying English (Language Skills);* 4th grade. L.W. Singer Co., 1961.

ANASTASIO, D., "Impressions" (The Arts: Music, Dance, Drama, Architecture); 4th grade. Part II *Cycles, Imphession, A Visit with Rosalind,* eds. C. Smith and R. Wardhaugh. Macmillan, 1975.

WHITNEY, ALMA, *Wonders* (Earth, Moon, Sun, Stars and Other Planets), 5th grade. Part I *Wonders, Outlets, Moonball,* eds. C. Smith and R. Wardhaugh. Macmillan, 1975.

ANASTASIO, D. and W. HALLIBURTON, "Dialogues: Part III" 6th grade. *Awakening, Journeys, Dialogues,* eds. C. Smith and R. Wardhaugh. Macmillan, 1975.

GLOSSARY

Acetylcholine. A chemical neurotransmitter thought to be instrumental in the transmission of nerve impulses at synapses and myoneural junctions.

Acoustic nerve. (Auditory nerve) See *Nerves*.

Amygdaloid nucleus. Nuclear mass located in the inferior horn of the lateral ventricle; connected with systems (limbic and reticular) subserving emotional reinforcement, motivation and recent memory. *Figs. 2-6; 2-7.*

Apgar score. A numerical expression of the condition of a newborn infant, usually determined at 60 seconds after birth, being the sum of points gained on assessment of the heart rate, respiratory effort, muscle tone, reflex irritability, and color.

Attention. A psychological process by which an individual conducts a search-and-sampling of the event in order to interpret it.

    diffuse a. When the threshold of many classes of immediate stimuli is the same, attention is scattered or diffuse.

    fiixation a. Inability to leave one stimulus for succeeding stimuli.

    selective a. Stimuli not relevant to the oriented stimulus are shut out by suppression of their neural potentials.

    set-to-attend. Its neurological correlate is the reticular-activating system.

Auding. Managing of auditory information, storage and retrieval. *Figs. 2-2; 2-10.*

Auditory perception of language. (Auditory comprehension; auditory discrimination) Organization and interpretation of units of speech symbols received through the ear. *Figs. 2-2; 2-10.*

Basal ganglia. (Basal nuclei) See *Corpus striatum.*

Behavior modification. Application of principles of operant learning in which the individual's responses are progressively reinforced in the direction of a desired pattern.

Broca's area. One of cortical organizing areas for motor speech, located in the inferior frontal gyrus in the left (major) cerebral cortex. *Figs. 2-2; 2-10.*

Cephalo-caudal waves. Generalized head-to-foot motor response patterns exhibited by infants.

Cerebellum. The part of the metencephalon behind the brain stem but connected with it by three pairs of peduncles. Plays a major role in coding temporal-spatial patterns of balance, rhythm, and movement. *Fig. 2-9.*

Cerebral lobes. Five pairs of lobes, one of each pair comprising the two cerebral hemispheres.

    frontal 1. That part of the cerebral hemispheres located in front of the central sulcus (Fissure of Rolando) and above the lateral cerebral fissure (Fissure of Sylvius) *Figs. 2-8; 2-9.*

    limbic 1. Part of the medial aspect of the cerebral hemispheres; c-curved structure encircling thalamus; includes cingulate and hippocampal gyri. *Figs. 2-6; 2-7.*

    parietal 1. Part of the cerebral hemispheres located above the lateral cerebral fissure (Fissure of Sylvius) and behind the central sulcus (Fissure of Rolando). *Fig. 2-9.*

    temporal 1. Part of the cerebral hemispheres below the lateral cerebral fissure (Fissure of Sylvius) and continuous posteriorily with the occipital lobe.

    occipital 1. Part of the cerebral hemispheres, located posterior to the parietal-occipital fissure; triangular area at the occipital extremity.

Cerebral palsy. A neurologic disability caused by pre-, peri-, or postnatal injury or disease of the central nervous system or by genetic defects, and most commonly exhibited in motor dysfunction. Sensory, intellectual and behavioral deficits may also be a part of the syndrome. Various clinical types are described as spastic, athetoid, ataxic, dysarthric, etc., but the delineations are not entirely accurate or mutually exclusive.

Cerebrum. Main portion of the brain, occupying the upper part of the cranial cavity; its two hemispheres, united by the corpus callosum, form the largest part of the central nervous system in man; basal nuclei (basal ganglia) and connecting structures also are derived from the telencephalon and hence are part of the cerebrum. *Fig. 2-9.*

    cerebral cortex. The convoluted layer of gray substance that covers each cerebral hemisphere.

Cingulate gyrus. Arch-shaped convolution in the limbic lobe, containing feedback circuits with other structures of the limbic system and with the reticular formation. *Figs. 2-6; 2-7.*

Cluttering. 1. Perceptual disorder reflected in a verbal manifestation of interruption of coding processes. 2. Language disorder characterized by rapid utterance with many elisions, transpositions, and omissions of significant speech sounds and word groups. Speech is generally jerky, explosive and non-melodic, thus obscuring meaning.

Cochlea. The essential organ of hearing; a spirally wound tube, resembling a snail shell, which forms part of the inner ear. Contains the Organ of Corti or sensory end-organs of hearing. *Fig. 2-2.*

Cochlear nerve. The cochlear branch of eighth cranial nerve (Acoustic nerve). *Fig. 2-2.*

    cell bodies I: Cell bodies in the spiral ganglion located in the modiolus of inner ear. Bipolar cells which send fibers peripherally to the spiral organ making up the inner ear and centrally through the internal acoustic meatus to the cochlear nuclei of the brain stem.

    cell bodies II: Ventral and dorsal cochlear nuclei. Two nuclear masses in the upper medulla with which primary auditory fibers of cochlear nerve synapse and which give rise to secondary order of auditory fibers.

Cognition. Simple awareness of knowing or being in possession of information. *Recognition* or *identification* of information derived from sensations from one or several modalities.

Competence. See *Linguistic competence.*

Conservation. 1. The maintenance of a structure as invariant during physical changes of some aspects. Implies an internal system of regulations that can compensate internally for external changes. 2. Piagetian term: the acquisition of a linguistic skill or schemata by which the amount or quantity of a matter stays the same without respect to any changes in shape or position. The ability to hold one dimension invariant in the face of changes in other dimensions.

Contentive words. Nouns, verbs, adjectives which generally but not exclusively make concrete reference to persons, objects, actions, and qualities. Antonym: functor words.

Coronal. A distinctive articulatory feature which a sound holds in common with others in a group or class of sounds. Thus /t/ and /d/ /θ/; /ð/ are generally assumed to possess a coronal feature.

Corpus callosum. Broad transverse band of fibers connecting the cerebral hemispheres. *Figs. 2-6; 2-9.*

Corpus striatum. A subcortical mass of gray and white substance in front of and lateral to the thalamus in each cerebral hemisphere. *Fig. 2-3.* basal nuclei. (basal ganglia) Gray substance of c. striatum making up the *caudate* and *lenticular n.* Some authors include in c. striatum subthalamic n. and red n. Functions: Through complicated circuitry with feedback loops and reciprocal connections with frontal lobe of cerebral cortex, subcortical nuclei, and brain stem, the basal nuclei 1) activate and integrate finely graded movement patterns employed in motor expression; 2) maintain steady muscular state involved in reciprocal innervation; 3) regulate emotional expression through its feedback circuitry with thalamus and limbic system.

Correlation coefficient.   An average constancy estimate for the group. Usually estimated by equivalent forms of the same test.

Cortical localization areas.   (extended from Brodmann's cytoarchitectural map) *Fig. 2-9.*

> **Area 19.**   Area in occipital anterior lobes and posterior temporal-parietal border zones associated with visual recognition and perception. Deficit: Visual-verbal agnosia.
>
> **Area 21-22.**   Areas in superior and middle temporal gyri and extending into parietal lobe, associated with the interpretation and recall of spoken language.
>
> **Area 37.**   Area in inferior temporal gyrus, associated with the formulation and recall of proper nouns and words. Deficit: Anomia, amnesic aphasia.
>
> **Area 39.**   Area of the angular gyrus in the superior temporal and parietal lobes associated with comprehension of symbols in reading, writing, and arithmetic. Deficits: Dyslexia, dysgraphia, dyscalculia.
>
> **Areas 41–42.**   (Wernicke's area) Area in superior temporal, inferior parietal and possibly border of occipital lobes, associated with the recognition of spoken language. Deficit: Auditory-verbal agnosia.
>
> **Area 44, 45.**   (Broca's area). Area in the inferior section of third frontal convolution, associated with the organization of motor speech. Deficit: Broca's aphasia.

Cortico-strio-ponto-cerebellar neural circuit.   A sensorimotor feedback loop affecting such complex motor behavior as speech by its regulation of timing and coordination of finely graded movement patterns. A significant system in phasic locomotor activities embracing chiefly the cortex, corpus striatum (caudate and lenticular nuclei), pons and cerebellum, but not excluding connections with the thalamus and midbrain. *Fig. 2-3.*

Co-variance.   See *Variance.*

Deduction.   An inference which has been made from formal premises or propositions.

Delayed auditory feedback.   See *Feedback*

Dichotic listening.   Test presumed to establish cerebral dominance through the input of simultaneous but different stimuli to each ear. Dichotic tasks involving recall of digit strings, word lists, nonsense syllables, and phonetic classes have been used which, on the basis of recall, normally suggest right ear-left brain dominance. A reversal of ear superiority (left ear-right brain) may take place for such non-speech modalities as melodies, sonar signals, and environmental noises. Validity of the interpretation of dichotic test results in ear asymmetries as they apply to dyslexia, learning disabilities, etc. has been questioned. —J. B. deQuiros.

Dichotic speech perceptions.   See *Dichotic listening.*

Discrimination. A process differentiating or detecting differences. A process by which one builds perceptions.

DNA (deoxyribonucleic acid). Any of the class of nucleic acids that contain deoxyribose, found chiefly in the nucleus of cells, and which functions in the transference of genetic characteristics and in the synthesis of protein.

Duration. The temporal attribute of sensations. In phonology, prolongation of sounds and non-sound intervals for the purpose of indicating stress, emotional overlay, prosody.

Dyslexia. 1. Perceptual deficit involving linguistic processing and affecting reading, speech, spelling and other sensorimotor integrative activities necessitating fine coordination. Obsolete: Word blindness. 2. Reading disability, one form of learning disability—Susan Ann Vogel.

Dysphasia. Impairment of an acquired ability to comprehend and express oral language.

Aphasia. Total or global impairment.

Dyspraxia. A sensorimotor disorder affecting the higher levels of neural organization and resulting in deficits in the cortical integration and motor expression of oral language. Imperfect comprehension and memory lapses also may contribute to coding disability. The resulting disruption in programming and sequencing affects all voluntary motor adjustments necessary for speech — respiration, phonation, resonation, and articulation.

Echolalia. Repetition of the final segment of a sentence or question, generally practiced by severely retarded children, selectively practiced by young normal children who respond to another's utterance in order to comprehend it or to keep up their end of the dialogue.

Ecology. Study of the relation of organisms to their environment. Study and function of nature. The community or individual and the non-living environment function together as an ecological system or eco-system.

Educable mentally handicapped. (EMH) Persons of subnormal mentality whose intellectual functioning (existing concurrently with deficit adaptive behavior) falls two or more standard deviations below the mean on standardized tests. On the Stanford-Binet or Wechsler Intelligence Scale for Children, a score of 65–70 would place a child in the EMH class. The term does not imply feeblemindedness. Synonym: Mental impairment (MI).

Embedding. A process of sentence recasting which places a proposition in a particular semantic role within another proposition.

Energy metabolism. The physiologic activities concerned with the intake, interchange, and output of energy.

Facilitation. The potential of certain neural assemblies and circuits to increase the integration and/or strength of the final response. The reticular activating system performs such a function.

Feedback. 1. Process of monitoring and modifying one's own responses, as in a cybernetic system. It includes both an internal form, where part of the response pattern is fed back into the system prior to effecting the response, and an external form, where the overt response is monitored. *Fig. 2-3.* 2. Negative mechanism restricting and correcting input, integration and output.

auditory f.   control system of the speech act in which output is returned to the input and integrative systems mediating auditory perception.

delayed auditory f.   Delay of speaker's speech to his ears in excess of the time of arrival of air- or bone-conducted sound of his speech.

haptic f.   A control system of the speech act in which output information is returned to the tactile and kinesthetic input and integrative areas mediating speech, thus providing a self-monitoring regulation of speech. tactile proprioceptive f. See *Haptic feedback*.

Feedforward.   In the perceptual and expressive processes of oral language, feedforward, a neurobiological control system increases neural activity, accelerates conductance and heightens the electrical potential in strategic cortical areas mediating the response. *Fig. 2-3.*

Figure-ground.   Ability to perceive salient central features which are separate and distinct from their surrounding background.

Fornix.   Arched fiber tract under the corpus callosum, connecting hypothalamus, thalamus, hippocampus and other nuclear masses in the limbic system. *Fig. 2-6.*

Frontal lobes.   See *Cerebrum and cerebral lobes*.

Fourth ventricle.   One of four cavities of the brain filled with cerebrospinal fluid; the floor of the fourth is the medulla-pons; the roof, the cerebellum. *Fig. 2-9.*

Functor words.   In contrast to contentive words, functors are forms, relatively small in number, which rarely contribute to the referent. They mark grammatical structure and modify meaning. Articles, prepositions, conjunctions, inflections, and auxiliary verbs are examples.

Generative grammar.   A system of explicit rules accounting for the basic structures of a language and which are capable of generating a number of grammatical utterances.

Genetic drive.   Inherited, built-in force or energizer that varies with the physical constitution of the genes and determines the potential of the nervous system.

Glia cells.   Cells of the supporting structure of nervous tissue (neuroglia) and in the cortex thought to have a functional purpose in addition to their nutritional and buffer support of the primary cortical neurons.

Grammar.   The rules which are basic to the morphology and syntax of a language.

Haptic perception.   See *Tactile-kinesthetic perception*.

Hemispherical dominance.   Refers to horizontal superiority, to the preeminence of one cerebral hemisphere over the other in such specialized activities as hand control, language, music, and analytical processes. *Fig. 2-8.*

Heschl's gyrus.   Transverse temporal gyrus which in the dominant hemisphere is intimately associated with the auditory perception of language.

Hippocampus. Gyrus in the floor of inferior horn of lateral ventricle of cerebrum; processing station of limbic system. Postulated role in emotional control and memory. *Figs. 2-6; 2-7.*

Holophrase. A single word functioning as a phrase or sentence, possessing an underlying cognitive-perceptual-action structure, and expressing intention and meaning.

Homeostasis. 1. The regulated balancing of nervous and endocrine factors in the organism in order to preserve an internal state of labile stability. 2. A tendency to stability in the internal environment of the organism achieved by a system of control mechanisms activated by feedback and feedforward.

Hypoglossal nerve. See *Nerves.*

Hypothalamus. Portion of the diencephalon forming the base of the thalamus, flanked medially by the third ventricle and caudally by midbrain. Its nuclear masses and circuits are responsible for such autonomic functions as the regulation of body temperature, for such endocrine activity as emotional control, and such visceral activities as hunger, thirst, etc. *Fig. 2-7.*

Illocutionary language. Performatory language in such dyadic social situations as thanking, requesting, describing, reporting, etc. Language characterized by intentional communication in which motor and vocal acts combine to secure attention and satisfaction of the child's immediate needs.

Inferior colliculi. See *Midbrain.*

Internal capsule. Great band of nerve fibers on the outer side of the thalamus and between the caudate and lenticular nuclei; continuous with the cerebral peduncles; contains great sensorimotor tracts to and from the cortex. *Fig. 2-3.*

Intonation. A synonym for prosody or the melodic patterns of language as used by some scholars. The melody resulting from variations in pitch, stress and duration in connected speech.

Kinesthetic perception (Proprioception). 1. Awareness and appreciation of those sensations derived from bodily movement including the position of the body in space, its static limb positions, dynamic movement patterns and sensitivity to direction. 2. Neurol. Proprioceptors respond to stimuli arising in the deeper tissues particularly in the locomotor system. They are concerned with movement, position and pressure and include the neurotendinous organs of Golgi, neuromuscular spindles, Pacinian corpuscles, and vestibular receptors in the membranous labyrinth. *Figs. 2-1; 2-3.*

Lateral lemniscus. Primary auditory tract, fibers of which originate in the cochlear nuclei of the opposite side and in the trapezoid body; they will synapse with nuclei in the inferior colliculi and the medial geniculate body. *Fig. 2-2.*

lateral lemniscus n. Diffuse cell groups in the pons contributing to the lateral lemniscus.

Learning disability. 1. "The child exhibits a disorder in one or more of the basic psychological processes involved in understanding or in using language, spoken or written, which may manifest itself in an imperfect ability to listen, think, speak, read, write, spell, or to do mathematical calculations. Such term includes conditions as perceptual handicaps, brain injury, minimal brain dysfunction, dyslexia, and developmental aphasia. The term does not include children who have learning problems which are primarily the result of visual, hearing, or motor handicaps, of mental retardation, of emotional disturbance, or of environmental, cultural, or economic disadvantage."—School Code of Illinois. 2. A rubric defying definition because it includes many multi-faceted syndromes. The term is described in terms of assets and deficits found in certain children, as in the following: "A child with learning disabilities is one with adequate mental abilities, sensory processes and emotional stability who has a limited number of specific deficits in perceptive, integrative, or expressive processes which severely impair learning efficiency. This includes children who have central nervous dysfunction which is expressed primarily in impaired learning efficiency."—National Council on Exceptional Children (CEC), St. Louis, April 1967.

Lexicon. 1. All linguistic signs, words or morphemes comprising a given language. 2. The stock of terms in a vocabulary. 3. An internalized dictionary representing the idiosyncratic properties of words. 4. A list of the morphemes of the language.

lexeme. A set of inflectionally related words.

lexical entry. An inventory of pairs of elements, each pair being called a lexical entry. Elements are the representation of the sound of a word, or of a part of a work; the representation of the meaning of the word, prefix, or suffix.

lexical meaning. Meaning which relates to words, word formatives and vocabulary.

Limbic lobes. See *Cerebrum and cerebral lobes.*

Limbic system. A primitive neural complex in the upper brain stem and cortex contributing to facilitation and inhibition in coding processes, chiefly through emotional reinforcement, recent memory, and mastery of purposive motor response. Nuclei in the hippocampal gyrus, hypothalamus, thalamus, and the basal section of the fronto-temporal cortex are included in the limbic system. *Figs. 2-6; 2-7.*

Linguistics. The study of languages, their origins, structure, and evolution.

linguistic competence. Comprehension of the meaning, structure, sound units, and prosody of one's language.

linguistic performance. The speaker's actual use of language. The demonstration of competence in the overt expression of listening, speaking, reading, and writing.

Localization areas.   See *Cortical localization areas.*

Loudness.   1. Physical intensity of a sound, measured in decibels and correlated in a logarythmic relationship with the physical energy of the stimulus. 2. Loudness perception: A subjective sensation, related but not linearly to physical intensity (amplitude), pitch (frequency), and stress; it is measured by the sone.

Mammillary bodies.   Two nuclear masses in hypothalamus providing a feedback circuit with the reticular system and other parts of the limbic system controlling emotional and behavioral patterns. *Figs. 2-6; 2-7.*

Mands.   Semantic intention of speech acts: demands, commands and requests.

Medial geniculate bodies.   Located on the posterior inferior aspect of the thalamus, they receive auditory impulses from the inferior colliculi and relay them to the temporal-parietal cortex. *Fig. 2-2.*

Medulla.   Lower part of brainstem extending from the pons to the spinal cord; developmentally an extension of the spinal cord. Eight of 12 cranial nerves exit from medulla. Great sensorimotor trunk lines decussate and continue their ascent or descent in the medulla. Autonomic centers for respiratory and circulatory control located in the medulla. *Fig. 2-3.*

Memory.   1. A process whereby organized time-space events are carried forward in time. 2. Neurol. The retention in the neural organization of a skeletal relationship among neurone assemblies that have responded together in earlier time-space events and reproduce this related complex when needed.

iconic m.   Employment of imagery and hence symbolic storage of visual, auditory, haptic patterns.

long-term m.   neurol. Long-term change in synaptic effectivness; shares a common neuronal locus with short-term m.

short-term m.   neurol. A depression in the electro-chemical current in the presynaptic terminal producing habituation as a result of the modulation in strength of a previously existing synaptic connection.

Mental impairment.   1. Complex developmental syndrome characterized by a) intellectual deficiency; b) learning disabilities; and/or social maladjustment. (See educable mentally handicapped, EMH.) 2. Reduced general intellectual and adaptive functioning apparent from the early developmental period. Classification of MI: borderline (IQ 70–84); mild (IQ 55–69); moderate (IQ 36–51); severe (IQ 25–39); profound (IQ below 20).

Midbrain.   (Mesencephalon). Section of the brain stem connecting the pons and cerebellum with the forebrain; in the ventral section are the cerebral peduncles; the tectum (roof) contains the superior colliculi (visual processing station) and the inferior colliculi (auditory processing station). *Figs. 2-2; 2-3; 2-9.*

Morpheme.   1. Smallest unit of meaning which may be combined to form words. Meaning may be lexical, relating to words, word formatives and vocabulary *or* grammatical, indicative of tense, possession, plurals, etc. 2. Smallest meaningful unit of language having a differential function. 3. Smallest unit of grammatical analysis.

free m.   Unit which has meaning when standing alone.

bound m.   Unit which must be joined to free morpheme in order to have meaning. Frequently a grammatical inflection which may indicate singularity and plurality in nouns, tense in verbs, negation, possession, etc.

Morphology.   1. Study of the building of words from smaller constituents. 2. The pattern of word formation, including inflection, derivation and composition. 3. Refers to change in word endings and word forms to denote tense, plurality, possessive and comparative. 4. Deals with the combination of morphemes into words.

Motivation.   Phenomena involved in the operation of incentives and drives. The genetically conditioned limbic and reticular-activating systems are active neurological agents in motivation. Motivation is determined both by intrinsic and extrinsic forces.

primary m.   Incentive derived from basic genetic drive.

secondary m.   Incentive derived from external forces.

Nerves.

afferent neuron.   A neuron which conducts a nervous impulse from a receptor to a center.

efferent neuron.   A neuron which conducts a nervous impulse from a center to an organ of response.

acoustic nerve.   VIIIth cranial nerve, having two roots, the vestibular branch originating in the vestibule and the semicircular canals, and the cochlear branch originating in the cochlea. The two branches mediate equilibration and audition respectively. *Fig. 2-2.*

cochlear nerve.   Branch of acoustic nerve (CNVIII) whose first cell bodies make up the spiral ganglion in the cochlea; second order neurons are ventral and dorsal cochlear nuclei. *Fig. 2-2.*

hypoglossal nerve.   XIIth cranial nerve providing both sensory (proprioceptive) and motor innervation to the muscles of the tongue. *Fig. 2-3.*

Neuronal assemblies.   A collection of neural circuits which have acted together in previous space-time events and will admit related circuits into the complex. Basis of cortical integration.

Nominals.   Noun phrases, as they are usually called, in generative grammar.

Nucleus ruber.   (Red nucleus) A distinctive oval nucleus centrally placed in the upper mesencephalic reticular formation. Directly connected with cerebellum, cerebral cortex, and thalamus. Probably an important part of the reticular activating and integrative system. *Fig. 2-3.*

Object permanence.   Child's perception and retention of object although it is no longer present in his immediate environment. Child uses the percept "apart from himself" and apart from the actual presence of person, object or event.

Occipital lobes.   See *Cerebrum and cerebral lobes.*

Ontogenic development.   Refers to the natural order of language development, from birth to adulthood, from non-verbal to verbal communication, and follows the normal course of developmental changes in
an individual.

Operant conditioning.   Process of establishing new or modifying learned
responses by which the sought response occurs spontaneously and upon
which the subject is given a reinforcer or reward. The increase in
frequency of target response is an index to the stability of the operant
behavior.

Optic chiasma.   Bundle of nerve fibers from the retina in which the fibers
from the nasal and temporal half of each retina cross the median plane
to enter the optic tract of the opposite side. *Fig. 2-9.*

Parietal lobes.   See *Cerebrum and cerebral lobes.*

Perception.   Interpretation and affective appreciation of information in all
its relational aspects.

global p.   Convergence of all sensory modalities in the perceptual act of
language—auditory, visual, tactile-kinesthetic, etc.

syncretistic p.   "Perception as a whole and nothing first."—Piaget.

perceptual set.   Appreciation of information based on past experiences,
both on perceptual and emotional level.

Perceptual-semantic development.   Growth in the comprehension and/or
expression of information in meaningful language.

Performative.   1. Utterances that occur as part of a child's actions (bye-bye
with waving). 2. A linguistic term referring to words which indicate
something in contrast to constantives which talk about something. 3.
Words declaring, demanding, commanding, requesting something; a
speech act. 4. The developing intentions in children's use of language.
5. The union of perceptual-semantics with the structure and phonology
of language.

performative language.   Early language of action or action-object which
the child as implicit agent uses to intervene in his environment.

Permutation.   Linguistical term. A transformation which converts one phrase
structure into another by substitution or displacement.

Phonatory development.   Maturation of the physical attributes of voice that
signal the principal linguistic characteristic subsumed in prosody or the
melody of speech. The primary vocal modifications are in pitch,
quality, intensity and duration. Some scholars equate stress and intonation patterns with prosody.

Phone.   Single speech sound represented always by the same single symbol
in a phonetic system. Example: /ʃ/ = *sh,* a single speech sound.

Phonemics.   The study of the phoneme, "a bundle of relevant sound features . . . a class of sounds, actualized or realized in a different
way in any given position" in the total utterance.—Mario Pei

Phonological development.   The growth of a sound system of language involving phonetic and phonemic combinations and contrasts to express
meaning. Development proceeds from prelinguistic vocalization to

morphophonemic maturation of sound patterns in syllabic combinations making up first words and word combinations based on the derivational structure of language.

Pitch.   1. Attribute of tone perceived by the number of vibrations per second, its intensity and overtone structure. The greater the number of vibrations per second, the higher the pitch. 2. Attribute of auditory sensation in which sounds are ordered on a scale from low to high, measurable through comparative discriminatory responses.

Pituitary body.   (Hypophysis) Small rounded organ attached by a stalk to the floor of the brain. Anterior lobe or anterior pituitary gland is the master gland of the endocrine system. *Fig. 2-9.*

Pons.   That part of the central nervous system lying between the medulla and the midbrain, ventral to the cerebellum. *Figs. 2-7; 2-9.*

Pragmatics of oral language.   1. Language development in the context and environment in which it is generated. Includes such factors as intention in communication, sensorimotor actions preceding, accompanying and following the utterance; the knowledge shared in the communicative dyad; and the elements in the environment surrounding the message. 2. Set of rules governing the use of language in context. Context is treated as an integral part of language structure rather than a cause of language, and meanings are seen as the result of the creative combination of utterance and social settings; thus meanings and context become virtually inseparable. 3. Study of linguistic acts and the contexts in which they are performed. 4. Study of speaker-listener intentions and relations and all elements in the environment surrounding the message.

Proprioception.   See *Kinesthetic perception.*

Prosody.   1. The melodic patterns of an individual's oral language, determined primarily by modifications of pitch, quality, loudness and time, and perceived primarily as stress and intonation. 2. A phonatory feature and linguistic function of voice dependent upon contrastive features of voice. 3. "A prefabricated system of temporal variability, *inherent in the organism* which permits the brain to process the meaning quickly."—D. L. Bolinger 4. Vocal response to the meaning and to emotional and attitudinal states of the human organism.

Referent.   1. The object, event or abstraction that is pointed to by oral or other symbolic signals. 2. Verbal response following directed attention to perceived objects and events in environment or to events available to one through thought. 3. That which is referred to by a verbal symbol. 4. Speech which stands for objects or relations (Leonard).

Reflex.   An involuntary movement in response to a stimulus originating in the skin receptor or muscle spindle and by connection of sensory neuron with motor neuron producing a muscular response. Five elements required for most spinal reflexes: 1) peripheral receptors, 2) sensory neurons, 3) internuncial neurons, 4) motor neurons, and 5) terminal effectors. Most common are two- or three-neuron arcs, either ipsilateral or crossed. True reflexes are rare since their arcs are subject to brain-stem and cortical activation and inhibition.

Reticular formation. Intricate neural network which forms most of the brainstem tegmentum; complex integrative system, involving both brainstem and cortical circuits.

   reticular activating-adapting system. Neural complex in the brain stem with cortical connections, associated with arousal and drivesetting functions and exercising control over the organization and direction of neural impulses in coding oral language. *Figs. 2-2; 2-3; 2-5.*

Retrieval interference. Disability in memory (recall) caused by reduction in potential of significant neuronal pool with the resulting introduction of conflicting circuits. Causes: Genetic defects, fatigue, emotional surcharge, trauma producing limbic and reticular disturbances.

Rhythm. 1. A harmonical succession of sounds, consisting in regular periodicity in a series of phonemes, constituting or contributing to measured movement or musical flow of language. 2. Synonym for prosody as used by some scholars. See *Prosody*. 3. Pattern of speech flow.

Ribonucleic acid (RNA). An RNA fraction of intermediate molecular weight, with a base ratio corresponding to the DNA of the same organism, which transmits information from DNA to the protein-forming system of the cell. In the nervous system, RNA acts as a neuro-chemical transmitter at the synapse and is thought to be an effective agent in neural integration and in the retention of learning.

Sequencing. 1. The order in which events or objects occur. 2. A succession of quantities, each derived from the preceding quantity by the same operation. (math.) 3. Continuous or connected series of things or events.

   sequencing rules. In linguistics an aspect of syntax which governs the order in which words may be combined into phrases and sentences.

Seriation. Ordering of items on the basis of a dimension, such as size, quality, or quantity.

Social learning theory. Language learning consists in the child's imitation and modeling of the social behavior and responses of significant others with or without reinforcement.

Somesthetic area. Cortical projection area in the postcentral gyrus for information initiated by stimulation of receptors in the skin, joints, muscles, and viscera; involved in conscious perception of somatic sensation.

Stress. 1. Intensity of utterance; special emphasis on a sound or sound group, the result of greater amplitude of the sound waves, producing relative loudness. 2. A variable referring to those phenomena of speech which are correlated with sensations of muscle movement in the production of speech articulation. Minimum unit of stress is the syllable, of which its most prominent component is the breath pulse. 3. Psychological force applied to a system, sufficient to cause strain or distortion in the system, or, when very great, to alter it into a new form.

Superior colliculi. See *Midbrain*.

Superior olivary nucleus. A complex of cell bodies dorsolateral to the trapezoid body, receiving cochlear fibers and contributing to the formation of the trapezoid body and the lateral lemniscus; an auditory processing station. *Fig. 2-2*.

Synapse. Functional unit of the nervous system. The region of junction between processes of two adjacent neurons, the place where a *functional* (not anatomic) connection is made permitting a nervous impulse to flow from one neuron to another. *Fig. 2-1*.

Syncretistic perception. "Perception as a whole and nothing first."—Piaget

Syntagma. 1. "A term designating the perceptual and communication unit of oral language, usually six or seven syllables, held by rhythmic constraints."—V. A. Kozhevnikov and L. A. Chistovich. 2. A tone group possessing a coherent internal structure, an hierarchical organization based upon temporal relations or rhythmic patterning.

Syntax. 1. Study of the rules or patterns of formation governing the form and structure of a language. Syntax and morphology = grammar.
syntactical development. The correlative maturation of phrases and sentences with perceptual-semantic growth.

Tactation (Taction). Sense of touch. Tactile perception of the environment, such as geometric information (size, shape, line and angle); texture, pain, and pressure derived from the sensory end-organs (touch corpuscles) in the skin and subcutaneous tissue.

Taxonomic orientation. That which deals with categories, e.g., parts of speech, sentence types, etc.

Tempo. Rate of speech sound flow. The rate at which morphemes, syllables, words and phrases are uttered, reflecting duration of silence as well as sound and hence the total communicative situation of speaker-listener.

Temporal lobes. See *Cerebrum and cerebral lobes*.

Temporo-parietal cortex. Portion of the lower parietal and upper temporal lobes of the brain in which the comprehension of auditory sequences of speech is mediated. Auditory centers of perception of oral language. *Figs. 2-2; 2-3; 2-10*.

Thalamus. Nuclear mass situated at the base of the cerebrum, projecting into and bound by the third ventricle. Considered by some authorities to be a part of reticular activating and organizing systems; by others a part of the limbic system controlling emotional and other behavioral patterns. *Fig. 2-7*.

Trapezoid body. Mass of transverse fibers extending through the central part of the pons and forming a part of the path of the cochlear nerve; after crossing the fibers become part of the lateral lemniscus. *Fig. 2-2*.

Variance. The square of the standard deviation.
co-variance. When factors are not independent, co-variance must also be analyzed.

Ventral and dorsal cochlear nuclei.   See *Cochlear nerve.*

Wernicke's Area.   Auditory perceptual and integrative area for comprehension of oral language. Field located chiefly in the upper temporal and lower parietal cortices. *Fig. 2-10.*

Word.   The smallest unit in a language that can be used alone as a sentence.

INDEX

A

Aphasia, linguistic confusion and,
    25–26
Articulation;
  language deficit, 174
  test, 173
  time lag, 174–75
Attention:
  controlling factors:
    communicative intention, 89
    eye contact, 90
    expectancy, 90
    motivational orientation, 89
    novelty, 89
    rate of change, 90
    response expectation, 90
    schematic number, 90
  deficits in language retardate, 91–95
    expectancy and intention, 91
    selective a. and perceptual style,
      92–93
    shift and fixation, 93–95
  facilitation, 95–97
  genetic drive and, 77–79
  neurogenic basis, 75–79
    reticular system, 75–77
    limbic system, 75–77

Attention (*cont.*)
  neuropsychological relation, motivation
    and, 88–89
  psychosocial aspects, 87–88
  teaching guide, 96–97
Auditory perception of oral language, 32;
    (fig. 2–2) 32; 53–62; (fig. 2–10)
    55
  auding process, 56–59
  auditory acuity vs., 61
  auditory-visual relation, 27
  central auditory dysfunction, 26–27
  deficits in, 60–62
  influence of tactile-kinesthetic feedback
    on, 56–57
  peripheral hearing impairment,
    influence on, 61–62
  primary auditory tract, 60
  right-ear superiority, 59–60
  of speech sounds, 56
  tests of, 60–61

B

Bennett, J., *cited* on syntax, 17–18
*Berry-Talbott Developmental Guide,
    Comprehension of Grammar,* 193

C

Causal, spatial-temporal relations, 136–39
Cazden, *cited,* 215, 228
Categorization, 263–67
Children's literary materials:
  chants and finger plays, 282
  rhymes, poems, choric verse, 282–83
  riddles, 282
  stories, 283–85
Chomsky, N. and Halle, M., 9–11, 17, 167–68
Choric verse, 253–54
Classroom-teacher cooperation, 239–40
Cluttering, 26, 246–47
Community resources, 240–41
Comprehension-expression of oral language:
  auditory perception, 32, 53–62
  Liberman, A. M., quoted on single sounds, 56
  neural variables, 119–20, 190
  summary, 64–66
  Table, 1–36 months, 141–46
Cranial nerves:
  auditory nerve, VIII cochlear branch (fig. 2–10) 55
  hypoglossal XII, (fig. 2–3) 33
  trigeminal V, mandibular section (fig. 2–3) 33
Crystal, D., *cited* on Prosody, 153

D

Distinctive feature theory, 166–69
  paradigm (Chomsky and Halle), (Table 5–3) 168
  weaknesses, 167–68
Dolch List, cited 258
Dyslexia, and spatial perception, 26

E

Early childhood education, 4
Environment in language learning:
  physical, 233
  psychological: "clinic-bound," 233
  social, 233–34

F

Feedback:
  in audition (fig. 2–2) 32
  in disease, 36–37
  neural integration in, 35
  in proprioception (fig. 2–1) 29; (fig. 2–3) 33
Feedforward, 34–35; (fig. 2–2) 32
  in auditory system (fig. 2–2) 32
  in language learning, 36

G

Gates Vocabulary List, *cited* 258
Global-ontogenic teaching program:
  basic concepts, 229–32
  characteristics of, 228–32
  terms:
    global, 229–30
    ontogenic, 230–32
"Grammar is all?", 183–84

H

Hallmarks of oral language, introduction
  developmental order and interdependence, 16–18
    phonatory development, 16–17
    phonological development, 17
    syntactic development, 17–18
  interdependence, 113
  teaching order, 19–20
Hemispherical dominance, 48–52
  definition, 49
  determiners of, 53
  development, 50–51
  functions, 49–50
  major hemisphere (left) (figs. 2–8, 50; 2–9, 54; 2–10) 55
    auditory perception in, 51–52
    tactile-kinesthetic perception in, 51–52
  minor hemisphere, 51–52
    musical pitch and quality, 51–52
    spatial discrimination, 52
    language functions, 52–53
  schema of (fig. 2–8) 50
  shift in, 52–53
    causes of, 52–53

Hippocampus, and limbic system, 45
Holophrastic expression:
 in beginning language development,
  210
 definition, 126
 examples, 207–208, 209
Home environment:
 active listening, 236
 case study, *Lennie,* 235
 emotional climate, 234–36
 learning set, 236
 practice laboratory, 237
 sensorimotor experiences, 237
 situational language experiences, 237–
  38
Homeostasis:
 failure of, in disease, 36–37
 and feedback, 36–37
 hypothalamus and, 35
 in language learning, 30, 36–37
 limbic system and, 35, 36–37
 reticular system and, 35, 36–37
Hypothalamus, and limbic system, 47;
  (fig. 2–6) 46; (fig. 2–7) 47

I

Intelligence:
 development of, 121–22
  Kagan's theory, 121–22
 and perception, 121
Intonation. *See* Prosody

J

Jakobson, R., cited on phonemic system,
  166

L

Language enrichment, 3, 7, 23–24, 137,
  245
Language learning:
 abstraction skills, 130
 in babies, 37–39
  body language (gestural language),
   207–9
  comprehension-expression, review,
   230–32

Language learning (*cont.*)
  comprehension of syllable strings,
   124
  early signs, 121
  first words, 126
  holophrase, 126
  Kagan's theory, 121–22
  object permanence, 122
  overextension of word meaning, 128
  phonatory development, 16–17
  phonological development, 17
  positive markers, 210–11
  prosodic development, 207–9, 210
  prosodic imitation, 125, 208–9
  syllable strings, 127–28
  symbolic play, 123
  word labels, persistence of, 128
Language learning:
 environment, 115–16
  physical, 233
  pleasurable reinforcement, 233, 234
  psychological, "clinic-bound," 233
  social stimulation, 233–34
 extension beyond home, 237–38
  Andy and circus, 238
 first words, 126
 gesture language, 129–30
 imitation in, 187–89, 221
 introduction to
  perceptual-semantic development,
   112
  semantic and lexical skills, 113–14
  syntactic skills, 114–15
 lexical development, 126–32
 motivation, 83–84
 neurophysiological determinants, 119–
  20, 190
 parental cooperation, 232
 phonological deviations, 174–76
 pragmatism in, 231–32
 semantic complexity, 132
 socioenvironmental influences, 189–90
 subordination of syntax in, 185–87
 subordination of syntax to pragmatic
  intentions, 185–87
 syntactic problems in, 192–201
 syntax and pragmatic intention, 185–
  87
 variables, 115–20
  health status, 117–19
  learning environment, 115–16
  neurophysical handicaps, 119–20
  special sensory impairment, 129
 vocabulary development, 131–32, 216
 Wh-questions, 131
 word order in, 185
Learning disabilities, 5

Lexical development:
early intermediate stage, 216
first words, 126
in language retardate, 217–18
later intermediate stage, 221
overextension of meaning, 128
pragmatic adaptation, 128
vocabulary development, 131–32
word labels, 128
Limbic system, 45–49
in aural coding, 61
Brown, G. W., quoted on, 48
composition, 45–48; (fig. 2–6) 46;
(fig. 2–7) 47
functions, 48–49
Linguistic constraints, 172
Linguistically handicapped children:
classification, 1–2
definitions, 1–2
examples, 2–3
Linguistics and oral language:
Chomsky, N., 9–11, 17, 167–68
evaluation of, 9–11
Staats, A., on, 9–10

M

Mean length of utterance (MLU), 196–97
Memory:
coding problems, 97
definitions, 97–98
genetic drive and, 77–79
language-retardation, 102–5, 222–23
perceptual mastery, 102–3
sensory-verbal transportation, 103
unisensory input, 103–4
retrieval interference, 104
retarded speech, 104–5
and limbic system, 48
neurogenic basis, 97–98
neurogenic basis of short-term m;
long-term m., 77
organizational strategies, 100–101
perception and m., 99–100
short-term and long-term m., 98–99
skills and strategies in training, 105–6
visual, auditory, haptic
transformations, 101–2
Mental impairment, 6
Learning Opportunities Program for, 6
Morpheme:
and phonological development, 169–70
definition, 169
relation to syntagma, 169–70

Motivation:
and attention, 89
defined, 79
determinants of:
competition, 81
sanctions, 81–83
sensorimotor exploration, 80–81
emotion in, 78
emotional factors in, 78–79
extrinsic, 79–80
genetic drive in, 77–79
in language development, 83–84
in language disorders, 84–87
and limbic system, 48
neurogenic basis, 75–79
limbic system, 75–77
reticular system, 75–76

N

Nervous system:
auditory system, (fig. 2–2) 32
cortical areas in perception-expression
(fig. 2–10) 55
diseases affecting language learning,
30, 36–37
dynamism of, 27
genetic deficit and, 28–30
hemispherical dominance (fig. 2–8) 50
integrative mechanisms in feedback
(fig. 2–3) 33
limbic system (fig. 2–6) 46; (fig. 2–7)
47
reflex arc, 37–39; (fig. 2–4) 38
reticular system (fig. 2–5) 42
RNA and, 28–29
sagittal section of brain (fig. 2–9) 54
sensorimotor circuits (fig. 2–1) 29
S-R concept, 37–38; (fig. 2–4) 38
Delburck quoted on, 67
synapse, basis of function, 28

O

Oral expression:
and language retardation, 140
nonverbal relations, 139
practice, 139–40
social nature, 139–40
social-prosodic context and structure,
139–40

Oral language acquisition, beginning
　　stage 1:
　behavior modification, 12–13
　modeling in, 11
　negative markers in retardate, 211
　phonatory markers:
　　action percepts, 207–9
　　prosody, 207–9, 210
　positive markers, 210–11
　presyntactic markers:
　　word order, 209–10
　social learning theory and, 11–12
Oral language acquisition, early
　　intermediate stage 2:
　expansion of interaction, 211–12
　isomorphic observations, 215–16
　negative markers in retardate, 217–18
　positive markers, 216–17
　prosody and syntactic relations, 212–
　　13
　sentence development:
　　constituents, 213–14
　　expansion, 215
　　freewheeling syntax, and, 214
　　syntactic developmental order, 213–14
　　wh question in, 214–15
Oral language acquisition, later
　　intermediate stage 3:
　embedding, 220
　negative markers in retardate, 222
　positive markers, 221
　sentence complexity, 219–20
　sentence length, 219
　syntactic advances, 218–19
　syntactic rules, 218
　use of superlative, 220
Oral language acquisition, continuing
　　education stage 4:
　perceptual-semantic advances, 223–24

P

Parents Respond (PR), 239, 265
　body language, 279
　pantomime, 279, 280
　problem solving, 281
Parkinson's syndrome, 45, 245
Perceptual-semantic development (3–5
　　years):
　synthesis of gestural and oral skills,
　　129
Perceptual-semantic development (6–9
　　years):
　advancing skills: classification,
　　causality, sequencing
　Boehm's *Test of Basic Concepts,* 135

Perceptual-semantic development (6–9
　　years) (*cont.*)
　Engelmann's *Basic Concept Inventory,*
　　135
　Piaget's theories, evaluated, 134–36
　pragmatic language materials, 135–36
Perceptual-semantic development (9–14
　　years):
　advanced perceptual processes:
　　decision-making, 138–39
　　problem solving, 138–39
　advancing skills, 136–39
　formal operational stage, 136–38
　Hayakawa's semantic principles, 138–
　　39
　pragmatic language materials, 137–38
Perception-expression of oral language:
　auditory perception, 32 (fig. 2–2)
　　32; 53–62; (fig. 2–10) 55
　　auding process, 56–59
　　auditory acuity vs., 61
　　deficits in, 60–62
　　influence of tactile-kinesthetic feed-
　　　back on, 56–57
　　peripheral hearing impairment,
　　　influence on, 61–62
　　primary auditory tract, 60
　　right-ear superiority, 59–60
　　of speech sounds, 56
　　tests of, 60–61
　neural integrative mechanisms, 53;
　　(fig. 2–9) 54; (fig. 2–10) 55
　　cortical areas associated with, (fig.
　　　2–10) 55
　sensory modalities in, 53–62; (fig. 2–1)
　　29; (fig. 2–2) 32; (fig. 2–3) 33;
　　(fig. 2–9) 54; (fig. 2–10) 55
　tactile-kinesthetic (haptic) (fig. 2–1)
　　29; (fig. 2–3) 33; (fig. 2–10) 55;
　　56–57; 62
　　influence on auditory perception,
　　　56–57
Perceptual-semantic development:
　abstraction and, 123–24
　categorization:
　　class inclusion-exclusion, 264
　　differences and similarities, 264–65
　　functional organization, 263–64
　　home activities, 265–66
　　problems of language retardate,
　　　266–67
　　taxonomic organization, 263–64
　comprehension of syllable strings, 124
　in continuing education stage, 223–24
　definition, 16–17
　early intermediate stage, 211–18
　early signs, 121
　embedding, 132–33

Perceptual-semantic development (*cont.*)
environment, 133–34
holophrastic expression, 126
intelligence and, 121
introduction to, 112
Kagan's theory, 121–22
in language retardate, 211, 217, 222
later intermediate stage, 218–24
object permanence, 122
pragmatic lexicon, 128
phonatory development and, 16–17
phonological development and, 17
and pragmatic intention in beginning
language, 210
prosodic imitation, 125
referent, identified by:
behavior relationships, 261–62
place relationships, 261
separation from complex, 262–63
use relationships, 261
relation of syntax, 133
semantic complexity, 132
sensory organization, 122–23
single-word labels, persistence of,
128
subordination of syntax to, 185–87
syllable strings, 127–28
symbolic play, 123
syntactic development and, 17–18
traumatic effects on, case study, 224
vocabulary, 131–32
wh-questions, 131
word order, 127–28
Phonatory development, 16–17, 152–62,
229 *See* Prosody
Phonological deviations in language
retardate:
articulation, 174
atypical phonological system, 175
neurophysical and anatomic deficits,
175–76
time lag and, 174–175
Phonological development, 17, 162–76,
230
child practices in development, 170–
71
early intermediate stage, 217
evolution, 163–69
imitation and, 170
International Phonetic Alphabet
(IPA), 163
in language retardate, 211, 218, 223
later intermediate stage, 221
phonemic system:
basis of order (Jakobson, R.), 166
chart (Table 5–1) 164
definition, 163
developmental bases, 163–64

Phonological development (*cont.*)
distinctive feature theory, 166–69
order of (Table 5–2) 165, 166
phone vs. phoneme, 163
Templin, M. on, 166
teaching practices:
articulation test, 173
dependence on linguistic constraints,
172
dependence on neurophysiological
equipment, 172–73
psychosocial environment and, 173
relation to oral language
remediation, 173–74
sound in isolation, 171–72
Piaget *cited* 134, 135, 138
Pragmatics and language learning,
Foreword, 18–19, 231–32
Problem solving, 256–57
Professional and nonprofessional aides,
240–41
Prosody:
adult overlearning, 154
attributes of, 153
bases of:
genetic, 154–55
moto-kinesthetic, 158–59
psychoneural, 155–56
sensorimotor, 156–58
basis of oral language, 62–64
contrasting features, 153
Crystal *quoted* on, 153
definitions, 62–63, 152–53, 154, 155
development, 156–57, 207–9, 210
in early internal stage, 216
in language retardate, 211, 217, 223
in later intermediate stage, 221
in relation to bodily movements, 62–
64, 208–9
features, 63
foreign language patterns, 154
functions of:
control of phonemic form, 161–62
control over grammar, 160–61
determinant of word order, 159–60
determinant of word perception,
159–60
organizer of meaning, 158
speaking-listening link, 159
temporal constraint on syllable
strings, 158–59
historical development:
Lashley, K. S. *cited,* 158
Liberman, A. M. *cited,* 158
Martin, J. G., *cited,* 158–59
Monrad-Krohn, G. A., *cited,* 158
imitation, 125
in language retardation, 157–58

Prosody (*cont.*)
  relation to perception-production, 158
  in speech arts, 157
  universality, 153–54
Psychosocial environment, 173, 187

R

Referent, 260–63
Reticular system:
  activating-adapting function, 40–43;
    (fig. 2–5) 42
  attention and, 41
  in aural coding, 61
  in coding oral language, 58–59
  French, J. D. *quoted* on, 41
  lesions of, 45
  linguistic handicaps and, 43–45
  and Parkinson's syndrome, 45
  summary of functions, 43–44
  tactile-proprioceptive tract in r. s. (fig.
    2–5) 42
  and voluntary motor activity, 45
Rhythm. *See* Prosody

S

Semantic and lexical skills:
  introduction to, 113–14
Semantics:
  Hayakawa's principles, 138–39
Sensorimotor responses:
  in beginning language development,
    210
Sentence length vs. complexity, 196–97
Sequencing (seriation), 136–39, 256–57
  forward and reverse sequencing, 267–
    68
  problem solving, 271–73
  space relations, 269–71
  temporal relations, 267, 268
Sex differences in language acquisition,
  206
Similarities-differences, 136–39
Situational teaching:
  activities in, classroom, 231–32, 234
  activities outside classroom, 234
  contractual relation, 232
  goals, 256–58
  parental cooperation, 232
  parents' notebook, 232
  Parents Respond (PR), 232

Situational teaching (*cont.*)
  physical environment, 233
  psychological environment, 233
  social environment, 233–34
    stimulation, 233–34
    pleasurable reinforcement, 233, 234
  teaching syllabus, 232
Special language teacher:
  creative abilities, 242
  educational background, 241
  nomenclature and, 3–4
    clinician, 3–4
    pathologist, 3–4
  organization, 241, 242
  personal qualities, 241
  physical stamina, 242
  preparation of, 4–7, 9–15
  teaching opportunities of, 4–7
Syntactic development, 229–30
  child vs. adult syntax, 184–85, 197
  contributing factors:
    imitation, 187–89
    neurophysiological factors, 190
    socioenvironmental influences, 187,
      189–90
  early intermediate stage, 216
  importance compared with other
    hallmarks, 185–87
  introduction, 59, 17–18
  in language retardate, 217–18, 220,
    222–23
  later intermediate stage, 221
  linguists' theories, 183–84
  pragmatic intentions and, 185–87,
  skills, 114–15
  subordination in language learning,
    87
Syntagma, 124, 159, 169–70

T

Tactile-kinesthetic perception. *See*
  Comprehension-expression
T.A.L.K. (Teaching activities for
    language knowledge), Foreword,
    3, 7, 23–24, 137, 245
Teacher-parent relationships, 238–39
Teaching language retardates:
  initial goals:
    child's responsibility for learning,
      243–44
    increase in volume of talk, 243
    motivating activities, 243, 244
    psycho-emotional adjustment, 243

Teaching methods:
  alteration of traditional, 14–15
Teaching perceptual-semantic skills:
  activities:
    cookie and juice party, 289
    Hunt in the Woods, 291
    social studies and science, 293
    Shutter-Snappers, 291–92
    Spring Garden, 289–90
  materials:
    artificial attributes of perception, 259
    categorization, 286–87
    comprehension-expression as a unit, 259–60
    problem solving, 288–89
    referent, 286–88
    sequencing, 287–88
    spatial relations, 286
  elementary organizational processes:
    categorizing, 263–67
    identifying referent, 260–63
    problem solving, 256–57
    sequencing, 256–57
  meaning-percepts, 255–57
  questionable practices, 258–60
  situational learning, 257
  vocabulary building, 258–59
Teaching prosody and phonology:
  to acoustically handicapped children, 246
  to clutterers, 246–47
  in combination with other hallmarks, 248–50, 253–54, 255
  gestural (body) language, 250–52
  to language retardate, 245
  melody patterning in verse and speech, 252–53
  priority of prosody, 244–46, 247–49
  prosodic speech, 254–55
  phonological and syntactic development, 253–54
Teaching syntactic development:
  appraisal in language lag, 197, 199–201
  appraisal of structure in free speech situations, 198

Teaching syntactical development *(cont.)*
  cooperation with others *(Parents Respond)*; colleagues, 198–99
  correlation with perceptual-semantic teaching, 185–87, 190–91, 194, 196, 198
  correlation with pragmatic functions, 196
  logical relationships, 192
  motivational problems, 186, 193–95
  psychosocial environment, 187, 196
  questionable methods:
    evaluation measures, 192–94, 195, 196–97
    exercises in elicited speech, 193–95
    objective tests, 195–96
    prediction vs. noun phrase, 191
    prepositions, 191–92
    relation to pragmatic needs, 193–94, 196
    rules vs. logical relationships, 192
  sentence length vs. complexity, 196–97
  tasks eliciting spontaneous speech, 193–95
  transfer value, 187
Tests and measurements, 7–8
Thalamus:
  and limbic system, 49

V

Vocabulary, *See* Lexical development

W

Wh-questions, 131